THE EFFECTIVE
SECURITY OFFICERS
TRAINING MANUAL

THE EFFECTIVE SECURITY OFFICERS TRAINING MANUAL

by

Ralph F. Brislin, CCP, MPA

Editor

Eric C. Lewis

Butterworth–Heinemann

Boston Oxford Melbourne Singapore Toronto Munich New Delhi Tokyo

Copyright © 1995 by Butterworth–Heinemann.
℞ A member of the Reed Elsevier group
All rights reserved.

 Recognizing the importance of preserving what has been written,
Butterworth–Heinemann prints its books on acid-free paper, and we exert
our best efforts to that end.

Library of Congress Cataloging-in-Publication Data
Brislin, Ralph F.
    The effective security officer's training manual / by Ralph F. Brislin.
        p.   cm.
    Includes bibliographical references.
    ISBN 0–7506–9610–9
    1. Private security services—United States—Handbooks, manuals, etc.
    2. Police, Private—United States—Handbooks, manuals, etc.
    I. Title.
    HV8291.U6B74   1994
    363.2'89'0683--dc20   94-25959
                                                                    CIP

British Library Cataloguing-in-Publication Data
A catalogue record for this book is available from the British Library.

Butterworth–Heinemann
313 Washington Street
Newton, MA 02158–1626

10 9 8 7 6 5 4 3 2 1

Printed in the United States of America

Table of Contents

Appendix I: Security Survey

Appendix II: Facility Diagram

Bibliography & Recommended References

Answer Key to Chapter Questions

Contributing Authors

James H. Clark
President, Clark & Associates, Cleveland, OH

Thomas J. Krena
Manager, Accident Prevention & Occcupational Health, Armco, Inc., Pittsburgh, PA

William R. Krob
Vice President of Operations, United Security Patrol, Inc., Cleveland, OH

Preface

The Effective Security Officer's Training Manual has been a labor of love for four years. Written and designed in a format that assists learning, the material is presented in a non-threatening, accessible fashion. Although most of the material contained within this manual has appeared in various forms and to varying degrees in other publications, I believe that we have designed this book in a manner that will lend itself to a variety of settings: to be studied independently, used in a classroom, provided as part of on-going training or professional development, and/or used in conjunction with other training media.

While many worthwhile security training manuals exist today, *The Effective Security Officer's Training Manual* conveys the written information more effectively than any of its competitors. Included is a 200-question multiple-choice final exam, which, once passed, certifies that the student has adequately absorbed the basic information needed to work effectively as a security officer.

Acknowledgements

Many people have given of their time and talent to assist in the publication of this manual. I would like to thank the following persons:

My wife, Becky Brislin
John Brislin
Harry T. Otto
Brian Zielke
Richard E. Justik
Jeremy Varner
Kay Ball
Jon Truax
Karen Moster
Dave Stofka
Mike Leonowski
and
Ron Hamm

THE EFFECTIVE SECURITY OFFICERS TRAINING MANUAL

Introduction to Security

Introduction to Security

As you read and study this Security Officer Training Course you should be aware that you are in one of the fastest growing industries in the United States. The purpose of this course is to familiarize you with the most important aspects of the duties of a security officer. We believe you will find this course easy to read, yet interesting and challenging.

What is Private Security?

Private security is made up of self-employed individuals and privately funded businesses which provide security and related services to other persons and businesses for a fee. Security is intended to protect and preserve activities / property without loss or disruption. Most security officers have no more legal power than the average citizen. However, some security officers possess police/arrest powers because they have been commissioned by a local, state, or federal government agency.

Private security: privately funded business which provide security and related services to other persons and businesses for a fee.

Security has existed since people began to inhabit the earth. Archeologists have discovered drawings attributed to early "cavemen" which describe how early inhabitants hunted and made war against other tribes or groups of people. The early inhabitants of the earth needed to protect themselves from not only invaders but from wild animals as well.

The first recognized set of laws is attributed to King Hammurabi of Babylon who lived about 2000 B.C. Hammurabi devised a legal code which was designed to regulate the behavior of people to one another and to society as a whole. The Code of Hammurabi described what punishment would be enforced against a person who violated the code. The old saying, "an eye for an eye, and a tooth for a tooth," is generally accepted to have been initiated in this code. Ancient customs and traditions which sanctioned improper behavior were legitimized in the Code of Hammurabi.

Code of Hammurabi: a legal code developed by King Hammurabi of Babylon around 2000 BC designed to regulate the behavior of people to one another and society as a whole.

Between 500-600 B.C. the Greeks developed procedures and implemented systems to protect strategic roads leading to and from their cities and to protect their vital interests from potential enemies.

Near the time of the birth of Christ, the Roman empire ruled much of the known world. The Roman army was well-organized and highly trained. Military units were utilized to protect their cities and the development of the first quasi-police department was considered to be that of the praetorian guard.

Law in the United States is based on ancient common law which was developed in England. In late 800 A.D., King Albert established the "King's Peace" which was an attempt to stop the private wars and battles which occurred between English noblemen who maintained private armies. The "King's Peace" called for certain punishment to be inflicted for violations of the law.

The development of law and the original criminal justice system continued in England for the next several hundred years. In 1750, the first plain clothes detective unit was formed and was known as the "Bow Street Runners." The members of this unit were responsible for running to the scene of a crime in the attempt to capture the criminal. In 1829 what is considered to be the first police department was formed by Sir Robert Peel who was Home Secretary of England. Sir Peel was responsible for the establishment of this uniformed, full-time police force. The English police term "Bobbie" for police officers, was the nickname derived from Sir Robert Peel.

In the United States, police departments were formed in several large cities during the 1800's.

Development of Private Security in the United States

Alan Pinkerton is recognized as the father of private security in the United States. In 1857 he founded the Pinkerton Detective Agency. He worked primarily for the railroads, thus most of the early work of Pinkerton's was catching train robbers. The Pinkerton Company served as an intelligence-gathering (spy) service for the Union army during the Civil War. In 1874 American District Telegraph (ADT) was formed to provide alarm detection services.

In 1859 William Brink founded a truck and package delivery service in Chicago. When Brinks carried its first payroll in 1891, it became the first armored car and courier service. In 1909 William J. Burns founded the Burns Detective

Notes

Praetorian Guard: considered to be the first type of formal security, developed by the Roman Military near the time of the birth of Christ, used to protect Roman citizens and property.

"King's Peace": developed in England in 800 A.D. by King Albert; an attempt to stop the private wars between English noblemen.

"Bow Street Runners": the first plain clothes detective unit created in 1750 in England; members were responsible for running to the scene of a crime in an attempt to capture the criminal.

Sir Robert Peel: Home Secretary of England who in 1829 established the first police department.

"Bobbie": nickname for English police officers attributable to Sir "Robert" Peel.

Alan Pinkerton: considered to be the father of private security in the United States; founded the Pinkerton Detective Agency in 1857.

ADT: American District Telegraph established in 1874 to provide alarm detection service.

Agency which provided security during labor strikes.

At the beginning of World War I the security industry began to grow because of concern about sabotage and espionage, but the growth slowed considerably during the Depression. During the 1940's, with the outbreak of World War II, the industry began to grow again.

Before awarding defense contracts, the government required that munitions suppliers begin security measures to protect classified materials and defense secrets from sabotage and spying. The Federal Bureau of Investigation (FBI) assisted defense contractors in ensuring their security was adequate. The government also granted the status of auxiliary military police to more than 200,000 plant security officers. For the most part, their jobs were to protect war goods, equipment and personnel. As a result of World War II, manufacturing companies became aware of the need for plant security and its value. After the war George R. Wackenhut and three other former FBI agents formed the Wackenhut Corporation. In 1955 the American Society for Industrial Security (ASIS) was formed. Today, there are over 25,000 members of ASIS. In 1968 the federal government required increased security for federal banks when Congress passed the Federal Bank Protection Act. In January, 1973 the Federal Aviation Administration (FAA) began to require the screening of all air passengers and carry-on baggage due to the number of air hijackings which were occurring.

Security Development and the Future

Security like most professions has continued to change amid rapid growth. More and more organizations are examining the training criteria of security companies to ensure that a satisfactory level of knowledge and professionalism exists.

Different definitions and terms are often used interchangeably to describe security.

- Private Police
- Security Police
- Plant Protection
- Facility or Plant Security

Notes

William Brink: *founded Brink's, the first armored car and courier service in the USA in 1891.*

William J. Burns: *founded the Burns Detective Agency in 1909.*

George R. Wackenhut: *founded the Wackenhut Security Corporation shortly after the end of World War II.*

ASIS: *American Society for Industrial Security, formed in 1955, now has over 25,000 members.*

- Loss Prevention
- Risk Management
- Loss Control
- Fire Protection
- Asset Protection
- Safety
- Hazardous Material Control

Security encompasses all of the above areas to a greater or lesser degree depending on the facility or industry where security officers are employed. This is not meant to imply that the term security is the same as all of the above terms. Rather, in the 1990's and continuing into the next century, security responsibility will continue to increase, provided training of security personnel is considered a good value and return of investment to corporations.

Security generally refers to the protection of people and/ or property in an effort to maintain what is considered normal conditions.

Loss Prevention refers to a management philosophy which invests money in the hope of preventing losses from occurring.

Risk Management involves recognizing risks that could result in losses and evaluating how to best reduce risk and loss. (Usually relating to insurance)

Loss Control refers to a management philosophy which recognizes that losses will occur but attempts to minimize or control losses at a predetermined level.

Law Enforcement refers to the actual enforcement of legal requirements which if violated will result in punishment to the offender.

Safety refers to ensuring that the workplace or conditions in the workplace are not inherently dangerous to people or if dangerous, that proper protection devices or procedures are implemented to ensure the continued well-being of people.

Fire Protection simply incorporates the equipment, devices, policies and procedures which are enforced to protect life and property from fire loss.

As you study the material in this manual in an effort to learn as much as possible with regard to security training, ask yourself, "What type of career or profession have I entered into?" Various studies have been highly critical of the security industry citing training inadequacies, poor selection and hiring practices, low pay, high turnover, intense competition, etc. If these studies are true, why would a person want to work as a security officer? This is a question which each individual employed in the security field must answer.

In their book, **Principles of Security**, Tillet and VanMeter state that it is well accepted that many persons enter the private security industry because of the "John Wayne Syndrome." This means that many persons desire to become security officers (and in many cases, police officers) because they can wear a uniform and in some instances, carry a gun. While those of us in the security profession may not like the term "John Wayne Syndrome," unfortunately in many cases security officers deserve the nametag. More and more companies for a variety of reasons are disarming security officers. The day is here when a person who wants to work in the field of security must be willing to provide service. There is little need for the "macho, tough-guy" approach to security. Security officers are promoted in large part based upon their ability to "serve" clients and security services companies are retained on their ability to satisfy their customers with quality service.

In 1980, the National Institute of Justice began a comprehensive study conducted by Hallcrest Systems, Inc., to evaluate the extent and nature of private security efforts.

This study included interviews with more than 400 people in law enforcement and all aspects of proprietary and contractual security, a survey of state agencies regulating private security and of 1,600 law enforcement and security managers. The study also formulated an economic analysis and forecast of the private security industry.

The findings and recommendations from this study and a later study, Hallcrest II, will be discussed in a later chapter, "Security Personnel".

Law enforcement and security professionals agree that training is essential. Police are not knowledgeable of security duties but private security equipment and resources could be made available to police departments.

Notes

John Wayne Syndrome: term used to describe persons who seek to work in security or law enforcement simply because of the uniform and perceived power of the position and equipment used. Only interested in the show aspect of the job.

Hallcrest I: a study conducted by Hallcrest Systems Inc., (founded in 1980 by the National Institute of Justice) The study evaluated the efforts of private security in the USA.

This manual is divided into several different modules or chapters. Every module covers a fundamental element in the training regimen of a security officer. In each chapter there is a glossary, questions, and points to remember in addition to the text, figures and charts. Also, the reader will find a handy section on each text page on which to make notes.

The purpose of this training program is to provide the information necessary in order for a person to successfully and properly provide a high level of service as a security officer or supervisor. Over the next several years, the security industry will continue to grow, diversify and change. The persons who study the material contained in this manual must realize that the single and only determiner of whether or not they are successful in the security industry, rests with themselves!

"The Quality of a person's life is in direct proportion to their commitment to excellence, regardless of their chosen field of endeavor."
-Vincent T. Lombardi

Notes

QUESTIONS

1. The first set of recognized laws were called:

    a. The Ten Commandments
    b. The Bill of Rights
    c. Writ of Habeas Corpus
    d. Code of Hammurabi

2. Name of the military soldiers who protected the interests of the Roman empire:

    a. The Vanguard
    b. The Right Guard
    c. The Victorian Guard
    d. The Praetorian Guard

3. In the late 800's A.D., King Albert established the _____ to stop the private wars between English noblemen.

    a. King's Peace
    b. Magna Carta
    c. Corpus Delecti
    d. Code of Hammurabi

4. What was the name of the first plain clothes detective unit formed in an attempt to capture criminals at the scene of a crime?

    a. Bowery Street Runners
    b. Main Street Runners
    c. Bow Street Runners
    d. Jones Avenue Sprinters

5.   He was responsible for the establishment of the first full-time police department.

    a. Alan Pinkerton
    b. William Burns
    c. Sir Walter Raleigh
    d. Sir Robert Peel

6.   He is recognized as the father of private security in the United States:

    a. Alan Pinkerton
    b. William Burns
    c. Sir Walter Raleigh
    d. Sir Robert Peel

7.   The management philosophy which stresses investing money in the hope of preventing losses:

    a. Loss Control
    b. Risk management
    c. Security
    d. Loss Prevention

8.   The name given to persons who desire to work in security or law enforcement because of the power and authority of the positions:

    a. Clint Eastwood Syndrome
    b. John Wayne Syndrome
    c. Robo-Cop Theory
    d. Mother Theresa Syndrome

THE EFFECTIVE SECURITY OFFICERS TRAINING MANUAL

Chapter I

Security Personnel

Security Personnel

Private security personnel currently greatly outnumber the number of law enforcement personnel. Private security is one of the fastest growing occupations in the United States, and it is in this field that you the reader of this manual have chosen to work either to supplement your income or to serve as the main source of your income. Many of you who are reading this manual are probably not doing much more than earning a meager way of living. There are several reasons why a security officer (especially in contract security) in many cases earns less than $5.00 per hour. One major reason is that most people believe that a person who works as a security officer is not talented enough to earn more money, so why should they be willing to pay more? Security officers will earn more money only when the business community recognizes that security officers can be talented, dedicated and possess a general knowledge that is essential in performing their job. Some businesses today are willing to pay a security officer considerably more than minimum wage but it is only because those businesses genuinely believe that they are getting their money's worth from their security services company or in-house (proprietary) group.

In the early 1970's a study was conducted by the Rand Corporation of the private security industry. This study was very critical of the private security industry. It stated that most security officers were uneducated, 60 year old, white men. Authors Ricks, Tillet and VanMeter in their 1981 book, **Principles of Security**, state, "it should be noted that the Rand Study was done with a small sample and in one geographic location (southern California) and it is generally agreed that their sample was not typical of the industry as a whole. It is interesting to note that the Rand Study is more often cited in the literature than the other research that has been conducted."[1]

In 1977 the Law Enforcement Assistance Administration (LEAA) funded another report on the private security industry. This report entitled: **Private Security: Standard and Goals** - from the *Official Private Security Task Force Report* was an attempt to define standards and goals for the private security industry. The Private Security Task Force Report was designed as a reference tool and guiding document for use by state and local criminal justice officials, members of the private security community and consumers of private security services and citizens. One goal of the report was that the private security industry would find the standards and goals useful as a means of evaluating the industry's position and role in the criminal justice systems and also as a means for improving the quality of its services and upgrading its image.[2]

The Private Security Task Force Report included ten (10) goals for Personnel Training in its report.

Goal 2.1 Training in Private Security
The responsibilities assumed by private security personnel in the protection of persons and property require training. Training should be instituted at all levels to insure that personnel are fully prepared to exercise their responsibilities effectively and efficiently.

Goal 2.2 Professional Certification Programs
Professional associations must study the feasibility of developing voluntary certification programs for private security managerial personnel.

Standard 2.3 Job Descriptions
Private security employers should develop job descriptions for each private security position.

Standard 2.4 Training Related to Job Functions
Private security employers should ensure that training programs are designed, presented, and evaluated in relation to the job functions to be performed.

Standard 2.5 Preassignment and Basic Training
Any person employed as an investigator or detective or guard or watchman, armored car personnel or armed courier, alarm system installer or servicer, or alarm respondent, including those presently employed and part-time personnel, should successfully:

Notes

Private Security Task Force Report: *report funded by LEAA in 1977, studied the Private Security industry and attempted to define standards and goals for the industry.*

1. **Pre-Assignment Training**
2. **Specialized Training**
3. **On-the-Job Training**
4. **Refresher/Ongoing Training**

Some states certify officers. The International Foundation of Protection Officers offers a certification program for $185/person.

Do you have a job description?

Does the training match the job?

1. Complete a minimum of 8 hours formal preassignment training.

2. Complete a basic training course of a minimum of 32 hours within 3 months of assignment. A maximum of 16 hours can be supervised on-the-job training.

Standard 2.6 Arms Training

All armed private security personnel, including those presently employed and part-time personnel, should:

1. Be required to successfully complete a 24-hour firearms course that includes legal and policy requirements—or submit evidence of competence and proficiency prior to assignment to a job that requires a firearm.

2. Be required to requalify at least once every 12 months with the firearm(s) they carry while performing private security duties (the requalification should cover legal and policy requirements).

Standard 2.7 Ongoing Training

Private security employers should ensure that private security personnel are given ongoing training by using roll call training, training bulletins, and other training media.

Standard 2.8 Training of Supervisors and Managers

Private security employers should provide effective job-related training for supervisory and managerial employees. Appropriate prior training, education, or professional certification should be accepted to meet this requirement.

Notes

What pre-assignment training is given prior to the start of a job?

Specialized training for officers carrying firearms is suggested.

Training while on the job.

In-Service Training - For Managers, set up in-service training programs for supervisors and managers.

Standard 2.9 State Authority and Responsibility for Training

A State government regulatory agency should have the authority and responsibility to accredit training schools, approve training curriculums, and certify instructors for the private security industry.

Standard 2.10 State Boards to Coordinate Training Efforts

Appropriate State boards and agencies should coordinate efforts to provide training opportunities for private security personnel and persons interested in preparing for security employment, through utilization of physical and personnel resources of area vocational schools and colleges and universities.

As a person employed in the private security profession you can determine for yourself whether your employer and state meet any of the goals and standards suggested by the Private Security Task Force Report.

As stated, Tillet and VanMeter write that it is well accepted that many persons enter the private security industry because of the "John Wayne Syndrome." This means that many persons desire to become security officers (and in many cases, police officers) because they can wear a uniform and in some instances, carry a gun. While those of us in the security profession may not like the term "John Wayne Syndrome," unfortunately in many cases security officers deserve the nametag. More and more companies for a variety of reasons are unarming security officers. The day is here when a person who wants to work in the field of security must be willing to provide service. There is little need for the "macho, tough-guy" approach to security. Security officers are promoted in large part based upon their ability to "serve" clients and security services companies are retained on their ability to satisfy their customers with quality service.

Hallcrest I

In 1980, the National Institute of Justice began a comprehensive study conducted by Hallcrest Systems, Inc.,

---

Notes

Some states regulate and certify security officer training programs.

Many community and technical colleges offer security training classes and programs.

John Wayne Syndrome: persons who are only interested in the <u>show</u> aspect of law enforcement.

Liability is also leading to unarming security officers. Let's emphasize serving through the ability to communicate and respond to the client's needs.

to evaluate the extent and nature of private security efforts. The study's objectives were:

- to gather information on the general character of the private security industry in the USA, updating previous research.

- to describe the contribution private security makes to crime control and order maintenance, and to identify opportunities for improvement.

- to describe the working relationship between private security and public law enforcement agencies, and to develop recommendations for improved cooperation and coordination.

This study included interviews with more than 400 people in law enforcement and all aspects of proprietary and contractual security, a survey of state agencies, regulating private security and of 1,600 law enforcement and security managers, and an economic analysis and forecast of the private security industry.

The following information summarizes the findings of the study:

1. **There will be continued growth in the private security industry.**

2. **Private security personnel outnumber sworn law enforcement by over a two to one ratio. The Bureau of Labor Statistics forecasts that about 215,000 new operating personnel will join private security employment by 1990. The most rapid growth in security occurred between 1978-1985 during an economic recession.**

3. **Between 1980-1985, private citizens undertook self-help measures against crime, including the use of locks, lighting, guns, burglar alarms, citizen patrols and security guards.**

4. Law enforcement executives surveyed rated the overall contribution of private security as "somewhat effective," but gave private security low ratings in ten areas, including quality of personnel, training received and familiarity with legal authority.

5. Police are inclined to stereotype private security guards as "heavy-handed" in their use of force and weapons.

6. Police feel that up to 12% of their time is taken up with responding to false alarms.

7. False alarms, "moonlighting" by police, and negative perceptions of private security competence have all contributed to a situation in which there is little formal interaction or cooperation between the police and private security.

The following recommendations were included in the Hallcrest I report:

1. Upgrade private security. Upgrading the quality of security personnel was the most frequent recommendation made by both the police and security managers. Both law enforcement and security personnel agreed on the need for statewide regulatory statutes for contract security, plus mandatory criminal background checks, and minimum levels of training for both proprietary and contract security officers.

2. Increase police knowledge of private security.

3. Expand interaction by sharing strategies which include identification of specialized investigative resources and equipment of private security that are available to police.

Notes

Law enforcement and security professionals agree that training is essential.

Police are not knowledgeable of security duties.

Private security equipment and resources could be made available to police departments.

4. Experiment with transfer of police functions to private security such as responding to burglar alarms.

Hallcrest II

Another study concerning the security industry was published in 1990 entitled: **The Hallcrest Report II: Private Security Trends (1970-2000)**. The purpose of this study was designed to identify:

- a profile of growth and changes in the private security industry over the past two decades.

- emerging and continuing issues and trends in private security and its relationship with law enforcement.

- present recommendations and future research goals in the interests of greater cooperation between private security and law enforcement.

The Hallcrest II report identified economic crime as posing a serious threat to society. It found that for the past twenty years two major components of economic crime have been white collar and ordinary crime which are identified as:

- crimes committed in the course of one's lawful occupation (i.e. a bank employee who steals funds while performing normal duties).
- a violation of trust
- a lack of physical force to accomplish the crime (the use of force was not needed).
- money, property or power and prestige to accomplish the crime
- intent to commit the illegal act
- attempt to conceal the crime

Statistics on economic crime vary and the costs are estimated to be well over $100 billion a year. The Hallcrest II study identified liability as one of the significant reasons for increase in indirect costs of economic crime. Liability

Notes

Could private security assume certain police functions (ie. issuing parking tickets, responding to burglar alarms.)?

Economic Crime: Criminal offenses that impact society financially.

usually takes the form of a lawsuit claiming inadequate or improper security. Frequently, private security companies are named as defendants in these lawsuits.

The Hallcrest II study also identified drug abuse as a major cause of economic crime in the workplace but drug prevention and treatment programs are rare in small companies.

The study estimates that the average annual rate of revenue growth for the private security industry will be 8% to the year 2000. By the year 2000, private security expenditures will reach $104 billion. Expenditures for public law enforcement will grow by only 4% during the same period, reaching $44 billion by the year 2000.

The study also estimates that employment in private security is projected to grow at 2.3% annually while law enforcement is expected to grow at an annual rate of only 1%. In the year 2000, the total employment in security and law enforcement will be 2.5 million people.

The rapid growth of the number of security personnel will continue. By the year 2000, the study projects there will be 750,000 contract guards compared to 410,000 proprietary security personnel. Employment in proprietary security will decrease over the next 10 years mostly because of increased contracting out of security. The report further states that until training, salary, and promotional opportunities are improved, turnover in private security will continue to be high.

Contract guard security managers surveyed by Hallcrest in 1981 reported an average annual personnel turnover rate of 121% with a high of 300%. Field and focus group interviews in 1989 disclosed a similar turnover pattern.

The Private Security Task Force reported a concept related to security personnel turnover that has been generally accepted as the "vicious circle": The vicious circle is created by factors which are typically regarded as "norms" within the security guard industry:

Notes

Random drug testing of current employees is relatively inexpensive but is not used extensively in industry.

Nearly 2 1/2 times as much money is spent on security than law enforcement.

Proprietary Security Officer: *person employed as a security officer by the organization where the person works.*

Proprietary security positions will continue to decline.

Contract Security Officer: *person employed by an agency but who physically works for another organization at their facility.*

This high turnover rate means for every security officer position, three to four people per year are required.

Because many security companies have low standards and high turnover rates, people tend to quit one company to work for another.

- little or no training
- low salaries
- marginal personnel
- little or no promotional opportunities
- ineffective performance

The study also reported that for at least the past 20 years, most contract guards have been hired at slightly above the minimum wage rate. Consistently, the salaries of in-house security personnel have been higher than those of contract guard personnel.

Ten years ago about 50% of contract guards earned between $3.35 and $4.00 per hour while the average wage for in-house security guards was about $6.50 per hour. The Hallcrest research staff estimates an average wage of $7.70 per hour for unarmed security guards in 1990. The average income of a police officer is about $24,000 or about 50% higher than the annual compensation of the average security guard.

While the Hallcrest II report indicates that in-house or proprietary security officers earn considerably more than contract security officers, it also pointed out that in-house positions are decreasing and the trend will continue. This would seem to indicate that individuals who are employed as in-house security officers should re-evaluate their current positions. Questions should be asked such as, "What other skills or responsibilities could I obtain or accept which may make me more valuable to the company?" Far too often in-house security officers make preposterous statements such as: "The company won't or can't replace me," or "Where are they going to get someone else as dedicated or loyal as us!" Far too often, security officers (both contract and in-house), fail to recognize the most essential element necessary for job security...client satisfaction. If the client believes and feels that they are receiving quality service from the current security staff and they believe they are paying a reasonable fee for those services, more than likely the existing service will be maintained. However, business climates change quickly. Executives who were our friends and allies

Notes

Wages for contract security officers are still near the minimum wage.

Police officers earn twice as much money as most security officers.

The trend will continue due to the cost cutting of industry.

Security positions are maintained only as long as the company or client feel they are "getting their money's worth" for security service.

today leave and are replaced by persons who may not share the same positive view toward the existing security provider. To borrow a phrase from a Chrysler automobile commercial, all security personnel should remember the three most important rules in business: **SATISFY THE CUSTOMER! SATISFY THE CUSTOMER. SATISFY THE CUSTOMER!**

RECRUITMENT OF SECURITY OFFICERS

The recruitment of most security officers is not very elaborate. Most security companies obtain the majority of their applicants as a direct result of newspaper advertising. In some cases, security companies will offer cash bonuses to their current employees if the person recommends someone who is hired and works a minimum of 90 days. In certain special situations such as recruiting security officers for summer amusement parks or concert halls, colleges and universities are visited by security agencies. Qualifications for these positions are normally minimal. Many agencies will request that the applicant possess a high school education or equivalent such as a G.E.D. In 1971 the United States Supreme Court ruled in the case Griggs v. Duke Power Co. that a high school diploma and standardized I.Q. tests could not be required as a condition of employment unless it could be proven that the education and tests were valid and non-discriminatory. A company can request all applicants have a high school diploma or G.E.D. but may have to show proof for "requiring" the diploma. A "clean" police record is a typical requirement which is asked for in the newspaper advertisement. Unfortunately, a person with a "clean" police record but who does not own a car and have a telephone at their home may quickly be denied an opportunity to work.

Selection standards for many security officer positions are virtually non-existent. Intense competition exists within the Contract Security industry. Often a security agency will be willing to pay the security officer only $4.25 per hour. Considering that many "fast food" restaurants offer $4.50 to $4.75 per hour to beginners, it is obvious why many persons who work in security are frustrated "police-types." A person can earn more, work in a cleaner and warmer environment

Notes

This is done through communication, service and performance.

Typically, security officer positions are advertised in local newspapers.

Recruitment: process of signing up or enlisting into an association as a member or employee.

Many companies request and may even require a person to have a high school diploma to work as a security officer.

G.E.D.: Graduate Equivalent Degree, test for non high school graduates that when passed receive the G.E.D. which is similar to a high school diploma.

and in many cases receive discounts on food purchases by working for McDonald's, Burger King, Wendy's, etc. When you consider the responsibilities that even a night watchman has as compared to the person who cooks hamburgers, does it make any sense for a person to work as a security officer for $4.25 per hour? The answer is yes, indeed! While anyone employed as a security officer earning at or near the minimum wage would gladly accept more money, these individuals work as security officers because they enjoy certain aspects of the work or they prefer a particular shift or location to work. For the most part, persons who are employed as security officers would not prefer to be flipping hamburgers!

Differences of opinion exist as to why many contract security officers earn a wage at or near the minimum. Various reasons are given for this fact:

- Hiring and training practices of most security companies are poor or non-existent.
- The client's idea of a trained security officer is a warm body who stays awake, and who can walk and chew gum at the same time.
- The contract security industry fails to regulate itself and because of intense competition, standards are usually seldom agreed upon.

Some experts argue for mandated state or federal regulations to govern the practices of security companies. Unfortunately, there is no one simple solution to this problem. In cases where one security company refuses to bid on a contract proposal because the standards/requirements of the position are so minimal, at least nine or ten other guard agencies will be more than willing to provide a quotation.

A favorite question to ask the prospective client during the proposal meeting is, "What do you want or expect the security officers who work at this account to earn?" Replies such as," "I don't care," "That's not my concern," or "I'll leave that up to you," are indicative of a client who expects the security officers to earn a minimum age. Clients who stipulate security officers wages and benefits (even if

Notes

Many people employed as security officers enjoy their work even though they earn little money.

One solution is to hire retired people with a proven work ethic who may only want to supplement their retirement income.

The cut throat aspect of the profession leads to the lack of integrity.

Many security agencies will "low ball" or propose a lower wage rate for security officers, in order to obtain a contract.

their rates are considered low) allow the competing security agencies to prepare bids which should enable for fair, value-comparison analysis.

Fortunately, some security agencies can offer stable employment with some reasonable potential for advancement which will allow a security officer to earn over $10,000 a year. Since some companies can provide better opportunities for persons who remain with the firm for 2-3 years, these agencies will often screen job applicants through the use of written honesty tests, drug screening and in some limited cases, psychological testing.

A significant point about the value even low-paying positions provide is that of supplementing income for the many people who work in the contract security industry on a part-time basis. Many college students and retired or semi-retired individuals work as contract security officers. These people provide a high degree of service to their employers and clients and are forgotten when the debate over the money problems of the contract security industry are discussed.

Training

Authors Ricks, Tillet and VanMeter state in **Principles of Security**, "there is no more important issue in private security today than the training (or rather the lack of it) received by private security personnel." 3.

The authors continue by stating that while there are a number of differences between private security and public law enforcement, the greatest difference is in the issue of training. Most states require 400 hours of entry level training for newly hired police officers but only a few states "require" training for private security personnel. If you are currently employed as a private security officer (contract or proprietary) recall to yourself the amount of training you received when you began your assignment. The primary purpose for this training manual is to provide a comprehensive, yet easy to read and understand course which will provide the security officer with the basic knowledge required to adequately perform his/her job. To be effective, training must be continuous and repeated often.

As noted earlier Standard 2.5 of the Private Security Task Force Report recommends 8 hours of formal pre-assignment training and 32 hours of additional training within 3 months.

While there is considerable debate regarding training for unarmed private security officers it is generally agreed by all security executives that some minimum amount of training is required for security officers who are armed. By design, this manual does not address armed security officer issues. Armed security officers should ask their employer or supervisor if their training is adequate.

JOB DESCRIPTION & PERFORMANCE EVALUATION

A job description (see sample at the end of this module) should detail the various information a security officer is to be knowledgeable of while on assignment. This job description should include:
- Job Title
- Date Job Description was prepared
- Breakdown of required duties
- Name & Title of Supervisor
- Explanation of Job Evaluation
    - how will performance be measured?
    - who will evaluate the performance?
    - what is considered satisfactory work?
    - what are the requirements for termination?

Performance or job evaluations should be conducted after the first 30 days of assignment and at least at the six month, one year time periods and twice a year thereafter. Job evaluations should specifically detail if the security officer is satisfactorily performing his/her job. Job evaluations should detail factual information such as:

- Days absent since last evaluation.

- Days late since last evaluation.

Notes

Evaluation: process of measuring how well a person works at a job or task.

- Number of reports submitted on a weekly, monthly and/or annual basis.

- Officer's daily appearance

- Competence in writing incidence reports

- Incidents of performance counseling since last evaluation.

- Record of Detex or "key" patrols and number of stations "hit/missed."

- Knowledge of job based upon an objective test of important aspects of the job. (This test can be prepared by the security officers.)

- Specific examples of attitude displayed (both proper and improper).

- Specific examples related to all subjective or "opinion" evaluations should be included in the evaluation.

- Officer oriented training session -- officers exchange ideas and suggestions.

Security Personnel

Once an organization has determined that it has a need for security officers important issues will have to be addressed regarding the number of officers to be employed and the type of service desired, contract or proprietary (in-house).

In order to determine the number of security officers needed an organization must determine the number of posts or stations which are to be manned by security personnel. Consideration must be given to the number of pedestrian, auto and truck entrances and the hours which they will be open. The number of patrols that a security officer is

Notes

Many times you can use fewer officers if they are well-trained, well organized, well-supervised, adequately scheduled and rewarded for their on-duty performance.

expected to make during a shift as well as whether these patrols will be conducted on foot or with a vehicle must be determined. Finally, consideration must be given to escort and special services required of the security department.

If a post is to be manned 24 hours a day, 7 days a week and 365 days a year, 4 1/2 security officers will be needed to operate the post. This assumes that each officer works 40 hours each week.

EXAMPLE:

Post 1 Hours of Coverage   Required Personnel

Monday-Friday	12 Midnight - 8AM	1.0
Monday-Friday	8AM - 4PM	1.0
Monday-Friday	4PM - 12AM	1.0
Saturday &	12 Midnight - 8AM	.4
Sunday	8AM - 4PM	.4
	4PM - 12AM	.4
	Total	4.2

To determine the approximate cost of operating one post 24 hours per day, each day of the year, multiply the total number of hours by the hourly cost of a security officer (24 hours per day X 7 days per week X 52 weeks per year equals 8,736 hours of coverage each year). If the average hourly cost of one security officer is $7.50, the yearly cost for operating one post 24 hours a day, 7 days a week would be $65,520.00.

Because of this expense organizations will often choose to use contract security officers rather than "in-house" personnel. In-house or proprietary security personnel are usually paid more than contract personnel. The primary reason for this is that proprietary personnel will usually receive an hourly wage at least equal to or near the lowest paid company employee. An organization that pays proprietary officers well below other employees, is stating

Notes

Security, even at low rates, is expensive.

Many "in-house" or proprietary security positions are filled by company employees who for one reason or another were offered a position as a security officer. Security is sometimes used as a "dumping ground" for employees who are injured or not considered high performers.

that security is not as important as other functions. Additionally, many business people believe that security officers serve only in limited roles, so the less they are paid, the better.

Usually by using contract security personnel, an organization can pay much less for coverage because the nature of the industry keeps rates low. An organization can imply that the reason the contract security officers are low paid is because of the security service company. In addition, if the organization is not satisfied with either the contract company or an officer in particular, a change can be made.

For years, security professionals have debated which offers better service for the money, contract or proprietary security. In all likelihood, the debate will continue into the next century. In general, persons who prefer proprietary security list the following reasons:

1. **Proprietary officers project a more favorable company image.**
2. **Proprietary officers are more loyal.**
3. **By using proprietary officers, selection of the officers is better.**
4. **Training of proprietary officers is better.**
5. **Proprietary security officers are more familiar with the facility they protect.**

While several reasons could be given for using contract security, the only meaningful reason is money. When all the reasons are examined, debated, reviewed and debated some more, contract security exists solely because it is less expensive than proprietary security. An organization which is choosing between using contract or proprietary security should determine precisely how much money they are willing to spend for the hourly pay rate, benefits, uniforms, training, etc. The assumption that because a contract security service is used, hourly pay rates, benefits, training and personnel selection will be substandard is incorrect. An organization when soliciting quotes for contract security service can stipulate the hourly rate the officer is to make, the benefits to be received, the type and amount of training and uniforms

Notes

These five reasons are generally not applicable to contract security companies whose clients are willing to pay for higher than average wage rates, training and benefits.

Money is always the major reason contract security is a popular alternative to proprietary security.

Another reason is that contract security guards can eliminate some of the familiarity that builds among company employees. A kind of outside-looking-in position is garnered. Developing a visible, yet not over-imposing position can lead to a very successful service.

and if desired, the right to interview all applicants before hiring. The advantage in using contract security with the stipulations noted above will allow for the security officer to receive fair wages and benefits but more importantly, the many personnel problems can be minimized. If the organization wants to transfer or remove an officer the contracting company can do so. Problems with union language, restrictive job requirements, and seniority considerations are normally not considered as restrictions when utilizing a contract security agency. Fairness in administering contract security personnel is necessary to insure good employee morale.

An organization which uses a contract security service can be very satisfied with the company provided the organization demands quality service and is willing to pay for quality service. Naturally, the contract security company must be able to deliver what it promises. Therein lies another problem with contract security. Security service companies will often reduce service in order to increase profits for a short period of time. Eventually, the client organization decides to change security companies and unfortunately, another company is selected which fails to serve the client's needs.

When reviewing a contract security company's billing rate the following information can generally be relied upon:

Hourly rate/labor costs	....	67%
Administrative costs	....	23%
Profit	....	10%
	Total	100%

Based upon the above information if a contract security company charged its client $8.00 an hour for service, approximately $5.35 will be paid to the security officer.

For the past 25 years there has been a steady increase in the use of contract security services. There is no indication this trend will reverse. A contract security company that delivers what it promises and does not sacrifice long-range

Notes

A contract security company must tailor the security officer to the position. Security companies should look at the long haul approach. Good service will generate more hours and more profit over the longer period of time.

The dilemma for people employed as security officers is: proprietary positions pay more than contract positions, however, proprietary positions are continuing to be eliminated.

goals for short-term profit, is considered a rarity. Those rare companies which do exist are very successful!

Summary

You should recall that this module detailed the 10 goals and standards published in the **Private Security Task Force Report.** While these standards and goals addressed different issues, the same theme was stressed: training is needed in private security.

The "John Wayne Syndrome" was described as an attitude displayed by many security officers who want to carry a gun and act like the actor, John Wayne. The basic type of recruiting performed in private security is through use of local newspapers' Help-Wanted ads.

For a variety of reasons including recruitment and training, low wages are normally paid to private security officers, particularly those who work for contract agencies.

Job descriptions and job evaluations were explained and are considered a "must" in an effort to insure a security officer performs his/her job successfully.

The cost of using security officer coverage was explained. Costs can be high depending on the number of hours of coverage provided and the hourly billing rate for that service. Typically, a post which is operated 24 hours a day, 7 days a week can cost over $65,000 a year.

Issues concerning the selection of proprietary or contract security were addressed. While there may be several good reasons for employing proprietary or "in-house" security, the main reason for using contract security is cost. Problems associated with the Contract Security industry could be minimized if the organizations which use contract security demanded more service and paid for this service.

Notes

SELECTED REFERENCES

1. Truett A. Ricks, Bill G. Tillet & Clifford W. VanMeter, Principles of Security: An Introduction, Anderson Co., 1981, p. 116.

2. Private Security: Standards and Goals, *The Official Private Security Task Force Report*, Anderson Co.,1977, p. 16.

3. Ricks, et. al., p. 122.

4. *Security Management*, "Views on the Hallcrest Report", February 1985, pp. 58-61.

5. William C Cunningham, John J. Strauchs & Clifford W. Van Meter, The Hallcrest Report II: Private Security Trends 1970-2000, Butterworth-Heinemann, 1990.

6. *Security Management*, "Hallcrest II: The State of Security", December, 1990, pp. 68-78.

QUESTIONS

1. Private security personnel outnumber law enforcement personnel.   True or False.

2. The Rand Study published in the early 1970's looked favorably on the private security industry. True or False.

3. In 1977 the LEAA (Law Enforcement Assistance Administration) funded a report entitled: Private Security: Standard and Goals from the Official Private Security Task Force Report.   True or False.

4. In the Private Security Task Force Report it recommended that training be conducted at all levels of security to insure that personnel are fully prepared to perform their job effectively.   True or False.

5. The Private Security Task Force Report recommended that private security employers should develop job descriptions for each security position. True or False.

6. The Private Security Task Force Report recommended that private security employees complete a minimum of 8 hours formal pre-assignment training. True or False.

7. The Private Security Task Force Report recommended that all private security personnel be required to successfully complete a _____ hour firearm course that includes legal and policy requirements.
      a. 2
      b. 12
      c. 32
      d. 24

8. The Private Security Task Force Report stated that supervisors and managers did not need job related training. True or False.

9. When a security officer acts tough and walks in a cocky, arrogant manner, he/she may be acting like:
      a. Bozo the Clown
      b. Moe, Larry or Curly
      c. Ronald Reagan
      d. John Wayne

10. Most security companies obtain most of their applicants as a direct result of

      _____.

11. What is the name of the 1971 case in which the U.S. Supreme Court stated that a high school diploma and standardized I.Q. tests could not be required as a condition of employment unless it could be proven that the education and tests were valid and non-discriminatory?
    a. Miranda v. Arizona
    b. Roe v. Wade
    c. Griggs v Duke Power Co.
    d. Terry v. Ohio

12. Authors Ricks, Tillet and VanMeter in <u>Principles of Security</u> state, "there is no more important issue in private security today than _____.
    a. Hourly wages
    b. Benefits
    c. Finding a good job
    d. Training

13. Job descriptions and job evaluations should be given to all security officers at least every year. True or False.

14. If a post is to be operated 24 hours a day, 7 days a week, 365 days a year, how many security officers would be needed to operate the post?
    a. 6
    b. 3
    c. 4.2
    d. 8

15. The main reason that contract security officers are used rather than proprietary is:
    a. Better training.
    b. Fewer problems.
    c. Money.

16. The author of this manual believes that a company when soliciting bids for contract security should specify the hourly pay rate, benefits and training a security officer is to receive. True or False.

17. Approximately 65-70% of a contract security company's billing rate should be paid to the security officer as an hourly wage. True or False.

18. Base on question #17, if a contract security company bills at a rate of $10 per hour, the security officer should receive between $_____ and $_____ as an hourly rate.

19. Contract security has been decreasing over the past 25 years. True or False.

20. It is generally agreed that some minimum amount of training is required for security officers who are armed. True or False.

SAMPLE SECURITY OFFICER PERFORMANCE EVALUATION
(CONFIDENTIAL)

NAME(print)_____

           (Last Name)   (First Name)   (Middle Name)

DATE OF EVALUATION_____DATE OF HIRE_____

POSITION_____FACILITY_____

IMMEDIATE SUPERVISOR_____

PURPOSE:

The performance appraisal has one prime purpose - improved performance. The appraisal procedure must not be mere display of appreciation for good work done or, on the other hand, an opportunity to reprimand the employee for poor performance. Rather, it is to serve as an opportunity to offer the employee advice and counsel regarding the strengths and weaknesses of the employee's performance.

OBJECTIVE:

To establish a performance appraisal system that will enable us to:

1. Objectively relate compensation to performance.
2. Focus maximum attention upon achievement of assigned duties.
3. Provide a tool which enables management to accurately assess individuals strengths and weaknesses, relate these assignments to current and future needs, and make staffing and organization plans accordingly.
4. Challenge the individual to continually improve performance and personal effectiveness.
5. Keep employees continually informed of their successes and failures so they know where they stand and are in a position to control their progress.
6. Place primary emphasis on employee self-development and intimately involve the individual in the planning and implementation of career objectives.

PERFORMANCE APPRAISAL - MECHANICS:

1. The performance appraisal is to be conducted quarterly and/or in conjunction with wage reviews. Performance appraisals, however, may not necessarily mean an increase in wages.

2. Definitions of the rating factors (unsatisfactory, meets requirements, exceeds requirements, exceptional) are as follows:

   A. unsatisfactory
   Performance does not meet acceptable standards and improvement is required.

   B. meets requirements
   Performance meets minimum acceptable standards in most instances.

C.   exceeds requirements
Performance is usually above minimum standards in most instances. Performs duties in a comprehensive manner. Usually accurate, timely, and decisive.

D.   exceptional
Duties conducted in a thoughtful and judicious manner with little or no need for direction, resulting in outstanding contributions on a continuing basis. Typically accurate, timely, decisive, and comprehensive in carrying out assignments and/or making recommendations. Aggressively seeks to expand scope of activity and assume additional responsibility.

3.   The focus of the appraisal is necessarily on past performance. The rating terminology used for each area should conform to the terms used above. Each area should be rated separately and the overall rating developed on cumulative basis.

4.   The performance appraisal and salary/bonus recommendation must be approved by Site Management, Corporate Office Management, and Client Management before the performance appraisal interview is held.

5.   The following numerical values should be applied to the respective rating factors:
        A.   Unsatisfactory - 0
        B.   Meets Requirements - 1
        C.   Exceeds Requirements - 2
        D.   Exceptional - 3

Description of Factors:

ATTENDANCE

No instances of tardiness or absenteeism = Exceptional
(1) instance of tardiness or absenteeism = Exceeds Reg.
(2) instances of tardiness or absenteeism = Meets Req.
(3) or more instances of absenteeism or tardiness in a quarterly period is unsatisfactory.

There are NO EXCEPTIONS for rating this factor.

QUALITY OF REPORTS, LOGS, & OTHER WRITTEN MATERIAL

"How well" are the reports & other written material produced? Spelling, neatness, completeness, accuracy? Is all information obtained when handling valuables situations?

Are there ever any discrepancies with this person's paperwork?

CONDUCT

Compliance with established work rules and policies. Does this person always respond in a professional and expedient manner? Have there been any counseling reports generated on this person for behavioral infractions other than attendance? Does this person avoid loitering in the security office and employee smoking areas?

INTERPERSONAL RELATIONS

Ability to work well with others; helpfulnesses to public, patients, and employees; relates well to supervisors and Hospital Administration. Consider any confrontations. Do they possess and utilize good verbal communication.

PROFICIENCY

Technical knowledge of own job; skill in using equipment such as radios, cameras, and established techniques. Thoroughness of patrols; Do they report open doors, safety hazards, suspicious persons and vehicles? Do they complete assigned tasks in an acceptable manner? Do they always answer telephones in an appropriate and courteous manner?

APPEARANCE

Does this person always report clean shaven? Is their uniform always neat, clean, and properly pressed? Are their shoes always shined? Is their hair neat in appearance?

DEVELOPMENT & INITIATIVE

Motivation; interest in the job. Are they attending or have they recently attended any security related schools, courses, etc. Any management courses? Does this person frequently request difficult special assignments? Does this person require constant or minimal supervision? Does this person make sound recommendations to improve the security program? Does this person frequently go above and beyond the "call of duty?"

FACTOR	UNSATIS.	MEETS REQ.	EXC. REQ.	EXCEPT.	PTS.
ATTENDANCE	____	____	____	____	____
QUALITY OF REPORTS	____	____	____	____	____
CONDUCT	____	____	____	____	____
INTERPERSONAL RELATIONSHIPS	____	____	____	____	____
PROFICIENCY	____	____	____	____	____
APPEARANCE	____	____	____	____	____
DEVELOPMENT & INITIATIVE	____	____	____	____	____

COMMENTS:

_____

_____

_____

_____

TOTAL POINTS____   _____

                          Employee's Signature

OVERALL EVALUATION

                          _____

POINTS   RATING   Supervisor's Signature

21   = Exceptional

14 to 20   = Exceeds requirements

7 to 13   = Meets requirements

Under 7   = Unsatisfactory

The following checklist should be completed when developing the rating for Appearance:

1.   Does this individual's appearance give an immediate impression of a professional security officer?

_____unsat.   _____meets   _____exceeds   _____except.

2.   Does this officer's bearing elicit a positive response from the public?

_____unsat.   _____meets   _____exceeds   _____except.

3.   Does this officer's appearance reflect a positive self image and pride?

_____unsat.   _____meets   _____exceeds   _____except.

4.   Is this officer always properly uniformed?

_____unsat.   _____meets   _____exceeds   _____except.

5.   Are this individual's uniforms always clean and serviceable?

_____unsat.   _____meets   _____exceeds   _____except.

6.   Measure this officer's personal appearance, personal hygiene, weight, hair style.

_____unsat.   _____meets   _____exceeds   _____except.

7.   Is this individual physically fit?

_____unsat.   _____meets   _____exceeds   _____except.

Total_____

Average_____

The following checklist should be completed when developing a rating for Interpersonal Relationships:

1.   Is this officer sensitive to the various ethnic and social groups?

_____unsat.   _____meets   _____exceeds   _____except.

2.   Does this officer have an insight into the types of problems that affect the organization?

_____unsat.   _____meets   _____exceeds   _____except.

3.   Does this officer's performance and interaction with employees, visitors, and patients reflect favorably on the image of the organization and security department?

_____unsat.   _____meets   _____exceeds   _____except.

4.   Does this officer try to look at things from the other party's point of view?

_____unsat.   _____meets   _____exceeds   _____except.

5.   Are employees, visitors, and patients generally satisfied with the way this officer handles situations?

_____unsat.   _____meets   _____exceeds   _____except.

6.   When possible, does this officer try to explain or give a rationale to people before taking action?

_____unsat.   _____meets   _____exceeds   _____except.

7.   Does this officer avoid a condescending or contemptuous attitude?

_____unsat.   _____meets   _____exceeds   _____except.

8.   Is this officer able to give consolation and emotional support to people in times of crisis?

_____unsat.   _____meets   _____exceeds   _____except.

9.   In interacting with employees, visitors, and patients does this officer empathize with their plight by being friendly, tactful, and understanding?

_____unsat.   _____meets   _____exceeds   _____except.

Total_____

Average_____

The following checklist should be completed when developing a rating for Proficiency:

1.   Is this officer able to defuse potentially bad situations?

_____unsat.   _____meets   _____exceeds   _____except.

2.   Does this officer have a grasp for investigative techniques and is the individual innovative in their applications?

_____unsat.   _____meets   _____exceeds   _____except.

3.   Is this officer versatile in his/her patrol function effectively handling a variety of situations? Do they report open doors, suspicious persons and/or vehicles?

_____unsat.   _____meets   _____exceeds   _____except.

4.   Does this officer respond as quickly as possible to service calls?

_____unsat.   _____meets   _____exceeds   _____except.

5.   Is this officer aware of Hospital and Company policies and procedures?

_____unsat.   _____meets   _____exceeds   _____except.

6.   Does this individual analyze data and assemble facts and information with accuracy and attention to detail?

_____unsat.   _____meets   _____exceeds   _____except.

7.   Is this individual's general outlook geared to providing service to employees, visitors, and patients?

_____unsat.   _____meets   _____exceeds   _____except.

8.   Does this individual place a high priority on employee, visitor, and patient satisfaction?

_____unsat.   _____meets   _____exceeds   _____except.

9.   Is this officer able to maintain control in stressful situations?

_____unsat.   _____meets   _____exceeds   _____except.

Total_____

Average_____

The following checklist should be completed when developing a rating for report writing:

1. Are this individual's reports complete, concise, accurate, and qualitative?

    _____unsat.   _____meets   _____exceeds   _____except.

2. Are this individual's reports often in need of correction for misspelled words?

    _____unsat.   _____meets   _____exceeds   _____except.

3. Would you be willing to turn this individual's reports into Administration as if they were your own?

    _____unsat.   _____meets   _____exceeds   ____except.

4. Does this individual's reports always contain "Who, What, When, Where, and How"?

    _____unsat.   _____meets   _____exceeds   _____except.

5. Does this individual listen to what others say and extract relevant information?

    _____unsat.   _____meets   _____exceeds   _____except.

6. Does this individual value and take pride in his/her work in the area of report writing?

    _____unsat.   _____meets   _____exceeds   _____except.

7. Does this individual handle patient valuable situations in manner consistent with current guidelines? Is all the necessary paperwork always completed properly?

    _____unsat.   _____meets   _____exceeds   _____except.

8. Is this individual able to communicate in writing his/her point of view of what really happened in an incident?

    _____unsat.   _____meets   _____exceeds   _____except.

Total _____

Average_____

The following checklist should be completed when developing a rating for conduct:

1. Is this individual empathetic when speaking to people on a person to person basis?

    _____unsat.   _____meets   _____exceeds   _____except.

2. Is this individual tactful in dealing with others?

    _____unsat.   _____meets   _____exceeds   _____except.

3. Are employees, visitors, and patients generally satisfied with the way this individual handles situations?

    _____unsat.   _____meets   _____exceeds   _____except.

4. Has this individual been counseled for any disciplinary actions during this rating period for anything other than absenteeism/tardiness?

    _____unsat.   _____meets   _____exceeds   _____except.

5. Does this individual use persuasion rather than authority, when possible?

    _____unsat.   _____meets   _____exceeds   _____except.

6. Does this individual avoid a condescending or contemptuous attitude?

    _____unsat.   _____meets   _____exceeds   _____except.

7. Does this individual's performance and interaction with employees, visitors, and patients reflect favorably on the image of the organization and the security department?

    _____unsat.   _____meets   _____exceeds   _____except.

8. Is this individual willing to be unpopular among peers in order to adhere to positive principles?

    _____unsat.   _____meets   _____exceeds   _____except.

9. Can this individual be relied upon to successfully complete sensitive assignments?

    _____unsat.   _____meets   _____exceeds   _____except.

10. Can this individual make sound decisions under stress?

    _____unsat.   _____meets   _____exceeds   _____except.

11.   Is this individual able to exercise restraint?

_____unsat.   _____meets   _____exceeds   _____except.

12.   Is this individual aware of how security is perceived in situations when officers congregate in the security office?

_____unsat.   _____meets   _____exceeds   _____except.

13.   Is this individual aware of how security is perceived in situations when officers eat at their post?

_____unsat.   _____meets   _____exceeds   _____except.

14.   Is this individual aware of how security is perceived in situations when officers are observed loitering in a particular area, such as designated smoking areas?

_____unsat.   _____meets   _____exceeds   _____except.

15.   Are this individual's decisions logically sound, as opposed to emotional or impulsive?

_____unsat.   _____meets   _____exceeds   _____except.

16.   Is this individual a willing worker?

_____unsat.   _____meets   _____exceeds   _____except.

17.   Is this individual able to control his/her emotions?

_____unsat.   _____meets   _____exceeds   _____except.

18.   How does this individual react to unforeseen events?

_____unsat.   _____meets   _____exceeds   _____except.

19.   Does this individual place a positive emphasis on the personal treatment of employees, visitors, and patients?

_____unsat.   _____meets   _____exceeds   _____except.

20.   Does this individual go out of his/her way to give assistance to employees, visitors, and patients?

_____unsat.   _____meets   _____exceeds   _____except.

Total_____
Average_____

This following checklist should be completed when developing a rating for Development and Initiative:

1. Is this individual self-motivated?

_____unsat. _____meets _____exceeds _____except.

2. Has this individual recently (past year) completed any security related courses in college?

_____unsat. _____meets _____exceeds _____except.

3. Has this individual recently (past year) completed any security related courses specifically designed for a healthcare setting?

_____unsat. _____meets _____exceeds _____except.

4. Has this individual recently (past year) completed any security related courses at any institution?

_____unsat. _____meets _____exceeds _____except.

5. Has this individual completed any management related courses recently (past year)?

_____unsat. _____meets _____exceeds _____except.

6. Is this individual a participating member in any security or healthcare related organizations?

_____unsat. _____meets _____exceeds _____except.

7. Is this individual willing to work nights, weekends, holidays and willing to change his/her personal schedule in order to meet company demands?

_____unsat. _____meets _____exceeds _____except.

8. Is this individual willing to "get involved" when necessary, acting decisively?

_____unsat. _____meets _____exceeds _____except.

Total_____

Average_____

THE EFFECTIVE SECURITY OFFICERS TRAINING MANUAL

Chapter II

Physical Security

Physical Security

Barriers can be divided into two types: natural and structural. Natural barriers are bodies of water, mountains, marshes, deserts or other terrain that occur without man's intervention. Structural barriers are walls, fences, grills, bars, or any other man-made structure. Both types of barriers are used to:

1) define property boundaries
2) deter entry
3) delay and impede unauthorized entry
4) channel and restrict the flow of traffic
5) provide for more efficient and effective use
   of security forces.

Perimeter Security

Perimeter protection refers to the use of barriers and manpower to surround and physically protect valuable material or information.

Great care should be taken to ensure that the structure to be protected receives maximum exposure, that means that if possible the structure should be placed in such a way that all four sides are visible. Also, landscaping precautions should be taken to be certain that large quantities of plants not be located within 50 feet of the structure.

Fencing

Fencing is usually used to protect large areas. There are three basic types of fencing:
1) chain link: used to secure permanent facilities.
2) barbed wire: used for less permanent facilities.
3) concertina wire: used in emergency or short
   term situations.

Characteristics of Chain Link Fencing:
- should be as straight as possible
- usually 8 feet in height
- erect fence 50 feet or more from the building or
  object to be protected

Notes

Reading for a Purpose
Look for these key words:
- Chain-link Fence
- Panic Bar
- Foot Candle
- Continuous Lighting
- Master Key
- Safes
- Floodlight
- Mechanical Locks
- Electronic Locks
- Combination Locks
- Deadbolt
- Vaults

Look for answers to these key questions:
- What are the various devices and instruments which are used in combination with one another to ensure adequate physical security?
- How effective is lighting in providing security protection?
- What role does a good key system play in providing adequate security?

Natural barriers served early civilization as an effective means of security.

Barriers allow for effective security.

- 11 gauge or heavier wire should be used
- mesh openings in the fence should be no larger than 4 square inches

Characteristics of Barbed Wire Fencing
- seldom used to protect perimeter due to unsightfulness and danger
- should be constructed of #12 gauge wire, twisted and barbed every 4 inches
- should be at least 8 feet in height

Characteristics of Concertina Wire Fencing
- consists of barbed wire clipped together at intervals to form cylinders weighing approximately 55 pounds; sometimes referred to as "razor ribbon"
- sections of fence are 50 feet in length
- one coil placed on another creates a fence of 6 feet in height
- can be laid quickly and easily retrieved, good for emergency situations
- difficult to cut

Protective Dogs

Protective dogs are used to provide either a physical or psychological barrier. The dogs are generally divided into two categories - sentry dogs and attack dogs.

Sentry dogs are usually kept on a short leash as they make the rounds with a security officer. They keep the handler alert and provide companionship and give confidence. They are most effective at night.

Some problems that may occur with the use of a sentry include: industrial noise will significantly interfere with hearing and a strong odor of oil will make it difficult for the dog's sense of smell. In addition, dogs are not used extensively since many security officers do not enjoy the animals and/or are incapable of handling sentry animals. To be effective the security officer and sentry dog must spend a lengthy period of time training together in addition to the care of the animal (food, cleaning, etc.).

Notes

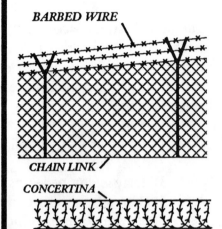

BARBED WIRE

CHAIN LINK

CONCERTINA

Protective Dogs provide a greater level of security than one security officer and is far cheaper than adding another officer. Dogs provide valued companionship to a security officer, especially at night.

How many security companies are you aware of that use dogs?

Guard or attack dogs are different from sentry dogs. Guard dogs usually patrol inside fenced areas and buildings without a human handler. Guard dogs will attack without command and are often used by car dealers, retail stores, scrap yards and warehouses. The decision to use guard dogs must be evaluated with regard to the significant liability factor in the event the animal attacks.

Building Service Security

The second line of defense is the actual building which consists of six sides:
- roof (very vulnerable)
- floor
- 4 walls

Windows

In addition to the roof, windows are extremely vulnerable to forced entry. Glass windows can be reinforced with metal bars or grates placed on the outside of the windows. Windows alarms, such as foil, are often used to protect windows. Window foil (which is similar to aluminum foil) is usually 3/8" - 1" in width and is taped onto the inside portion of a window. An electrical current passes through the foil in a non-alarm status. The foil forms an electrical current which continuously passes. If the foil is torn or broken thereby causing a disruption in the electrical current, an alarm is sounded. Typically, liquor and jewelry stores use window foil alarms on large store front windows.

In addition to the window foil alarms, vibrator or glass breakage alarms can be discretely placed on the inside of a window. In the case of the vibration alarm, if the window is jolted an alarm will sound. A glass breakage alarm sounds once glass in the window is broken or cracked.

Since windows are commonly used in residential and industrial settings, it is important to have at least a basic understanding of how glass is made and how windows are secured so that they remain in place.

Notes

A "junkyard dog" describes a mean and vicious animal and is synonomous with the phrase, "mean-as-a-junkyard dog!"

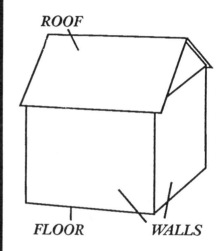

Window glass is usually installed in one of three ways:

1) putty
2) molding which may be nailed to the window
3) the window frame may be grooved so that the glass can be inserted in the grooves and then clamped into place with glazing compound.

Glass can be reinforced to minimize damage. Plastic can be adhered to glass to resist shattering.

Tempered glass is treated to resist breakage by placing a piece of regular glass in an oven bringing it almost to its melting point, then chilled rapidly. A skin forms around the glass which strengthens the glass three to five times its normal strength. Tempered glass is also more resistant to heat.

Laminated glass (used in street level windows and display glass) is made of two sheets of ordinary glass which are bonded to an intervening layer of resilient plastic material. Laminated glass which is about 5/16" in thickness is shatter resistant.

Bullet proof glass is actually bullet resistant and is constructed of laminated glass and plastic. Bullet resistant glass is 3/4" - 3" thick.

Wired glass has been used in the past by many institutions, particularly schools but is generally considered to have limited acceptability. Wire is inserted between two sheets of glass during processing and when dry the wire is secure.

Plastic glass such as acrylic glass is much lighter than regular glass. Generally, plastic glass is more expensive but it is easier to install because of its lightness.

Doors

Special precautions need to be considered when installing doors to insure that the door and/or frame cannot be easily removed to allow for unauthorized entry. Close attention must be paid to fire codes, especially the Life Safety Code which usually requires all doors to open outward. Doors can be alarmed to allow for exit but local fire codes must be reviewed before exit doors are locked. A relatively recent development has been the "delayed panic door release".

Notes

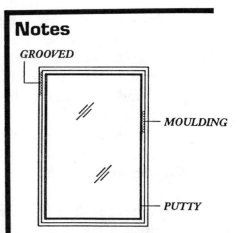

GROOVED

MOULDING

PUTTY

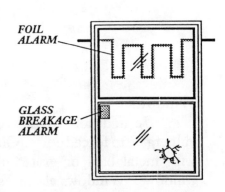

FOIL ALARM

GLASS BREAKAGE ALARM

DELAYED PANIC DOOR RELEASE

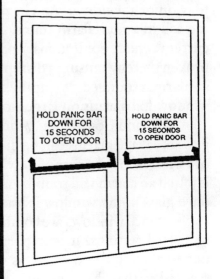

HOLD PANIC BAR DOWN FOR 15 SECONDS TO OPEN DOOR

HOLD PANIC BAR DOWN FOR 15 SECONDS TO OPEN DOOR

Notes

This device requires a person who is exiting to hold the handle down for 15 seconds before the latch is released and the door is opened. The purpose for the "delay release" is to allow for a reasonable level of security (i.e. while the door handle is held down, a camera could record the identify of the person trying to exit) while insuring safety controls are met.

Security Lighting

Security or protective lighting serves as a deterrent for potential criminal activity. A study of six areas in California by the National Criminal Justice Information and Statistics Service showed that in 69% of the burglaries studied, the point of entry was not illuminated.[1]

Today, even the smallest communities provide for street lighting in their budgets. As protective lighting has developed, it has come to serve many functions. The National Evaluation Program on Street Lighting Projects outlines the varied uses:

Security and Safety
- Prevent Crime
- Alleviate Fear of Crime
- Prevent Traffic (Vehicular and Pedestrian) Accidents

Community Character and Vitality
- Promote Social Interaction
- Promote Business and Industry
- Contribute to a Positive Nighttime Visual Image
- Provide a Pleasing Daytime Appearance
- Provide Inspiration for Community Spirit & Growth

Traffic Orientation and Identification
- Provide Visual Information for Vehicular and Pedestrian Traffic
- Facilitate and Direct Vehicular and Pedestrian Traffic Flow.[2]

Lighting basically serves three purposes:
1. advertises the owner or facility manager's product or service during the evening hours.
2. assists in pedestrian and vehicular traffic.
3. deters unauthorized entries and exits from the facility and may aid in apprehension of assailants.

In planning for an effective protective lighting layout one must take into consideration the following:
1) size
2) brightness
3) contrast
4) time

Size
Larger objects require less light than smaller objects. Larger objects reflect more light.

Brightness
Light color reflects more light than dark color. A building which is painted white will need less lighting than one which is painted a dark color. Brightness is the level of light.

Contrast
Coarsely textured objects tend to absorb light whereas smooth surfaced objects tend to reflect light.

Time
Time refers to the fact that greater illumination is required for areas that are visually complex or crowded.

Lighting Terminology

1) Candle Power - One candle power is the amount of light emitted by one standard candle. This standard has been established by the National Bureau of Standards and is commonly used to rate various systems.

2) Foot Candle - One foot candle equals one lumen of light per square foot of space. The density or intensity of illumination is measured in foot candles. The more intense the light, the higher the foot candle rating for the light.

Notes

3) Lumen - One lumen is the amount of light required to light an area of one square foot to one candle power. Most lamps are rated in lumens.

4) Brightness - Brightness refers to the ratio of illumination to that which is being observed. High brightness on certain backgrounds makes observation difficult. Brightness therefore, should not be too low or too high relative to the field of vision.3

As an example, the sun on a clear day supplies about 10,000 foot candles of light to earth. It is generally accepted that 100,000 foot candles of light is the upper tolerance limit for light striking the human eye.

Lighting can provide a psychological deterrent to convince a "would-be" attacker that penetration attempts would likely lead to detection and/or apprehension.

Types of Protective Lighting

Continuous is the most common type of lighting. With continuous lighting a series of fixed lights are installed so that a protected area is flooded with overlapping "cones" of light.

A second type of lighting is glare protection which is used often is illuminating the perimeter of a facility. Lighting with floodlights is a form of glare protection. Floodlights can be mounted on poles, roof lines or on top of a building's walls or fence. High-Pressure Sodium floodlights have become very popular in recent years. The High-Pressure Sodium lights emit an orange light that provides for greater illumination than the Mercury-Vapor lights which emit a blue light. In addition, High-Pressure Sodium lights use less energy than Mercury-Vapor lights. A 400 watt High Pressure Sodium floodlight produces illumination equal to a 1,000 watt Mercury-Vapor floodlight. Many electric utility companies provide a service which allows its customers to convert from the Mercury-Vapor lights to High-Pressure Sodium for a nominal charge.

A third type of lighting is controlled lighting. As the name implies, this type of lighting is designed to light a particular area in a controlled fashion. It is generally used to light facilities or areas which cannot use glare protection lighting. Parking lot lighting used by most hospitals and

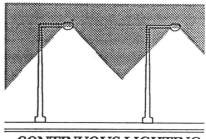

CONTINUOUS LIGHTING

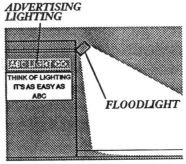

GLARE PROTECTION

colleges is an example of controlled lighting. Controlled lighting allows for sufficient illumination but does not cause glare which could prove dangerous to motorists.

Finally, lighting can be supplemented with movable lighting and emergency lighting systems. Movable lighting became extremely popular with NCAA football games the past five years. Many stadiums such as Notre Dame's and Ohio State's do not have permanent lighting. Television networks induced many colleges and universities to move their Saturday afternoon games to late in the afternoon or into the evening hours in order to televise the games during prime time. Large banks of lights were transported on movable cranes or "booms" and were elevated above the stadium. These movable lights provided illumination similar to the fixed lighting systems.

In summary, when a lighting system is being considered security needs, safety concerns and cost must all be addressed.

Locks & Keys

Locks and keys have existed in a variety of forms for centuries. This discussion will focus primarily on four types of locking systems:

1) Mechanical
2) Electro-mechanical
3) Electronic
4) Combination

Mechanical

Mechanical locks utilize some barrier arrangement of physical parts to prevent the opening of the bolt or latch. The three functional assemblies are:

1) the bolt or latch which actually holds the movable part (door, window, etc.)
2) the tumbler array which is the barrier that must be passed to move the bolt.
3) the key or unlocking device which is specifically designed to pass the barrier and move the bolt.

Notes

Types of Mechanical Locks

Warded Lock - is the lock longest in use, first developed in the first century B.C., easily vulnerable, key is not resistant to weathering, homes built in the early 1900's can be found to have warded locks (skeleton type design).

Lever Lock - was developed in the 18th century, offers greater security than the warded lock, keys can be cut to different dimensions to operate the lock which is known as master keying, still used in cabinet and locker installations and bank safe deposit boxes, susceptible to picking but precautions during lock design and manufacture can reduce this to a low level.

Pin Tumbler Lock - was an important development in the 19th century by Linus Yale; it is now the most widely used type of lock in the United States, the maze/obstacle segment is different from other locks:

Conventional Tumbler - always has its keys pins equally spaced in one row only.

Plug - rotates the key when properly inserted and permits the bolt to be drawn or "thrown" by rotary action.

Shell - the immovable housing where the plug is fitted; the pin tumblers extend from the shell into the plug thereby preventing the plug from turning.

Wafer Tumbler Lock - utilizes wafers (flat metal discs) to bind the plug to the shell.

A common use of keys and locks for convenience and ease of operation is master keying. Master keying refers to the ability of one key or a set of keys to unlock more than one lock. While master keying affords convenience, three problems occur as a result:

1) proper accountability of master keys must be maintained.
2) a lock is easier to manipulate because of the ability of different keys to unlock it.
3) maintenance of the system is increased because of the additional keys.

Notes

WARDED KEY

LEVER KEY

PIN TUMBLER LOCK

Electro-Mechanical Locks

Electro-mechanical locks operate either entirely through electrical energy or with an electrical release feature as an adjunct to any standard mechanical lock. Usually, electro-mechanical locks use 115 volts of AC power. In an effort to make these types of locks more secure, the lock is enclosed in a metal container which is physically resistive to outside energy sources and will not release the bolt unless the exact electrical energy level is received.

Electronic Locks

Electronic locks utilize certain combinations or sequences of events to occur before the control circuit will deliver electrical energy to the mechanical or latch release. Locks of this type include card key systems.

Combination Locks

Dial type combination locks operate by aligning gates on tumblers to allow insertion of a fence on the bolt. These locks offer better security but are more expensive. Most combination locks are manufactured with two to six tumblers, each with a slot or notch cut into its edge. When all these notches are aligned by the proper turning of the dial, an arm (fence) drops into a slot created by the alignment and the locking bar can be retracted from the strike to open the lock.

Key Systems

A key is the standard method of allowing entry through a locked door as well as relocking the door. Most key locks are designed to accept only one key which has been made and cut to fit the lock. Keys and keying systems are generally divided as follows:

1) Change key: standard key that fits a single lock within a master key system or to any other single lock unnumbered by such a system. Numerous locks can be "keyed alike" to accept only one key.
2) Maison key: type of submaster very common in apartment houses and office buildings. This key unlocks apartment and the main entrance door.

Notes

3) Master Key System: by splitting the bottom pin into two or more segments, two different cuts or combinations of different keys will raise the bottom pins to the shearline which allows for unlocking.
4) Submaster: opens all locks of a particular area or grouping within a facility.
5) Master Key: opens all locks in the facility that are part of the master key system.
6) Grand Master: opens every lock in a key system involving two or more master keys.
7) Control Key: maintenance key which removes the core from the housing and allows for recombinating the lock; useful when keys are lost.

Key Control

Key control is vital if an effective lock and key system is to exist. It is generally recommended that a person who has security responsibility (of some sort) be designated as the key control person. This individual would issue all keys, note changes in personnel who possess keys, review all requests for new keys and conduct regular inventories to ensure that all keys are properly accounted. A written log on all key and lock transactions should be maintained. Grand Master keys should not be routinely issued. Instead they should be securely stored for use in an emergency. Likewise, master key issuance should be restricted. A loss of a master key compromises all of the locks which were part of the master or sub-master system. All keys should be identified by coding or marking along with a notation that the key is not to be duplicated.

Types of Lock Bolts & Latches

Deadbolt: A deadbolt does not contain a spring and it must be manually moved into the strike by turning a key or thumb turn. Deadbolts provide a greater degree of security but fire codes must be reviewed to ensure that proper precautions are taken before the installation of a deadbolt lock.

Springloaded Latch: A springloaded latch provides a minimum level of security since the latch can be withdrawn from the strike whenever force is applied to the latch itself.

Notes

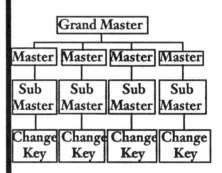

Springloaded Deadbolt Latch: A springloaded deadbolt latch operates in the same manner as the springloaded latch except an extra latch (bar) is located on the side of the latchbolt.

In summary, locks and keys provide only a reasonable level of security. If an attacker desires entry a good lock and key system will only delay the assault but this delay is important and may serve as a deterrent in that the attacker feels he/she may be observed. Naturally, the benefits of a lock and key system are enhanced if careful planning is undertaken during the installation of the system and proper key controls are in place and enforced. Nearly 50% of all illegal entries occur by the intruder entering through a door. A basic lock and key system which is utilized to its fullest extent can reduce the illegal entries.

Safes

A labeling service is provided by Underwriter's Laboratories (UL) and the Safe Manufacturers National Association (SMNA) which defines the level of protection each safe can be expected to provide.

Record Safes & Fire Protection

Paper is destroyed at 350° F. while electronic data records (computer storage media) can be destroyed at 150 F. It is necessary that moisture be built into the insulation of the safe to help remove heat during a fire. As long as there is sufficient moisture to displace the heat, the contents will be protected. Moisture cannot be replaced in the insulation of a safe that has been in a previous fire. For this reason, a safe that has been exposed to a fire while not showing signs of damage on its surface, should be replaced.

Labels on safes which describe their fire-resistive characteristics can usually be found on the back of the safe's door or in the interior of the safe.

An example of the UL and SMNA ratings is shown below:

SMNA Designation	UL Designation
A	350° F. - 4 hours
B	350° F. - 2 hours
C	350° F. - 1 hour

Notes

All three classes are given three tests: fire exposure, explosion and impact. Insulated file safes designated as a Class D or E provide far less protection from both fire and impact.

As an example: if a safe were rated "Class A" by SMNA and 350° F. - 4 hours by UL this means that the safe would withstand temperatures up to 2000° F. for four hours. During this four hour timeframe the temperature of the interior of the safe would not exceed 350° F. which would allow this safe to protect documents.

Class "C" safes are the most popular and commonly used safes.

Electronic Data Processing Record Protection

Since electronic data processing records begin to deteriorate at 150° F. and at humidity levels of more than 85%, these records are often protected by using a "safe within a safe." This is done with a container that has a sealed inner insulated repository, in which the EDP material is stored, and an outer safe protected by a heavy wall of insulation.

Safes Designed to Protect Money

Safes which are designed to protect money or other forms of negotiables (such as checks) differ greatly from the fire resistant safes. Since fire resistant safes contain a great deal of insulation to protect the safe's contents from heat, these safes are more susceptible to burglary and robbery.

Robbery - Resistive safes will prevent thefts when there is no actual assault on the safe itself. Chests with key locks, lockers and wall safes with either key or combination locks fit this category. Robbery - Resistive products require steel bodies and doors of less thickness than is required for burglary - resistive safes. Robbery - Resistive safes afford a satisfactory level of security in protecting money and other valuables provided "force" is not used to open the safe. Remember that robbery involves the taking or attempt of taking something of value from a person by force, the threat of force and/or violence. Robbery - Resistive safes provide only some protection against robbery.

Burglary - Resistive safes differ greatly from robbery - resistive safes. Burglary - Resistive safes will resist attack by tools, torch or explosives in direct proportion to their

Notes

construction. These safes are constructed of reinforced or solid steel. Remember that burglary is the unlawful entry of a building to commit a felony or theft. Burglary differs from robbery in that in most cases the burglar is attempting to steal from another person without their knowledge, such as a person breaking into a business after closing to steal from a safe. When a robbery is committed, the victim knows immediately of their loss since they are being forced by the assailant to give up their property.

Vaults

Vaults differ from safes in that vaults are larger and are part of the building structure. Vaults should have walls of 12" reinforced concrete, steel doors and a combination lock.

The Insurance Services Office classifies safes. An example of some of these classes is described below:

Class	Doors	Walls
B (Fire Resistive)	Steel less than 1" thick.	Body of steel, or iron less 1/2" thick.
ANY IRON OR STEEL SAFE HAVING A SLOT THROUGH WHICH MONEY CAN BE DEPOSITED.		
C (Burglar Resistive)	Steel at least 1" thick.	Body of steel at least 1/2" thick.
SAFE BEARING LABEL "UL INSPECTED KEYLOCKED SAFE KL BURGLARY		
E (Burglar Resistive)	Steel at least 1 1/2" thick.	Body of steel at least 1" thick.

Notes

SUMMARY

Physical security consists of barriers which are either man-made or natural. Natural barriers are bodies of water, mountains, marshes, deserts and other terrain. Barriers define property boundaries and provide for better use of security forces.

Perimeter protection consists of fencing, protective dogs, buildings, windows, doors and lighting.

Locks and keys are essential in any type of security program. Locks can be mechanical, electro-mechanical, electronic or a combination type. The Warded lock has been used longer than any other lock. The Lever lock provides better security than warded locks. Lever locks are still used in cabinets and lockers. The Pin Tumbler lock was developed in the 19th century and is the most widely used lock in the USA. It is important that proper records of locks and keys are maintained. Deadbolts are a good security device used in many locks. Deadbolts must be physically moved with a key or thumb turn and are difficult to force open.

Safes are usually designed to protect valuables from fire or burglary. Underwriters Laboratories (U.L.) and the Safe Manufacturers National Association (S.M.N.A.) test and label safes which describe their level of protection. Safes are designed to protect computer records and money or other valuables. Safes may be robbery resistive or burglary resistive.

Vaults differ from safes. Vaults are larger and are part of the building. They should have walls of 12" reinforced concrete, steel doors and a combination lock. Vaults usually provide a higher degree of protection than safes.

FOOTNOTES

1. Truett A. Ricks, Bill G. Tillet & Clifford W. VanMeter, Principles of Security: An Introduction, Anderson Co.,1981, p. 55.
2. Ibid, pp. 56-57.
3. Ibid, pp. 58-59.

Notes

QUESTIONS

1. Natural/Structural barriers are used to:

    1. define _____ _____.
    2. _____ entry.
    3. _____ and _____ unauthorized entry.
    4. _____ and _____ the flow of traffic.
    5. provide for _____ _____ _____
        of _____ _____.

2. Name the three types of fences and when they are used.
    1. _____ : _____
    2. _____ : _____
    3. _____ : _____

3. What is the difference between guard dogs and sentry dogs?

    _____

4. For security purposes a building consists of six sides. Name them.
    1. four _____
    2. _____
    3. _____

5. List 3 ways windows can be made less vulnerable.
    1. _____
    2. _____
    3. _____

6. List the three purposes lighting serves.
    1. _____
    2. _____
    3. _____

7. What are the three types of protective lighting?
    1. _____
    2. _____
    3. _____

8. What are the four types of locking systems?
    1. _____
    2. _____
    3. _____
    4. _____

9. What is master keying?

    _____

    _____

10. What should the duties of the key control person be?

    _____

    _____

11. What is built into the insulation of a fire resistant safe to protect the safe's contents?

    _____

12. If a safe is rated Class A by SMNA and 350° F. - 4 hours by UL what does this mean.

    _____

13. Electronic data processing (computer) records begin to be destroyed at _____ F. and at humidity levels of _____%.

14. Burglary resistive safes differ greatly from other safes because they are constructed of:

    _____

15. What are vaults?_____

    _____

    How do they differ from safes? _____

Practical Exercises and Questions

1. **Describe the barriers existent at the facility where you work?**

2. **Are any security lock-up procedures in conflict with the Life Safety Code?**

3. **Does exterior perimeter lighting seem sufficient? Are lights replaced when found to be inoperable?**

4. **Who is responsible for key control? Are adequate records maintained? How often is a key inventory conducted?**

5. **Are combinations to locks changed when an employee with access leaves the organization?**

THE EFFECTIVE SECURITY OFFICERS TRAINING MANUAL

Chapter III

Patrol Prodcedures

Patrol Procedures

The primary purpose of security is to prevent and deter loss. A key element in this strategy is the use of patrols conducted by security officers. Patrolling is defined as the act of moving about an area to provide protection and to conduct observation.

Patrols have existed since security measures were first implemented. **Security Supervision** states, "Patrols are necessary to insure the integrity of the overall security program. Frequent and total coverage of the protected area is needed to provide the most timely discover and correction of security, safety and fire hazards."

Fire Prevention

Patrols can be very effective in the overall role of fire prevention provided the security officer is attentive to equipment which may have been unintentionally left on by an employee. Examples would include: coffee pots, typewriters, copier equipment and certain machinery or equipment which a security officer can turn-off, provided they have received instructions to do so. Equipment such as personal computers should never be turned off by a security officer since information stored in the computer's memory may be lost if the equipment loses power.

While patrolling, a security officer should be observant to fire hazards such as the improper storage of combustible or flammable material, blocked fire exits, exposed wiring, fire extinguishers which are inoperable or in accessible, and equipment which may be malfunctioning. It is essential that prior to any patrols, a security officer has been instructed as to -- what to look for when patrolling; how to determine when an abnormal situation exists; and what to do and who is to be notified to report an abnormal situation.

Notes

Reading For A Purpose
Look for these key words:
- **External Patrol**
- **Internal Patrol**
- **Loss Prevention**
- **Pattern Variations**
- **Ingress**
- **Egress**
- **Watchclock**
- **First Patrol**
- **Sixth Sense**

Look for answers to these questions:
- **What are the purposes of patrolling?**
- **What is the significance of the first patrol?**
- **What equipment should be carried while patrolling?**

Patrolling: moving around an area to provide protection.

Combustible materials: *materials which burn when heated to the ignition temperature of the material.*

Reporting to work 10-15 minutes early allows the arriving officer to learn essential information from the officer who is going off duty.

Theft Prevention

While patrolling, a security officer must know what doors and windows are normally open/closed, locked and unlocked. Again, if a door or window is open when it is to be closed and locked, what action should the security officer take? Does he merely close and lock the door and note the same on his shift report, or should someone be immediately notified? There are many situations when, depending upon the circumstances, the police are to be notified if a certain door or window is found unsecured.

Often, while patrolling a security officer will notice that there are several other persons in the facility. How does the security officer know that these persons are authorized to be in the facility? Do employees and visitors wear identification badges? Are certain areas restricted from access for certain employees? It is essential that prior to patrolling a security officer obtain as much information as possible as to what employees/visitors are in the facility? When are these persons scheduled to depart? After they depart, which areas are to be secured? Once all of this information has been obtained, a security officer should not be startled to find other persons in the facility, assuming these persons are authorized. Much of this information should be known by the security officer who is going off duty.

A final part of theft prevention when patrolling will occasionally require a security officer to inspect equipment being removed from the facility. The security officer must know what material can be removed from the facility with proper paperwork and authorization. Are shipping documents, or material removal passes provided to the security officer before removal? If no paperwork is required, the security officer should note in their shift log the identity and description of the person removing the material and what material was being removed.

System Failures & Accident Prevention

Usually, a security officer conducting a patrol in an industrial or manufacturing environment should note a

Notes

It is wise to have a patrol checklist for the officer.

Security Officers must arrive to work early enough to talk to the officer they are relieving to obtain information.

System Failures include problems such as heating and air conditioning systems malfunctioning, or machinery or other equipment which is not operating properly.

potential safety hazard (leaking pipe, water on the floor, etc.) virtually every time a patrol is conducted. This is due in large part to the vastness and age of many facilities. Even though, potential safety hazards may have been previously reported and not corrected, a security officer cannot take for granted that he/she can simply ignore the hazard and not document what has not been corrected. Security officers must be certain that a condition previously reported is known to the proper management officials, before deciding not to document the hazard again believing that, "Nothing ever gets fixed around this place!" Failure to document safety hazards may cause the security officer and their employer to be liable for damages which result from a hazard.

External Patrols

"External patrol covers the grounds, parking areas and streets surrounding the facility buildings. The basic purpose of the external patrol is to protect vehicles and persons entering or leaving the grounds, to provide surveillance of persons attempting to use unauthorized exits, to prevent the carrying of unauthorized property from the facility, and to prohibit or discourage unwanted persons from enter the facility."1

A security officer conducting an external patrol will greatly enhance the overall level of protection provided to a facility. By constantly observing and noting any changes or discrepancies with doors, windows, lights, etc., a security officer can determine unusual situations, which if reported can be properly investigated.

Vehicle Patrols

Vehicle patrols can support external patrols either by supplementing foot patrols or in place of them. A prerequisite for each security officer prior to operating a motorized vehicle is to possess the necessary state driver's license. Additionally, some security personnel may be required to show proof of insurability prior to their operation of a vehicle.

Notes

When in doubt, always make out an incident report: make sure all patrol reports are written in professional language.

External patrols: patrols of an outside area.

Also always note the vehicles that are left on the grounds for extended periods of time.

All security officres should possess a valid driver's license and maintain proper insurance.

A vehicle offers a security officer mobility while providing protection from the elements. Additionally, a vehicle permits a security officer to carry more equipment which can be readily used when needed.

Security vehicles are of all types, shapes, and sizes. Some are battery powered while many are automobiles, trucks, or vans which are utilized as the security department vehicle. No matter what type of vehicle is used, appropriate maintenance and care must be given the vehicle to insure it is functional when needed. Daily and shift vehicle logs should be utilized to document levels of fuel, oil, water, tire pressure, etc. Mileage has to be documented and verified according to IRS regulations. If any problems develop with the security vehicle, they should immediately be noted in the vehicle log. All damage to a security vehicle must be noted immediately. Unfortunately, since several persons usually drive a security vehicle, wear and tear of the vehicle is often accelerated. Some security managers restrict driving of a vehicle to only two or three persons.

Bicycles

Recently, many security departments, especially those that serve a multi-facility or campus-type settings such as colleges and universities have incorporated the use of bicycles and tricycles as part of their vehicle patrols. The advantages of a bicycle include dramatically reduced maintenance costs as well as the fact that the purchase of a bicycle is a fraction of any other type of motorized vehicle. Additionally, many individuals who utilize bicycles enjoy the physical exercise which occurs when conducting patrols. Disadvantages of bicycles include their restricted use during inclement weather and during hours of darkness. Some resistance toward required bicycle use may also exist initially but this resistance is usually for only a short time. Industrial-type tricycles have become popular with many departments since they are usually easier to operate.

No matter what type of vehicle is used when conducting external patrols, the purpose is the same. . . observation. A security officer must put forth an effort while

Notes

Whenever a security officer arrives on duty, any vehicle which will be used should be inspected prior to use. Any damage should be noted immediately. Problems develop when a vehicle sustains damage which is unreported for more than one shift.

Vehicle patrols assist with effective observation.

patrolling that increases the likelihood that if something abnormal or unusual were to occur on the exterior of the facility, he/she would notice the event. Far too often, external patrols become very routine, tedious and boring. The security officer finds himself day-dreaming, listening to the vehicle radio, smoking a cigarette and/or in general, just waiting for time to pass. Usually it is during these times that an unexpected event occurs in the parking lot and the security department is then reacting to the event rather than actually preventing or deterring an incident.

While conducting an exterior patrol, security personnel must be aware of the normal routine and behavior of all individuals who enter and exit the facility. A security officer must know that the behavior of an observed individual appears normal (i.e. when walking to their vehicle they do not appear frightened or in a hurry) or unusual (i.e. a person continues to sit in a vehicle 10 minutes after leaving the facility). The point to be made is that it is often difficult to distinguish between the behavior of an individual preparing to commit a crime and the innocent employee or visitor who may be having a problem of some kind. The key point is that as security personnel, we remain alert and make reasonable inquiries such as, "May I help you?" to individuals whose behavior appears unusual. By taking an active interest in learning what is routine from unusual and by investigating suspicions, hunches or observations, security personnel will greatly increase their probability of success in providing effective loss prevention.

INTERNAL PATROL

Purpose

Internal patrols are a key element of an overall loss prevention program and is an integral part of the daily duties of security personnel. Generally, internal patrols are conducted for the same reason as external patrols; to observe, act and report on abnormal or unusual conditions. As part of internal patrols, security personnel should include the following:

Notes

Officers should continually be on the alert and pay attention to the areas about them.

It is here when the officer should stay away from the "John Wayne Syndrome."

Loss prevention: A management philosophy based on the concept of establishing policies which deter or prevent loss.

Internal Patrols: Patrols made inside a facility to observe, act and report on abnormal or unusual conditions.

* Checking doors & windows, correcting & reporting abnormal conditions (i.e. open, closed, locked, unlocked)
* Checking machinery and/or maintenance instruments
* Observing fire protection equipment (sprinklers, risers, fire exit, etc.) for proper condition.
* General Observations

Notes

Assigned Areas

Usually internal patrols are arranged in some sort of systematic manner which includes the times and routes of the patrols. Often a facility of considerable size will have various internal patrols which may be conducted simultaneously by two or more officers or may be alternately patrolled at pre-arranged times. Whatever the situation, it is essential that security personnel remain in their assigned patrol areas unless requested to aid or assist someone. If the security officer is required to leave his assigned patrol area, a supervisor or other officer (if practical & possible) should be notified. This absence from the assigned area should also be noted in the appropriate logs. Unfortunately, incidents will occur in an area that is patrolled by a security officer. Without fail, if security did not observe the incident in any manner, questions will be asked by management as to where and what was the security officer doing during the time of the incident.

The need for up-to-date reports before leaving your shift is essential.

First Patrol

Whenever one security officer is relieving another at the change of shifts, after the normal discussion of events on the preceding shift, the relieving officer will often conduct a patrol of the facility. This patrol is the most important one since it is at the beginning of a shift. At this time, a security officer should note and correct any unusual occurrences. By documenting and correcting any problems during the first patrol, a basis of comparison will be established which may prove invaluable at a later time.

Often, conflicts develop between security officers when one security officer notes in the log doors or windows they found unlocked. Security officers should not attempt to embarass their fellow officers. Simply put, state the facts and give no opinion.

During this first patrol, the professional security officer will note the doors and windows which are opened or unlocked but should be closed and locked. Lights which are left on should also be noted. Particular attention should be given to those areas where problems have occurred in the past such as vending machines, cafeterias, restrooms, conference rooms and executive offices.

During subsequent patrols, the professional security officer will be able to quickly determine if something is out of place because of the diligence paid during his/her first patrol.

Pattern Variations

Virtually every security textbook stresses the importance of varying the route and time of patrols. No two security officers conduct their patrols in the exact same manner. One officer may pay close attention to open doors and windows while another walks through out-of-the-way places. The point to be made is that even patrols made in a reliable yet systematic routine diminish the effectiveness of patrols. Employees of the protected facility will often joke that they can set their watch to the patrols of a security officer.

In an effort to break monotonous, routine patrols, security officers should be encouraged to be creative during their patrols; staggering the time and route of patrols. Merely conducting a patrol while simply "going through the motions" serves little use.

ENTRANCE & EXIT POINTS

The easiest and simplest way to enter a facility is through an entrance or exit. Usually these points of ingress and egress are controlled either by a receptionist, security officer, lock, camera or some other access control mechanism. However, some entrance ways are not controlled adequately especially visitor and employee entrances. Even with sophisticated electronic security devises, compromises occur. That is why, as part of an internal or external patrol, the

Notes

First patrol: the first patrol of a work shift.

Be sure to note any unusual observances in your written logs.

Pattern variations: Varying the route and time of patrols.

Give a position report over the radio when doing patrols.

Ingress: Entrances or ways into a facility.

Egress: Exits or ways out of a facility.

64

security officer should review activity at entrance and exit points.

Persons, who intend to steal from a facility or commit some other sort of act which would damage an organization, will usually enter or exit the building the easiest and quickest way possible. An observant security officer visible at entrance and exit points may never apprehend a criminal but will no doubt prevent some losses from occurring.

WATCHCLOCK ROUNDS

The use of a watchclock to record the time at which a security officer was at a particular location is still in use today. Many companies have changed to a computerized version of the watchclock which serves the same purpose, to provide supervision with a tool to document and evaluate the patrols of a security officer. A record is produced which allows for a proper evaluation to be conducted on the time and route of patrol.

A major problem with the watchclock system is the "punching the clock station" becomes the primary objective of the security officer as opposed to observing, correcting and reporting on anything which appears out of the ordinary.

Proper care and maintenance of the watchclock is required to insure proper operation. Damage to the unit is the primary cause for reliability problems. Any damage to the watchclock should be immediately noted in the daily shift log.

KEYS

Keys are usually carried by a security officer during patrols. Many departments have restricted the number and type of keys a security officer possesses while on patrol. A good rule of thumb is for the officer to carry with him only those keys required to effectively conduct a patrol and respond to requests for doors to be unlocked. Some persons may argue that a security officer should carry an entire set of keys so that in any situation, at any time, access to a particular

Notes

Crime prevention is an essential element of security.

Watchclock: clock device carried by a security officer to document patrol sequence and location of stations.

Officers should not hurry through patrols "just to punch the clock." The most important thing is the patrol itself.

If the watchclock is accidentally damaged, report it at once.

Keys are an important tool of security officers when conducting patrols.

Lock Boxes which contain a master key for use by the fire department can be used to improve access during an emergency.

area could be gained. However, a greater likelihood exists that keys will be lost or misplaced, thereby compromising the entire key system as opposed to a devastating fire that went uncontrolled because a key to unlock an area was not at immediate disposal.

It is important for security personnel to know the key system so that undue delay and embarrassment does not occur because the officer was struggling to find the right key to unlock an area. In addition, serious credibility problems may exist for the security department when a security officer misplaces the keys or accidentally takes the keys home. Many departments place a large key ring around all of the security keys to decrease the likelihood of loss or misplacement.

Radio Communication

Two-way radio communication is also essential and commonplace in most security departments. Radio communication provides quicker response to a problem and affords added protection for a security officer should an injury occur or other problems develops.

It is essential that security personnel be properly trained in the use of two-way radio equipment. Additionally, proper radio etiquette must be practiced by security personnel while using two-way radios. Persons who are unfamiliar with radio etiquette tend to verbalize and babble. This impoliteness appears as unprofessional and creates embarrassment to both the security officer and the entire department. Two-way radio communication may be a shared process with other departments. One must always remember, you never know for certain how many other people are listening to the conversation. When speaking on the radio, a person should assume he is speaking in public. Items of a sensitive or confidential nature should be discussed on a restricted channel or better yet, over the telephone or in person.

Notebook

All security personnel should always carry a small notebook and pen with them at all times while on patrol.

Notes

When changing shifts, make sure keys are exchanged or are left on a key rack for both shifts to note.

Radios are expensive and are an essential part of security communication. Protect them accordingly
a) Good language and diction are important in radio use.
b) It is not an entertainment device.
c) Do not hold radio too close when speaking.
d) Do not cut in on someone else's conversation.
e) Use a number system or code system for identification.

If it's n ot written down...it didn't happen.

Anything of significance should be noted in this notebook as a patrol is conducted.

Flashlight

In order to properly view all areas when patrolling, at least a minimal amount of lighting is required. A security officer needs to know what lights are to be turned-on or off during off-shifts. If lighting is extremely poor, a handheld flashlight will be required. Some departments require security officers to provide their own flashlights. Officers must know if they are permitted to carry large flashlights which may "double" as nightsticks.

PROBLEMS IN PATROL

When patrolling, a security officer may come upon a variety of problems that are not encountered on a daily basis. These include traffic accidents and involvement with unruly persons. At these times, it is extremely important for the security officer to maintain composure and to handle and control the situation in a professional manner. At all times a security officer must consider his safety and the safety of others before rushing into a situation.

At times, a security officer may actually come upon a crime in progress. Again, safety is of prime consideration. Information should be gathered as quickly as possible and this information must be forwarded to the appropriate emergency response units at once! Be certain to be in a position to communicate to arriving emergency units the situation at hand.

A security officer must remember that normally he/she will not come into contact with these special problems. However, on occasion, an emergency will occur which will require the officer to rely on their previous training in order to safely and professionally handle the incident.

Notes

Provide your own flashlight, if necessary.

Remember the liability involved when dealing with a person. Let's again stay away from the John Wayne Syndrome.

Look and listen before rushing into a situation where "angels fear to tread."

Always give your position to arriving safety units. Be certain you know exactly where you are located.

Common sense: is an added requirement when dealing with a problem.

USE OF SENSES

Security officers when patrolling will rely upon their natural senses to determine if conditions are normal or abnormal.

Sight
Sound
Touch
Taste
Smell

A security officer will use their sense of vision to recognize familiar objects in familiar places. Additionally, vision will inform the security officer if an obvious change in the surroundings has occurred since his last patrol.

The sense of hearing will enable a security officer to distinguish glass breakage and malfunctioning equipment from normal operations.

The sense of touch will allow the security officer to determine a possible fire in progress by touching a door prior to entering an area. Malfunctioning equipment may also be hot to touch. Finally, the sense of touch will allow a security officer to come to the aid of an injured person.

It is essential that a security officer learn what is a normal situation from an abnormal situation. When a security officer believes that a condition may be "abnormal", further investigation and follow-up is required.
Does a security officer know who should be contacted to report an abnormal condition?

The sense of smell allows an officer to distinguish normal aroma from acidic, chemical, or burning fumes.

The Sixth Sense

Many times a person is said to have a "sixth sense". This is normally meant as a compliment to the person. What is often meant is that the person always seems to know what is going on around them. Certain teachers, particularly those in the elementary grades are credited with having this "sixth sense". This "sixth sense" whether referring to a teacher, coach, parent or supervisor, is the ability of someone to know what is about to occur, or the ability to know who is being truthful, or what appears out of the ordinary and does not seem "just right." Another term for this sixth sense is intuition or insight. Usually, intuition or insight is developed from experience. Experience permits an individual to sense what is abnormal or unusual. As security officers it is vital to learn as much about the facility as possible. Then, when confronted with a situation which does not appear normal, the security officer should investigate further in order to determine if the situation requires further attention or action.

Sixth Sense: Knowing what is going on around you - identifying a problem before it happens.

Footnote:
1. **Hospital Security**, Russell L. Colling, (Butterworth Publishers: Boston, 1976) p.113.

Summary

The primary purpose of security is to prevent and deter loss. Patrols are necessary to insure the integrity of the overall security program. When doing a patrol, the security officer should be aware of the following problems during coverage of a protected area. Possible fire hazards through the improper storage of combustible materials, exposed wiring, inoperable fire equipment, or employee carelessness. While patrolling, the officer should note unlocked doors and windows, unatuhorized personnel on the premises, and, as a final part of theft prevention, inspect equipment being removed from the facility. The security officer should also note potential safety hazards that can lead to the prevention of possible accidents. There are two types of patrols. They are internal and external. External patrols are those that cover the grounds, parking areas and streets surrounding the facilty. External patrols are either done on foot or with the support of a vehicle. No matter what vehicle is used, appropriate maintenance and care must be given to the vehicle to insure it is functional when needed. The most important aspect of an external patrol is observation. You must become attuned to what is normal and abnormal. Internal patrols are a key element of an overall loss prevention program. Security personnel should be aware of the same abnormal or unusual condition that are part of an external patrol. Internal patrols should be arranged in some sort of systematic order with added significance placed upon the first patrol. Sometimes staggering the time and route of patrols will break up the monotony and take away a "going through the motions" attitude. Some locations still use the watchclock. The officer should not hurry through patrols "just to punch the clock," but remember the patrol itself is the most important element. All security officers should be trained in correct radio etiquette and always assume that he or she is talking to the public. When doing a patrol, a security officer may come upon a variety of problems. He should maintain his composure and consider the safety of himself and the safety of others. When encountering a problem, it is wise many times to call upon one's senses, and above all utilize the one sense that separates a good security officer from an incompetent security officer: that sense being common sense.

Notes

Questions - True-False

1.   The primary purpose of security is to prevent and deter loss. _____

2.   Observation is the basic aspect of both external and internal patrols. _____

3.   When doing patrols, a notebook is not necessary. _____

4.   Failure to record safety hazards could bring liability to the security officers and their employer. _____

5.   A good rule to follow is that a security officer should carry all the keys on his person while doing rounds. _____

Match the Following - Best Answer

_____ 1. Patrolling
_____ 2. External Patrol
_____ 3. Internal Patrol
_____ 4. Simultaneously
_____ 5. First Patrol
_____ 6. Pattern Variations
_____ 7. Egress
_____ 8. Ingress
_____ 9. Sixth Sense
_____ 10. Loss Prevention

a. Changing patrol routes
b. Exit of the facility
c. Act of moving about an area to provide protection
d. Patrol within the facility
e. Entrance to the facility
f. Covers grounds and parking lots
g. Being aware of your surroundings
h. Patrolling at the same time
i. Purpose of Internal Patrol
j. Will establish a basis for comparison
k. Time a security officer was at a particular location

Questions

1.   When making a patrol, what should the security officer be aware of?

2.   What are external patrols and what do they include?

3.   What is the value of the first patrol?

4.   What should an officer do with his keys during a patrol?

5.   What is the importance of a notebook during patrol?

6.   Choose one - What would you do if you encountered a(n) a) accident or b) crime in progress during a patrol.

THE EFFECTIVE SECURITY OFFICERS TRAINING MANUAL

Chapter IV

Electronic Alarm Systems

Electronic Alarm Systems

Electronic alarm systems provide another element of defending a company's assets from loss. An intrusion alarm system which will detect unauthorized entries into a building must be evaluated as to the cost of the alarm system versus the value of the items that are to be protected. For good overall security, there must be a balance between services, equipment and alarms. A system must:

1) be planned to operate without major problems.
2) be economically feasible for the property or building which is being protected.

Alarms can function in a variety of ways and serve a variety of needs. Alarms can be used to:

1) detect fire
2) detect an unauthorized entry
3) notify authorities during an emergency
4) monitor equipment and report malfunctions

The need for an alarm system and the type must be evaluated according to the needs of the owners of the facility. Some facilities will be more prone to burglary or robbery while another may be more likely to be damaged as a result of fire.

There are five basic components to any alarm system: 1) a sensory device, 2) a control unit, 3) an annunciator, 4) a power source and 5) an alarm circuit. These will be explained in greater detail on the following pages.

Sensory Device: initiates the alarm signal as a result of sensing a stimulus or condition to which the system has been designed to react. Heat and smoke detectors and door contacts are examples of sensory devices.

Control Unit: is the final point for all sensors and switches in the alarm system; the control unit is usually housed in heavy metal, tamper resistant cabinets; the elements within the control unit are arranged to receive signals from the sensors and to relay these signals to the appropriate final point within the control unit.

Annunciator: is a visual and/or audible signaling device which indicates activation of the alarm system; a particular type of annunciator is selected depending upon the circumstances and location of the alarm system and the

Notes

Reading for a Purpose
Look for these key words:
•Sensory Device
•Control Unit
•Annunciator
•Alarm circuit
Look for answers to these key
        questions:
•What are alarms used for?
•What types of sensors exist?
•How are alarms received?
•What are disadvantages to an
        alarm-only system?
•What is the false alarm
        problem?

System Components

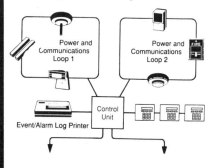

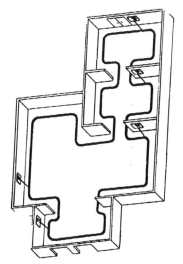

Courtesy of Wells Fargo Alarm Systems

71

desired or required response. (Example: a bank would utilize a "silent" annunciator alarm to report a robbery while a school would use horns, sirens and lights to annunciate a fire.)

Power Source: a 110 volt power system which is generally filtered to provide the proper current and voltage normally used; an emergency power source or battery back-up system should also be included.

Alarm Circuits: used to transmit signals from the sensors to the control unit which in turn transmits the signals to the local or remote annunciator alarm unit; alarm systems are either open or closed circuit systems: open circuit: an electrical line which does not have a flow of current present until switch or relay is closed completing the circuit.

Closed circuit: an electrical line with current flowing through it; any change in this electrical current flow will initiate an alarm.

In addition, systems can be arranged by a direct method of alarm notification or by a loop system. The loop system is referred to as the McCulloh Loop (named after its inventor) which is a circuit which has two or more sensors, switches or systems on the same circuit. The greatest advantage of the direct system is that when an alarm is received the exact location of the alarm is known. With a loop system, only a general area of the alarm is known.

As discussed earlier, alarm sensors can take a variety of forms. Basically, there are three types of alarm sensors:
1) perimeter or point of entry
2) area protection
3) object protection

In a thorough security system all three types of alarm sensors may be utilized in an effort to provide a high level of security.

Sensors are designed to initiate alarms under several different conditions:
1) when a surface or area being protected is penetrated
2) when a power failure occurs.
3) when the sensor is opened, grounded or shorted out.
4) when the sensors fails due to age or wear.
5) when the container which houses the sensor is opened.

Notes

DIRECT SYSTEM

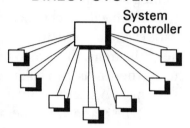

LOOP SYSTEM

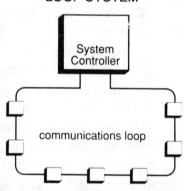

Perimeter protection will usually be a gate or door that, when opened, annunciates an alarm.

Area protection will often be a motion detector located within a room or hallway to detect unauthorized access.

Object protection would be used to protect an item such as a safe, display cabinet, jewelry box, etc.

Sensors can be of various types:

Electro-Mechanical

Electro-mechanical sensors are considered to be reliable but may be costly. They are designed to place a current carrying conductor between an intruder and the area to be protected. The conductor carries the current which keeps a holding relay in an open position. If the current flow stops for any reason the device releases the relay and allows the contacts to close so that an alarm circuit is activated.

Foil

Foil is usually installed on glass and is a thin metallic tape which carries an electrical current. Once the foil is broken, cut or torn the electrical current is interrupted thereby causing an alarm. Foil serves as a psychological deterrent. The cost of foil is small but its installation requires considerable time.

Intrusion Switches

Intrusion switches are used on windows, doors and skylights. The switches are made of two electrical contacts, one is installed on the opening surface (door or window) while the other is installed on the fixed surface. When the surface (door or window) is closed the two contacts provide a closed circuit so there is a continuity of current flow. When the surface is opened the contacts separate and the electrical circuit is broken and the alarm is signaled. These switches are always installed on the inside or the side of the material to be protected.

Magnetic Switch

Magnetic switches consist of one part magnet and a switch assembly connected to an actuator. The switch is usually mounted on the fixed surface with the magnet fastened to the opening surface. When the surface is closed, electrical current flows. When the surface is opened, the magnetic field is broken and an electrical circuit is activated and the alarm is signaled. **Protection of Assets** authors Walsh and Healy state that the most efficient magnetic switch is a balanced magnetic type that will activate an alarm upon the increase, decrease or attempted substitution of an external magnetic field.

Wire and Screen Detectors

Wire and screen detectors are used to enhance security for windows and can provide a valuable service to the home security system owner. Wire is woven into the window screen. If the screen is cut as well as the alarm wire, an alarm will be activated since the electrical current flowing through the wire has been interrupted. Screen detectors, while providing a good level of security, are not inexpensive.

Pressure Mats

Pressure Mats are designed to initiate an alarm when a weight of 5-20 pounds per square foot is applied to the surface. Pressure Mats utilize electrical wiring placed within a rubber or plastic coating which is normally hidden underneath carpeting. Pressure mats are suited for carpeted office areas but are most widely used in home security systems.

Soundwave and Microwave Sensors

Soundwave and Microwave sensors are based on the "Doppler" principle according to authors Walsh and Healy. Doppler was an Austrian scientist who discovered that "microwaves or soundwaves are disturbed by movement."[1] Sensors which utilize this principle have a transmitter that sends a wave pattern and then receives it. As long as the pattern being received is the same as the one being transmitted a stable condition exists. A distortion of a wave-pattern caused by movement is detected thereby initiating an alarm. Soundwave or ultrasonic employs soundwaves of a higher frequency than the human ear. Sensors of this type are usable only inside a building. Audio noise does not affect the sensors nor does air currents. However, if heating/air conditioning air currents move displays suspended from a ceiling, the display movement may activate an alarm. Radar detectors work in the same manner as ultrasonic but the radar wave is different. Radar can be used outside. Radar waves do not permeate construction such as plaster walls.

Notes

WIRE/SCREEN
DETECTORS

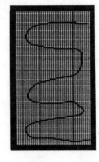

PRESSURE MAT
(Under Carpet)

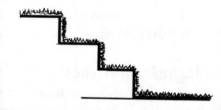

DOPPLER SENSOR

Capacitance Sensors

Capacitance sensors are large electronic sensors that radiate energy and detect change in the capacitive coupling between an antenna and ground. These are normally low in cost and are suitable for outside use.

Vibration Sensors

Vibration sensors use a sensitive contact microphone which is installed indoors on the surface to be protected. Vibrations caused by someone attempting to penetrate the surface are picked up and transmitted to an amplifier that initiates an alarm. These are not considered useful outside.

Audio Sensors

Audio sensors are microphones which are activated when sound initiates the alarm. Audio sensors are used for vaults.

Light Sensors

Light sensors operate on the principle if there is a change of light or if a beam of light is interrupted. The use of a photoelectric cell is the simplest means of changing the transmitted light beam through a propeller-like baffle. The receiver must be tuned to a frequency which matches the RPM of the motor and vibrations in speed caused by temperature change.

Receipt of Alarms

Alarms can be received at a number of different locations. Local alarm systems sound a generating device on the outside of the building to call attention to the alarm. Advantages of using a local alarm system include:

1) psychological deterrent (intruder knows he's been detected.
2) damage should be minimized since the intruder hears the alarm.
3) the alarm is inexpensive to install and easy to maintain.

Many sprinkler systems have local annunciating systems which consists of a bell which rings as water flows through the sprinkler riser.

Notes

There are some disadvantages in using only a local alarm system which include:
1) easy to defeat because of their simplicity.
2) the intruder will probably not be apprehended.
3) the alarm may be disregarded if no one is nearby to hear the alarm.

A second type of alarm system is the central station. With the central station alarm system the alarm is not heard by the intruder and is called a "silent" alarm. Police are normally notified immediately of the alarm which aids in apprehension since the intruder is not aware of the alarm. Many alarm companies provide a monitoring service for the central station systems. This will require the company who desires the coverage to test the system on a regular basis to insure effectiveness. This type of system uses telephone lines to carry the alarms. Direct lines or use of a loop system may be employed to provide the service.

A third type of alarm answering system is the direct police or fire department termination. The advantage of this type of system is obvious: a quick response should be given to the alarm. However, in many cities the police and/or fire department are not permitted to receive the alarms directly unless the facility is a school. church or other public building.

The final type of alarm receipt system is proprietary termination. With this type of system a facility monitors its own alarms by using either security officers, maintenance or other employees to respond to alarms. Advantages of the proprietary system include:

1) system can be designed to meet the needs of the owner.
2) the system is operated and controlled by the owner.
3) functions can be virtually unlimited if designed properly.
4) line security is enhanced since the alarm line begins and ends on the owner's property.
5) system can be cost effective if designed properly.

Notes

System Components

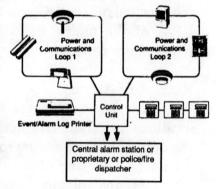

Disadvantages of the proprietary system include the cost of providing personnel to monitor the alarms and additional costs if the system has not been designed properly. Even by using a proprietary system, security guard patrols will often still be needed.

False Alarm Problem

If most police officers were asked what they believe is the single greatest problem with alarm systems they would probably answer without hesitation that false alarms are the greatest problem. Between 90 - 98% of all alarms are false. False alarms are a result of:

1) user error or negligence
2) poor installation or servicing
3) faulty equipment

More than 50% of all false alarms are due to user error or negligence. Because of poor installation and service, many states and local governments have developed standards for installing and servicing alarm systems. False alarms affect police in three ways:

1) encourage poor police searching of protected premises.
2) poor attitude toward the alarm user and alarm industry.
3) belief that intrusion alarms are more trouble than they are worth.

Solutions to the false alarm problem include:

1) sell the system correctly; consider the environment, habits and routines of subscribers, don't overprotect.
2) don't use space protection excessively.
3) instruct the subscriber on the proper use of the system.
4) reinstruct the subscriber at frequent intervals.
5) train and retrain alarm company employees on procedures and troubleshooting techniques.
6) maintain system in proper working order.

Notes

Closed Circuit Television Systems (CCTV)

Close Circuit Television or CCTV systems play an important role in an overall security system. CCTV systems support the security officer in the observation and surveillance of the facility and areas that are to be protected.

While CCTV systems are not necessarily inexpensive, in recent years because of technological advancements, these systems are much less in cost than in previous years. CCTV systems are most effective when incorporated into a security program that uses security personnel. CCTV cameras can be utilized to minimize security officer coverage and related expenses. It should not be believed that cameras can completely replace security staffing.

CCTV cameras support security in several ways:

1. Allows for hidden surveillance of an area which is vulnerable to theft.
2. Allows for the positive identification of persons and/or material prior to granting entrance or exit privileges.
3. Provide a deterrent to crime when cameras are visible to employees and visitors.
4. When used in conjunction with a video tape recorder, records of thefts or other incidents are permanently recorded.
5. Provides better utilization and efficiencies of security personnel.

CCTV cameras are used widely in retail operations, hospitals, officer complexes, factories, and parking decks. Monitors allow a person to view what the camera is scanning. If security personnel are required to monitor several cameras, care should be taken to ensure that observation of the monitors is designed in such a manner to allow for proper effectiveness.

A term seldom used in security is ergonomics, a science that focuses on human capabilities and limitations in the design of jobs, workstations, tools and equipment. Camera monitors which are placed in a security office or control center to be monitored by one person who is also required to answer the telephone, sign in visitors, communicate with

Notes

CCTV Terminology
Pan & Tilt camera: camera which has mechanical components which allow it to be moved up and down and from side to side from remote controls.

Fixed camera: camera which is permanently mounted which views one area constantly; this camera cannot be moved for alternate viewing.

Console: an arrangement of CCTV monitors, switches and devices that houses all of the equipment necessary to monitor cameras, alarms...

Switcher: device that alternates the monitoring of cameras in order that one (or more) monitors can be used to view more than one camera. Four cameras may be monitored by one CCTV monitor that alternates or "switches" screens every 3-5 seconds.

other personnel via two-way radio, page employees over a public address system, etc...., will have great difficulty in effectively monitoring cameras.

Security consoles (see exhibits) assist in providing security personnel with proper ergonomic design to ensure cameras are effectively monitored.

References
[1] Timothy J. Walsh & Edward J. Healy, The Protection of Assets Manuals, Merritt Company, (Santa Monica, CA: 1986).

Notes

ACCESS CONTROL SYSTEMS
"A Modern Tool for the Security Officer"

Access Control can mean many things to many people, but for purposes of this discussion, we will define access control as "An electronic means of controlling access and identifying users."

Basic access control systems employ the use of a card, and are typically the one or two door variety. They simply identify a card as valid or invalid, and on that basis, allow or deny access. The system does not identify the valid card to a particular user, and their is no hard copy report or other record of entry. In short, it is no more than an electric key. The system does not identify who has what card, or even what card is used. If a card is coded for that door, then the system allows access. If it is not, then access is denied.

The more sophisticated systems have the ability to identify a particular card to an assigned user of the card. When the card is presented to the card reader, the system not only permits or denies access based on the validity of the card, but also can identify the user by name, employee I.D. number, and by access level. Beyond that, the system can also permit or restrict access by time, date, day of week, and as many as fifty access authorization levels, depending on the sophistication of the system.

These systems are every bit as important for what they record as what they control. Every entry or "transaction", is recorded in the system. Larger access control systems can automatically log, display and print out upwards of 1.5 million transactions. For an average larger system, this could be as much as six months worth of access information.

The ability to perform audit functions adds to the value of the access control system. Now you can answer these questions: Who went through what door? How often? What time of day or night? Did a person attempt access through a door that they shouldn't have? This information becomes very valuable when an incident occurs such as a theft, or accident. The audit trail that can be retrieved from the access control system may eliminate as well as identify suspects. Who was in? What time? Why did Mr. Smith attempt to enter a restricted area? As the capacity of personal computers continues to increase, the ability to store and retrieve

Notes

Card access systems which substitute as an "electronic key" are popular for use in hotels.

Systems such as this are very useful in restricting access and identifying who has entered and exited a facility. These systems do not necessarily prevent theft but can assist in identifying possible suspects after a theft has occurred.

information will continue to increase as well. Already, the access control system is being utilized for such automation functions as Guard Tours, Time and Attendance, Telephone Call Accounting and Pricing, Doctor Registry's in health care facilities, Copier Control and Pricing, and other automated functions that either save or generate revenue for the user organization.

PERFORMANCE

What is the performance criteria that a company needs to look at in deciding whether to install an access control system to replace a key system or other means of access control?

1. Is the Card valid? It must establish the identity of the card user.
2. Is the system reliable? Every time John Smith presents his card, it must validate his presence.
3. Is the system easy to use? It must not slow normal work flow, or make ordinary tasks difficult.
4. Is the system secure? It must be resistant to counterfeiting or duplication of the card.
5. Is it durable? The system must be rugged and have a long life expectancy.
6. Is the system hardened to its environment? The system must be physically adequate to protect against force or manipulation.
7. Is the system easy to maintain? It should offer some internal guidelines for troubleshooting for the system.

SYSTEM TECHNOLOGY

There are many types of card access technology in use in various facilities and applications. Some of those that you will likely encounter include:

Notes

Security personnel may use a card access system to record their patrols.

Time and attendance capability serves to replace the standard manual timeclocks still used in many organizations. As costs for telephone calls and copier use continue to increase, a card access system can be incorporated to control and identify use.

Notes

Hollerith Readers -- Punched holes in card. When inserted in the reader, provides a momentary contact closure to release a locked door. Sometimes seen in hotel rooms. Insert reader. — Inexpensive, but easy to duplicate.

Magnetic Stripe Readers -- Reads the characters on magnetic tape affixed to card. Most popular because so much information can be stored on tape. Insert or swipe reader. — Relatively inexpensive, but easy to duplicate, and potential for vandalism, because it is a contact device.

Proximity Readers -- Each card is individually tuned and can be read when in close proximity of reader. Non-contact and virtually never wears out. Can often be used without taking out of wallet or purse. Non contact. — Expensive, can be duplicated, thick card.

Bar Code Readers --Inexpensive, and good for low security areas. — Easily duplicated, some errors or false reads. Good for dual technology cards, but not for high security.

Wiegand Readers -- Imbedded wire, almost impossible to duplicate. Offers higher level of security than others. Non-contact for low vandalism. Insert or swipe, non contact.

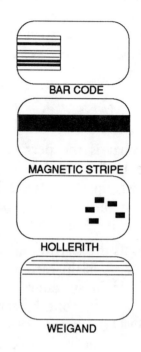

Biometric Systems

Retina scanners -- Identifies user's unique retinal blood vessel pattern.

Hand geometry -- Measures the user's unique hand

Fingerprints -- Identifies user's unique fingerprints.

Voice verification -- Computer identifies user's voice pattern within previously established parameters.

These are expensive systems designed for high security applications, however as they gain acceptance, prices will move downward.

VIDEO BADGING INTEGRATION

The video badging system incorporates a digital video ID system with the door access control system. It positively identifies the user by displaying the card holder's picture on the monitor at the security guard's desk the instant the card is passed through the reader. The value of the digital video image is that it allows the guard to see an image of the person passing through the door. Secondly, the video imaging system allows a quick and easy means of keeping, storing and upgrading the employee photo I.D. file, since it is stored on a digital disk rather that on hard film.

ACCESS CONTROL DEVICES

Doors, locks or barriers commonly referred to as turnstiles work in conjunction with card access systems. As a card reader scans and accepts a card, a signal is transmitted to a barrier to open, unlock or release a barrier in order for access to be granted. Most barriers or turnstiles are designed to prevent unauthorized access to an area and yet blend with the decor and aesthetics of the facility where they are installed.

Turnstiles are also used to direct and maintain crowd control at sports stadiums and arenas, amusement parks and offices and factories. Special attention must be given to the type and style of turnstile which would be accepted at a facility.

USER FRIENDLY

The modern card access systems have become quite user friendly, with one and two key stroke commands for the security guard operator. The manufacturers have learned over the years that not everyone is computer literate, and have built their systems on that basis. Most new systems come with easy to understand user prompts and menu screens. The systems also provide basic troubleshooting commands to help identify problems, and conditions that are not normal. Many even tell us what to do if certain conditions exist.

Perhaps the simplest, but most important feature of these modern systems is that they can tell us immediately who went through what door, or which door is propped open or ajar.

Notes

CONCLUSION

As a security officer, it is not necessary for you to understand the internal workings of a personal computer driven access control system to take advantage of its conveniences. It is important however to note the basic instructions. Once you have that understanding, you can master the system at your own pace. It is also important to understand that the modern access control system is nothing more than another tool to assist you in protecting the facility to which you are assigned. The sooner you give in to that notion, the sooner you will be able to use it to its maximum capability.

References
1. Honeywell Product And Services Manual, *Honeywell Protection Series*, (Minneapolis, 1990).
2. John Ericson, "The Archives", *Security Management Magazine*, ASIS, June 1991, p. 27..
3. Richard L. Mourey, "Its in the Cards", *Security Management Magazine*, ASIS, July, 1989, p. 17.

Notes

SUMMARY

An electronic alarm system must be planned to operate without major problems and be economically feasible for the property or building which is to be protected. Alarms can be used to detect fires, unauthorized entries and/or monitor equipment and report malfunctions.

The five basic components to any alarm system are:

1. a sensory device

2. a control unit

3. an annunciator

4. a power source

5. an alarm circuit

Systems can be arranged by a direct method of alarm notification or by a loop system.

There are three types of alarm sensors:

1. perimeter or point of entry

2. area protection

3. object projection

Sensors are designed to initiate alarms when a surface or area being protected is penetrated, when a power failure occurs, when the sensor is opened, grounded or shorted out, when the sensor fails due to age or wear or when the container which houses the sensor is opened. Sensors can be of many different types including: foil, intrusion switches, magnetic, electro-mechanical, wire/screen, pressure mats, soundwave, capacitance, vibration, audio and light.

Alarms can be received at a number of different locations such as local, central station and proprietary.

False alarms are the greatest problem with electronic alarm systems. Between 90 - 98% of all alarms are false. More than 50% of all false alarms are due to user error or negligence.

Alarms and alarm systems are like locks, fences and other barriers in that they can provide a reasonable level of security only if used according to specifications and in conjunction with other security devices. Proper training and indoctrination of all security personnel with the alarm system is critical if the system is to work as intended.

Closed-circuit television systems support security personnel in observing the facility and areas which are vulnerable to theft or vandalism. The use of CCTV cameras in conjunction with security personnel can improve the effectiveness and efficiency of the security program.

Notes

QUESTIONS

1. Alarms can be used to:
    a. detect _____.
    b. detect an _____ _____.
    c. _____ authorities during an _____.

2. What is the greatest advantage of direct method alarm notification?

    _____

3. Name the three basic types of alarm systems.
    1. _____
    2. _____
    3. _____

4. Name two types of alarm sensors suitable for indoor use.
    1. _____
    2. _____

5. Name two types of alarm sensors suitable for outdoor use.
    1. _____
    2. _____

6. What are the advantages of a local alarm system?
    1. _____
    2. _____
    3. _____

7. What are the disadvantages of a local alarm system?
    1. _____
    2. _____
    3. _____

8. What are the four types of alarm answering systems?
    1. _____
    2. _____
    3. _____
    4. _____

9. List the two advantages and two disadvantages of the proprietary termination system?

    1. _____

    2. _____

    1. _____

    2. _____

10. False alarms are usually a result of:

    1. _____

    2. _____

    3. _____

11. 50% of all false alarms are due to _____.

12. List two things that can be done to reduce the number of false alarms.

    1. _____

    2. _____

ACCESS CONTROL

SURVEILLANCE   CAMERA

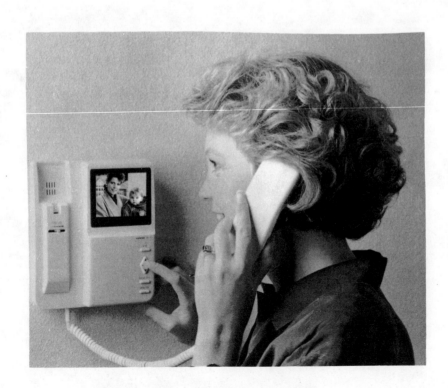

VIDEO ENTRY SECURITY SYSTEM

EXHIBITS

ACCESS CONTROL

SECURITY CENTER CONSOLES

ELECTRONIC ALARMS

MICROWAVE/PASSIVE INFARED MOTION SENSOR

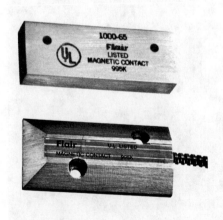

1½" Gap

FLOOR MOUNT CONTACTS   SCREW TERMINALS

ELECTRONIC ALARMS

PHOTOELECTRIC INTRUSION DETECTOR

PASSIVE INFARED DETECTOR

THE EFFECTIVE
SECURITY OFFICERS
TRAINING MANUAL

Chapter V

Investigations

Investigations

Conducting a security investigation is a primary function of any security organization. Most security officers and supervisors will be called upon to conduct preliminary investigations due to a theft, injury or other type of incident. Most of these investigations will be of a non-criminal nature but are, nevertheless, important since they may result in civil litigation.

Types of Security Investigations

In any type of investigation there are usually two phases. Most security officers will be involved with preliminary investigations. O. W. Wilson described the preliminary investigation as follows:

P	Proceed to the scene with safety & dispatch.
R	Render assistance to injured.
E	Effect arrest of perpetrator.
L	Locate and identify witnesses.
I	Interview complainant & witnesses.
M	Maintain scene & protect evidence.
I	Interrogate suspects.
N	Note all conditions, events, & remarks.
A	Arrange for collection of evidence.
R	Report incident fully & accurately.
Y	Yield responsibility to investigators.[1]

Care should be given in minimizing destruction of evidence when treating victims. A second step at the scene is to gain control of the situation so that further injury to victims is minimized. This may require an officer requesting assistance from other security personnel and, possibly, from public emergency services (i.e. police, fire, rescue).

PROCEED TO THE SCENE
* Get there as fast as possible.
* Get there safely, don't violate laws or become reckless.
* Think as you are en route:
  • What might you come into contact with?
  • Rely upon past experiences to help you. Have you had similar incidents? In some cases it may be a situation involving the same people or equipment.

Investigations: The gathering of facts and their evaluation to determine a given purpose.

Preliminary investigation: the first phase of an investigation.

Follow-up investigation: the second phase of an investigation.

The most important consideration of any investigation is to proceed to the scene as quickly as possible. Persons who are injured should receive priority attention.

* Begin to make mental notes:
  * Will you have to call for outside emergency services?
  * Will there be someone else at the scene who will assume responsibility or will you be the person in charge?

Render Assistance to the Injured
Once at the scene, attempt to quickly analyze the situation and prioritize what must be done.

1. Provide first aid to the injured or remove a person(s) from harm's way (i.e. fire).
2. Identify the need for additional assistance, radio for additional help and if necessary call for police and fire units to respond.
3. Attempt to stabilize the situation by treating the injured, calling for assistance, and providing general direction.

EFFECT ARREST OF PERPETRATOR

If a criminal offense has occurred resulting in a serious injury caused by a vehicular accident or assault, attempt to keep all parties at the scene. If you are not certain of the facts be cautious about arresting or even detaining persons. Be extremely cautious in pursuing individuals off the grounds of your facility. You must remember what legal authority and power you possess. Additionally, your organization may not want you to pursue possible suspects. Instead, you may only be required to provide the police with a physical description of the alleged suspects.

LOCATE & IDENTIFY WITNESSES

Upon arrival at the scene and once you have determined who requires first aid, attempt to identify anyone and everyone who may have knowledge of what occurred. Ask witnesses to remain in the area until you have had a chance to talk to them. It is critical in this situation that you have a notebook and pen at your disposal. Attempt to interview those persons who were actually involved, whether they are the alleged victims or perpetrators.

Notes

If you find you are questioning yourself as to whether to call for additional assistance... CALL FOR ASSISTANCE IMMEDIATELY. When in doubt, call for assistance.

Encourage people to remain at the scene until you have obtained assistance.

Remember to protect yourself and your employer from civil and/or criminal charges resulting from your actions.

Attempt to project a calm and cool manner. Try not to become excited. Take deep breaths an attempt to maintain your professional demeanor at all times.

INTERVIEW COMPLAINANT & WITNESSES

As mentioned, if a person requested your presence at the scene, this should be the first person you speak to after you have arrived on the scene. Naturally, if persons are injured or their safety is in danger, you must wait to interview the complainant.

Many security officers are not proficient in interviewing persons simply because they have not had much experience in this area. It is essential at this time that the security officer maintain his/her composure and demonstrate a cool and calm demeanor. Security officers who demonstrate coolness under pressure instill confidence with witnesses.

The best place to start the interview process is at the beginning by obtaining the following:

Date & Time of Accident   _____

Date & Time of Report   _____

Name of Person   _____

Address of Person   _____

Phone Number   _____

Social Security Number   _____

An effective opening statement without directing or prejudicing the witnesses is to say, "Tell me what happened!" Often, other witnesses present will interpret and interject their own opinions of what happened. If possible, walk away from the other witnesses in order that the main witness can talk without interruption. If this is not possible, you may have to ask the other witnesses to please be quiet until you have an opportunity to talk with each of them. If the witness is upset or extremely excited you may have to continue to prompt them with additional questions such as, "What happened next? Then what?" "What did the person do or say then?" This type of interview may continue for several minutes.

Notes

As soon as possible and when practical, you need to talk with the person who requested your presence.

Complainant: person who notifies the appropriate authorities of a situation or incident.

It is essential to obtain the name, address and phone number of all witnesses. Ask to see driver's licenses to verify their identities.

"Tell me what happened!"

If it is necessary to ask that the person repeat a portion of the story in order for you to gather all of the facts, then ask them to do so.

Once the witness has completed telling his/her story, you should repeat the story to him/her based upon what you've written in your notes. Any changes in his/her story should be marked with an asterisk * to remind you that a portion of his/her story changed. This may not necessarily indicate the person is lying, however, it may reflect that the facts are not as clear as first thought.

After the main witness or complainant has been interviewed, other witnesses must be interviewed until everyone has been spoken to concerning the incident. In many situations because of time constraints and/or the number of witnesses involved, more than one security officer will be required to conduct the interviews. It therefore becomes critical that each officer explore the interviews in similar fashion to be certain as many facts as possible are gathered. Remember, you are on a fact finding mission. Obtain as much information as possible. Normally, it is at this time when witnesses will be the most cooperative and truthful.

MAINTAIN SCENE & PROTECT EVIDENCE

When dealing with incidents which may be criminal in nature, it is extremely important to attempt to gather as much evidence as possible. The job of the security officer in attaining this objective may be extremely difficult. Fingerprints, footprints, tire marks, torn clothing, etc... which may be essential in a criminal investigation may be altered or destroyed unintentionally, especially if first aid must be rendered to victims. As security officers become more proficient in responding to crime scenes, valuable evidence can be preserved prior to the arrival of the police.

As quickly as possible, a security officer must attempt to cordone off the area from sightseers and people who are just simply curious. Three inch wide yellow and black tape provides a good resource in notifying sightseers to refrain from crossing into the crime scene area. Careful attention should be given to not touching any possible evidence with exposed hands or fingers. Often, the main responsibility of a security officer will be to maintain the integrity of the crime scene until the police arrive.

Notes

Repeat to the witness everything he/she has told you. Use a phrase such as, "Now in order for me to understand what happened, let me repeat to you what you said."

Gather as much information as possible.

One of the most difficult aspects of conducting a preliminary investigation is in maintaining the scene and protecting the evidence.

An excellent investigator will have accumulated a great deal of knowledge and experience in the field. With investigation, there is no substitute for experience.

Security officers who work for banks, museums, hospitals and/or colleges will usually be more familiar with crime scenes due to the nature of their jobs as opposed to security officers who work in manufacturing or office facilities. In addition, officers in manufacturing and office settings may not have the frequent contact with the public.

INTERROGATE SUSPECTS

O.W. Wilson includes interrogating suspects as part of the Preliminary Investigation. Interrogation is vastly different than conducting an interview. In fact, John Reid and Associates note the differences between the two:

Interviews are non-threatening in nature, less structured where notes are taken. Miranda warnings are not required during an interview when the interview is being conducted by a law enforcement/government official. Often, interviews may not be conducted with absolute privacy.

Normally, interrogations are conducted near the conclusion of an investigation after all possible leads have been researched. Any interrogation should be conducted in absolute privacy, in an office or room which prevents distractions or interruptions.

A situation may arise which provides the security officer with an opportunity to ask a suspect a questions such as, "Bill, why did you hit Ed?" A security officer may be fortunate and receive an admission from the suspect. In general, interrogations are conducted only after an extensive investigation has revealed as many facts as possible regarding the incident.

NOTE ALL CONDITIONS, EVENTS & REMARKS

Sometimes during an emergency, which requires a security officer to render first aid or assist in other emergency procedures, actual notetaking may not be possible. However, as soon as possible after an incident, the security officer must reconstruct the order of events. If little or no notes were taken, before writing an incident report, the security officer should make notes of all relevant conditions, starting with when he/she was first notified of the incident.

Notes

Few security officers will be in a situation requiring them to interrogate a suspect.

Interviews: Non accusatory conversations with a person where little evidence exists implicating the person.

Interrogations: Accusatory, one-sided discussions where the suspect is under suspicion for a crime or offense and where evidence exists which supports the suspicion.

Notetaking is an essential part of any preliminary investigation.

The following items may be of critical importance when documenting the incident:

- Date
- Time
- Location
- Weather Conditions
- Witnesses
- Complainant
- Physical Descriptions
- Clothing
- Odor or smells
- Statements made by victim, witnesses or suspect

The essential parts of any report are the facts. Names, descriptions of individuals, vehicles, buildings, surroundings, correct dates and times are critical when attempting to reconstruct on paper what actually took place.

Often a report is written several minutes or several hours after an even has occurred. People who can provide answers may no longer be available for questioning.

Every security officer or supervisor should always carry a pen and small pocket notebook in order to document key facts as they occur. Names, titles and even descriptions can often be quickly noted even during an emergency. This information can prove to be critical months later.

The following are some helpful hints to remember when you are reconstructing the incident from your notes in preparation for writing your report:

1. Write what happened in chronological order. What happened first, then what happened next, and next, etc...
2. Be sure to include all names, positions, titles, and department numbers of all employees.
3. Include names, addresses and, if possible, social security numbers of all non-employees who either witnessed or were involved.
4. Explain in plain, simple English what happened. If you mention a building by its name or number, give its location as well. Remember, many people who read this report are not as familiar with directions and location as you are.

Notes

Assume nothing! Gather as many facts as possible.

5. When you begin to write your report, constantly refer to your notes. Don't include your opinion or comments and don't editorialize. You can give your opinion or comments about the incident in person to your superior.

6. Don't discard your notes. Keep them until your superior advises you to discard them.

7. Write your report before you leave work. Leaving the job before your report is written gives a bad impression of your security department.

ARRANGE FOR COLLECTION OF EVIDENCE

In any type of incident where an accident has occurred or when a crime has happened, evidence exists. Sometimes evidence is obvious and apparent and easy to collect. Other times however, evidence is difficult to see and may be difficult to collect. Imagine a theft from an office area. Evidence could include:

- fingerprints
- footprints
- broken glass
- scratches or dents
- broken glass
- forgotten burglary tools
- torn clothing

Evidence from a car accident may include:

- skid marks
- broken glass
- damaged vehicles
- empty liquor containers

Assuming that all injured parties have been cared for, the security officer must (as discussed earlier) protect all evidence and maintain the integrity of the (crime) scene. Usually, this will entail an officer cordoning or blocking off the area from all bystanders. If evidence may be lost or damaged due to the weather or something else, the security officer should collect the evidence. Care must be used when

Notes

There is no excuse for a report not being written prior to a security officer leaving work.

gathering evidence. Putting additional finger or footprints onto evidence will only serve to delay or impair the investigation. Evidence preservation kits including plastic bags are convenient ways for even novice security officers to succeed in the gathering of evidence which may be destroyed if not immediately recovered. This evidence must be carefully sealed with the name, date and time, and name of the person recovering the material. Evidence must be properly stored and secured for safekeeping.

REPORT INCIDENT FULLY AND ACCURATELY

In the manual **Effective Report Writing for the Security Officer**, specific outlines are presented which assist the security officer in obtaining all the facts necessary to write a clear and accurate report.

Common mistakes made by security officers when writing reports include poor grammar, misspellings, poor penmanship, inaccurate statements and in general, offering opinions or commentary when it is not appropriate. A favorite saying used by many security directors is a quote from Dragnet detective, Joe Friday, "Just the facts, ma'am!" Far too often personal opinions are interjected into a report when it is totally inappropriate.

YIELD RESPONSIBILITY TO INVESTIGATORS

As mentioned throughout this chapter, most investigations conducted by security officers are of the preliminary variety. Once an investigator has arrived at the scene, the security officer should relinquish control of the investigation. A word of caution: some security directors may prefer to retain some control over an investigation prior to relinquishing authority to a law enforcement detective. If an actual crime has occurred the security officer may have no choice but to yield to a detective.

References

Colling, Russell L., Hospital Security, (Butterworth Publishers, Boston, 1977) p. 141.

Notes

Maintain an accurate "chain of evidence" record which notes the date and time the evidence was collected and who has had possession of the evidence.

A well-written report reflects favorably for the security officer and entire security department.

The security director, manager or representative should be notified as soon as possible and informed of the incident.

Summary

A security investigation is the primary function of any security organization. An investigation involves the gathering of facts and the evaluation of them to determine a given purpose. There are two phases of any investigation. They are referred to as the preliminary investigation and the follow-up investigation.

The most important consideration of any preliminary investigation is to proceed to the scene as quickly as possible. Pay close attention to those injured, do not destroy any evidence, and make sure you have total control of the situation.

If a criminal offense has been committed, encourage people to remain at the scene until you have obtained assistance. Be extremely cautious not to exceed your authority.

When you are at the scene, the security officer should locate and identify witnesses, interview the complainant and witnesses and make as many mental notes as possible.

The officer should make every attempt not to prejudice the witnesses. For that reason, a good opening remark might be, "Tell me what happened." It may be necessary to ask the person to repeat his or her story. After they have completed their story, repeat the story to them based upon what you have written in your notes. Any changes should be marked with an asterisk (*). Make sure you speak with all witnesses. You are on a fact-finding mission. Obtain as much information as possible.

One of the most difficult aspects of conducting a preliminary investigation is in maintaining the scene and protecting the evidence. The security officer should cordon off the area from sightseers and people who are just curious.

Most security officers are involved in interviews, not interrogations. The difference between an interview and an interrogation is that interviews are non-accusatory conversations whereas interrogations are accusatory, one-sided discussions where the suspect is under suspicion for a crime or offense.

The security officer should note all condition, events and remarks. The following items may be critical when documenting an incident: date, time, location, weather conditions, witnesses, complainant, physical descriptions, clothing, odor or smells, and statements made by victim, witnesses or suspect.

Notes

After the interviews are complete, the security officer should arrange for the collection of all the evidence. All evidence should be carefully sealed with the name, date, and time, and the name of the individual recovering the material. Evidence should be properly stored and secured for safekeeping.

The last and very important task of a security officer would be to report the incident fully and accurately.

Notes

Questions

Fill-in

1. An investigator involves the _____ of facts and the _____ of them to determine a given purpose.

2. The first phase of an investigation is referred to as the _____ investigation.

3. The second phase may be referred to as the _____ investigation.

4. Care should be given in minimizing destruction of _____ .

5. An officer should always take written notes and begin to make _____ notes.

6. One of the most difficult aspects of conducting a preliminary investigation is in maintaining the _____ and protecting the _____ .

7. Non-accusatory conversations are called _____.

8. One-sided discussions where the suspect is under suspicion are called _____.

Exercises

1. You have been dispatched to the scene of a preliminary investigation. In what order would you complete the following:

_____Arrange for collection of evidence

_____Interview witnesses

_____Interrogate suspects

_____Report incident fully and accurately

_____Effect arrest of perpetrator

_____Yield responsibility to investigators

_____Locate and identify witnesses

_____Render assistance to injured

_____Maintain scene and protect evidence

_____Note all conditions, events, remarks, etc.

2. There are six important facts you should obtain when doing an interview. What are they?

   _____

   _____

   _____

   _____

   _____

   _____

3. Which items may be critical when documenting an incident:

   _____

   _____

   _____

   _____

   _____

   _____

   _____

   _____

4. List 3 of the 4 common evidences found at a car accident:

   _____

   _____

   _____

5. For the evidence at a theft, we would look for:
   torn clothing
   broken glass
   Can you name 3 more?

   _____

   _____

   _____

THE EFFECTIVE SECURITY OFFICERS TRAINING MANUAL

Chapter VI

Report Writing

Report Writing

Written reports have existed since men and women were first able to read and write. Documents such as the Bible and Koran have existed for thousands of years. These books are considered to contain detailed reports of mankind's years on earth during the past 5,000 years. Because past events were recorded in writing, permanent records exist which allow generation to generation to learn the exact same information. The comment, "If its not written, it didn't happen", is of particular importance in the study of history.

For security personnel, written reports are used for several purposes:
1. to provide a permanent record of an incident
2. to verify the job duties performed
3. to explain confusing events
4. to provide evidence in a legal proceeding
5. to provide information for follow-up action

Provided that security reports are clear, concise and accurate, a security department will maintain a high degree of credibility within an organization. Security logs and reports are subject to being used in court proceedings both civil and criminal. It is essential that security personnel factually record all information in their logs and reports which answer the following:

- WHO?
- WHAT?
- WHEN?
- WHERE?
- WHY?
- HOW?
- CONCLUSIONS?

Answering the above mentioned questions seems very simple, but security officers will often fail to answer these basic questions. In fact, many times, security officers fail to write reports or document incidents whatsoever. When information is not documented and a security officer is called at home to answer a question, the credibility of the officer and the entire security operation is damaged.

Notes

Reading for a Purpose
Look for these key words:
•Shift/Daily Log
•Incident Reports
•Material Passes
•Visitor Logs
Look for answers to these
    questions:
•What should you include in
    your daily log?
•Why is note-taking important?
•Why do security companies
    keep records of logs?
•What kinds of logs will you be
    expected to keep?

All security reports must always answer the following: Who? What? When? Where? Why? How? and conclusions

There are no legitimate reasons or excuses for a security officer failing to document an incident or situation with a written report, prior to the end of the workshift. If necessary, remain at the worksite until the report has been completed.

The following guidelines are suggested to ensure that reports are written in an acceptable, professional manner.

1. Document everything! If as a security officer you have to pause and ask yourself if something should be written down, you have answered the question...WRITE IT IN YOUR LOG!

2. Write clearly and neatly! Few adults possess penmanship skills which are neat and easy to read. It is suggested that all reports be either printed by hand or typed.

3. Report all the facts! Don't give your opinion. Simply state the facts. Rememeber the classic line from Sgt. Joe Friday of the television series Dragnet, "Just the facts, maam."

4. Protect the information contained in logs and reports! Never allow anyone to read information in a security log or report unless you know for certain they are permitted to do so by your superiors. Often, union officials or department managers may ask for a copy of a security log or incident report. A good rule of thumb if you are unsure if they are permitted to review the information is to reply. "I'm sorry, but I can't release that information. I will note on the report that you have requested a copy. If my supervisor grants permission to release the information, I will be happy to provide you a copy."

5. Know what information your supervisor wants included in security reports. Often. security officers include information in reports which is not necessary. Remember to keep things simple. The KISS (Keep It Simple, Stupid) approach is always preferrred. In addition, conflict between security officers, may occur when one officer documents information in their report, (such as finding a door open) which an officer on the preceeding shift should have found. Know what your supervisor wants documented in reports. Don't intentionally try to embarrass the preceeding shift officers. Just, state the facts!

TYPES OF SECURITY REPORTS

Most security departments use a variety of reports including:

- Shift Logs or Daily Logs
- Vehicle Logs

Notes

Keep your logs current. Don't write information in your log before it happens. Example: Security officers will often complete a log an hour or two in advance. This is unprofessional and dishonest!

Don't insert your personal opinion or comments into a report. Simply report what happened!

Never allow an unauthorized person to read a report. Often, information contained in written reports is extremely confidential and sensitive.

Security personnel receive some legal protection against defamation/slander when their written reports contain accusations implicating another person. This protection is based on the legal principle of "privileged communication." Security reports, provided their distribution is restricted to only only authorized and privileged persons, would normally fall under the protection of "privileged communication."

- Visitor/Contractor Logs
- Material Control Passes/Logs
- Incident Reports

These may cover a wide variety of events such as fire, theft, injury, safety hazard, maintenance or housekeeping item, etc...

SHIFT/DAILY LOGS

These logs are used to document all of the significant events which occur during a particular shift. For example:

- Officer's Name
- On Duty Time
- Name of Officer Relieved
- Notation as to obtaining keys, card access devices, etc.
- Times of all Patrols
- Notation of any unusual observations after first patrol:
- Number of Personnel/Vehicles on Site
- Doors/Windows open or unlocked
- Coffee pots which are on
- Special note or instructions regarding visitors, contractors or a delivery which is expected
- Equipment out of service and status (fire sprinkler system out of order due to repair)
- Pick-Up and Delivery Times of parcels
- Condition of security equipment (note any problems with CCTV cameras, radioes, etc.)
- Times of Officer's breaks for lunch or restroom
- Unusual phone calls
- Alarm Notification (Type of alarm and time)
- Notation of incident
- Off-Duty Time
- Name of relieving officer
- Notation as to keys and equipment given to arriving security officer

Notes

Shift or daily log reports will be the most common and frequent type of reports written by security officers. Often, for these reasons, they are the most boring. Security officers only create problems for themselves and their departments when they fail to note the most basic facts and incidents which took place on their shift.

VEHICLE LOGS

Vehicle logs are maintained by security personnel to document most vechicular traffic at a facility. Usually, this is primarily restricted to pick-up and delivery of material.

Trucks which are entering a facility normally stop at the main security post for the following reasons:

1. Weight Measurement — Many facilities have scales which all in-bound and outbound trucks must drive upon to have their weight recorded.

2. Driver Assistance — Many truck drivers will be entering a facility for the first time. The security officer will need to instruct them on where they need to go to pick-up or deliver their shipment. Often, the security officer will need to call the shipping or receiving department in order to obtain the necessary information for the driver.

3. Recording tractor and trailer numbers. — The proper recording of tractor and trailer numbers by security officers is extremely important. Often facilities are either waiting for a delivery of material which is called a "hot" load, or a trailer has already been loaded and is awaiting shipment. Accurate recordkeeping of trailer numbers by security personnel will insure that the correct shipments are taken by the drivers. Security personnel are often the final "check and balance" to ensure a shipment leaving the facility is correct.

4. Recording of "Manifests" and "Bills of Lading." — "Manifests" are documents which are given to a truck driver which represents the cargo or material they are removing from a facility. At many facilities, security personnel are required to inspect "Manifests" prior to a driver departing to ensure they have been given the proper shipment. The number of the manifest will often be noted on the vehicle log. "Bills of Lading" are documents which represent the material a driver has in his possession that is being delivered to a

Notes

It is essential that all security personnel understand the shipping and receiving routine at every facility.

Take nothing for granted! Verify all paperwork to ensure that all outbound trucks have the correct cargo.

Always remember to be professional and polite when dealing with drivers. They can often be rude and insulting. If their pick-up or delivery is delayed, they will often become frustrated and angry. This anger will often be directed to security personnel.

facility. Usually, security personnel will only inspect a "bill of lading" to determine where a driver should be directed with their shipment.

5. Time In / Time Out — The times that a driver arrives and departs from a facility are also very important. Often, deliveries and shipments are scheduled in advance. It is essential that drivers be on time and are prompt when entering and leaving a facility. Drivers are often given times when they are to be at a facility. If a driver is early or late in their arrival, their delivery or shipment may not be immediately processed. Security personnel must be certain to accurately record all times.

6. Seals and Locks — Many trailers are "sealed" and/or locked prior to departing a facility. A "seal" is a device which is placed into the latch of doors of a trailer. These seals cannot be removed unless they are broken, cut, or otherwise removed. Seals are stamped with a number which is also placed on the manifest or bills of lading. The purpose of a seal is to determine if a shipment has been opened or tampered with prior to its destination. Seals also can serve as locks. Security personnel will generally inspect a "sealed" trailer to be certain the seal has been properly secured and that the number on the seal matches the number on the manifest or bill of lading. If a security officer suspects that a load has been tampered with or the seal number is improper, a shipping or receiving supervisor should be immediately notified.

VISITOR/CONTRACTOR LOGS

Visitor and Contractor logs are normally maintained by security to document the visitors who are entering the facility and contractors who are working at the facility.

Most visitor and contractor logs require the following:

1. Date & Time of visit.
2. Employee or person to be visited.
3. Escorted/Unescorted Visitor. Some facilities will allow for certain visitors to enter a facility and after the person they are to visit has been notified, they are permitted to walk or drive their vehicle unescorted into the facility. By unescorted, it is meant that an employee does not have to be

Notes

with the visitor at all times. Some facilities never allow for unescorted visits at a facility. Therefore, an employee must always escort the visitor.

4. Material Entering the Facility. Many facilities (especially those which are government contractors and defense contractors) will require visitors to announce to security personnel what material they are bring into a facility. Items such as tape recoders and cameras will normally be prohibited from entering the facility.

5. Materials Leaving the Facility. Visitors who are often vendors may be removing certain material from a facility for testing, or engineering or manufacturing modificiation. If a material control pass is not used to document this fact, the material may be noted on the bottom or back portion of the visitor pass.

6. Time Departed — It is essential that security personnel properly note the time a visitor or contractor departs a facility. In the event of an emergency such as a plant evacuation, it is critical that emergency officials know precisely who is in or out of a facility. To a far lesser degree, associates or other employees where the visitor or contractor is employed may call for the person or inquire to when they departed the facility.

As previously noted, it is essential that security personnel maintain accurate records of all visitors and contractors who enter a facility. Situations may occur regarding questions to the timeliness of warranties or maintenance agreements at a certain facility. When the visitor or contractors logs are reviewed, it may be proven that the manufacturer representative was in fact at the facility during the warranty timeframe. The point to be made is that while it is often boring and tedious, the proper maintenance of visitor and contractors logs can be essential to the overall operation of a facility.

Visitor and Contractor Logs are usually retained for several years.

MATERIAL CONTROL PASSES/LOGS

Most facilities have some sort of recordkeeping control of the material, tools or equipment which is occasionally removed from a facility by employees. Usually, employees are borrowing a tool or taking home a personal computer or typewriter to complete an assignment. Most Material Control Passes or Logs will contain the following information:

- Date and Time
- Name of Employee/Person Removing the Material
- Description of material
- Ownership (Company or Personal Property)
- Length of time material is to be borrowed
- If the material is not to be returned, the reason why? (Example: scrap lumber, etc.)
- Person Authorizing property removal

While material control/property passes seem to provide a means of ensuring company property is returned, often proper follow-up of material control passes is not conducted. Problems develop in that while security may know when material is removed, security is often not notified when material is returned. Security personnel should audit material control passes frequently and follow-up with employees who still have material which should have been returned. **Practical Example:** A security mananger was contacted by an employee who stated that she would soon retire and she would like to purchase the company's typewriter that she had at home. It seems the female employee had removed the typewriter some five years previously on a material/control pass. She had never returned the typewriter because no one had ever called her to ask her when she would return it.

INCIDENT REPORTS

Many security departments use separate forms for serious incidents. These are called Incident Reports. The purpose of documenting incidents via Incident Reports rather than recording them in the Daily/Shift logs is that special notice or attention is given to an incident when a separate report is written. Incidents such as attempted thefts, fires, incidents involving employees, vehicle accidents, property damage, etc... would be examples of when an Incident Report should be written. It is suggested that a brief notation be made in the Daily/Shift Log such as: "incident involving employee Pete Smith, see Incident Report number ___."

The following questions must be answered when writing an Incident Report:

- WHO?
- WHAT?
- WHEN?
- WHERE?

- WHEN?
- WHY?
- CONCLUSIONS?

NOTETAKING/FIELD NOTES

The essential parts of any report are facts. Names, descriptions of individuals, vehicles, buildings, surroundings, correct dates and times are critical when attempting to reconstruct on paper what actually took place.

Often a report is written several minutes or several hours after an event has occurred. People who can provide answers may no longer be available for questioning.

Every security officer or supervisor should always carry a pen and a small pocket notebook in order to document key facts as they occur. Names, titles, and even descriptions can often be quickly noted even during an emergency. This information can prove critical months later.

The following are some helpful hints to remember when you are reconstructing the incident from your notes in preparation for writing your report.

1. Write what happened in chronological order. What happened first, then what happened next, and next, etc.

2. Be sure to include all names, positions, titles and department numbers of all employees.

3. Include names, addresses and, if possible, social security numbers of all non-employees who either witnessed or were involved in the incident.

4. Explain in plain, simple English what happened. If you mention a building by its name or number, give its location as well. Remember, many people who will read this report are not as familiar with directions and locations as you are.

5. When you begin to write your report, constantly refer to your notes. Don't include your opinion or comments and don't editorialize. You can give your opinion or comment about the incident in person to your superior.

6. Don't discard your notes. Keep them until your supervisor advises you to discard them.

7. Write your report before you leave work. Leaving the job before your report is written gives a bad impression of your security department.

RECORDKEEPING, STORAGE & USE OF COMPUTERS

Security reports and logs should be kept secure under safekeeping. Many security departments maintain these records for several years. Besides the fact that these reports, when retained, are valuable in proving or disproving claims against an organization, many security departments keep track of all incidents and categorize them by event. By tracking incidents, security managers are better prepared to conduct investigations such as theft and accidents.

Many security departments have personal computers available for their security officers to directly input their reports. Other departments use computers to track incidents and these reports are often inputed by a secretary.

As stated previously, it is essential that all security reports be written factually, clearly and neatly. Provided this is accomplished, prior to a security officer going "off-duty", a security manager should never be embarrassed over the quality of written reports.

SUMMARY

Written reports have existed for thousands of years as shown by documents such as the Koran and Bible. Security reports are written to: provide a permanent record of an Incident; verify the job duties performed; explain confusing events; provide evidence in a legal proceeding; and provide information for follow-up action.

Security reports must be clear, concise and accurate. Security logs and reports may be used in court proceedings. It is therefore essential that information pertaining to: who, what, when, where, when, why, and how are always answered. Security officers often fail to answer these basic questions which damages the credibility of the entire security organization.

Security reports must document all events which occured, must be written clearly and neatly, all facts must be reported factually, the inforamtion must be protected, and security officers must know what their supervisors want them to include in their report...

Most security departments use a wide variety of

reports, including: Shift or Daily logs; Vehicle logs; Visitor/ Contractor logs; Material Control Passes; and Incident Reports. Notetaking is the essential foundation upon which well-written reports are built. The essential parts of any report are the facts. Names, descriptions of individuals, vehicles, buildings, surroundings, correct dates and times are critical when attempting to reconstruct on paper what actually took place.

Often a report is written several minutes or several hours after àn event has occurred. People who can provide answers may no longer be available for questioning.

Every security officer or supervisor should always carry a pen and small pocket notebook in order to document key facts as they occur. Names, titles, and even descriptions can often be quickly noted even during an emergency. This information can prove to be critical months later.

Security reports and logs should be kept secure. Besides the fact that these reports when retained are valuable in proving or disproving claims against an organization, many security departments keep track of all incidents and categorize them by event.

Many security departments have personal computers available for their security officers to directly input their reports.

It is essential that all security reports be written factually, clearly and neatly. Provided this is accomplished, prior to a security officer going "off-duty", a security manager should never be embarrassed over the quality of written reports.

Notes

QUESTIONS

1.   Name the five purposes for security reports.

        1). _____

        2). _____

        3). _____

        4). _____

        5). _____

2.   Name the seven questions which must be answered in every security report or log.

        1). _____

        2). _____

        3). _____

        4). _____

        5). _____

        6). _____

        7). _____

3.   It is proper and acceptable for a security officer to include their personal opinion and commentary when writing security reports? True or False _____

4.   Even though a department manager or union official may be allowed to read an incident report concerning an employee, the security officer on duty should not permit them access unless prior approval has been given by a superior? True or False

      _____

5.   Security reports which document the daily activity of a security officer are called:

      a. Vehicle Logs

      b. Contractor Logs

      c. Material Pass Logs

      d. Shift/Daily Logs

6.   List as many items as possible that a security officer should include in their Shift/Daily Activity Log.

    1.)_____

    2.)_____

    3.)_____

    4.)_____

    5.)_____

    6.)_____

    7.)_____

    8.)_____

7.   Name five items that should be included in all Vehicle Logs.
1.)_____
2.)_____
3.)_____
4.)_____
5.)_____

8.   Explain the purposes of "seals."

_____
_____
_____

9.   Explain the difference between an Escorted and Unescorted visitor.

_____
_____
_____

10.   Name the seven suggested requirements that are contained for Material Control Passes or Logs.
1.)_____
2.)_____
3.)_____
4.)_____
5.)_____
6.)_____
7.)_____

11.   Incident Reports are used by many security departments to report significant or serious incidents which should be separate from the normal shift logs. True or False

12.   What is the term for documenting events in the order in which they occurred?

_____

13.   If a security officer does not have time to write an Incident Report regarding a serious accident before their shift ends, the officer should:

       a. Go home and write the report the following day.
       b. Ask the person who is relieving the security officer to write the report.
       c. Ask permission from their supervisor to work over for the time necessary to complete
           the report.
       d. None of the above.

14. Name one reason why security logs and reports are retained by security departments.

_____

Security Logs -- Practical Suggestions

The primary purposes of a security logbook are:
- To provide a primary record of security officers' time on and off duty.
- To provide a precise and factual record of what duties are performed and when they are performed.
- To record unusual events (incidents) and observations.
- To keep a record of equipment and other special items that are entrusted to the care of the security officer.
- To provide evidence to clients and the company that may be used to settle disputes or legal proceedings.
- To ensure proper notifications are made regarding unusual conditions when a supervisor or a client representative is called.

Certain items should always be recorded when making log entries.
- Itemize significant equipment received at the start of your shift, especially the number of keys received. (Radios, Detex clock, charger, cash box, paychecks, etc.)
- Log each door or gate that is locked or unlocked during your shift.
- Log all doors or gates found unlocked, which are normally locked.
- Log any item that is delivered to the guard station (paychecks, packages, etc.) and any item picked up. Ask for identification before allowing pick-up if you do not know the individual.
- Log all visitors and employees entering or leaving the facility during non-working hours unless a special form is provided for such use.
- Make all entries in ink -- preferably black.
- Print all entries to ensure legibility.
- Use precise time entries. Round off no more than to the nearest five minutes.
- Make an entry for every hour, even if nothing significant occurs. For example, "Access control at guardhouse -- all appears normal."
- Check and log the condition of all vending machines (especially change machines) on all patrols.
- Log the time of each patrol. (start and finish)
- Write things down -- take credit for your good work. It is better to write down too much than too little.
- Log all phone calls made by you or anyone else. You are only protecting yourself should a telephone abuse situation come up at your posted facility.

Do not do the following things in the log book:
- Do not doodle or write anything not security related.
- Do not log anything before the time in which it occurs.
- Do not use abbreviations or ditto marks.
- Do not sign off duty before your relief arrives and is fit to perform his or her duties.
- Do not enter personal opinions or write derogatory comments about co-workers, client employees or your supervisors.
- Do not white out or erase anything in the log book. If you make a mistake, draw a line through the error, initial the entry and make the corrections.

DAILY REPORT OF SIGNIFICANT OCCURRENCES	
DATE *6-1-92* **TIME PERIOD FROM** *0800* **TO** *1600*	
LOCATION *GATEWAY INDUSTRIAL PLANT*	

TIME	REMARKS
0745	OFFICER JOE JONES ARRIVES ON DUTY, TO RELIEVE
	OFFICER PETER SMITH.
0800	RECEIVED KEYS, FLASHLIGHT, ACCESS CARD AND
	WATCHMAN PATROL CLOCK FROM OFFICER SMITH.
	SMITH OFF DUTY.
0815	PATROLLED MAIN PARKING LOT TO DETERMINE
	VEHICLES ON SITE:
	1. BLUE CHEVY PICK-UP TRUCK #383-LOV
	2. WHITE HONDA ACCORD (4-DOOR) #135-PQV
	3. BLACK OLDS "88" (4-DOOR) #250-PMT
0830-0930	CONDUCTED PATROL OF INTERIOR (OFFICES AND PLANT)
	THE FOLLOWING ITEMS WERE OBSERVED:
	1. INTERIOR HALLWAY DOOR IN ENGINEERING DEPT.
	WAS UNLOCKED. SECURED AT 0845.
	2. EXTERIOR DOOR TO EMPLOYEE'S LUNCHROOM IN
	DEPT. #20 WAS UNLOCKED. SECURED AT 0900.
	3. COFFEE POT WAS ON IN PAYROLL/ACCOUNTING
	AREA. TURNED OFF AT 0915.
0930-0945	TOOK BREAK IN GUARD OFFICE. NO PHONE CALLS.

CONTINUED ON OTHER SIDE: YES NO   OFFICER IN CHARGE *Joe Jones*

TIME	REMARKS
0945-1000	TWO SALARY EMPLOYEES, BILL WARREN AND JIM LESLIE,
	SIGNED-IN TO GO TO WORK IN ENGINEERING.
1000-1100	INTERIOR PATROL - NOTHING UNUSUAL REPORTED
1100-1115	PATROLLED MAIN PARKING LOT TO DETERMINE
	VEHICLES ON SITE:
	SAME THREE VEHICLES, PLUS:
	1. GREEN FORD ESCORT # 212-PQM
1115-1200	ABBREVIATED INTERIOR PATROL - NOTHING UNUSUAL
1200-1230	OBSERVED THREE MAINTENANCE EMPLOYEES EXIT
	THE FACILITY. CONDUCTED PACKAGE INSPECTION.
	INCIDENT WITH JIM ARNOLD. (SEE INCDENT REPORT)
1230-1330	CONDUCTED INTERIOR PATROL - NOTHING UNUSUAL.
1330-1345	TOOK BREAK IN GUARD OFFICE.
1345-1445	CONDUCTED INTERIOR PATROL - NOTHING UNUSUAL.
1445-1500	POSITIONED IN GUARD OFFICE. ONE PHONE CALL
	FOR JIM LELIE FROM MR. NEIL ANTHONY.
1500-1545	ABBREVIATED INTERIOR PATROL - NOTHING UNUSUAL.
1545	RELIEF OFFICER, JOHN GENTRY, ON DUTY.
	TURNED OVER ALL KEYS, FLASHLIGHT,
	ACCESS CARD AND WATCHMAN CLOCK.
1555	MADE ONE-MINUTE PHONE CAL TO SPOUSE.
1600	OFFICER JONES OFF-DUTY
	Joe Jones

SECURITY DEPARTMENT

INCIDENT REPORT

NATURE OF INCIDENT		REPORT NO.

☐ Theft of Property ☐ Liquor Violation

☐ Vandalism ☐ Other _____

_____
Date and Time of Report

☐ Trespassing _____

_____
Date and Time of Incident

☐ Time Card Violation _____

_____
Location of Incident

☐ Unauthorized Entry/Exit

REPORT IN DETAIL: Who   What   When   Where   How   Why

Complainant	Clock or Social Security No.	Department of Address
Offender	Clock or Social Security No.	Department of Address
Witness	Clock or Social Security No.	Department of Address

DESCRIPTION OF INCIDENT: _____

_____

_____

_____

_____

_____

_____

_____

_____

_____

_____

_____

_____

_____

_____

_____

Estimate of Theft or Damage $_____   REPORTED BY:

Continued on Reverse Side? ☐ Yes   ☐ No

_____
Security Officer   Badge No.

Page ____ of ____

INCIDENT REPORT

REPORT NUMBER (FACILITY)

NO. 1988-B

TYPE OF INCIDENT	GRID OCCURRENCE	REPORTING DATE	COMPLAINT NUMBER (Security Use Only)

Owner/Victim _____ Address _____ Phone _____

Reported By _____ Address _____ Phone _____

Address of Incident _____ Type of Place _____

Time of Incident _____ Date of Incident _____ Day of Week _____

WHAT OCCURRED? (Include any suspects and/or witnesses)

_____

_____

_____

_____

_____

_____

_____

_____

_____

_____

_____

_____

_____

_____

Total Value $ _____

(If more space is required, continue on supplement.)

Police Advised ☐ Yes ☐ No (If yes, give officer's name, city and describe action taken by police above.)

POLICE DEPT.	OFFICER/CAR NUMBER	POLICE REPORT NUMBER

Signed _____ Department _____ Telephone Ext. _____

Approved _____ Date of Approval _____
(SUPERVISOR'S SIGNATURE)

Alarms: Weather Conditions:

False ☐ Yes ☐ No   Windy ☐   Rain ☐   Snow ☐   Lightning ☐   Clear ☐

DAILY GUARD TOUR REPORT

GUARD *(PRINT NAME)*		EMPLOYEE NO.	SHIFT	DATE	
LOCATION	RELIEVED BY *(PRINT NAME)*			EMPLOYEE NO.	

INSTRUCTIONS:

1. SEE REVERSE SIDE FOR AN EXPLANATION OF EACH ITEM.
2. INDICATE ANSWER BY PLACING AN "X" IN THE PROPER COLUMN. EACH ITEM MUST BE CHECKED.
3. EXPLAIN ANY UNUSUAL CIRCUMSTANCES IN "REMARKS." REFER TO APPLICABLE ITEM NUMBER.

	YES	NO		YES	NO
1. TOURS, STATIONS MISSED			15. FIRES		
2. SPECIAL INSTRUCTIONS RECEIVED			16. SPRINKLER HEADS BLOCKED		
3. CLASSIFIED CONTAINERS OPEN			17. RISER VALVES BLOCKED, CLOSED		
4. VAULTS, SAFES OR FILE CABINETS OPEN			18. SAFETY HAZARDS		
5. CLASSIFIED INFORMATION VIOLATIONS			19. RUBBISH ACCUMULATION		
6. THEFTS, ATTEMPTED THEFTS			20. MAINTENANCE REQUIRED		
7. SUSPICIOUS ACTIVITIES			21. BURNED-OUT LIGHTS		
8. TRESPASSERS			22. BROKEN LOCKING DEVICES		
9. WINDOWS, DOORS UNLOCKED			23. HEALTH HAZARDS		
10. EQUIPMENT, LIGHTS, WATER ON			24. PARKING LOT VIOLATIONS		
11. ALARMS ACTIVATED			25. PERIMETER BARRIER HAZARDS		
12. DEFECTIVE EQUIPMENT			26. COMPLAINTS BY EMPLOYEES		
13. FIRE DOORS, EXITS, LANES BLOCKED			27. PROPRIETARY INFORMATION VIOLATIONS		
14. FIRE HAZARDS			28. OTHER THAN ABOVE (Explain in Remarks)		

REMARKS *(PLEASE PRINT)*

_____

_____

_____

_____

_____

_____

_____

_____

_____

_____

DISTRIBUTION: WHITE - *MANAGER, SECURITY & ADMIN. SERVICES*   CANARY - *GUARD - FILE AT LOCATION*

SECURITY GUARDS DAILY DUTY LOG

SECURITY GUARD _____

SUPERVISOR-IN-CHARGE _____

(PLEASE PRINT ALL INFORMATION BELOW)

DATE _____

DUTY HOURS _____

TIME	LOCATION	REMARKS	DISPOSITION	TIME COMPLETED

GUARD'S SIGNATURE _____

DAILY REPORT OF SIGNIFICANT OCCURRENCES	
DATE TIME PERIOD FROM TO	
LOCATION	
TIME	**REMARKS**

CONTINUED ON OTHER SIDE: YES   NO   OFFICER IN CHARGE _____

DAILY TRUCK RECORD

COMPANY OR CARRIER Please Print	TIME		D.P.S.	DATE: _____ REMARKS
	IN	OUT		

PROPERTY RECEIPT

1. RECEIVED FROM Last First Middle	2. DATE	3. HOUR
4. ADDRESS Street City State	5. CENTRAL COMPLAINT NUMBER	
6. Describe Articles Received, Give Serial Numbers if Available	7. PROPERTY BOOK	
	Book No.	Page No.

8. Officer's Signature	9. Badge Number	10. Organizational Element

PROPERTY REMOVAL PASS

NAME_____DATE_____TIME_____
DEPARTMENT_____EXT. OR PHONE NO. _____

QUANTITY   ITEM   LOCATION (Removed From)

_____   _____   _____

_____   _____   _____

_____   _____   _____

_____   _____   _____

_____   _____   _____

_____   _____   _____

TOTAL NUMBER ITEMS REMOVED_____PERMANENT [ ]

                                                                    _____
DATE TO BE RETURNED BY_____TEMPORARY [ ]   DEPARTMENT HEAD

DISTRIBUTION: SEND ENTIRE FORM TO THE SECURITY DEPARTMENT

Fire Extinguisher Maintenance Checklist Location	Type	J a n	F e b	M a r c h	A p r i l	M a y	J u n e	J u l y	A u g	S e p t	O c t	N o v	D e c
LOWER Level													
Hamilton Wing	ABC-20												
Hamilton Wing	CO2-15												
Hamilton Wing	ABC-20												
Boiler Room	ABC-10												
Boiler Room	ABC-10												
Boiler Room	CO2-15												
Boiler Maintenance	CO2-15												
Boiler Entrance	CO2-15												
Computer Room	Halon												
Johnson Wing	ABC												
Johnson Wing	ABC												
LaRoue Wing	ABC												
LaRoue Wing	ABC												
Auxiliary Storage	CO2-5												
Maintenance Storage	CO2-5												
Maintenance Storage	CO2-5												
Maintenance Shop	CO2-15												
Maintenance Shop	CO2-15												
Power Room	ABC												
Power Room	CO2-15												
Fire Pump Room	CO2-15												
Officer's Initials	Date												

CONTRACTORS LOG	Time	Time	Time	Time	Time	Time	Lot	Lot	Lot	Lot	BADGE	DATE: _____
Company Name & Signature	IN	OUT	IN	OUT	IN	OUT	A	B	C	D	#	License #

THE EFFECTIVE SECURITY OFFICERS TRAINING MANUAL

Chapter VII

Legal Aspects

Legal Aspects of Security

Security officers usually possess one of three different kinds of authority:

1. they possess authority because they are citizens and/or property owners.
2. they possess authority granted to them by deputation or commissioning from public law enforcement agency (least common).
3. they possess authority which is a mixture of their powers as civilians and certain special requirements which were added by a special law or ordinance.

Security Officers with Only Citizen Powers

Security officers who possess only citizen powers are the most common in the U.S. For the most part, security officers function as an agent for their employer. The security officer has only the power and authority of their employer. Think of a security officer with only the power of a private citizen in this way: whatever authority a private citizen has to protect himself and property from harm, a security officer working for that business or owner has the same authority, no more - no less.

Security Officers with Special Commissions

Some security officers have been granted special police or peace officer powers (*commissioned*) by a local, state or federal government authority. Usually, when a security officer has this type of power, it is limited to the grounds and buildings of the employer. What makes this security officer different from a police officer is that the security officer's power exists only when they are working and only when they are on the property of their employer. Many security officers who work for retail stores have arrest powers for shoplifting incidents. These powers exist because the security officer is

Notes

Reading For A Purpose
Look for these key Words:
- commissioned
- U. S. Constitution
- shopkeeper laws
- self defense
- tort
- defamation

Look for Answers to these questions:
- What are the three types of security officers?
- Where do their powers come from?
- When can a security officer detain a person?
- When can a security use force?

Commissioned: act by a federal, state or local agency which authorizes or sanctions individuals with special legal authority.

working for a shopkeeper. Most states grant a merchant, shopkeeper or their agents (security officers) the right to detain a person when there are reasonable grounds to believe that the person has shoplifted. Usually, the merchant or security officer has the authority to request identification from the suspected person; to verify their identification and to make a reasonable inquiry as to whether the person has unpaid merchandise in their possession. Some states allow for the suspected shoplifter to be *detained* or held until the police arrive. Many security officers who work for railroads have the full power and authority of police officers while either on railroad property and/or while working on behalf of the railroad.

Security Officers who are Policemen/women

Some full-time police officers work part-time as security officers and they make up the third type of security officers. The particular state where the policeman or woman works will determine the requirements for an officer who works part-time as a security officer.

Basis of Authority

After the Revolutionary War with England the founders of the United States met to form and revise what is known as the United States Constitution. The Constitution was enacted on September 17, 1787, and is made up of seven articles which among other things establishes the offices of President and Vice-President, Congress and the Supreme Court. The Constitution did not specify how much power and authority private citizens have to protect themselves and their property. However, the Constitution did grant to states the ability to provide for the safety of people and their property. From this part of the Constitution, private security has its power.

The Bill of Rights

The original *Bill of Rights* was made up of ten amendments to the Constitution which were became law in 1791.

Notes

Detention: *the stopping of a person preventing their freedom of movement for the purpose of identification of the person and/or ownership of property.*

U.S. Constitution: *enacted on September 17, 1787, made up of seven articles which established the offices of President and Vice President, Congress and the Supreme Court and serves as the basis for all laws in the United States.*

Bill of Rights: *originally 10 amendments added to the U.S. Constitution in 1791, designed as protection for citizens from certain actions by the federal government.*

The Bill of Rights was created because people worried that their new country (USA) would restrict their lives in the same way England had. Since 1791 other amendments have been added to the Constitution. This course will only discuss the 4th and 5th amendments which directly and indirectly affect the security profession. The purpose of the discussion of the 4th and 5th amendments is to provide a basis of knowledge to the security officer which will allow him or her to understand fully one of the major differences between their profession and that of a police officer.

4th Amendment

The 4th amendment protects citizens from unreasonable searches and seizures. Specifically, the 4th amendment states that people have a right to be secure and that "their persons, houses and papers" cannot be illegally searched. In order for these items to be searched, in most cases a search warrant must be obtained which describes the place to be searched and the persons or things which are to be seized. Many people misunderstand the importance of the 4th amendment and how it pertains to security officers. In many court cases throughout the U.S. and with only few exceptions the following statement is fact:

THE PROTECTION GIVEN IN THE 4TH AMENDMENT AGAINST UNREASONABLE SEARCHES AND SEIZURES DOES NOT PERTAIN TO PRIVATE CITIZENS. THE PROTECTION OF THE 4TH AMENDMENT AGAINST UNREASONABLE SEARCH AND SEIZURE APPLIES ONLY TO GOVERNMENT INTRUSIONS AND NOT TO UNLAWFUL ACTS OF PRIVATE CITIZENS.

The point to be made here is not that security officers can act in a reckless or improper manner for if they do they could be liable for civil or even criminal action. However, it is important to note that unless a security officer is commissioned, deputized or in some other way granted peace officer or police powers, the security officer is not held to the search and seizure restrictions which affect law enforcement personnel. That is why security officers can conduct package inspections of employees and their belongings as people enter and exit a facility. In almost every instance, inspections

Notes

4th Amendment: an amendment to the U.S. Constitution which protects citizens from unreasonable searches and seizures by government officials.

of vehicles, persons and their property can be made by a security officer at anytime. **Please note: some companies have entered into agreements with their employees (or the employees' union) which specify if and how inspections and/or searches are to be done.** Therefore, inspections may be restricted or perhaps even prohibited because of company policy. In addition, if a security officer is commissioned, deputized, is a full-time police officer working as a security officer or is working as a security officer for a government agency, the 4th amendment will probably apply. These security officers will fall into the same category as police officers relative to search and seizure.

5th Amendment

The *5th amendment* to the U.S. Constitution prohibits several actions by the government against a citizen. The most important and most recognized prohibition is that a citizen is protected from "self incrimination" or testifying against themselves. A famous U.S. Supreme Court case was decided in 1966 and as a result of the ruling the famous Miranda decision was made into law. From this ruling came the "Miranda Warnings":

1. A person has the right to remain silent.
2. If a person decides to talk, anything the person says can be used against them in court.
3. A person has the right to an attorney.
4. If a person cannot afford an attorney, the court will provide one at no cost.

All of these warnings must be told to the person or suspect in a way that the suspect clearly understands. Because the Miranda warnings were based on the 5th amendment to the Constitution and because the amendments pertain only to protection from government officials, the Miranda warnings do not have to be given by security officers when questioning suspects. Once again, an exception may exist if the security officer has been commissioned, deputized or given police powers. Some security departments may require their personnel to give the Miranda warnings. However, in most cases, it is not required.

Notes

5th Amendment: an amendment to the U.S. Constitution which protects citizens from "self-incrimination," allows for consultation with a lawyer before police questioning.

Miranda Warnings: also known as a person's "rights," police are required to recite the warnings to a person who is a suspect or who has been arrested for a felony.

Detention and Arrest Powers

Generally, security officers do not have broad powers to make arrests as compared to police officers. Private security officers have at least the same type of *arrest powers* as private citizens. For the most part and as previously discussed, owners of stores and their employees or agents have limited authority to detain a person suspected of shoplifting. Also, many states allow shopkeepers or their employees to arrest persons but only when certain conditions have been met.

Security Officers with Authority to Arrest
For Felony or Misdemeanor

Laws differ from state to state regarding the authority for citizens to arrest when a *felony* crime has been committed. For you, as a security officer, it is important to know the law for the state in which you work. For purposes of this discussion it is necessary for you to understand what a felony crime is: A felony is an offense that is so serious that a person (who commits a felony) can be sentenced to jail for one year or more or in the case of murder a person can be executed. For the most part, felony crimes are always more serious than *misdemeanor* crimes. Misdemeanor crimes are ones that can cause a person to be sentenced to jail for less than one year. Many security officers, because of the nature of their work are not expected to ever make an arrest. Company policy will always dictate whether an officer is expected to make arrests. In most states a private citizen can arrest another person when a felony has been committed in the person's presence and the person making the arrest reasonably believes the person he/she is arresting, committed the felony. Again it is stressed, many security officers are not expected to arrest persons. One reason for this is that if a security officer is mistaken and the person he/she arrested did not in fact commit the felony, the security officer and his/her employer may be sued.

Notes

Arrest Powers: given to police, peace officers and in certain instances citizens, allowing for the legal arrest of a person.

Felony: a criminal offense which is punishable with a sentence of more than one year in jail.

Misdemeanor: a criminal offense which is punishable with a sentence of up to one year in jail.

Shopkeeper Laws

Most security officers who are expected to make arrests will fall under the category of laws which give a merchant, store owner, their employees and/or their agents authority to detain a person suspected of shoplifting. It is important to know that the various laws referred to as *shopkeeper laws* pertain to those businesses which are primarily retail/wholesale establishments which are selling goods to the public. Laws vary from state to state but in most cases a storeowner or his/her employees or agents may detain a person suspected of shoplifting for a reasonable period of time to determine the identity of the person and if they in fact have unpaid merchandise in their possession.

Security Officers with Peace Officers' Authority to Arrest

The final category which will be discussed is security officers who possess police or special peace officer's authority to arrest. As a general rule security officers who possess police power must follow the same requirements as police officers.

Felony Arrests

A peace officer has authority to arrest without a warrant if he/she has reasonable grounds to believe that a felony has been committed and that the person arrested committed the felony. You may ask yourself what is the importance of the term "reasonable grounds?" For the security officer, police officer or private citizen the importance of reasonable grounds cannot be minimized. Stated simply, "reasonable grounds" means that a ..."reasonable, prudent and discrete person would believe that a felony has been committed and that the person being arrested committed it." The more information obtained, from whatever the source, the better the chances are of proving that reasonable grounds for the felony arrest did exist."1 In summary, security officers must ask themselves this question, if a reasonable, uninterested, third person were given the same information as the security officer, would that person have

Notes

Shopkeeper Laws: rights of a merchant, store owner, employees or agents of the store owner the right to detain a person for determining their identity and ownership of property.

Reasonable Grounds: theory that a reasonable person would make certain assumptions founded on sound, logical factors.

acted in the same manner and arrested the person?

Misdemeanor Arrests

"In most states, the law provides that a peace officer may not arrest for a misdemeanor unless it is committed in his presence".2 By "in his presence" authors Bilek, Klotter and Federal in LEGAL ASPECTS OF PRIVATE SECURITY explain that while the officer does not have to witness the entire misdemeanor crime occur, he/she must witness some part of the crime still in progress. A security officer must utilize primarily his/her senses of sight and hearing in determining if a misdemeanor offense is taking place.

Authority to Arrest with a Warrant

The 4th Amendment to the Constitution states that a *warrant* will be issued only upon probable cause which is supported by an oath which describes in particular the person or things to be seized. Arrests with a warrant are almost exclusively reserved for police officers but in certain situations a security officer with police powers may arrest with a warrant. A warrant must be obtained from an issuing official such as a magistrate or judge. The warrant will have to be supported by probable cause. This means that the person issuing the warrant must determine that through his/her independent evaluation of the facts he/she believes probable cause exists for the person or things in the warrant to be seized. Several other requirements such as the identity of the offense must be clearly defined. Provided all of the requirements of obtaining a warrant are met the person making the arrest will be protected from civil liability even if the person is not guilty of the crime for which they were arrested.

The Use of Force

Force may be used in the making of an arrest, but the security officer must be aware that to use force will greatly increase the chance that a civil suit will be filed against the officer and his/her employer. Because of the increased

Notes

Warrant: *legal document issued by a judge or magistrate which gives government officials authority to arrest a person and/or search and seize the contents of their person, property or home.*

Probable Cause: *reasonable or probable grounds to believe that the person who is to be arrested has committed the crime he/she is being arrested for. In order to make an arrest, a law enforcement officer must reasonably believe that guilt is more than a possibility.*

threat of a lawsuit, the security officer must be certain that force is necessary to make an arrest. Consider this: an arrest of a person is made at the height of emotions. An individual who is 5'6"" tall and weighs 150 pounds may normally not act like a world class boxer or wrestler. However, if the person is enraged (for whatever reasons: intoxicated, etc...) two or three officers who are each over six feet in height and weigh over 200 pounds may have difficulty in controlling and finally arresting the person. Human tendency is to retaliate when attacked. Remember, that if force is used to accomplish an arrest, the facts surrounding the incident may be viewed weeks or months later during the "cool of the day." While it may appear obvious to a person witnessing the arrest that force was necessary to make the arrest, some three to six months later a jury comprised of people who are grandparents, school teachers, musicians, doctors, engineers and businessmen may be making the final decision as to whether the force was necessary and reasonable. Keep in mind that current or former boxers, wrestlers or people who just enjoy a good fight will likely not be members of the jury determining if the force used was necessary and reasonable. In general, a police officer or private person (security officer) may use force necessary to make a valid arrest provided that the force used in making the arrest is equal to the nature and extent of resistance by the person who is to be arrested. In other words, if you have the choice of either sitting on or holding a person to the ground versus hitting them with your fist, it would be wiser, to not hit the person. Most courts determine the proper measure of force by the reasonable person theory. This theory is, would an ordinary, prudent and intelligent person with the same knowledge in a similar situation as the security officer have used the same amount of force? Most states view differently the amount of force used in the making of a felony arrest from a misdemeanor arrest.

Force Used in a Felony Arrest

Some states allow that any force necessary to make an arrest short of deadly force, may be used to affect an arrest. Please note: most of these state statutes apply to police officers. As a general rule, except when acting in *self-defense* a security officer when making an arrest without a warrant

Notes

A security officer may use force only in certain situations and only if the force used is reasonable.

Reasonable Person Theory:
Would an ordinary, prudent and intelligent person with the same knowledge and information make the same decision as the security officer?

Self Defense: justifiable act of protecting oneself from harm.

and only with the suspicion that a felony has occurred, cannot kill a suspect in order to make the arrest. This means that a security officer would only be justified in killing a suspect, if the security officer's life is in danger. Another word of caution for all security officers: keep in mind that once again a judge or jury may be reviewing your actions at a later time. If you took the life of another person because you were in fear of your life, will the judge or jury agree with you? Many security officers and their companies have been found liable for the deaths of persons killed by security officers. In many of these situations (which will be discussed in greater detail in the section: CIVIL LIABILITIES FOR SECURITY OFFICERS the security officer was found to have escalated the emotions at the time of the incident. A security officer who reaches for a nightstick, mace or even their revolver may very well have increased the likelihood for violence. Remember! The two most important things to an individual are his/her freedom and life. These values must be respected when compared to the importance of property being damaged, destroyed or stolen.

Amount of Force for a Misdemeanor Arrest

In general a security officer cannot use force which could injure or kill a person who has committed a misdemeanor. An officer can use only deadly force when necessary to protect himself/herself from death. Force in many cases cannot be used by a security officer who has only private citizen authority. Laws vary according to state. **Please consult with your employer as to what your state allows.**

Authority to Detain

In most situations a security officer does not have authority to detain suspects. An exception which would allow for detention is for shoplifting suspects. The U.S. Supreme Court granted police officers the authority to detain a person when unusual conduct is observed which leads the police officer to believe that criminal activity may occur. The Supreme Court decision was decided in 1968 in the Terry v. Ohio decision. Terry, along with three other men, was observed by a police officer acting suspicious in

Notes

A security officer can only use deadly force if they believe they are in immediate danger of suffering serious bodily injury or death.

Terry v Ohio: A 1968 U.S. Supreme Court case which gave police the authority to "stop and frisk" a person suspected of committing or about to commit a crime

downtown Cleveland. The police officer asked them their names and when one of the three mumbled something, he grabbed the individual and "patted him down." He felt a pistol in one of the suspect's coat pocket. The three men were arrested and based upon their appeal to the U.S. Supreme Court the case was decided which allows police to detain persons who behave suspiciously. The authority to detain or "stop and frisk" does not apply to security officers unless they have been given the authority of a peace officer by a licensing procedure or by state law. When authority to detain has been granted that authority can be applied to wherever the suspected criminal activity takes place.

Criminal Liabilities of Security Personnel

Most security officers only have the same authority as any private citizen. Often, when criminal charges are filed against a security officer it is for one of the following offenses:

- *assault*
- *battery*
- *homicide*
- *discharging a firearm*

It is important to know what each offense means:

<u>assault:</u> an attempt or threat, using force or violence to harm another person.

<u>battery:</u> the actual touching of a person with intent to injure or harm another person.

<u>homicide:</u> killing of a person by another, ranges from first degree murder to involuntary manslaughter.

<u>discharging a firearm:</u> use of a firearm for unjust cause which may injure another.

Protection of Self

Self-defense is a recognized standard for the justifiable use of force. However, for the claim of self-defense to be valid a person cannot have been the aggressor in the conflict. A person cannot start a fight and then claim that they acted in self-defense. A security officer must also believe that the other person was going to kill or seriously injure them. The danger of serious harm or death must be

Assault: a criminal or civil offense, an attempt or threat to use violence to harm another person.

Battery: a criminal or civil offense, the actual unlawful touching of another person with intent to injure or harm another person.

homicide: killing of a person by another, ranges from first degree murder to involuntary manslaughter.

discharging a firearm: use of a firearm for unjust cause which may injure another.

real and immediate and it must be clear that a person had no other choice of action other than to defend him/herself. The justifiable use of self-defense will also have to have been viewed as reasonable, which is measured by an objective third party's viewpoint. In other words, would a reasonable person in the same situation, act in the same way in protecting him/herself?

The use of deadly force in self-defense must clearly be justifiable. A security officer who stands 6'0" and weighs 200 pounds could not be justified in the killing of a person who clearly could not have created the fear of death or serious injury in a reasonable person. If a 12 year old boy who weighs 100 pounds strikes the security officer with his fist, the use of a gun by the officer would not be justified. If the youth threatened the security officer with a knife or other weapon the use of a gun may be justified. The point to be made here is that the law expects security officers to act in a reasonable manner using good judgment. Instead of using deadly force which kills the person, a security officer might have been able to retreat to prevent injury or perhaps have called the police. Once again, a security officer must remember that his/her uniform and badge while giving some authority does not allow for actions which are not justified. For a security officer to use force when the facts of a case suggest that force was not necessary, it will clearly result in liabilities against the officer.

Use of Force in Protecting Others

The law also allows for a person to use force to protect someone else. Employees may use force to protect their employer and the employer can do the same for the employee. The same general principle applies to the use of force in protecting others as with the use of force in self-defense: would a reasonable person in the same situation believe that someone was about to be bodily injured by another and that the threat of bodily injury was real and immediate? If the facts support that the threat was real, then the use of force to protect another would be justified. This does not mean that deadly force can be used against a person when "less than deadly force" could protect the victim and the security officer. The force which would be justified is that which

Notes

Security officers must always act in a reasonable manner using good judgement.

If a security officer uses force against a person, and it is determined later that force was unnecessary or unreasonable, a civil lawsuit will probably result.

Use of Force: Permitted to protect self, employer or other employees. Force must be reasonable and that the threat of bodily injury was real.

Force may be used to stop a physical attack. Once the attack is stopped, the force must stop.

stops the attack. Once the attack is stopped, force can no longer be used.

Use of Force in Protecting Property

The law allows for a person to defend his/her property from invaders. A person may also hire other people to protect property. The force which is permitted depends on the nature of the invasion. If a person is trespassing on property, force cannot be used until a request to leave is made or unless it is clear a request is meaningless. Deadly force can be used to protect property only during a forcible felony. A person may use deadly force to protect one's self and property during an armed robbery. In short, non-deadly force can be used to protect property. Deadly force can be used only when there is a reasonable belief that a dangerous felony (rape, robbery, murder, ...) is about to be committed on or in the property. A bank security officer may be justified in the use of deadly force to prevent an armed robbery. A security officer working in an office building may be justified in using deadly force to prevent a rape. A retail store security officer would not be justified in using deadly force against a shoplifter who steals merchandise and runs out of the store without having threatened anyone.

Civil Liabilities for Security Personnel

As discussed previously a security officer can be charged for a criminal offense if his/her actions are judged to have violated the law. In addition and equally important to know is that a security officer can be sued in a civil court. This type of action comes under the broad notion of Tort Law. A "*tort*" is an act or failure to act, which causes injury or loss to another person. Tort law allows for a victim to sue an individual for actions which have injured the victim. Tort law allows for compensation to be paid to the victim. The types of tort offenses which generally impact the private security profession will be discussed at this time.

Notes

The use of deadly force should always be a last resort and only when a felony involving force is occurring.

Tort: a civil wrong, an act or omission which causes injury or loss to another person.

Assault and Battery

As discussed earlier a criminal charge of assault and/ or battery can be claimed against a security officer. Additionally, a civil charge or intentional tort claim alleging assault/ battery can also be made against a security officer. A battery occurs when an unauthorized touching or contact occurs. It is not necessary to prove that any real harm resulted but only that the contact was not authorized. Assault requires that at least some threatening gesture occur. In addition, the victim must have thought the gesture would result in harm. It is especially important for a security officer to remember that their actions, tone of voice, gestures and the like may be viewed as threatening. Remember! Most security officers wear uniforms which can add to the fear a person may feel when confronted.

False Imprisonment

False imprisonment involves the unauthorized restraint of a person's freedom. The only elements necessary to create liability for false imprisonment are detention and its unlawfulness.3 A false imprisonment charge may be sustained even if the detention was brief. It is also important to remember that a person does not have to be physically restrained to claim that they were falsely imprisoned. Words, gestures, threats or the perception that they do not have freedom of movement may constitute false imprisonment. Many storeowners and their employee/agents receive some protection from false imprisonment when they detain a person based upon a reasonable belief the person had unpaid merchandise in their possession. In addition, if a shopper consented to the detention a claim of false imprisonment cannot be sustained. Security officers who work in the retail profession should obtain detailed instructions from their company's attorneys as to the exact wording they should use when they attempt to detain a shopper. Some companies have their security personnel stop a person by saying, "Excuse me, I am a security officer for the ABC Company, I believe you have unpaid for merchandise from our store in your possession. Would you please walk with me to the store's security office where we can discuss this in private?"

Notes

Battery: *unauthorized touching or contact.*

Assault: *actual threatening of a person.*

False Imprisonment: *the unauthorized and unlawful restraint of a person preventing their freedom of movement.*

It is advisable whenever possible to recover at least some of the stolen merchandise immediately so that the shoplifter does not have an opportunity to discard the merchandise. Naturally, each situation is different which may require the security officer to change his/her approach to suspected shoplifters.

Emotional Distress

The offense of intentionally inflicting emotional distress can be affirmed in civil court if the behavior by a security officer is judged to be outrageous. The security officer must pay special attention when dealing with children, the elderly, the sick, the handicapped or pregnant women. Society views treatment to those groups differently than from other people. In order to recover for emotional distress, the victim must have suffered severe mental pain. As has been stressed continually in this chapter, security officers must remember that their actions will be reviewed at a later time when emotions are not high. Under these circumstances, someone may judge that the actions of the security officer were severe or outrageous. The actions of a security officer are viewed differently than the actions of a private citizen. A uniformed security officer gives the appearance of authority and many people may mistake them for a police officer. It is critical that a security officer conducts himself or herself in a manner that is judged at all times to be proper and reasonable.

Defamation

Defamation is a tort which takes two forms, libel and slander. Libel is defamation in a written form while slander is defamation other than in writing. Defamation affects a person's reputation. Defamation could be in the form of pictures, speech or any form of communication between people. Publication of the alleged defamatory remark is the most important requirement to prove defamation. The remark must have been heard, read or received by some third person other than the victim. Therefore, defamatory remarks exchanged within earshot of only the two people involved will not constitute defamation.4 Some remarks are considered privileged and may be excluded from being

Notes

Emotional Distress: A type of civil lawsuit brought against a security officer in which the actions of the officer are alleged to have been outrageous and which caused severe mental pain or distress.

Defamation: pictures, speech or any form of communication (oral or written) which unjustly harms a person's reputation.

Libel: defamation in written form.

Slander: defamation in oral or verbal form.

considered in a defamation charge. Truth is always a defense against a charge of defamation. A security officer should always be careful as to what they say about a person who is suspected of wrongdoing. To say, "I caught this thief trying to break into a car", may be grounds for a claim of defamation if the assumed thief was actually the owner of the car who had locked his keys in the vehicle. Pretending to be "Dirty Harry" serves no purpose. Simply do your job and always treat people with respect whether you believe they deserve it or not.

Invasion of Privacy

A security officer may face a charge of invasion of privacy if actions reveal the officer intruded upon the victim's expectation of privacy. An intrusion of privacy could take the form of an unauthorized entry into a person's home or vehicle. Phone tapping may also result in an invasion complaint.

Invasion of Privacy: violation of a person's expectation of privacy.

Negligence

A charge of *negligence* against a security officer and his/her employer may be claimed if the security officer "failed to act". Failure to escort an employee to their vehicle at night may constitute negligence if such escorts were provided in the past or upon request. Negligence could also be claimed if a security officer operated a vehicle in a negligent and reckless manner while on patrol. Another example of negligence would be if a company which hires security officers employed a person who had a history of felony crimes such as rape and robbery. If the person were to commit a similar crime while on duty as a security officer, the security company would be liable for a charge of negligence in the hiring of the ex-felon.

Negligence: absence of due diligence, failure to conduct oneself with due regard to the safety and rights of others, can also be a failure to act when required.

Monetary Remedies — Torts

Generally, civil courts grant monetary awards to victims of torts such as assault, battery, false imprisonment, negligence, defamation, etc... Besides a security officer being held financially liable for damages because of a tort action, the security company which employs the officer may

Compensatory Damages: compensate an injured person for injuries. Money which makes good or replace the financial loss/cost.

be held financially liable. A court may award medical expenses and/or lost profits or wages due to a personal injury. In addition to the previously mentioned compensatory damages, punitive, monetary damages can be granted if the conduct of the person afflicting the injury is considered reckless or outrageous.

References

1. Arthur J. Bilek, John C. Klotter, and R. Keegan Federal, **Legal Aspects of Private Security**, (Anderson Publishing; Cincinnati) p. 96.

2. Ibid.

3. Ibid, p. 159.

4. Ibid, p. 163.

Notes

Punitive Damages: compensate a person and punish the person responsible for the injury/actions.

Summary

Private security is made up of individuals and companies which provide security and related services to other businesses or persons for a fee. Alan Pinkerton is considered to be the father of private security. Private security grew dramatically during World War I because of the threat of espionage and sabotage.

Security officers can possess three different kinds of legal authority, the most common being citizen power.

The U.S. Constitution was enacted in 1787 and established the offices of President, Vice-President, Congress and the Supreme Court. The Bill of Rights was originally made up of 10 amendments to the Constitution which protected citizens from certain actions by the federal government. The 4th Amendment protects citizens from unreasonable searches and seizures. The 5th Amendment protects citizens from self-incrimination. The Miranda warnings developed from the 5th Amendment.

Private security personnel may have the authority to arrest a person based upon their rights as a private citizen, or because of their deputations or commission as a police/peace officer, or because of Shopkeeper laws.

Force may be used in the making of an arrest but only that force which is required. The Supreme Court granted police officers the authority to detain a person when unusual conduct is observed which leads the police officer to believe criminal activity may occur.

Private security officers can be charged in criminal court if they overstep their authority. Usually, a security officer would be charged with assault, battery, homicide or discharging a firearm.

Self defense is a recognized standard for the justifiable use of force but only if a person did not start the conflict. A person can use deadly force if their life or someone else's is in immediate danger. Deadly force can be used to protect

Notes

property only when a forcible entry of a building/dwelling has been made.

Besides criminal charges, civil charges can also be filed against a security officer if their conduct is judged to have been unreasonable and/or negligent. A security officer could be financially liable to another person for this unreasonable behavior.

Notes

Questions

1. What are the three types of authority a security officer may have:

    1. _____
    2. _____
    3. _____

2. Private security derives its' power from:

    a. U.S. Supreme Court
    b. Declaration of Independence
    c. U.S. Constitution

3. What amendment protects citizens from unreasonable searches and seizures?

    a. 1st
    b. 4th
    c. 5th
    d. 10th

4. What amendment protects a person from "self incrimination?"

    a. 1st
    b. 4th
    c. 5th
    d. 10th

5. The amendments to the U.S. Constitution legally restrict only the authority of government officials. True or False?

6. Generally, a security officer would normally need a search warrant to inspect an employee's lunchbox or briefcase? True or False?

7. The Miranda warnings are a result of a U.S. Supreme Court case which based its' findings on the _____ amendment.

    a. 1st
    b. 4th
    c. 5th
    d. 10th

8.   Write the Miranda warnings.

    1. _____

    2. _____

    3. _____

    4. _____

9.   Security officers who have no special authority or power are not required to give the Miranda warnings to suspects?   True or False.

10.   The Miranda warnings have been in effect for over 100 years?   True or False.

11.   What determines the amount of force which may be used when making a felony arrest?

_____

12.   In most situations a security officer does not have the authority to detain suspects. What is an exception that allows for detention?

_____

13.   What is the purpose of private security?

_____

_____

14.   Unless a security officer is commissioned, deputized, or in some other way granted peace officer or police powers, the security officer is not held to the search and seizure restrictions? True or False.

15.   Security officers who possess only citizens powers are the most common in the United States? True or False.

16.   The _____ amendment to the U.S. Constitution prohibits several actions by the government against a citizen.

17.   In most situations a security officer does not have the authority to detain suspects. True or False.

18.   What is meant by "Shopkeepers' Law?"

_____

_____

19. What is assault?

_____

_____

20. What is battery?

_____

_____

21. A _____ is a "failure to act" which causes an injury or loss to another person.

22. _____ _____ is the unauthorized restraint of a person's freedom.

23. A criminal charge of _____ _____ could be proven against a security officer if their actions are judged to be outrageous.

24. There are two types of defamation. _____ is defamation which is written. Defamation which is other than written is _____.

25. A charge of _____ could be made against a security officer for failing to act.

IMPORTANT SECTIONS OF THE U.S. CONSTITUTION

PREAMBLE: We the people of the United States in order to form a more perfect Union, establish Justice, insure domestic Tranquility, provide for the common defence, promote the general Welfare, and secure the Blessings of Liberty to ourselves and our Posterity, do ordain and establish this Constitution for the United States of America.

Article I: Section One establishes the Congress of the United States, which shall consist of a Senate and House of Representatives.

Article II: establishes the office of President

Article III: Section One establishes the Supreme Court

Article IV: grants every state the right to govern and protects each of them against invasion.

Amendments

Amendment I: establishes Freedom of religion, speech and freedom of the press.

Amendment II: right of citizens to bear arms.

Amendment III: in peacetime, no soldier can be quartered in anyone's home without permission.

Amendment IV: the right of people to be secure in their persons, houses, papers, and effects, against unreasonable searches and seizures, shall not be violated, and no warrants shall be issued except for probable cause, supported by oath, or affirmation, which describes the particular place to be searched, and the persons or things to be seized.

Amendment V: no person shall be held to answer for a capital crime unless indicted by a Grand Jury, except in cases involving the military; no person shall be charged with the same offense twice; no person will be forced to testify against him or herself; no person will be deprived of life, liberty, or property, without due process of law; nor shall private property be taken for public use without just compensation.

Amendment VI: a person accused of a crime has the right to a speedy and public trial, by an impartial jury; the accused has the right to question his accusers, and has the right to an attorney.

Amendment VII: right of an accused to have a jury trial.

Amendment VIII: prevents excessive bail, excessive fines and cruel and unusual punishment.

Amendment IX: all rights in the Constitution shall be retained by all people.

Amendment X: all other rights and powers not prohibited by the Constitution are reserved to the States or to the people.

Amendment XIV: States are prohibited from enacting any law which deprives any person life, liberty, or property, without due process of law; nor can any State deny equal protection of the law.

PRACTICAL EXERCISES & QUESTIONS FOR THE SECURITY OFFICER

LEGAL ASPECTS

1. Identify the powers and legal authority you possess on your current job.

2. What state statutes apply to your role as a security officer?

3. Can you become commissioned in your city, county, or state? If so, how would you go about obtaining a commission?

4. What is the state statute for shoplifting?

5. Is there a city ordinance which regulates shoplifting?

6. Are you considered a government official? Do you work for a bank or federal agency?

7. Is a package inspection policy in place at your place of work?

8. Are you allowed to inspect packages which are entering or leaving the facility?

9. What occurs and what are your instructions if a person refuses to show you what they are carrying into or out of the facility?

10. If you don't have a package inspection policy and are considering one, you should answer the following questions:

     a. Are there incidents of theft at your facility? How much? When? Are records kept of reported thefts?

     b. Are employees part of a union?

c. How many security officers would be needed to conduct package inspections?

d. Is there a property removal system?

e. Consider posting a notice from your Labor Relations department which explains to employees the reasons for an inspection policy, when it will begin, and how employees are to conduct themselves.

f. What will a security officer do if an employee refuses to comply with the inspections? Will the employee be disciplined? Will witnesses be needed if its just the word of a security officer against an employee?

g. What will a security officer do if suspected stolen property is uncovered during an inspection?

h. Will briefcases be inspected? Vehicles? Purses? Duffle bags?

i. Will salary employees also have their packages inspected?

11. What is a security officer to do at this facility if they suspect an employee of theft?

12. Are the police ever to be called about a suspected theft? Who has the authority to call them?

13. What is considered a felony in this state?

14. What is the company's policy on detaining or even arresting a person?

15. Who must be notifed to sign a police complaint against an employee or trespasser?

16. Is a security officer permitted to carry a firearm at this facility? A nightstick? Handcuffs? Mace?

17. What is the state law and company policy on authority? When if ever, is a security officer permitted to use force?

18. What is a security officer permitted to do if struck or hit by a person?

BASIS OF AUTHORITY

United State Constitution
September 17, 1787

| Office of the President and the Vice President | U.S. Congress: Senate and the House of Represent- atives | Bill of Rights | U.S. Supreme Court |

Freedom of speech and religion

Right to bear arms

Soldiers cannot be housed in a citizen's home in peacetime

Protection against unreasonable search and seizure

Rights of the accused-
    Protection from self-incriminatior

Right to a speedy trial; to question witnesses

Right to a trial by jury

Protection against excessive bail and punishment

Rights retained by the citizens

Rights retained by the states under constitution

State Constitution

| Statutory Laws passed by state legislature | Laws created by court decisions |

THE EFFECTIVE SECURITY OFFICERS TRAINING MANUAL

Chapter VIII

Testifying in Court

Testifying in Court

COURT TESTIMONY/DEPOSITIONS/ADMINIS-TRATIVE HEARINGS

INTRODUCTION

One of the most important aspects of the security officer's responsibilities is his ability to communicate effectively in a legal or administrative setting. The presentation of all of the material gathered in an investigation and reported in the documentation is all important, but only when it is presented effectively in the setting of an administrative hearing, deposition, or court testimony is its true worth known.

Some of the best street policemen and the most well trained private security officers fail in their mission, not because they did a poor job investigating or because they didn't gather the information properly. They fail, because they lack the ability to present it properly in a deposition, hearing or in court testimony.

The ability to make a good presentation in court, in deposition or in an administrative hearing is no different than writing a good report, or communicating with another individual verbally.

When providing information for an administrative hearing, deposition or court hearing, the single most important and constant element that is always required is the TRUTH. Nothing else is acceptable when attempting to accurately depict an event. To provide anything else, is to diminish the quality of your testimony as well as your credibility. Once lost, neither can be recovered.

In preparing to testify, it is important to distinguish what you know from what you think. For example:

What you know is what you have first hand knowledge of. What you think is your opinion, based on information you have received. If you witness an accident, where you see an employee fall down, your observation is "What you know".

Notes

Reading For A Purpose:
Look for these key words:
- Testify
- Subpoena
- Perjury
- Deposition
- Expert Witness
- Administrative Hearing
- Impeach

Look for answers to these questions:
1. Is a security officer permitted to review his/her notes before testifying?
2. What is the difference between testifying in court and giving a deposition?
3. How does a security officer prepare for testifying?

Testify: To give statements in court which serves as evidence.

Security personnel must always report information factually and truthfully, no matter the outcome!

If you arrive on the scene of such an accident after the fact, and the victim and others report to you what happened, and from that information you make a conclusion about the accident, then that is what you think. This is now your opinion.

Unless you have been called as an EXPERT WIT-NESS, you are not being called to court to present your opinion, you are being called to present the information that you have gathered, or, that which you have first hand knowledge of.

PREPARATION

Preparation for testimony in any setting, whether it be an administrative hearing, deposition, or trial, begins at the moment you are assigned to take a report or investigate an incident. Everything you do from that point forward should be with the thought that you will someday be testifying to it in a formal setting. With that in mind, it is imperative that you take the necessary steps to do a thorough investigation, concise report, and careful follow-up.

REVIEWING EVIDENCE, REPORTS, AND NOTES

Before you appear for testimony, study the material that you have collected. Whether it is an incident report, memorandum, or just the material in your officers notebook, make sure you are familiar with it, and what it means in the context of the incident at hand. Remember, you can only testify as to what you know, or what you have learned from your investigation or involvement. If you have taken pictures of an incident, make sure that they are properly labeled and stored so that you can explain each of them, why you took them and what they depict.

Let's assume for a moment that you are being called to testify in the case of a break-in, where an employee has been accused of the crime. In the course of your investigation, you took a picture of a window that had the glass broken out of it. It may have little significance to the uninformed, until

Notes

Take down information from witnesses exactly as it is given to you.

Expert Witnesses: Persons who are qualified to give testimony as to their opinion; expert testimony can be based on personal knowledge or observations or upon opinion expressed in response to a hypothetical question.

It is essential that any notes, reports, statements or photographs are organized, filed and properly stored for later use.

you explain that it shows that the glass is broken out, rather than broken in, which is consistent with the evidence that this was an inside job.

ADMINISTRATIVE HEARING

If you are preparing to give testimony in an administrative hearing, you will want to review your notes and any reports that you have made on the incident in question. Just as you have written your report in a chronological fashion, so to, you will want to present your testimony in an organized and chronological fashion.

In an administrative hearing, you often have the opportunity of presenting the whole story of what occurred as you know it. In a court or deposition setting, you may only be able to respond to specific questions that are asked. In any case, it is important to be clear and concise in your delivery. DO NOT abuse the privilege when someone asks you to present information on a specific subject. Remember, what you have to say is important, but it is only important if you present it properly.

NEVER offer your opinion as part of your testimony, unless you are testifying as an expert, which is a different situation entirely.

DEPOSITION

A deposition is your recorded testimony under oath, usually conducted in the privacy of an attorney's office or conference room. Typically, those present include; one or more attorneys representing either side of an issue about which you will be deposed, a court reporter, and you the witness. Their is no judge present to rule on objections or to guide procedure.

In preparation, you will want to spend time reviewing your notes and reports of the incident in question. Likely, you will spend time in advance of the deposition reviewing your material and testimony, with an attorney who represents the interests of the side for whom your testimony will be favor-

Notes

Administrative Hearing: *Formal review of an incident or event in which witnesses are heard; normally conducted within businesses, organizations, or government agencies.*

Chronological: Listing of events in the order of their occurrence.
An administrative hearing would include grievance or arbitration hearings involving employees represented by a union.

Deposition: Legal proceeding where testimony is recorded under oath.

able. The attorney will review likely questions that you will be asked. You should also be prepared for questions that are unexpected or not relevant to the issue at hand. Just as in court, another attorney present may object to the question. You should stop testifying immediately. Wait until the attorneys have discussed the objection, and then proceed with your testimony only after you have been instructed to do so.

For an attorney who represents interests opposite of what you will testify to, a deposition may be nothing more than an opportunity to create a written record of what you say, in order to later impeach you in court. This is not something that you need worry about. Your job is to convey the truth.

The opposing attorney may ask questions of you that call for incomplete answers or answers that are out of context. It may be necessary for you to ask the attorney to repeat the question in a way that you understand, or that will allow you to explain some piece of information in greater detail. You cannot control any of this, and you should not be disturbed by this process. The opposing attorney is looking for possible lies or inconsistencies in your testimony. If you are well prepared, and listen carefully to the questions, you can offer concise and truthful answers, and if necessary, be able to explain any questions later in court.

COURTROOM TESTIMONY

In preparation for your testimony in court you will want to review your notes, reports, and all other relevant materials. The attorney who has called or subpoenaed you to testify in court will likely review his questions with you in advance of the court hearing or trial. This will give you an opportunity to know what will be asked of you in advance, and it will give the attorney the opportunity to see how you will answer. The attorney may wish to coach you to the extent that with some answers, he may simply wish you to answer yes or no, and on others, he may ask you to provide some detail. This is an acceptable practice, and is designed to help you to be a better witness.

Notes

Impeach: Create doubt in the mind of the listener.

Subpoenaed: Act of summoning or requiring a person to appear in court and possibly testify.

It is only the unscrupulous attorney that would ask you to perjure yourself. Remember, you know what the truth is. If someone asks you to present information in your testimony that is contradictory to the truth, tell them no. Perjury is a crime, and you are the one who could be punished, not the attorney. Fortunately, the vast majority of attorneys are fair and honorable, and would not make such a request.

Get to know the turf. It is often helpful to visit the courtroom in advance of the trial. See where the witness stand is, the jury box, the judge's bench, and where the prosecutors or plaintiff's attorney and defendant's attorney are situated.

If you have never testified before, it is a good idea to sit in on a trial as a spectator. This gives you the opportunity to see how witnesses perform. Identify the things that they do well and those which they do not do well. Remember, that other than the judge and attorneys, who are at home, the court room it is a foreign environment to most people. The more familiar you can become with it, the less foreign it will be when you are sitting in the witness stand. A call to your municipal clerk of courts will tell on what days trials are scheduled.

Remember, when you are sitting in on a trial, that it is usually a very tedious process. It is not at all like the television image of Perry Mason asking the $64,000 question, and the witness blurting out a confession. In fact, most cases never even get to trial. Each however must be prepared as though it will.

TESTIMONY TIME

When it is time to testify, their are several things that you can do to help your image as a witness.

If you are required to wear a uniform while on duty, then you will likely wear one when you go to court. Make sure that it is clean and pressed, all badges, brass, insignias and other parts of the uniform are all neat, shined and in good

Notes

Perjury: Considered one of the most serious offenses; statements which are made by a person which are accepted as factual and truthful, but are actually false, and are provided in an effort to mislead the court, jury, or person who is conducting the proceeding.

Notes

repair. Shoes should be shined, hair and beard neatly groomed. If you are not on duty, or do not wear a uniform, then a dark suit with a white shirt and matching tie. Women should consider a dark business suit or dress, clean and pressed blouse, shoes shined, and if worn, jewelry and makeup that is not distracting. Remember, that while it is important to look clean and well groomed, you never want your listener(s) to be distracted from what you are saying by what you are wearing. Always sit up straight, but in a comfortable and relaxed manner. You want to convey that what you have to say is as important to you as it is to the people to whom you are speaking.

When testifying in an administrative hearing or deposition, answer the questions directly. Look at the questioner, but do not stare into his eyes. Sometimes direct eye contact, especially during testimony, can be intimidating. To look away can convey to the listener a sense that you are being distant, disinterested or even deceptive. A comfortable posture is to look at the questioner's forehead, mouth, or some other spot on the face. This conveys a sense of interest without being intimidating or confrontational. Your goal is to be informative and cooperative.

When testifying in court, look at the questioner while the question is being asked. When it is time to respond, turn to the jury. A good posture is to make eye contact with each of the jurors, moving from one to the other. When you have completed your answer, turn back to the attorney who is asking the questions in preparation for the next question. A jury is the group for whom your testimony is intended. They are the ones who will decide on the value of your credibility and weigh it against that of other witnesses and evidence.

KNOW THE FACTS

- Read everything you have written or done with regard to the incident, crime, etc.

- Summarize information so that you understand it completely and can explain it clearly and concisely.

Notes

- Know what will be asked of you.

- Rehearse with prosecutor or attorney

- Anticipate that difficult or trick questions may be asked and prepare for them.

A SPECIAL NOTE ON DEPOSITIONS

A deposition is your testimony under oath, a written statement admissible in court. Unlike a trial or hearing, where a jury and others can see your facial expressions, annunciation of key words, and the way you respond, a deposition is a written statement typically taken in a private setting, where one attorney is able to ask you questions, and a court reporter is present to record the questions and your answers.

An attorney may be present to object to inappropriate questions, but you may still be required to answer, and a judge will rule on the objection at a later time. Often times, an attorney will attempt to use what you testified to in a deposition, to contradict what you testify to later in court. It is most important to answer carefully and concisely in a deposition.

TESTIFYING

1. Don't bring anything to court with you that you have not discussed with the attorney, and that you do not want the other side to have.

2. Listen closely to the question. Pause before giving your answer so that you can formulate a well thought out response. Remember, you probably know the answer, and it is a matter of presenting it for the court.

3. Speak clearly, and loud enough to be heard. What you have to say is important, so make sure you can be heard. Speak slowly and deliberately.

4. Speak directly to the jury, if there is a jury. To the judge, if no jury. Even though an attorney is asking you questions, it is the jury or judge that will be weighing your testimony.

5. Never get angry. Part of the game playing that goes on in court is an attempt to discredit witnesses by confusing them.

6. Answer the questions as they are asked. Do not elaborate beyond yes or no, unless you have discussed it with the attorney in advance. If the answer to a particular question is yes, then answer yes. If the question requires more of an answer, then you should answer the question concisely with only that information that specifically answers the question. If the questioner wants more information, it is his/her responsibility to ask another question. **Never volunteer information.**

7. ALWAYS ALWAYS ALWAYS tell the truth. It is better to say I don't know or I don't remember, than to make a guess.

8. Attorneys will sometimes ask confusing questions that ramble on and may even be several questions combined into one. When this happens, it is acceptable to respond by either asking the attorney to repeat the question, or to point out that they have actually asked more then one question. You may then proceed to answer the questions one at a time.

9. Don't be anxious. An anxious person is often willing to be eager to please, or can be easily drawn into an argument. The best way to avoid anxiety is to be well prepared.

UNDERSTANDING THE ORGANIZATION OF A TRIAL

The trial begins with opening arguments from both the plaintiff's or prosecuting attorney, and the defendant's attorney. In any trial, the plaintiff or (in a criminal matter) prosecution, presents its side first. The defense then presents its side. You will testify during the presentation by the side that called you as a witness. After both sides have presented their case, both are then permitted to present closing arguments. If this is a jury trial, then the judge will issue instruc-

Notes

Example of asking too many questions: A defense attorney asked a witness if the witness had observed the defendant injure the plaintiff in a bar-room fight. During the fight, the plaintiff's right ear was seriously injured, allegedly by the defendant. When questioned, the witness testified that he did not see the defendant bite the right ear of the plaintiff. The defense attorney should have stopped asking questions, but he continued. "Well, Mr. Witness, if you did not see the defendant bite the ear of the plaintiff, what did you see?" The witness replied, "I saw the defendant spit the ear out of his mouth!" (Apologies to Giles T. Black)

tions before allowing the jury to retire to deliberate. If there is no jury, then the judge himself will retire to deliberate.

Some of the terms and procedures you are likely to hear before and during your testimony are defined below.

Arraignment-Where defendant appears after the Indictment by the Grand Jury. Appearance is before a judge of the Common Pleas or Superior Court for the purpose of making a plea of guilty or innocent. This is also where the indictment is read to the defendant.

Complaint-Sets forth the facts and describes the offense for which the person was arrested.

Cross-examination-This is the challenge to your testimony by the opposing side. While it their opportunity to discredit you, it provides you with an additional opportunity to explain what happened to the jury. If you have prepared well, then you can take best advantage of this "opportunity".

Deposition-An oral testimony taken by the opposing attorney with a court recorder present to record all the proceedings.

Defendant-The person against whom a civil or criminal action is brought.

Direct-examination-The direct-examination is the telling of a story from your point of view. This is the part of your testimony that you can control, because you can prepare for it.

Grand Jury-An exparte hearing where the state presents its evidence against the accused. They then have the option of returning a true bill for indictment or a no bill.

Investigation-Your examination of the incident in question.

Jury-Those persons selected to hear testimony and render a verdict in the matter presented to them.

Objection-Brought by one side or the other with regard to the

Notes

question being asked of the witness, or, the witness's answer. When you hear an attorney object, stop talking immediately, and wait for the judge to rule on the objection. The judge will either overrule the objection, in which case you will be asked to continue with your answer, or sustain the objection, which would then require the questioning attorney to ask a different question.

Plaintiff-The party who brings suit or court action against another.

Preliminary Hearing-Used to determine whether a crime has been committed and whether there is probable cause to believe that the accused is responsible for the crime.

Prosecutor-In a criminal case, the one who brings the accusation against the suspected guilty party to court.

Trial-Where the case against the accused is held, either in a municipal, common pleas or federal court.

Witness-A person who provides sworn testimony in the case.

TECHNIQUE

It is important for you to be comfortable. Speak in a manner that is comfortable to you.

Speak to the jury in a loud and clear voice. Do not make gestures or wear clothes that distract from what you are saying. If an attorney acts hostile, and attempts to intimidate or rattle you, remember that he is a trained actor. This is his stage, and you are merely a prop.

One way to communicate that which is important, is to not buy in to the negative comments or demeanor. If for example, an attorney on cross-examination attempts to rattle you by making negative comments, do not focus on the comments, but on the question. You do not have to respond to comments, only to questions.

Make eye contact with the jury. People equate eye contact with sincerity. They assume that someone who will not look them in the eye has something to hide.

In a deposition, make eye contact with the questioner, but do not stare or glare. A good technique is to focus on the questioner's mouth.

In an administrative hearing, make eye contact with the questioner. Again, as some questions may be heated, it is a good practice to focus on the mouth, rather than the eyes.

References: <u>Legal Aspects of Private Security</u>, Arthur J. Bilek, John C. Klotter, R. Keegan Federal , (Cincinnati: Anderson Publishing Co.), 1981.

Notes

SUMMARY

Testimony about any incident is and should be the most satisfying part of any police or security investigation. It is the opportunity to carry what you have learned in your investigation and put down in your report to a proper conclusion in the due process. It is the opportunity to present what you have gathered to a higher authority for disposition. Unfortunately, it is the area where some good security and police investigators often fall short.

Getting ready is the single most important element. Once you begin testifying, you have no place to hide. You don't have a chance to change what you have done. If you have made mistakes, don't be afraid to admit to them if you are asked.

Don't be one who falls short. Be prepared from the beginning. Always assume that your involvement in any incident will eventually result in your testimony, either in a hearing, deposition or court.

Be prepared and you will be satisfied with your presentation!

Notes

QUESTIONS

1. What is the single most important aspect of testifying in an administrative, deposition or court room procedure?

_____

2. Court testimony is nothing more than?

_____

3. What is the difference between an administrative hearing and a court hearing?

_____

4. What is unique about the Deposition Process?

_____

5. Why is appearance important?

_____

6. When does preparation for testimony begin?

_____

7. What is the role of the defendant in a trial?

_____

8. Explain direct-examination.

_____

9. Explain cross-examination.

_____

10. Who is the Plaintiff in a civil court proceeding?

_____

THE EFFECTIVE SECURITY OFFICERS TRAINING MANUAL

Chapter IX

Internal Threat

Internal Threats to an Organization

Many would argue security officers can do little to prevent or deter threats to an organization by its employees. However, an observant and properly trained security officer can assist in uncovering intentional theft.

A study by the U.S. Chamber of Commerce estimates that 30% of all business failures are caused by employee dishonesty. Most security professionals would agree that losses from employee dishonesty (theft) are far greater than non-employee loss. Employees who are trusted completely are in excellent positions to steal from a company without being caught. Companies that develop a policy which clearly states that dishonesty will not be tolerated have taken the first step in coping with the increasing problem of employee theft. The U.S. Chamber of Commerce estimates that $40 billion is stolen each year from American businesses.

Many companies are uncomfortable in dealing with and addressing this serious problem for several reasons:

1. Executives don't believe the problem exists.
2. Executives are unsure what to do about the problem if they believe it exists.
3. Executives simply believe that there is nothing that can be done (cost effectively) to solve the problem, so they consider theft as a cost of doing business.
4. Executives believe that more serious problems occur when a theft investigation is conducted such as problems with the union, employee morale, fear of a "witch hunt", too many people may lose their jobs and the "business just can't afford that."
5. Executives are concerned that the investigation could involve "key" people. People who live in glass houses shouldn't throw stones!

Notes

Reading For A Purpose
Look for these key words:
- inventory
- need/desire
- rationalization
- opportunity
- embezzlement

Look for the answers to these Questions:
1. What are the indications of theft?
2. What are symptoms of dishonest employees?
3. In what ways can a company prevent or deter internal theft?

Employees steal the greatest amount of cash, material and property from American businesses.

$40 billion is $40,000,000,000.

Many managers are ignorant and naive about internal theft.

People unfamiliar with loss prevention strategies are not certain what to do about employee theft.

Why spend more on security than the value of the property?

Often investigations last several weeks and create a distraction to the day-to-day operation of the business.

High level managers may be involved in improper behavior.

THEFT INDICATORS

Security professionals generally agree that indications of theft almost always come about in one or more of the following three ways:

1. Inventory shortages
2. Evidence or other indications discovered during facility inspections. (i.e. holes in fencing)
3. Information received (anonymous letters, calls)

Inventory Shortages are normally revealed at the end of the year when an annual inventory is taken. Some companies conduct inventories on a more frequent basis. In fact, some companies maintain a perpetual inventory. This means that on any day, information should be available which would inform a person that the inventory or amount of product not yet sold is the same as what the paperwork indicates. Provided the inventory is the same as the paperwork, shortages would not be revealed. If there is less inventory than what the paperwork reports then a shortage exists. This would be called a negative variance for the inventory. If there is more inventory than what the paperwork shows a positive variance exists. Just because an inventory shortage exists on paper, does not mean that there is in fact a shortage. It also does not mean theft is occurring. Normally, financial auditors will attempt to determine the reason why the paperwork does not match the inventory. Sometimes, explanations are found which indicate that theft does not exist. However, explanations are not always right. Therefore, many times, investigations are begun by a security manager or investigator. Many times, a security officer will not even know the results of the inventory.

Evidence or other indications discovered during facility inspections may imply theft is occurring. An observant security officer may notice evidence of theft during routine patrols. A security officer may see that the fence has been cut or that outbound truck shipments of goods are occurring at unusual times. A security officer who changes the pattern of his/her foot patrols may stumble into a theft because they surprised the thieves. A security officer can be of great help

Notes

A perpetual inventory allows a company to know at all times if a shortage exists within it's in-process or finished product.

Negative variance: indicates that less inventory actually exists than what inventory records report.

Positive variance: more inventory actually exists than paperwork reports.

Negative variance with regard to an inventory may be the result of theft, poor management controls, or miscounts of the actual inventory.

By knowing what usual behavior and patterns are, the observant security officer will recognize that which is unusual. Unusual behavior or patterns should be reported to a supervisor at once.

to the detection and prevention of theft by learning their job completely. This includes knowing exactly what he/she is to do regarding the use of all logs such as:

- Incoming/Outgoing Vehicle reports.
- Visitor & Outside Contractors reports.
- Property passes.
- Incident reports.

Another important way to uncover evidence which may indicate theft is occurring is to conduct package/lunchbox inspections as employees and visitors exit the facility. In the Legal Aspects module of this manual you learned what legal requirements (if any) must first be considered before conducting inspections. However, if you are expected to conduct package inspections, they should be conducted in a thorough manner. Large thefts have been uncovered because a security officer noticed an employee or visitor trying to carry property out of a building without proper authorization. Package inspections are only effective if they are conducted on a regular basis and only if a clear policy exists which explains to all employees and visitors the reasons for the inspections, how they will be conducted and penalties for persons who violate the policy. Violations of the policy include attempted theft and refusal to submit a package to inspection by a security officer. If a clear policy does not exist, package inspections are virtually useless.

The third indication that theft may be occurring is information is received of possible thefts. Sometimes, a security officer may receive information from an employee that theft is occurring. The job of a security officer is to report the information to his/her superiors. A security officer is not to try to verify for him/herself if the information is true or not. A security officer can gain respect and esteem from superiors by reporting this information in a timely fashion without opinion or conjecture on the part of the officer. As Sgt. Joe Friday used to say in Dragnet, "Just the facts, ma'am." Sometimes the information is accurate, sometimes it is not. It is not the job of a security officer to determine this. Report the facts and give an opinion only when asked.

Notes

Package inspections aid in theft deterrence and signify a message to all employees and visitors that theft is taken seriously.

Very often, anonymous letters or phone calls are received by security personnel or members of management. About 50% of the time the anonymous information proves to be factual. People report information anonymously for different reasons. Among them are revenge and a desire to see dishonest employees apprehended.

SYMPTOMS OF DISHONEST EMPLOYEES

There can be many indicators that an employee is stealing from their employer. Some of these indicators or symptoms may be evident to a security officer. Remember! These are just indications a person may be stealing. Unless you know for certain that an employee is engaged in theft, do not assume that they are stealing.

Employee Appears to Live Beyond their Means

This means that it "appears" a person has a lifestyle which may indicate they are receiving money from another source, separate from their job. A person who drives an expensive car, takes luxurious vacations or who just spends money recklessly MAY be involved in theft. Or maybe the person earns a lot more money than you think. Or maybe their spouse earns a lot of money. Or maybe their family is wealthy. Or maybe they inherited money or won the state lottery. Whatever the reason, a security officer would be very wise not to guess. If you observe lifestyle patterns which appear strange, your observations should be reported discretely to your supervisor. Your observations and/or opinions should not be discussed with anyone else. A person could be charged with ruining a person's reputation by careless comments. Be observant though! You may see a behavior that indicates a serious problem exists.

Dislike for Policies & Procedures

Some persons who steal never like to follow policies and procedures. These people always want to do things their way. Once again, this is only an indication of possible theft. Never assume a person who dislikes following procedures is a possible thief.

Bitterness toward the Organization

Persons who decide to steal sometimes tell themselves that they deserve more from the company. Perhaps, they feel they should have been promoted or received more money for their work. Maybe they're jealous that someone else has a better job. Regardless of the reason, many employees who steal are bitter at the company for one reason or another. Stealing is their way of "setting things straight."

Notes

Professional security officers never speculate or relay information (gossip) about a person that they do not know for certain is truthful.

Be very careful with this symptom. Many people have legitimate other sources of income that few people are aware of.

Usually if an employee is truly living beyond his/her means, clear evidence is often available during an investigation to substantiate the facts. Once again, simply report your suspicions to your superior.

Example: employees who remove property without a proper property pass.

Many honest employees who would never steal may be bitter toward their employer. Resentment of one's employer just makes it easier to rationalize why a person steals.

Gambling Habit

In almost every organization some limited form of gambling is always present. Gambling may take the form of football pools or be more serious such as "numbers" games or illegal horse race betting. Some people play cards every week for enjoyment and win or lose very little. However, much like alcohol addiction, some people become "hooked" on gambling. When this occurs, a person will eventually suffer losses. They may not be able to "cover their loss" so they begin to steal from their place of employment. Again, this is not to say that people who gamble are thieves. This does mean that people who gamble and lose a lot are more likely to steal than persons who do not gamble and lose money. If you ever learn of or receive information that a person has a serious gambling habit, discretely report this information to your supervisor.

Alcohol/Drug Abuse

Persons who have an alcohol or drug addiction may steal from an organization because of their habit. As in the previous examples, if you receive information, report it to your supervisor.

ELEMENTS OF THEFT

In almost every employee theft situation the following elements are evident with the person:
- Need or Desire
- Rationalization
- Opportunity

Need or Desire

This refers to the fact that people steal for a reason. People steal because they have a problem (such as alcohol/drug dependency or gambling habit) that they do not share with anyone else. Maybe they have a psychological need to steal. Perhaps they are a kleptomaniac or suffer from some other from of mental illness. Finally, they may just have a blatant criminal tendency or habit whereby they steal for no apparent reason other than for personal gain.

Notes

Employees with severe gambling habits are likely to steal when given an opportunity. These persons are usually borrowing money from other employees. In large factories, it is not uncommon for "loansharking" to exist. This is when a person loans another person money at a very high interest rate.

Besides the fact that people with an abuse problem need money, their lives are often out of control.

A person must __want__ to steal.

Kleptomaniac: a person with a psychological need to steal.

Rationalization

The human mind can rationalize or explain the reason for any type of behavior. Theft is not different. People who steal tell themselves they're good persons. They rationalize their stealing in several ways:

- "I only took what was being thrown out."
- "I was only borrowing it."
- "It's O.K. I'm underpaid."
- "Management gets their bonus. This is mine."
- "It's all right. I see the boss do it."

Naturally, none of these rationalizations or excuses, make it all right to steal. People make up these excuses because they don't like to think of themselves as bad or evil people. They tell themselves they are not thieves because the reasons for their actions are right. These people are not facing the facts. Theft is theft. No amount of rationalization will make the thefts O.K.

Opportunity

Opportunity is the final element of theft to be reviewed. The opportunity for theft is an element that an observant security officer can help in reducing. You have probably heard someone called an "opportunist."

This person takes advantage of an opportunity. Perhaps this person is a shrewd consumer and only buys things when they are on sale or after they have been on display for a long time. A thief who is "opportunistic," takes advantage of the situation. A thief who steals a car that had the keys left in the ignition may be called opportunistic. An employee thief who carries a computer out an unlocked door after business hours may also be called opportunistic. As a security officer, you will see conditions that if not corrected can make it very easy for a theft to occur unnoticed. Learn your job well! Learn what is routine and what is not. Learn what doors and offices are to be locked. When you find them unlocked during the time they should be locked, examine the situation more closely. If you can't find someone in authority who can explain the reason the doors/offices are unlocked, lock them! Write down things or people who seem to be out of place. People will usually steal only when they believe they can do so without being observed. An alert and effective

Notes

Rationalization: justification of one's actions.

Since a person never likes to consider that they are evil or "bad", or that their actions are wrong, the human mind can develop hundreds of reasons for unacceptable behavior to be explained. Listen to children! They rationalize their improper behavior constantly.

Opportunist: an individual who takes advantage of a situation, usually with little regard for moral principles.

A thief will take advantage of an opportunity to steal. As security officers, we must attempt to minimize opportunity. Consideration must always be given that a business must operate efficiently. Often, the person in charge of the operation will not reduce the opportunity for theft because the operation is impacted. Security professionals are always searching for the proper balance between security and convenience.

security officer may prevent theft simply because they are diligent. This means they follow their procedures consistently at all times. They enforce the rules and regulations with everyone they come into contact. This type of security officer is on top of their job. This security officer earns their pay!

TYPES OF INTERNAL THEFT

While a security officer may be limited in discovering internal theft, it is valuable to know the types of theft.

Money & Financial Items

Areas which are prone to theft include cash offices, accounts receivables, petty cash and cash disbursement departments. A security officer should be familiar with the physical location of each of these areas. If an officer is expected to routinely patrol through these areas they need to know which offices and cabinets are to be locked. Whenever found to be open, the areas should be locked and a report submitted. Items such as cash, airline tickets and payroll checks could be stolen. Thorough patrols and effective package inspections are two areas where the security officer can aid in loss prevention of financial items.

Merchandise or Material

A security officer may discover merchandise or material thefts during routine patrols. Officers who work in wholesale and retail establishments which sell goods to the public are more likely to better trained to spot possible theft since goods are normally stacked on shelves. Goods which are prone to theft include:

- computers and related accessories
- video cassette recorders
- automotive parts and accessories

The list can go on and on. In brief, anything that is popular and which is purchased by many people is likely to be stolen.

Material thefts may include anything that is used in the manufacturing of a product. Metals such as copper, aluminum, silver, gold, titanium, etc. are prone to theft. Tools of all types along with maintenance supplies (gloves, light bulbs, extension cords, etc. are also likely to be stolen.

Notes

If an area which contains cash is found unsecure, lock it up and immediately report the same to your supervisor.

Know in advance what actions you are to take if you find merchandise has been left in an area for the thief to return. Many organizations will want the merchandise to remain in the area where it was found and to have security conduct a surveillance, in the hope of apprehending the thief. Other companies may want the material placed in safekeeping by the security officer.

To deter and prevent material and merchandise thefts, organizations implement internal controls which are often directed from the finance or accounting department. Even with controls, theft occurs and is often covered-up by inflating the actual quantity of a product during inventory. In addition, damaged items are often stolen and are either repaired and sold as new. As stated often in this manual, a security officer can greatly assist his/her organization by being alert. A security officer should check trash and scrap bins on regular basis. Thieves will often hide their goods in trash or scrap bins with intentions of returning later to recover the items.

Embezzlement

Embezzlement is a criminal offense. It occurs when an employee who has been given authority to use company property as a part of their job decides to take control of the property and use it for their own benefit. Usually money is thought of when the term embezzlement is used. A payroll clerk who issues payroll checks but then begins to steal checks would be guilty of embezzlement. Many other internal theft incidents may be considered embezzlement. In almost every instance of embezzlement there is nothing a security officer can do to prevent or detect the theft.

Theft of Time

The theft of time by employees is a serious problem which affects American business. Employees who report off from work for sickness but who are not ill is an example of time theft. However, it is not a security officer's responsibility to investigate. A security officer's responsibility in reporting theft of time occurs when an employee deliberately by-passes control procedures such as signing in/out of the facility. If a security officer is aware of an incident of this type it should be reported to the security supervisor. An employee may either refuse to follow recognized time reporting procedures or falsely input their time. Provided the security officer reports the incidents to their supervisor there is nothing more to do.

Notes

Embezzlement: criminal offense - converting or illegally using the property of another, thereby violating a trust.

Employees will often punch in timecards of their friends and co-workers. When this is observed by a security officer, he/she needs to report this information to a supervisor.

Theft of Information (Industrial Espionage)

Theft of information is a major problem especially for companies in highly technical industries. As one company develops a new product a competitor may be trying to steal it. As discussed in the section on theft of money, a security officer cannot do much to prevent information theft. The officer can be certain that doors and office areas are locked during required hours. The officer can be certain to challenge persons in highly sensitive areas during non-business hours. The officer can be certain to obtain proper identification from all employees and visitors entering the facility. Finally, the officer can be certain to make appropriate package inspections of all articles that leave the facility. This assumes the organization has a package inspection policy and the officer has been properly trained to enforce the policy.

Internal theft can also be committed by computer fraud or within the purchasing department. Security officers will not normally be involved with computer security. Theft problems in purchasing could occur as a result of supplier companies receiving contracts because they are bribing or supplying "kickbacks" to purchasing employees. A "kickback" is when a supplier gives money or "kicks - back" money or gifts to the person who awards the contract. Kickbacks are illegal but still occur. Security officers can offer no real assistance in preventing this form of internal theft other than reporting any suspicious activity or information.

THEFT DETERRENT STRATEGIES

Hopefully, the organization where you work as a security officer has a strict policy regarding employee theft. In addition, a policy should exist that tells employees how to conduct business with suppliers. Many companies have a Code of Business Conduct. The Code addresses proper and improper behavior. It also explains under what conditions, if any, an employee can accept gifts or entertainment from a supplier. Often, suppliers try to influence purchasing department employees by giving them expensive gifts, offering free use of vacation homes and a number of other illegal inducements.

Notes

Trash is an excellent source of information for a competitor. The U.S. Supreme Court has ruled that, once trash has been abandoned or given away, the original owner cannot claim the information was important, sensitive or proprietary. If a security officer finds sensitive information in the trash, this should be reported immediately to his/her supervisor.

Kickback: when a supplier gives money or rewards for special considerations.

Theft Deterrent Programs: measures available to screen applicants for employment. E.g. Honesty tests.

Code of Business Conduct: a set of rules that address proper and improper behavior.

Other theft deterrent programs include the screening of all applicants for employment. This screening may include that the applicant complete a paper and pencil honesty test or some other psychological exam. Reference checks and background investigations can also be completed on applicants. These checks may uncover that the applicant is not suited for work because of past dishonesty.

SUMMARY

An observant and properly trained security officer can assist in uncovering internal theft. The U.S. Chamber of Commerce estimates that 40 billion dollars is stolen each year from American businesses. Many U.S. businesses are uncomfortable in dealing with this serious problem for a number of reasons. Among those mentioned are, the belief that a problem does not exist, nothing can be done about it, fear of a "witch hunt", and that an investigation could involve "key" people.

There are a number of indicators of theft. Inventory shortages, evidence secured during investigations, and information received from other sources. An observant security officer may notice evidence of theft during routine patrols. A fence may be cut or a truck with goods on board leaves the facility at an unusual time which may tip off an officer to potential thefts. A diligent security officer can deter theft by knowing his or her job completely. Knowing one's job includes noting incoming and outgoing vehicles in a daily log, logging visitors and contractors or service personnel, checking property passes and carefully writing coherent incident reports.

Another way to uncover evidence is through package or lunch box checks. Package inspections are only effective if they are conducted on a regular basis and only if a clear policy exists which explains to all employees and visitors the reasons for the inspections, how they will be conducted and the rights and penalties involved.

Notes

To deter theft a company should: 1) Have a clear written policy stating that theft will not be tolerated and will result in termination and/or criminal prosecution. 2) Have a loss prevention awareness program directed to all employees. 3) Employ a security staff that is well-trained and effective.

An alert security officer may also recognize characteristics of a dishonest employee. Does an employee live within his/her means? Does he or she show a dislike for policies and procedures and do things his or her own way? Does an employee openly harbor bitterness toward the organization and is convinced that the company owes them something? And finally, does the employee show evidences of a gambling habit, alcohol or drug abuse? It is the duty of the security officer to report those symptoms or evidence to his or her supervisor.

In almost every theft situation, three elements of theft surface. The need and desire to steal, rationalizations or excuses to steal appear, and the opportunity to commit theft exists. It is in reducing the opportunity to steal that the security officer can be most helpful. Learn your job well. Learn what is routine and what is not. An alert and effective security officer may prevent theft simply by being diligent.

A security officer is limited in discovering internal theft, but he can notice cash or petty cash available in an office, goods such as computers that are accessible and employees who steal time from a company by not signing in or signing out. Any irregularities should be reported and noted in daily logs.

Many organizations are now using Codes of Business Conduct. They are also screening applicants for employment by conducting paper and pencil honesty tests or some other psychological testing programs. But after all is said and done, it is the alert, well-trained, and diligent security officer that can help with the problem of internal theft.

Notes

QUESTIONS

Short Answer

1. Why are many companies uncomfortable in dealing with the problems of theft? Give 4 reasons.

2. How can a security officer notice evidence of theft during a routine patrol? Give 3 ways.

3. What are some of the characteristics of theft? Give at least 4 characteristics.

4. How can a security officer reduce the opportunity for theft?

5. How does the kleptomaniac differ from the disgruntled or bitter employee?

6. How can a "theft of information" be harmful to an organization?

Multiple Choice/True-False

1. A study shows that _____ % of all business failures are caused by employee dishonesty.
    A. 10
    B. 20
    C. 30
    D. 40

2.   The U.S. Chamber of Commerce estimates that _____ billion dollars is stolen each year from American businesses.
        A. 40
        B. 10
        C. 20
        D. 5

3.   Many executives believe that there is no cost effective answer to the problem of theft. True or False

4.   Most companies will go all out to solve theft problems. True or False

5.   If there is less inventory than the paperwork reports, it is called a positive variance. True or False

6.   Legal requirements should first be explored before package inspections are conducted. True or False

7.   Which of the following is not a sign that an employee may be dishonest?
        A. employee lives beyond his means
        B. employee has a bitterness toward the company
        C. employee does not display a gambling habit

Matching

Match the following terms with their correct definitions.

1. Opportunist	A.	"I saw it, I took it"
2. Kleptomaniac	B.	less inventory than paperwork shows
3. Rationalization	C.	"scratch my back, I'll scratch yours"
4. Kickback	D.	more inventory than paperwork shows
5. Positive Variance	E.	"I don't know why, I just took it, I had to"
6. Negative Variance	F.	An excuse for one's actions

Practical Exercises

1. During a routine exterior patrol of the facility, you notice valuable finished product has been placed in an isolated area near the employee parking lot. What do you do?

2. You receive information from an employee who wants to remain anonymous that five engineers recently attended an out-of-town National Football League game. Tickets were provided by a vendor along with free room and board at a resort. What do you do?

3. While working late one night you receive a phone call from a person who identifies himself as a businessman with an operation near your facility. He states that he is preparing to discard several years of paperwork and asks for the name of the waste removal company used by your facility. He also asks for the time of day they arrive at the plant for trash pick-up. Do you provide the caller with the requested information? If not, why not?

THE EFFECTIVE SECURITY OFFICERS TRAINING MANUAL

Chapter X

Fire Protection

Introduction to Fire Protection

Fire protection in the United States has developed only as a result of the loss of human life and property. Unfortunately, development continues only because the loss of life and property continues.

On October 9, 1871 the most famous fire in the U.S. began when, as legend has it, Mrs. O'Leary's cow kicked over a kerosene lamp. The fire destroyed much of Chicago. Fire Prevention Week is now celebrated during the week of October 9th each year in memory of this disaster.

As a result of a fire on December 30, 1909 at the Iroquois Theater in Chicago, which killed 602 people, improvements were mandated in the construction of fire protection for theaters.

On May 4, 1908 in Collinwood, Ohio 175 persons (mostly school children) were killed in a fire at the Lakeview Grammar School. Because of this fire, school fire drills were established.

Four-hundred ninety-two (492) persons, mostly servicemen, were killed when a fire swept through the Coconut Grove nightclub in Boston, Massachusetts on November 28, 1942. As a result of the Coconut Grove fire, regulations improving exits and installation of emergency lighting equipment were made law.

In 1958 ninety-five people died in Chicago's Our Lady of Angels Elementary school. Because of this fire schools everywhere are now inspected.

In May of 1976 over 175 people died at the Beverly Hills Supper Club near Covington, Kentucky when fire engulfed the nightclub.

In January of 1981 over 75 people died at the MGM Grand Hotel in Las Vegas, Nevada, as a result of a fire. Unfortunately, progress in the development of fire protection in the United States seems to occur only after people are killed in fires.

Fire departments are more advanced today in attempting to save lives and property from fire. The objectives of most fire departments in the U.S. are:

1. Prevent fires from starting.
2. Prevent loss of life and property when fire starts.
3. Confine fire to the place where it started.
4. Extinguish fires.

Notes

Reading For A Purpose:

Look for these key words:

- Carbon Dioxide
- Combustible
- Conduction
- Convection
- Deluge System
- Dry Chemical
- Dry Pipe
- Flammable
- Flammability Range
- Flash Point
- Foam
- Halon
- Ignition Point
- Radiation
- Standpipe
- Wet-Pipe

Look for Answers to these Questions:

- What are the chances for a business to survive after having suffered a serious fire?
- What is meant by the fire triangle?
- What are the various types of fire extinguishing systems?
- What is security's role in fire protection?
- What are the objectives of most fire departments in the United States?

The Great Chicago Fire
Fire protection for places of assembly
School fire drills
Revolving exit doors and emergency lighting
Inspections of schools
Fire regulations were ignored

Over 8,000 persons die each year in the U.S. as a result of fire. Most deaths are the result of breathing smoke or toxic gases. Usually, the victim is a child or elderly person. Most of the time these persons become confused and panic in a fire. Teenagers make-up the lowest percentage of deaths. The United States has more direct property loss, than any other country as a result of fires.

A study was conducted of 20,000 industrial fires. Of these 20,000 fires, 16,000 occurred while the plant or facility was operating. Nearly one-half (50%) of the facilities which had caught fire and were heavily damaged were never rebuilt. Out of the nearly 50% which were rebuilt (10,000), nearly one-third of these (some 3,300) were bankrupt in just three years. So by looking at the results of this study you can see why it is so important to prevent fires from starting. The chances are about 50-50 that if the plant or building where you currently work burns to the ground, you and all of your co-workers will be out of a job.

*ESTIMATED U.S. BUILDING FIRE CAUSES

	Percent of fires	Percent of dollar loss
Heating and cooking	16	8
Smoking and matches	12	4
Electrical	16	12
Rubbish, ignition source unknown	3	1
Flammable liquid fires and explosion	7	3
Open flames and spark	7	4
Lightning	2	2
Children and matches	7	3
Exposures	2	2
Incendiary, suspicious	7	10
Spontaneous ignition	2	1
Miscellaneous known causes	2	6
Unknown	17	44
Total	100	100

*Bugbee, Percy, Principles of Fire Protection, NFPA, Boston, 1978, p. 25.

Notes

Through fire inspections of existing facilities, fire departments attempt to prevent fires. The actual extinguishment of a fire is the final objective, preceded by preventing loss of life and property and preventing the spread of fire.

Because of their age and lack of mobility, children and older persons make up the highest numbers of deaths caused by fire.

Most industrial fires occur when a plant or facility is open or operating.

Fires are often devastating for businesses whether or not insurance covers the financial loss.

The greatest percentages of fires are started from: heating and cooking; smoking and matches; and electrical sources.

What is Fire?

Fire is unpredictable. It is a rapid, self sustaining, oxidation process accompanied by the evolution of heat and light of varying intensities. How's that for a definition? What that means is that fire spreads quickly and while there is enough air filled with oxygen (O2) fire will continue to burn. All the time it burns the fire will give off heat and light while the temperature of the fire increases and decreases. Four things are needed for a fire to continue to burn. These are:

1. Fuel
2. Heat or source of ignition
3. Oxygen (21% of air is oxygen)
4. Reaction time of oxidation or the chemical chain reaction of fire.

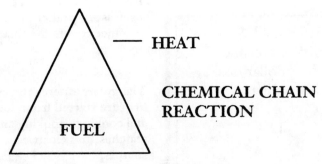

OXYGEN

HEAT

CHEMICAL CHAIN REACTION

FUEL

A fire will continue to burn until:

1. the combustible material (fuel) is either totally consumed or removed.

2. the level of oxygen in the air is reduced enough to stop the fire from burning.

3. the combustible material is cooled below its ignition point.

4. the flames are chemically inhibited.

Let's look at that again!

1. Fire will continue to burn until the material which is burning is either completely burned up or until it is removed from the fire. A log burning in a fireplace is a good

Notes

If there is not enough oxygen for a fire to continue to burn, a human being will not have sufficient oxygen to breathe.

Combustible: *Liquids which are classified by NFPA with a flash point at or above 100° F (37.8° C)*

Extinguish fire by:
1) Removing fuel
2) Reduce Oxygen
3) Cool the fuel
4) Break the "Chain-Reaction"

example: Once a fire has started in a fireplace, it will continue to burn as long as there is wood to burn. If the wood is used up or taken from the fireplace, the fire will stop.

2. Fire will continue to burn until the oxygen (O2) is lowered to a level where the fire cannot burn. A good example of this is when a pan with grease on the top of a stove catches fire. When you put the lid on top of the pan, the fire is extinguished because there is no air with oxygen for the fire. Fire needs oxygen in the same way a person needs oxygen to breathe. If there is no air, no oxygen, a person will suffocate. If a fire is denied oxygen, it will also suffocate and no longer burn.

3. Fire will continue to burn until the material on fire (fuel) is cooled so much that the fire stops. Can you think of an example of how a material is cooled below its ignition temperature. You're right if you thought of water! Water can be placed on many fires which will cool the material to the point where the fire will stop. (Note: Water is not used on all fires.)

4. Fire will continue to burn until the flames are chemically inhibited. This means that the fire will stop when the chain reaction which occurs between the heat, fuel and oxygen is stopped. Remember that! It will be discussed in greater detail later.

Heat Transfer

When an object is on fire, heat is transferred from that object to other objects which are not on fire. Any type of heat transfer occurs in one of three ways:

1. Conduction

2. Radiation

3. Convection

Conduction occurs when two objects are physically touching one another. If two objects are touching and one is burning, the second will become hotter and hotter and many times will eventually begin to burn. A good example of conduction heat transfer is when a piece of paper is laid on top of a hot pipe or stove. If the pipe or stove are hot enough (usually about 350 degrees F.) the paper will begin to burn.

Radiation is when heat travels in space. The degree of heat transfer depends on the size of the objects involved and their distance from one another. Heat from the sun is an

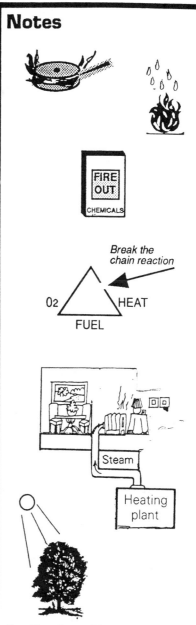

Notes

Break the chain reaction

O2   HEAT

FUEL

Steam

Heating plant

Conduction: *Heat energy which is transferred by direct contact between the heat source and another object.*

Radiation: *Heat energy that travels through space by waves or rays in a straight line from the heat source to surrounding areas and objects.*

181

excellent example of radiation heat transfer.

Convection is when heat is transferred by circulation of gas. Hot gases, vapors and liquids rise and the temperature of the material is gradually increased. Think of a "force fan" gas furnace. Gas vapors are ignited and air is heated in the chamber of a furnace until a fan "forces" the heated air from the chamber out into a room.

Heat Sources

There are four (4) major sources of ignition or heat energy:

1. Chemical
2. Electrical
3. Mechanical
4. Nuclear

Chemical

Fire is basically a form of chemical reaction, a chemical reaction process known as oxidation. Oxidation is a process which usually produces heat. Since air is the primary source of oxygen, the amount or flow of air will directly affect the rate of burn. Occasionally, an organic substance such as hay may ignite spontaneously. This occurs because the hay will give off heat due to the natural process of oxidation. Usually, when heat is given off from an organic matter the rate at which the heat is released is so slow and the area around the matter so large, the heat does not build-up. Should a build-up of heat occur such as wet hay in a barn loft, spontaneous ignition may result. When this occurs it is an example of a chemical form of ignition.

Electrical

Energy which is required to move electrical current through a substance will form heat. "When electrical current flows through a wire or another conductor, such as copper or another conductor such as silver, the resistance is low with the result that not much heat will be produced".[1] Potential fire hazards can exist because of electrical heat energy. These are:

Notes

Convection: Heat energy transferred by circulation of a gas such as air or a liquid via air currents.

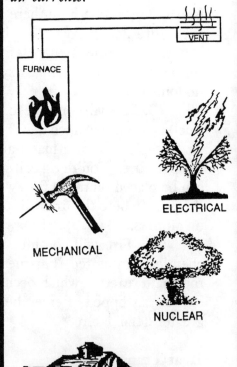

Fire hazards: conditions which make the possibility of a fire more likely.

1. Resistance
2. Arcing
3. Sparking
4. Static
5. Lightning

Resistance is caused by overloading electrical conductors. A common cause of fires is overloading electrical circuits by plugging in too many lights and appliances.

Arcing occurs when a good electrical connection is not made in a switch or fuse blank, the electrical energy will jump or arc across the space.

Sparking is different from arcing in that it is continuous.

Static occurs when an electrical charge exists on the surfaces of two materials which have been brought together and then separated. If the materials are not grounded the two surfaces will eventually emit a static spark.

Lightning is another form of electrical energy. A properly installed lightning rod will provide proper protection from lightning.

Mechanical

Energy which is generated when two objects are rubbed together is called mechanical. The friction transforms the energy into heat. Friction is the cause of many fires in industry.

Nuclear

Heat energy which is released from the nucleus of an atom is nuclear. Nuclear energy is used primarily in the generation of electricity.

Flammable and Combustible Liquids

Material burns because vapors are heated to the point where burning begins and continues. The lowest temperature at which enough vapor will be given off to form a flammable mixture with air is known as the material's flash point. These vapors form near the surface of the material and with the proper mixture of air, ignition will occur provided there is an ignition source. Consider lighter fluid. If a match is placed near a charcoal briquet which has been soaked in lighter

Notes

Resistance: Electrical condition which occurs when electrical conductors are overloaded; heat build up starts which could start a fire

Arcing: Electrical condition which occurs when a good electrical connection is not made and electrical energy jumps or arcs across a space

Flammable: Material which as a liquid has a flash point below 100° F (37.8° C); as a gas will burn in normal concentrations of oxygen in the air

Flash Point: The lowest temperature at which enough vapor is given off to form a flammable mixture with air

fluid, ignition will normally occur even if the match never actually touches the charcoal. If the match is not close enough to the briquet to ignite the vapors, ignition will not occur.

Another important term to be familiar with is ignition point. The lowest temperature at which a material must be heated in order to start self-sustained combustion or burning is known as ignition point or ignition temperature. The ignition point of most wood is approximately 350 degrees Fahrenheit. This means that if a small amount of wood were placed near a hot pipe, once the temperature of the wood reaches 350 degrees F. it would ignite automatically without another source of flame.

Flammability limit is another term which is important to know when discussing fire. Flammability limit describes the minimum level of mixture of air to vapors below which a flame will not burn. A mixture of air and vapors below the flammability limit means that the mixture is too lean and therefore will not burn. Consider how a carburetor works in a car. The flammability limits of gasoline are 1.4% - 7.5% These percentages mean that between 1.4% of gasoline vapors mixed with air and 7.5% of vapors mixed with air, gasoline will ignite. For a carburetor, the normal mixture of gasoline vapors with air is 5% If too much gas is in the carburetor (above 5%) the gasoline will not ignite and the carburetor is considered "flooded". If a person will wait until some of the gasoline evaporates, the carburetor will eventually rid itself of the excess vapors and will normally start. Examples of flash point and ignition temperatures of gasoline and kerosene are:

	Flash Point	Ignition Temperature
Gasoline	-45° F.	536° F.
Kerosene	100° F.	410° F.

In the above chart flash points are more critical. For gasoline, provided the right mixture of air to gasoline vapors exist and provided the temperature of the air directly above the gasoline liquid is above minus 45 degrees Fahrenheit, the gasoline will ignite. In most of the USA during most of the year the temperature will normally be higher than minus 45 degrees F. That is why gasoline is so versatile in vehicles. If however, you happen to be in northern Canada in the middle of February you may find the temperature of the air is colder

Notes

Ignition Point/Temperature:
The lowest point or temperature at which a material must be heated in order to start self-sustained combustion or burning

Flammability Limit/Range:
The range of a gas or vapor in which the gas will burn or explode in air; below a certain point the mixture of gas and air will not burn, and above a certain point the mixture will not burn

Fahrenheit: Temperature scale that registers the freezing point of water as 32° F and the boiling point as 212° F under normal atmospheric conditions

Celsius: Temperature scale that registers the freezing point of water as 0° C and the boiling point as 100° C under normal atmospheric conditions; centigrade

than minus 45 degrees F. If that is the case, sufficient gas vapors will not be given off and the vehicle will not start. Kerosene on the other hand would not give off enough vapors to ignite from a flame unless the temperature of the air immediately above the surface of the liquid is at least 100 degrees F. That is why kerosene is safer for use in homes than gasoline. With kerosene a flame source must be placed immediately above the kerosene until the temperature of the kerosine at the source of the flame is 100 degrees F. Gasoline on the other hand would not have to be heated to such a high temperature and therefore ignites and explodes much easier than kerosene.

The Factory Mutual Insurance Company gives seven suggestions for properly controlling flammables. They are:

1. Segregate the hazard by distance (don't put too much in the same area).
2. Confine or enclose the hazard by using proper containers.
3. Ventilate to prevent explosive mixtures.
4. Install explosion venting where needed.
5. Eliminate sources of ignition.
6. Educate those involved as to the hazards and proper safeguards.
7. Provide adequate fire protection.

Another important term is fire loading. Fire loading describes what occurs when too many combustibles or flammables are put into one area. One 55-gallon drum of kerosine may be proper storage. Six 55-gallon drums of kerosine may be considered excessive thereby creating an unsafe, fire loading problem.

Extinguishing Fires

Water is the most commonly used substance in fire protection. Water is used in fire hoses and sprinkler systems. At ordinary temperatures water is relatively stable. A fire will be put out only when water is felt at the source of the fire or combustion. Once the ignition temperature of the material is cooled by the water to a point where flame cannot continue the fire will be extinguished. Water has a great cooling effect. When water is sprayed onto a fire,

FIRE LOADING

Fire loading: when too many combustible or flammables are put into one area.

steam results. Steam indicates that the fire is cooling. Steam is important in extinguishing a fire. When water is converted into steam the volume of water increases at about 1,700 times. Large volumes of steam displace an equal volume of air and in a fire situation the steam causes oxygen to be reduced. When oxygen is reduced, the fire will also be reduced.

Water is used primarily in sprinkler systems which were first designed in 1878. Sprinklers are generally considered to be 95% successful at extinguishing fire. The 5% failure rate is primarily the result of human error. A sprinkler system cannot work if a valve which controls the water flow is closed. If a sprinkler system is properly maintained, it will normally work as it was intended. Most sprinkler systems are of the "wet-pipe" type. In a wet-pipe system, water is maintained in the sprinkler system at all times under pressure. Usually, sprinkler heads are closed with a small amount of solder. The solder is designed to melt at a temperature of between 135 degrees F. and 500 degrees F. depending on the type of sprinkler head. Most sprinkler heads are designed to open at 165 degrees F. (The temperature at which solder melts.)

Dry Sprinkler Systems

A dry-pipe sprinkler system provides protection from freezing since water is not contained in the sprinkler piping. Instead, a moderate amount of air is pressurized in the sprinkler pipes. When the solder to the sprinkler head melts, the air is released. Water which is stored behind a valve rushes through the pipes to the open head where it then discharges. The dry-pipe system is especially useful in those areas where freezing occurs.

Deluge System

For areas which need extra fire protection a deluge system is often used. These systems are normally controlled by heat/temperature detectors. When a detector senses heat it signals an alarm which automatically releases the water. Deluge systems have open sprinkler heads at all times. There is no solder which keeps the head closed. As the name implies, a deluge system is designed to literally deluge or flood an area with a great amount of water in a short period

Notes

Wet-Pipe Sprinklers: Sprinkler system which is under water pressure at all times so that water is discharged immediately when an automatic sprinkler head opens.

Dry-Pipe Sprinklers: Used in areas which may freeze; the sprinkler piping contains air or nitrogen under pressure instead of water, when a sprinkler opens the pressure is reduced, a dry-pipe valve is opened and water flows from the sprinklers

Deluge System: Used in extra hazard occupancies, sprinkler heads which are open at all times so that when the water comes on, the entire area is flooded

of time. Deluge systems are used for high hazard areas such as flammable liquid dispensing areas.

Standpipes

In order to provide a readily available means to manually fight a fire, many buildings contain standpipes. Standpipes are classified by the size of their hose connections. A Class I system is a 2 1/2" hose which allows fire departments to provide a great amount of water to a fire. A Class II system is a 1 1/2" hose which is designed to be used by building occupants until the fire department arrives. These hoses are lightweight, woven jacket and rubber line. Class III systems have connections for both 2 1/2" and 1 1/2" hoses. Water for the standpipes is usually provided by city water mains, pressure tanks, automatic fire pumps or gravity tanks.

Foam Extinguishing Systems

Foam extinguishing systems have been used for many years, particularly in the petroleum - chemical industry. Foam breaks down and vaporizes its water content under attack by heat and flame. When other fire extinguishing agents are used with foam, the foam may become ineffective. This is especially true if water is used in conjunction with foam. One of the most common methods of using foam is by a fire department truck hoseline nozzle.

Carbon Dioxide Systems

Carbon dioxide (CO_2) is a non-combustible gas that for many years has been used to extinguish certain types of fires. Carbon dioxide reduces oxygen in a fire to a point where it will no longer support the fire. Carbon dioxide will not conduct electricity. It is heavier than air and, when released from a cylinder, is about -110° F. which turns into dry ice. Carbon dioxide can 1) be discharged onto the surface of a burning material by fixed piping or by hand extinguishers or 2) the area can be flooded with the gas until the entire atmosphere in the room is converted to carbon dioxide. Since carbon dioxide removes oxygen in the air, care must be taken when people may be exposed to the gas. A concentration of about 9% carbon dioxide can cause a person to lose consciousness in a short time.

Notes

Standpipe: Pipe and hose system in buildings which are used to provide water in a fire; can be dry or wet systems

Foam: Fire extinguishing agent used especially in the petro-chemical industry for extinguishing flammable liquid fire.

Carbon Dioxide: CO_2 a non-combustible gas that reduces oxygen in a fire; will not conduct electricity, is heavier than air and when released from a cylinder is about -110° F.

Carbon Dioxide extinguishing systems are popular for controlling and extinguishing flammable material fires.

Persons need to be extremely careful when re-entering areas where CO_2 was recently discharged.

Halon Systems

Halon is a material made of hydrogen and carbon. The number of Halon such as 1211 or 1301 was developed by the U.S. Army Corps of Engineers and indicates the chemical composition of the material. Halon 1211 and 1301 are the only two agents recognized by the National Fire Protection Association (NFPA) as fire extinguishing halon. Both are widely used in the protection of electrical equipment, airplane engines and computer rooms. Since both Halon 1211 and 1301 rapidly vaporize in fire, they leave little residue to clean up. How halon works is not fully understood but there is some chemical reaction as the agents are very effective in extinguishing fire. Halon 1211 is used in fire extinguishers and is more toxic than Halon 1301 which is used to protect computer rooms. The low toxicity of Halon 1301 allows it to be discharged safely from total flooding systems where people are located. Contrary to some belief, Halon 1301 does not remove oxygen from the air as in the case of carbon dioxide.

Dry Chemical Extinguishing Systems

Dry chemical extinguishing agents consist of fine powders that effectively smother a fire. Dry chemical has been found to be an effective extinguishing agent for fires in flammable liquids and electrical equipment. Dry chemical is stable both at low and high temperatures. The ingredients in dry chemical are non-toxic. It is believed that the discharge of dry chemical into flames breaks up the combustion reaction. Dry chemical systems are not recommended for telephone switch board or computer protection because of their powdery residue.

Notes

Halon 1211: A Hydrocarbon, (bromochlorodifluoromethane), used in aircraft engine protection and fire extinguishers; toxicity level prevents its use in flooding of occupied spaces.

Halon 1301: A Hydrocarbon, (Bromotrifluoromethane), least toxic of the halons; used to protect computer facilities.

Halon has, in recent years, become less popular because of concerns over the environment. With further EPA restrictions enacted, CO2 systems will be a more acceptable alternative to Halon.

Dry chemical: Finely divided powders that effectively extinguish a fire when applied by a fire extinguisher, non-toxic.

Dry chemical powder resembles baking soda. The dry chemical in a dry chemical fire extinguisher is placed under pressure within the extinguisher cylinder. When pressure is released, the dry chemical powder escapes.

SUMMARY

Notes

Fire protection in the United States has developed only because of the loss of human life and property. National Fire Prevention Week is celebrated each October in the United States to remember the great Chicago fire of 1871. Countless other tragedies have occurred in the USA. As a result, fire regulations are strengthened and fire protection improved after each disaster.

Most fire departments attempt to keep fires from starting, prevent loss of life and property when fire starts, confine fire to the place where it started and extinguish fire. Nearly 8,000 people die each year in the USA from fires. Most of these deaths are children and elderly persons caused by smoke inhalation.

Fire is unpredictable, rapid and self-sustaining. Fire burns because of fuel, heat, oxygen and a chemical chain reaction which occurs during burning. A fire will continue to burn until one of the four is removed.

Heat is transferred by conduction, radiation and convection. The four major sources of ignition are chemical, electrical, mechanical and nuclear.

Material burns because vapors are heated to the point where burning begins. The lowest temperature at which enough vapor is given off to form a flammable mixture with air is the material's flash point. The lowest temperature at which a material must be heated to start burning is ignition point or ignition temperature.

Water is the most commonly used substance in fire protection. Water is primarily used in sprinkler systems which can be either wet or dry systems, deluge or standpipe variety. Foam is used to extinguish fires involving petroleum or chemicals. Carbon dioxide is a non combustible gas which is used to extinguish certain types of fire. Halon 1211, Halon 1301 and dry chemical powders are also effective fire extinguishing agents. Halon is used to protect computer rooms and aircraft.

Footnotes
1. Bugbee, Percy. *Principles of Fire Protection*. NFPA, (Quincy, MA, 1978) p.58.

QUESTIONS

1. From the study cited in the material, how many of the 20,000 facilities studied were open for business after a fire?
    a. 8,000
    b. 18,000
    c. 20,000
    d. 4,000

2. Name the four objectives of most fire departments.
    1. p_____ fires from s_____.
    2. p_____ loss of l_____ and p_____ when fire starts.
    3. _____ the fire to the place where it started.
    4. _____ fires.

3. Over _____ persons die each year in the United States as a result of fires.
    a. 10,000
    b.   100
    c.   8,000
    d. 80,000

4. Most deaths from fire are as a result of:
    a. burns
    b. smoke inhalation (breathing smoke/gas)
    c. jumping from buildings
    d. heart attack

5. In the study of 20,000 industrial fires _____ % of the businesses were never rebuilt.
    a. 25
    b. 75
    c. 33
    d. 50

6. The following four elements are needed for fire to continue to burn.
    1. _____
    2. _____
    3. _____
    4. _____

7.   Fire will continue to burn until:
    1. the burning material is _____ or _____.
    2. _____(O2) is lowered to a level where the fire cannot burn.
    3. the burning material is _____.
    4. the flames are _____ inhibited or stopped.

8.   How is heat transferred?
    1. _____
    2. _____
    3. _____

9.   Name an example of conduction heat transfer.
    _____

10. The four major sources of ignition are:
    1. _____
    2. _____
    3. _____
    4. _____

11. Flash point is:
    a. the temperature at which water freezes.
    b. what occurs when a match is ignited.
    c. the lowest temperature at which enough vapor is given off to form a
       flammable mixture with air.
    d. the temperature at which water boils.

12. The Factory Mutual Insurance Company gives seven suggestions for properly
controlling flammables. List them.
    1. _____
    2. _____
    3. _____
    4. _____
    5. _____
    6. _____
    7. _____

13. What is the most commonly used substance in fire protection?
    _____

14. Sprinkler systems are generally considered to be 95% successful at extinguishing fires.
What is the 5% failure rate due to?
    _____

15. Name the three types of sprinkler systems.
     1. _____
     2. _____
     3. _____

16. Dry chemical systems are not recommended for telephone switch board or computer protection. True or False.

17. Name the two types of Halon.
     1. _____
     2. _____

18. What type of halon is used to protect computer rooms?
     _____

19. Carbon dioxide will conduct electricity. True or False.

20. Foam is used as a fire extinguishing agent in what two industries.
     1. _____
     2. _____

21. What is a standpipe? _____

Fire Protection Practice Worksheet

1. What types of fire protection equipment are located at the facility? Who inspects? How often? Who inspects fire extinguishers?

2. Define fire hazards? Storage of flammable and combustible liquids? Special instructions/precautions?

3. Items to look for during a patrol:

   - Fire extinguishers

   - Blocked aisles

   - Sprinkler risers

   - Storage of materials

   - Fire exits and fire doors

   - Open electrical panels

4. Do you have maps indicating where all of the fire extinguishers and sprinklers are?

5. Who is called to repair an impaired system? Is the insurance company called? Fire department? Added fire watch patrols? Restrict cutting and welding and smoking? Suspend operation?

6. What special precautions are taken for sprinkler systems in winter? Dry valve systems? Anti-freeze systems? Insure heat is on?

7. Are there standpipes? Wet or dry? Are you trained on how to use a fire hose? Fire pump? Fire extinguisher?

FIRE PROTECTION

Conduction, Convection and Radiation

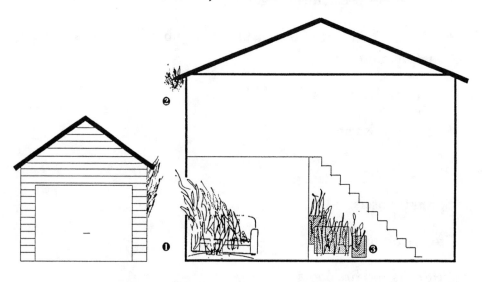

❶ Radiation—garage ignited by radiated heat from couch fire

❷ Convection—eaves ignited by convected heat from fire coming out of window

❸ Conduction—storage behind noncombustible wall ignited by conducted head

INTEGRATED FIRE SYSTEM DIAGRAM

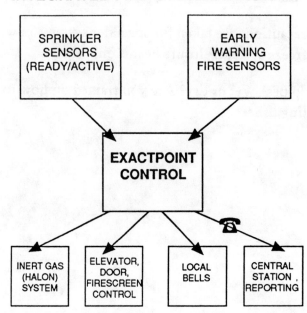

SPRINKLER SYSTEM MONITORING DIAGRAM

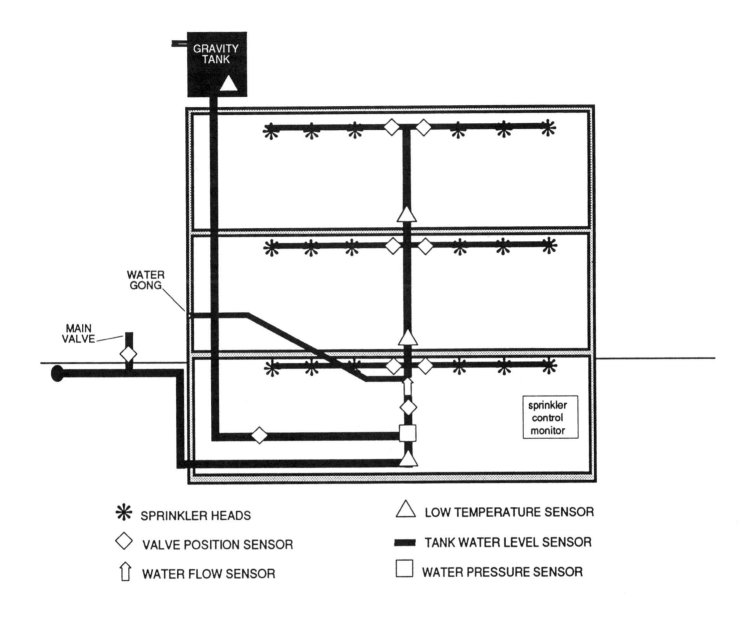

GRAVITY TANK

WATER GONG

MAIN VALVE

sprinkler control monitor

✳ SPRINKLER HEADS	△ LOW TEMPERATURE SENSOR
◇ VALVE POSITION SENSOR	▬ TANK WATER LEVEL SENSOR
⇧ WATER FLOW SENSOR	☐ WATER PRESSURE SENSOR

FIRE PROTECTION

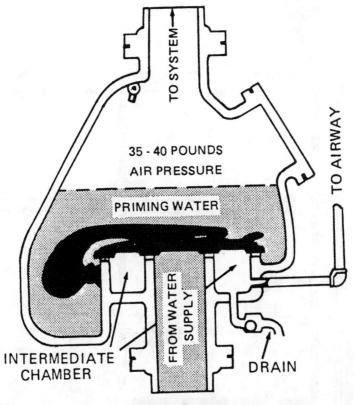

TO SYSTEM

TO AIRWAY

35 - 40 POUNDS
AIR PRESSURE

PRIMING WATER

FROM WATER SUPPLY

INTERMEDIATE
CHAMBER

DRAIN

DRY-PIPE SPRINKLER VALVE

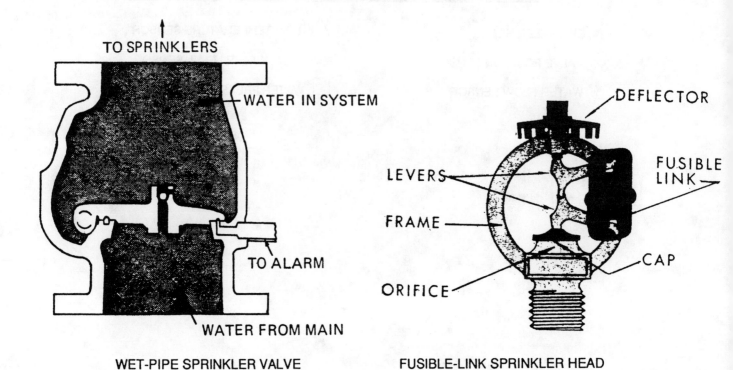

TO SPRINKLERS

WATER IN SYSTEM

TO ALARM

WATER FROM MAIN

WET-PIPE SPRINKLER VALVE

DEFLECTOR

LEVERS

FUSIBLE
LINK

FRAME

CAP

ORIFICE

FUSIBLE-LINK SPRINKLER HEAD

Fire Protection Exhibit -- Fire Extinguishers

EXTINGUISHERS HAVE THEIR LIMITS.

A portable fire extinguisher can save lives and property by putting out a small fire or containing it until the Fire Department arrives.

Portable extinguishers are not designed to fight a large or spreading fire. Even against small fires, they are useful only under the right conditions:

- An extinguisher must be large enough for the fire at hand. It must be readily available and in working order, fully charged.
- The operator must know how to use the extinguisher quickly, without taking time to read directions during an emergency.
- The operator must be reasonably strong to lift and operate the extinguisher.

BUY EXTINGUISHERS CAREFULLY.

A fire extinguisher should be "listed" and "labeled" by an independent testing laboratory.

The higher the rating number on an A or B extinguisher, the more fire it can put out. But high-rated units are often the heavier models. Make sure you can hold and operate the extinguisher you are buying.

Remember that extinguishers need care and must be recharged after every use.

For a pressurized extinguisher, ask your dealer how to have it serviced and inspected. It must be recharged after any use: a partially used unit might as well be empty.

If you are considering a disposable fire extinguisher, keep in mind that it can be used only once. Then it must be discarded and replaced.

You may need more than one extinguisher. In your home, for example, you may want an extinguisher in the kitchen as well as one in the garage or workshop.

Each extinguisher should be installed inplain view near an escape route and away from potential hazards such as heating appliances. Ask you local Fire Department for advice on the best locations.

Also ask you Fire Department about training and practice inuse of portable fire extinguishers. Many departments offer training sessions for the public.

WHEN TO FIGHT A FIRE...

Fight the fire only if all of the following are true:
- Everyone has left or is leaving the building.
- The Fire Department is being called.
- The fire is small and confined to the immediate areas where it started (wastebasket, cushion, small appliances, etc.)
- You can fight the fire with your back to a safe escape route.
- Your extinguisher is rated for the type of fire you are fighting, and is in good working order.
- You have had training in use of the extinguisher and are confident that you can operate it effectively.

If you have the slightest doubt about whether or not to fight the fire - DON'T! Instead, get out, closing the door behind you.

THE EFFECTIVE SECURITY OFFICERS TRAINING MANUAL

Chapter XI

Safety

Safety

Another fast growing profession is that of safety. Since the Occupational Safety and Health Act (OSHA) became law in the United States on April 28, 1971, and created the Occupational Safety and Health Administration (OSHA), industry has changed dramatically. If you work for a business affecting commerce, a "safe and healthful" workplace must be provided to all employees. In addition, many states have also adopted and in some cases expanded upon regulations which apply to businesses which operate within state boundaries.

The OSHA law requires employers to furnish to employees a place of employment free of recognized hazards that cause or are likely to cause death or serious physical harm. Employers must also post the official statute in order to notify all employees of their rights and obligations under the law.

Most large businesses have a formal safety program which defines every employee's role in promoting on-the-job safety. Various colleges and universities now offer degrees in safety management, industrial hygiene and environmental affairs.

The role of security officers in an organization's safety program will often be very limited. However, in recent years, many safety professionals have recognized that security officers can provide a valuable resource in an observation, and emergency preparedness functions in the safety program. Modern thinking security managers have recognized that if security departments can provide added services, such as in safety, job security can be enhanced.

OSHA INSPECTIONS AND INVESTIGATIONS

The Occupational Safety and Health Administration is a division of the Federal Department of Labor. Places of employment may be visited by OSHA officials "without delay and at reasonable times" for purposes of inspection and investigation. Inspections can be conducted at businesses which have higher than normal industry accident rates, if a serious accident occurs, or if selected on a random basis.

Notes

Reading For A Purpose
Look for these key words:
• OSHA   • Form 200
• OSHA Inspection
• Alleged Violations
• Citations   • Insurance
• OSHA Penalties
• Recordkeeping
• Recordable Incidence Rate
• Lost Workday Case Rate
• Lost Workday or Severity Rate
• Loss Control
• Bloodborne Pathogens
• Worker's Compensation
• Liability   • Disabilities
Look for answers to these key questions:
• Why is OSHA important to a company?
• What would you do if asked to handle an OSHA inspection?
• Can the cost of OSHA alleged violations be significant?
• What can accidents tell you about a company?
• What role can you play in a company's loss prevention/control program?
• How can security professionals assist in workers' compensation matters?
• Should security guard companies be concerned with insurance matters, such as general or products liability?

When considering furthering one's education, a degree in safety management should be evaluated.

Security officers can play an important role in a safety program.

Employees may request an inspection by notifying OSHA in writing, of their belief that a violation of a safety or health standard which threatens physical harm or imminent danger exists . When an inspection is made at the request of an employee, a complete inspection ("wall-to wall") may be made at the discretion of the OSHA Area Director and may not be limited to only the employee's initial complaint.

Employers have the right to request a warrant from an OSHA compliance officer. The Department of Labor will not reveal the name of the employee who made the initial complaint and an employee cannot be terminated or harassed for filing a complaint. OSHA will not automatically make an inspection each time it gets a request, but they must make an inspection when they believe a violation or danger exists. If OSHA decides an inspection is not warranted, they must notify the employee, in writing, of its decision.

If a compliance officer asks for an employer or union representative to accompany him on the inspection, the employer must allow it. In addition, the compliance officer can ask to speak to a reasonable number of employees during the inspection. As a security professional, you may be called upon to deal with an OSHA inspection. The information following is an outline of how to initially conduct an inspection and what to do after the inspection is completed.

OSHA INSPECTION

A. What to do if an OSHA compliance officer arrives at your facility.
   1. Be courteous
   2. Ask to see identification - if in doubt, contact the local OSHA office for confirmation.

B. Timetable of Events
   1. Introduction and meeting usually held with facility or plant manager and union representative.
   2. Review of records
   • injury/illness report forms; log 200; workers' compensation first report to state

---

Notes

"Wall-to-Wall" inspection: name given to a total and complete safety inspection of a facility by an OSHA compliance officer.

Warrant: Legal document which allows for the search of property.

Keep written notes of all meetings and discussions.

3. Opening conference
- introductions: names, addresses
- purpose of facility visitation
- results of records review
- intentions

4. Review of programs
- offer what your facility is doing for injury/illness prevention
- if possible, have the union attest to the cooperative spirit that exists in injury/illness prevention activities

5. Inspection
- answer questions precisely; don't get too detailed or too verbose
- don't volunteer information unless specifically asked to do so
- the compliance officer may request to interview employees privately; do not resist
- question alleged violations; make sure you and the compliance officer have an accurate understanding
- the compliance officer may wish to take photographs. If possible, take the identical picture with your camera
- keep it moving; do not linger if at all possible
- if something is pointed out, attempt to repair it immediately. If the compliance officer is to return the next day, actually go back to each discrepancy to show it was fixed
- show a genuine interest in making your plant the safest possible

6. Closing Conference
- compliance officer will review alleged violations
- dates will be determined when alleged violations are to be remedied. Seek the latest date possible
- a discussion of rights under the law will be discussed
- the compliance officer will return to the area office to have the area director determine violations and their dollar penalties

7. Citations
- will be mailed to the plant

Notes

195

- post a copy of the citation near each violation for three working days or until the violation has been corrected, or whichever one is later
8. Abate & Pay
- send your abatement response letter via registered mail. Discuss what was corrected, when, and in some cases, how
- send payment within 15 days

C. A follow-up inspection may take place to do the following:
1. to verify if the citations are posted
2. to determine if violations have been corrected
3. to determine if employees have been protected by some temporary measure if a long abatement is necessary
4. new alleged violations may be cited if observed during this follow-up

D. Appealing Citations
1. Informal Conference
a. call and schedule an informal conference with the area OSHA Director within 15 days to:
- obtain a complete understanding of the specific standards cited in the citation
- discuss methods to correct alleged violations
- negotiate for elimination of citations that you have a good argument against or to reduce proposed penalties (union representation is barred from offering any input into this process)
- extend abatement dates
- this informal conference does not extend the 15 day period allowed to contest or pay the proposed penalties

7. Formal Contest
a. You can formally contest a citation through written notification to the OSHA Area Director within 15 working days, Monday through Friday, excluding federal holidays.

(1). Clearly state which of the following you are contesting:

Notes

Abatement: Formal written response to a citation which attempts to reduce, lessen, or eliminate any penalty or fine; reasons are normally explained why a condition existed and what ahs been done to remedy the situation.

Organizations must be aware that a condition or hazard which was not cited as part of the first inspection, may be cited during a follow-up inspection.

- citation or aspects of the citation
- penalty
- abatement date
- any combination
(2). Post a copy of this letter near the posted citation until the issue is resolved
b. The contest will be heard in a pretrial conference with the OSHA Area Director. You may attend with an attorney (OSHA will have an attorney present)
c. If the issue is not resolved, the case goes to the Occupational Safety and Health Review Commission
d. Appeal to full Commission
e. Appeal to U.S. District Court
f. Appeal to the Court of Appeals
g. Appeal to the U.S. Supreme Court

CITATIONS

If the OSHA Compliance Officer finds an alleged violation of any safety requirement, a formal report or citation will be issued. The citation will advise you of the specific alleged violation found and the time allowed to either remove or correct the alleged violation. If alleged violations are not corrected within the agreed abatement period a penalty will be assessed equal to the amount of the initial penalty dollars per day for each day of not complying with the citation. Serious violations carry a mandatory penalty of up to $7,000. Other-than-serious alleged violations typically do not result in penalties, but penalties of up to $7,000 may be issued by the OSHA Regional Administrator if circumstances warrant. Willful violations of any standard can be assessed penalties between $5,000 and $70,000. Criminal willful violations can include a jail term of up to six months against an executive of the organization in addition to the monetary penalty. Repeat violations can have a maximum penalty of $70,000. Citations, when received in writing, must be posted at or near the place where the violation occurred. Companies may appeal citations, and they have 15 working days to do so. A company can also request an informal conference to discuss or appeal with the OSHA Area Director possible penalty reductions, and extensions of abatement dates.

Notes

Citation: Written legal document which describes a violation or infraction of the law.

In recent years, company officials have been charged in criminal court for alleged willful violations of safety at their workplace.

RECORD KEEPING REQUIREMENTS

OSHA regulations require all establishments to maintain records of occupational injuries and illnesses which involve medical treatment (other than just first aid), lost workdays, restriction of work or motion, loss of consciousness, fatalities, or transfer to another job be recorded in a log (OSHA Form 200).

OSHA Log

OSHA requires statistics be maintained for all injuries, illnesses and lost workdays so that objective data is provided which measures a company's overall accident experience. Companies with active accident prevention programs will generally have a better accident history than those companies who fail to have a program.

In recent years large penalties have been assessed by OSHA against companies who misrepresented the injury/illness history and OSHA injury logs. Penalties in excess of one million dollars have been levied because companies were allegedly reporting accident information and history falsely. Many companies continue to misunderstand the OSHA reporting system. There are generally three types of accident/injury rates that OSHA requires companies to monitor:

- OSHA Recordable Incidence Rate
- OSHA Lost Workday Case Incidence Rate
- OSHA Lost Workday Incidence Rate

OSHA Recordable Incidence Rate measures the number of injuries or illnesses based on 100 full-time workers at a facility. Since many companies have less than or more than 100 employees, a rate is obtained by using a formula based upon 100 full-time workers. This formula allows for companies which operate similar businesses to be compared to determine their safety program effectiveness. For example, by using this formula a sign company which employs 10 full-time workers can be compared against a sign company which employs 50 full-time workers. This formula allows a person to make inter industry comparisons, trend

Notes

analysis over time or comparisons among companies regardless of size. The formula to calculate the incidence rate is:

$$\frac{N \times 200{,}000}{AMW}$$

N = the number of injuries and/or illnesses recorded

200,000 = the base for 100 full-time workers who work 40 hours per week, 50 weeks per year (100 workers x 40 hours per week x 50 weeks per year = 200,000

AMW = The total hours worked by employees during the reporting period

Let's assume a company had 10 injuries or illnesses that were considered to be "recordable" by OSHA over a period of one year. Let's also assume the company had 350 full-time workers at the facility who worked a total of 700,000 hours during this same year. Following is the calculation to determine the OSHA Recordable incidence rate:

Formula:		Example:
$\dfrac{N \times 200{,}000}{AMW}$	=	N = 10 (Recordable Injuries/ Illnesses) x 200,000 <hr> 700,000 (Total Hours worked by all employees during the reporting period)

10 x 200,000 = 2,000,000
2,000,000 / (divided by) 700,000 = 2.85
2.85 = OSHA RECORDABLE INCIDENCE RATE

The 2.85 incidence rate (the number of injuries/ illnesses per 100 full-time employees) could then be used as a basis for comparison among other firms in the same industry. Usually, a company's accounting department would be able to provide the total hours worked by all employees during the reporting period. The number of recordable incidents of accidents or injuries must be maintained by someone within the organization (typically safety, human resources or medical personnel).

The Lost Workday Case Incidence Rate measures the number of occupational injuries or illnesses cases involving lost or restricted workdays. A lost workday case is one in which an employees suffers an injury or illness which causes him/her to miss one full shift of work. Sometimes the employee may only miss one day or if they were seriously injured they may miss several days of work. A restricted workday case is one in which an employee suffers an illness or injury that causes him/her to not be able to complete the full scope of their job due to medical restrictions for one or more shift. The Lost Workday Case Incidence Rate measures the number of injuries or illnesses cases which result in time missed from work or restricted from performing his/her normal duties. If a person was injured but did not miss any time from work or was restricted at work, it is not calculated with this formula.

The formula to calculate Lost Workday Case Incidence Rate is:

$$\frac{NL \times 200,000}{AMW}$$

NL = the number of injuries or illnesses which resulted in lost or restricted workdays.

200,000 = the base for 100 full-time workers who work 40 hours per week, 50 weeks per year (100 workers x 40 hours x 50 weeks = 200,000).

AMW = the total hours worked by employees during the reporting period.

Let's go back to our previous example where a company had 10 injuries or illnesses which were considered to be "recordable." Upon further investigation you learn that of the 10 injuries or illnesses, only 5 resulted in employees missing time from work or who were restricted while at work.

To determine this company's Lost Workday Case Incidence Rate you need to calculate the following information:

Formula: Example:

$$\frac{NL \times 200{,}000}{AMW} = \frac{5 \text{ (Injuries which resulted in lost or restricted workdays)}}{5 \times 200{,}000}$$

NL= Number of injuries/illnesses which resulted in lost or restricted workdays.

divided by:
700,000 (Total Hours worked by all employees during the reporting period)

5 x 200,000 = 1,000,000
1,000,000 divided by 700,000 = 1.42
1.42 = LOST WORKDAY CASE INCIDENCE RATE

The 1.42 Lost Workday Case Incidence Rate can then be used as a basis for comparison among other firms in the same industry.

The final accident rate which we are learning about is the Lost Workday Rate or Severity Rate. This measures the total number of lost and/or restricted workdays which results from recordable injuries or illnesses. This rate is important since it measures how serious or SEVERE injuries are at a facility.

For example: An injury where an employee falls and sprains an ankle and misses 5 days of work is not as SEVERE as an injury where an employee falls and injures his back and misses 90 days of work.

Let's go back to our previous example where a company had 10 injuries/illnesses which resulted in only 5 employees missing time from work or who were restricted while at work. Upon further investigation you learn that while only 5 employees missed time from work, 200 lost workdays resulted only from the 5 injuries.

To determine this company's Lost Workday Rate or Severity Rate you need to calculate the following information:

Formula:

$$\frac{NO \times 200,0000}{AMW} = $$

Example:
200 (Lost Workdays)
200 x 200,000

700,000 (Total Hours Worked by all employees during the reporting period)

NO = Number of lost or restricted workdays
200 x 200,000 = 40,000,000
40,000,000 divided by 700,000 = 57.14
57.14 = SEVERITY RATE (or lost workday rate)

The 57.14 rate which is the number of workdays lost or restricted per 100 employees can then be used as a basis for comparison among other firms in the same industry.

A review of the examples previously discussed reveal the following:

OSHA RECORDABLE INJURIES/ILLNESSES

1. Joe Brown - Burned Hand - No lost workdays
2. Peggy Smith - Sprained Wrist - No lost workdays
3. Jim Johnson - Broken Leg - 100 lost workdays
4. George Artwell - Sprained Ankle - 5 lost workdays
5. Bill Williams - Cut Hand - No lost workdays
6. Jill Humphrey - Dislocated Finger - No lost workdays
7. Brad Sommers - Sprained Back - 25 lost workdays
8. John Grant - Burned Hand - No lost workdays
9. Betty Williams - Sprained Back - 50 lost workdays
10. Adam Jones - Sprained Back - 20 lost workdays

Totals

10 Recordable Injuries=2.85 Recordable Incidence Rate
5 Injuries w/ lost workdays=1.42 Lost Workday Case Incidence Rate
700,000 Hours Worked by all employees=57.14 Severity Rate

In the example used, the facility did not have a poor OSHA Recordable Incidence Rate, and its Lost Workday Incidence Rate was one-half of the incidence rate. However, the facility's Severity Rate was extremely high. What assumptions can be made about this facility? One assumption is that while their OSHA Recordable Incidence Rate and Lost Workday Incidence Rate are not significant, their Severity Rate is extremely high. This would indicate that while not many injuries occur at this facility, when accidents do occur, they are serious. If the Severity Rate were to continue to increase, an accident may eventually result in a fatality.

The reason so much emphasis has been placed on explaining the various injury reports is that many managers and supervisors do not understand the importance of these records. It is not uncommon for organizations which do not have a formal safety department to fail to properly record and understand the reporting requirements. It is not the purpose of this manual to make security officers experts in accident recordkeeping. If, however, security personnel can fill an existing void at their place of work and serve as a valuable source of information, then they will have improved their credibility among management.

Loss Control/Loss Prevention

Security departments can provide a valuable resource in more areas than just simply the knowledge of OSHA recordkeeping requirements. A Loss Control or Loss Prevention philosophy is one where accidents which cause a financial loss are prevented. Since not all accidents will be prevented, those accidents which do occur should attempt to be controlled to minimize financial loss. Loss Control has a direct impact on an organization's profits. Accidents increase an organization's expenses. When expenses are greater than revenue, a company suffers a financial loss. Companies which continue to experience financial losses will ultimately be forced to go out of business.

In many organizations security professionals play a key role in Loss Control as first aid responders and members

---

Notes

A high Severity Rate means that besides many injuries being serious, employees miss a lot of work when injured. Since employers have to pay for these injuries with workers' compensation, accident insurance and replacement workers, severity rate is extremely important.

Loss Control: Management philosophy to minimize or control losses.

Loss Prevention: Management philosophy to avoid losses from occurring.

of a facility's emergency/recovery teams. Comprehensive emergency/recovery plans establish an organization's system for dealing with emergencies. Formal identification of possible emergency situations will enable management to develop realistic recovery plans which will expedite return to normal operations after an emergency. Many times security personnel are an integral part of emergency response and first aid teams. (See further information in the Emergency Preparedness module.)

In many organizations, emergencies will happen. How well a company has planned, organized and trained will decide how serious the emergency becomes. Therefore, those that want to keep losses to a minimum should take measures before an emergency occurs.

First, management should identify the types of emergencies the organization should prepare for, using a list of potential emergencies, such as fire, explosion, hazardous chemical spill/release, internal/external leaks of explosives or flammable gas, severe or multiple injuries, natural disasters (hurricane, floods, earthquake, tornado, etc.). Once a list of potential emergencies has been assembled, procedures can be developed to deal with each one. The procedures should include:

- What Can be Done?
- What Equipment is Necessary?
- What People are Needed?

Procedures should be kept in an Emergency Manual. The manual would contain all information necessary to respond to each emergency, and would include such information as:

- building floor plans showing utility lines, means of egress, fire fighting equipment
- diagrams of important chemical or utility systems, and fire extinguishing systems
- telephone numbers of key company personnel, police fire, civil defense, town/city and county services (water, electrical, phone, etc.)

- chemical spill procedures
- evacuation procedures
- names and phone numbers of outside contractors who can assist with special problems

An emergency response team should be assembled to assist in the preparation of the manual, and to react professionally when an emergency arises. Teams must be trained both in the classroom and with practice drills to make sure that everyone understands their role and the equipment to be used. To expect employees to expose themselves to hazards during emergencies without adequate training or safety equipment is not prudent and would complicate, not control, the problem(s).

If security officers are called upon to respond to first aid emergencies, they should be familiar with the OSHA regulation 1910.1030, Occupational Exposure to Bloodborne Pathogens. This regulation became effective on March 6, 1992, and requires precautions for employees who may be exposed to blood or other potentially infectious materials. This regulation requires an exposure control plan, employee training, recordkeeping, review of possible engineering to minimize or eliminate exposures, personal protective equipment, hepatitis B vaccinations, post exposure follow-ups, signs and labeling and housekeeping controls.

Insurance

Depending upon the losses and regulations of the state where a company operates its business, insurance will generally consist of one of the following:

1. The company insures loss through a private insurance company.
2. The company is self-insured; it sets aside money to pay for losses.
3. The company insures loss through a state fund.

The size of the company and its financial condition will determine, in large part, which type of insurance program they will have.

Notes

Especially security officers who work in hospitals or those who are expected to administer first aid or CPR may be required to comply with all of the sections of the OSHA regulation.

Review AIDS chapter for further information.

Companies insure their business against financial losses from the some of the areas which include:

1. Workers' Compensation
2. Comprehensive Public Liability
3. Product Liability
4. Fire
5. Business Interruption
6. Automobile Damage

Workers Compensation

Employee on-the-job accidents are covered by a Workers' Compensation policy. Basically, if an employee is injured as a part of their job, their medical expenses will be paid, and they may also receive a portion of their normal weekly salary. Workers' Compensation benefits for injuries are usually scheduled by law. The different types of disabilities are normally:

1. **Death** - fatality due to an occupational injury or illness.
2. **Permanent Total Disability** - the employee is unable work in any type of employment.
3. **Permanent Partial Disability** - loss of a member or part of a member of the body or a permanent injury which partially prevents the employee from doing his or any other job.
4. **Temporary Total Disability** - temporarily impairs the employee from performing his regular job or any other job.
5. **Temporary Partial Disability** - temporarily impairs the employee's ability to work at his job.

Most states set "schedules" with a specific limit of compensation for permanent partial disabilities or loss of use or amputation of body parts. Employees who suffer work related injuries with **permanent partial disabilities** are awarded dollar amounts based upon a percentage for a specific number of weeks. **Permanent Total Disabilities and Temporary Total Disabilities** are usually compensated for as long as the disability exists or for a long period such as 500 weeks. Employees who accept the award may still be able to

Notes

Does your employer pay the workers' compensation insurance to the state, to a private company, or are they "self-insured."? "Self-insured" companies pay for losses directly with little or no insurance in effect.

Schedules: *Determined by state workers' compensation agency which identifies the financial compensation afforded as a result of a specific injury or illness.*

receive additional dollars if they can prove their employer acted with negligence or malice in not preventing the injury. To reduce minor injury claims, most states require a minimum waiting period of three to seven calendar days (including Saturday and Sunday) of time lost from the job, before allowing for any compensation for lost wages. Medical expenses are paid from the inception of the injury. Most states also require an employee to report an injury to his employer within two years.

Finally, for those employees who have suffered severe injuries, rehabilitation centers have been established either by the state or by private enterprises. These centers may rehabilitate the injured employee or provide for new job skills training.

Security Investigators are utilized by many organizations to verify injury claims by employees which may appear to be false. Often, an investigator will conduct surveillance of the injured person which will normally include videotaping the person's movements. Fraud is a serious problem affecting workers' compensation plans. By verifying the actions of the injured party, objective data is usually obtained which will either support of disprove the injury claim.

Comprehensive Public/Product Liability

Because companies deal not only with employees but with customers as well, many businesses maintain liability insurance. Most liability insurance has two types of coverage, bodily injury and property damage.

Companies who make or sell products to vendors who sell them to retailers or directly to the customer, will generally maintain product liability insurance. Product liability insurance provides protection for a company against claims for bodily injury or death to any person by reason of consumption, handling, or use of any product produced or distributed. A manufacturer may be held liable for conditions in the product produced which causes injury to persons or damage to property. Liability for injury or damage is increased when products such as drugs or medicine are found to be inherently dangerous.

Notes

Many companies with proprietary security departments hire employees who were injured in the factory to work as security officers.

Some employees may act as if they were injured when they were not, in order to receive financial assistance.

Liability Insurance: Protects a person or company from financial claims resulting from alleged actions which cause injury to another party.

Automotive manufacturers, toy makers, medical companies, airlines, etc. all maintain some type of product liability insurance.

Virtually all security guard companies are required by the states where they do business to provide a comprehensive General Liability policy which provides financial protection in the event damages occur which are the result of actions (or failure to act) on the part of security employees. Usually, these policies financially protect a security company against charges of false imprisonment, assault and battery, emotional distress, etc. Security companies pay insurance premiums for General Liability Insurance Policies. Premiums ranging from $500,000 - $5,000,000 per year in coverage are common in the security industry.

Security's Role in Safety

Far too often, security managers have failed to recognize or understand the important role that security personnel can provide in an organization's safety/loss control program. This module on safety is not intended to transform security officers into Certified Safety Professionals. It is believed, however, that the information presented will at a minimum allow for security personnel to provide a resource to their organization in performing essential safety functions and safety awareness. If security officers impress or educate a client, manager, or employee with their understanding and awareness of an effective safety program, their credibility will be enhanced.

Finally, if security officers' interest in Safety/Loss Control is heightened, they should consider obtaining further training in the profession.

Notes

General Liability Insurance for security companies is very expensive. Security companies who have hiring and training standards and programs will pay less for insurance than companies who do no do a good job when hiring security officers or who have no training program.

Security departments must continually strive to assume more responsibility in areas which may be outside the general, recognized and accepted role of security in the past. Security personnel who are able to give a "value-added" service to their employer (i.e. safety) will go a long way to insuring their job security.

Safety Summary

Safety management is a fast-growing industry in large part because of the implementation of the Occupational Safety & Health Act (OSHA) of 1971. This law established the Occupational Safety and Health Administration (OSHA) which requires businesses to provide a "safe and healthful" workplace for all employees.

Many organizations have a formal safety program in order to comply with OSHA that the workplace is free of recognized hazards that may cause death or serious injury.

The role of security officers in safety programs has generally been limited, however in recent years many safety managers have recognized the role of security as a resource. Security officers can inspect and report potential safety problems.

The Occupational Safety & Health Administration is a division of the Federal Department of Labor. Workplaces may be inspected by OSHA Compliance Officers "without delay and at reasonable times." Employees can request an OSHA inspection by writing the agency. OSHA is under no obligation to report the identity of the employee who made the complaint. A company is not permitted to take any actions against an employee who filed a complaint with OSHA.

f during an inspection, the OSHA inspector finds an alleged violation of any safety standard, a formal report or citation will be issued. Serious violations carry a mandatory civil penalty of up to $7,000. Other-than-serious alleged violations typically do not result in penalties, but can carry a penalty of up to $7,000 also.

OSHA regulations require all establishments to maintain records of recordable injuries and illnesses. In recent years several large companies have received heavy fines for allegedly misrepresenting OSHA recordable injuries. Recordable Incidence, Lost Workday Case, and Lost Workday Rates enable companies to measure their safety performance and the effectiveness of their safety program.

Security departments can be a valuable resource in a company's overall loss prevention program.

Insurance provides financial protection for a company against claims of Workers' Compensation, public liability, product liability, fire, business interruption and automobile damage.

Workers' Compensation insurance pays the residual expenses and a portion of an employee's weekly pay if an on-the-job accident occurred. Workers' Compensation benefits for injuries are usually scheduled by law and include: death, permanent total disability, permanent partial disability. Most states require a minimum waiting period of three to seven calendar days of time lost from the job before allowing for any compensation for lost wages. Medical expenses are paid from the date of the injury.

Most companies carry liability insurance for bodily injury and property damage. Companies who make or sell products which are sold to the public will often have product liability insurance. This protects a company against claims for injury or death caused by the product.

Besides General Liability insurance, most companies carry fire insurance. Insurance rates for fire are based on the value of the contents of the building plus a rating given by the Fire Rating Organization.

Notes

Questions

1. What does the acronym OSHA the abbreviation stand for?

    _____

2. The OSHA Law requires that all employers provide employees with:

    a. Well paying jobs with insurance benefits
    b. A "safe" workplace
    c. First Aid training
    d. A "Safe and Healthful" workplace

3. Employers are required to post the official statute regarding OSHA. True/False

4. According to the author, the role of security officers in many organizations is:

    a. limited
    b. not limited
    c. not well defined
    d. receiving more emphasis
    e. a,c,d.

5. Federal OSHA Compliance Officers work for:

    a. The Congress
    b. The Secretary of HEW
    c. The Secretary of Labor
    d. The Secretary of Commerce

6. Employees may request an OSHA inspection by:

    a. notifying management
    b. majority vote by all employees
    c. notifying OSHA in writing
    d. telephoning the Secretary of HEW

7. The Labor Department must reveal to an employer the name of the employee who made the initial complaint. True/False

8. An employee can be terminated for asking for an inspection. True/False

9.   Whenever an OSHA Compliance Officer finds a violation of any safety hazard a
        _____ may be issued to the employer

        a. ticket
        b. citation
        c. reward
        d. penance

10.   An organization can be fined up to $_____ a day for not complying with an OSHA
        inspection report

        a. $50
        b. $1,000
        c. $7,000
        d. $70,000

11.   Criminal willful violations of any standard can result in a penalty of _____.
        and a punishment of _____ in jail against an executive of the organization

        a. $ 7,000 /3 months
        b. $10,000 /3 months
        c. $ 1,000 /6 months
        d. $70,000 /6 months

12.   Companies have _____ working days to appeal OSHA violations

        a. 10
        b. 15
        c. 20
        d. 1

13.   What are the three types of accident/injury rates that OSHA requires companies to
        monitor?

1._____

2._____

3._____

14.   The 200,000 hours used in the OSHA injury rates formula equate to 100 full-time workers who work 40 hours per week, 50 weeks per year. True/False

15.   The Lost Workday Case Incidence Rate measure only the number of injuries or illnesses which resulted in time missed from work. True/False

16.   What does Lost Workday or Severity rate measure?

_____

17.   Loss Control or Loss Prevention are terms which describe a philosophy of attempting to prevent or reduce financial loss. True/False

18.   Companies will generally have insurance to protect their business from financial loss against

1. _____

2. _____

3. _____

4. _____

19.   Name the five types of Workers' Compensation disabilities which are usually scheduled by states.

1. _____

2. _____

3. _____

4. _____

5. _____

20.   Usually Workers' Compensation insurance takes effect immediately after an injury. True/False

21.   Name the two types of liability insurance.

1. _____

2. _____

Practical Exercises and Questions

1.   Who is the person responsible for safety at the facility where you work?

2.   Who maintains all of the OSHA records?

3.   Are the OSHA incidence rates publicized and well known by most employees?

4.   Are security personnel utilized for observation, inspection and reporting as part of the overall safety program?

5.   What safety hazards exist for security personnel while performing their job duties?

Bureau of Labor Statistics
Log and Summary of Occupational
Injuries and Illnesses

NOTE: This form is required by Public Law 91-506 and must be kept in the establishment for 5 years. Failure to maintain and post can result in the issuance of citations an assessment of penalties. (See posting requirements on the other side of form.)

RECORDABLE CASES: You are required to record information about every occupational death; every nonfatal occupational illness; and those nonfatal occupational injuries that involve one or more of the following: loss of consciousness, restrictions of work or motion, transfer to another job, or medical treatment (other than first aid). (See definitions on the other side of form.)

Case or File Number	Date of Injury or Onset of Illness	Employee's Name	Ocupation	Department	Description of injury or illness
Enter a nonduplication number that will facilitate comparis on s with suppleme ntary records.	Enter Mo./day.	Enter first name or initial, middle initial, last name.	Enter regular job title, not activity employee was performing when injured or at onset of illness. In the absence of a formal title, enter a brief description of the employee's duties	Enter department in which the employee is regularly employed or a description of normal workplace to which employee is assigned, even though temporarily working in another department at the time or injury or illness.	Enter a brief description of the injury or illness and indicate the part or parts of body affected.

Typical entries for this column might beL Amputation of 1st joint right forefinger; Strain of lower back; contact dermatitis on both hands; Electrocution—body. |
(A)	(B)	(C)	(D)	(E)	(F)

OSHA NO. 200

215

U.S. Department of Labor

For Calendar Year 19 _____   Page ____ of ____

Form Approved
O.M.B. No. 44R 1453

| Company Name |
| Establishment Name |
| Establishment Address |

Extent of and Outcome of INJURY

Type, Extent of, and Outcome of ILLNESS

Fatalities	Nonfatal Injuries					Type of Illness							Fatalities	Nonfatal Illnesses				
Injury Related	Injuries With Lost Workdays				Injuries Without Lost Workdays	CHECK Only One Column for Each Illness (See other side of form for terminations or permanent transfers.)							Illness Related	Illnesses With Lost Workdays				Illnesses Without Lost Workdays
Enter DATE of death. Mo./day/yr.	Enter a CHECK if injury involves days away from work, or days of restricted work activity, or both.	Enter number of DAYS away from work.	Enter number of DAYS of restricted work activity.		Enter a CHECK if no entry was made in columns 1 or 2 but the injury is recordable as defined above.	Occupational skin diseases or disorders	Dust diseases of the lungs	Respiratory conditions due to toxic agents	Poisoning (systemic effects of toxic materials)	Disorders due to physical agents	Disorders associated with repeated trauma	All other occupational illnesses	Enter DATE of death. Mo./day/yr.	Enter a CHECK if illness involves days away from work, or days of restricted work activity, or both.	Enter a CHECK if illness involves days away from work.	Enter number of DAYS away from work.	Enter number of DAYS of restricted work activity.	Enter a CHECK if no entry was made in columns 8 or 9.
(1)	(2)	(3)	(4)	(5)	(6)	(a)	(b)	(c)	(d)	(e)	(f)	(g)	(8)	(9)	(10)	(11)	(12)	(13)

ILLNESSES

INJURIES

Certification of Annual Summary Totals By _____ Title _____ Date _____

OSHA No. 200

POST ONLY THIS PORTION OF THE LAST PAGE NO LATER THAN FEBRUARY 1.

FOLD

216

THE EFFECTIVE SECURITY OFFICERS TRAINING MANUAL

Chapter XII

AIDS & HIV

Human Immunodeficiency Virus (HIV) & Acquired Immune Deficiency Syndrome

Acquired immune deficiency syndrome (AIDS), an infectious and fatal disease first diagnosed in 1981, has within its first decade become a devastating epidemic. In the United States (U.S.) 115,984 people with AIDS have dies; this is 63% of all U.S. AIDS cases reported through June 30, 1991, (Centers for Disease Control (CDC), 1991, p.13). According to CDC 1991 estimates between 0.8 and 1.2 million, approximately 1 out of every 250 individuals, in the U.S. now has the human immunodeficiency virus (HIV) infection, which causes AIDS. The incubation period from HIV infection to AIDS can take 10 to 12 years during which time people are infectious but often asymptotic and unaware of their HIV infection. The discovery of the virus, HIV, in 1984 and the scientific knowledge gained from the subsequent study of the HIV have significantly changed the medical community across the country. This knowledge about AIDS/HIV disease is now also requiring sweeping changes in our society's educational, psychosocial, legal, and penal systems.

What Causes AIDS?
AIDS is caused by the HIV virus. AIDS is the most advanced stage of infection with HIV. Although HIV has been found in several body fluids, only blood, semen, and the vaginal secretions have been proven in spreading the infection. HIV infects the cells of the immune system. When the HIV enters the bloodstream, it begins to attack certain white blood cells, the T-lymphocytes. Substances called antibodies are produced by the body to fight the virus. A simple blood test can detect these antibodies within a period of 2 weeks to 6 months after infection. (Nevertheless, during this period between a person's having become infected and getting a positive test result, as well as forever after, the person can still infect others through unprotected sexual contacts and through blood to blood contacts.) The antibodies cannot stop the HIV from multiplying. HIV eventually destroys the person's immune system, leaving him or her vulnerable to opportunistic infections, which may eventually cause death. One of the most common opportunistic infections contracted by persons is a severe type of pneumonia.

Notes

Reading For A Purpose
Look for these key words:
- AIDS   • HIV
- PCP   • KS
- AIDS Myths
- T-Lymphocytes

Look for the answers to these
    Questions:
1. What are the symptoms of AIDS?
2. How does AIDS kill?
3. How does a person avoid contracting AIDS?
4. How does a health-care worker protect him or herself from the trans mission of AIDS from one person to another?
5. Will everyone who has contracted the HIV/AIDS die within a few years?

HIV: Human Immunodeficiency Virus -- virus infection that causes AIDS.

T-lymphocytes: certain white blood cells which are first attacked when the HIV virus enters the bloodstream.

Pneunocystis carinii pneumonia (PCP) very rarely occurs among individuals with normally functioning immune systems. Kapose's sarcoma (KS), a type of cancer, also occurs frequently among AIDS infected persons.

As many as 60% of AIDS patients have neurologic symptoms, which may be due to opportunistic infections, cancer, or infection of the brain by HIV. These symptoms may include motor problems, inability to concentrate, and memory loss, progressing to severe mental deterioration.

Why or how the AIDS virus moved to man no one knows, but when it did it embarked on an intercontinental killing spree. Apparently the AIDS virus lurked in the United States for several years before it was noticed. Finally, in 1981, the killer disease was identified in Los Angeles and New York. Then in 1984, researchers in France and the U.S. independently reported isolating and identifying the virus causing AIDS.

The term AIDS is a shortened version of Acquired Immune Deficiency Syndrome. With AIDS, the normal functioning of the immune system is severely impaired, and victims become vulnerable to infections and other diseases that rarely affect the average person.

Acquired	Refers to a disease that is not genetic, inherited or contracted from the environment
Immune	Refers to body's protection system against any particular disease
Deficiency	Refers to a gap in the body's immune system which leads to an increase in illnesses
Syndrome	Refers to a set of symptoms which occur together

HOW DOES ONE GET AIDS?

Homosexuals - Approximately 75% of those individuals affected by AIDS have been homosexual or bisexual. However, heterosexual women and men who have not been IV drug users or exposed to blood products can and have developed AIDS.

Notes

Pneunocystis carinii pneumonia: a severe strain of pneumonia that is difficult to catch with a normally functioning immune system.

Kapose's sarcoma: a type of cancer that occurs frequently among AIDS infected persons.

Intravenous Drug Users - This is a growing category of concern because addicts are so prone to carelessly use contaminated syringes and needles when in a hurry to get a fix.

Persons who Receive Unscreened Blood Products - Fortunately, since testing has been introduced for all blood products, this category has been reduced to a very small number.

Babies of AIDS-Infected Mothers - The HIV virus can be passed from mother to child before birth, at birth or through nursing.

IS THERE A BLOOD TEST FOR AIDS?

Laboratory test can detect antibodies to the HIV virus, thus identifying carriers and screening blood products for AIDS exposure.

HOW LONG DOES IT TAKE FOR AN HIV BLOOD TEST TO SHOW POSITIVE?

There is no sure answer for this question, but approximately six months' time is frequently required, after exposure to the HIV virus, for antibodies to be detected on the HIV blood test. However, the person's body fluids can infect another person during this time.

DO ALL PERSONS CARRYING HIV VIRUSES GET AIDS DISEASE?

While all carriers are contagious and may pass the virus on through blood or semen, it is probable that not all carriers will actually develop the AIDS disease. The best estimates at this time are that between 50% and 90% will develop AIDS, but is must be stressed that there is not enough history to say emphatically that the number will not be 100%.

ARE ALL PERSONS WHO ARE CARRYING THE HIV VIRUS INFECTIOUS?

Yes, whether or not they have any symptoms of the AIDS disease itself and whether or not enough time has elapsed for them to show a positive blood test. Once infected, a person is infectious for the rest of his or her life.

Notes

Some persons have contacted the HIV virus or AIDS through blood transfusions. For the past several years, donated blood has been tested to screen for the HIV virus and AIDS.

HOW LONG DOES IT TAKE FOR SYMPTOMS OR AIDS DISEASE TO APPEAR?

The answer is simply not known. Initially, it was felt that the disease would become apparent within six months to ten years after exposure to the virus, but it probably is a threat for the lifetime of the individual.

HOW IS AIDS TRANSMITTED?

A. *Sexual Activity* —Rectal sex is the most common cause of sexual transmission because the lining of the rectum, unlike the lining of the vagina, is not made to withstand sexual intercourse and will tear and bleed easily. However transmission through vaginal and oral sex is not only possible, it is happening with alarming frequency.

THE RUGGED VAGINAL MUCOSA

The vagina is lined with multiple layers of tough, fluid-proof squamous cells which allow it to withstand childbirth and intercourse without injury can block entry of the HIV virus. Nonetheless, heterosexual women are more at risk than heterosexual men because of how easily the vaginal wall can be abrased.

THE FRAGILE RECTAL MUCOSA

The rectum and colon are lined with a single layer of fragile, permeable, columnar-shaped cells which allow absorption of fluids into the bloodstream. These cells tear and bleed easily, providing immediate access into the bloodstream for the HIV virus.

B. *IV Drug Abuse* —Intravenous drug abusers can be exposed to the AIDS virus through blood-contaminated needles or syringes. It is extremely important that clean, disposable needles and syringes be used at all times by addicts or anyone receiving a hypodermic needle injection.

C. *Other Causes*

HETEROSEXUALS HAVING SEX WITH AIDS CARRIERS

The potential for the spread of AIDS by heterosexual intercourse can be as high as homosexual intercourse if unprotected sex is engaged in. In vaginal sex, transmission of the HIV virus is more limited but can occur. Persons who originally acquire the HIV virus through vaginal, heterosexual intercourse constitute a very small percentage of the AIDS patient population, with women outnumbering men by 3 to 1. It should be noted that some populations of female prostitutes carry a percentage of positive AIDS tests of over 50%. The majority of those who test positive have been IV drug users, but rectal and oral sex practices are also common among prostitutes.

BABIES BORN TO MOTHERS WHO CARRY THE HIV VIRUS

PERSONS RECEIVING UNSCREENED AIDS-CONTAMINATED BLOOD PRODUCTS

WHAT SHOULD YOU KNOW ABOUT THE HIV VIRUS?

The HIV virus lives in several fluids contained in the body but is transmitted through the blood, semen and vaginal fluids. If transmission occurs during sexual activity, the virus goes from one person to another through the vagina, penis, mouth or rectum. Up to one in three people exposed to the virus through rectal sex or IV drug use may develop AIDS, according to the National Cancer Institute. This is much higher than reported by early studies.

For all its ferocity, except for rectal sex and IV drug use, AIDS is relatively hard to get. The virus is very fragile outside the body and is quickly killed by heat, drying and disinfectant chemicals. This explains why AIDS is not spread through casual contact such as handshaking, hugging, drinking from common glasses, using toilet seats, etc.

Notes

WHAT ARE THE SYMPTOMS OF AIDS?

AIDS is a complex illness that develops gradually over time, and any of its symptoms can occur with many other diseases. The presence of any of these signs does not in itself indicate AIDS, but persons in high-risk groups with these symptoms should be alerted to see a physician.

WEIGHT LOSS
Loss of 10 pounds or more in two months, that does not appear to be related to a known cause.

FEVER
Elevated temperature or night sweats unrelated to a cold or other infection, that do not improve on their own.

FATIGUE

Severe fatigue that persists for no known reason, despite normal periods of rest and adequate diet.

PERSISTENT DIARRHEA
With no apparent cause.

SHORTNESS OF BREATH
Unassociated with exertion and especially associated with a dry cough unrelated to smoking.

SORES
In mouth, nose or anus that don't quickly heal.

ENLARGED LYMPH NODES
Swollen glands in the groin, neck, or armpit not associated with injuries or infections.

HOW DOES AIDS KILL?

The HIV virus does not in itself damage organs. By overwhelming the immune system, the virus permits a variety of infections, cancers and other diseases the opportunity to spread throughout the body, eventually resulting in death. These "opportunistic" infections are the hallmark of the presence of AIDS and are listed here in order of frequency of occurrence.

1. *Pneumocystis carinii is a lung infection caused by parasites.* Under normal conditions this pneumonia occurs only in cancer or transplant patients taking drugs which suppress immunity.

2. *Kaposi's sarcoma is an especially virulent skin cancer.* This normally rare cancer usually arises in the skin and produces characteristic purplish blotches or bumps before it spreads internally.

3. *Candidiasis is a fungal infection that commonly affects the mouth, esophagus and vagina of AIDS victims.*

4. *Cryptococcosis is a fungal infection that can cause meningitis* (infection of the brain and spinal cord).

5. *Cytomegalovirus infections can cause meningitis and colitis.* They are usually detectable in AIDS victims' blood.

6. Atypical bacterial infections can crop up anywhere in the body. A frequently seen infection is one which infects the bone marrow and liver.

6. *Herpes simplex is a virus that can cause ulcerating anal and oral herpes sores.* Any viral infection may attack AIDS patients, but herpes infections of the skin, mouth or genitalia are common.

7. *Cryptosporidiosis is an organism that causes prolonged diarrhea.*

8. *Toxoplasmosis is caused by protozoa that infect the brain and lungs.*

HOW TO AVOID AIDS IN YOUR LIFE

- DO NOT engage in anal sexual intercourse
- DO NOT have sex with multiple partners or persons who have had multiple partners
- DO NOT have any type of sexual contact with persons known or suspected of carrying the AIDS virus
- DO NOT participate in IV drug use and do not have sex with persons who do
- DO NOT use inhalant nitrates (poppers). Their role as a co-factor for Kaposi-Sarcoma in persons with the AIDS virus is being investigated.
- DO NOT engage in recreational drug and alcohol abuse. These activities are strongly associated with non-compliance with safe-sex techniques designed to prevent the spread of AIDS.

- Communicate with partner concerning past sexual history
- Always use latex condoms
- Avoid any sex that may cause injury or bleeding
- Avoid anal genital contact
- Avoid open-mouth, intimate kissing when open sores exist in the mouth
- Avoid contact with any body fluids (semen, blood, feces, urine, saliva)

EXPLODING THE MYTHS

None of these activities will transmit AIDS:

Working with AIDS carriers
Eating with AIDS carriers
Hugging AIDS carriers
Sharing restroom facilities
Drinking from common glasses
Touching common fixtures
Swimming in public pools
Petting animals

PREVENTING TRANSMISSION OF AIDS TO HEALTH-CARE WORKERS AND PERSONS CARING FOR AIDS VICTIMS

ALL PERSONS whether they are suspected of carrying AIDS or not, especially those in emergency care settings in which the risk of blood exposure and infection is increased, should be treated with these precautions:

• Gloves should be worn for touching blood and body fluids, mucous membranes, or non-intact skin of all patients for handling items or services soiled with blood or body fluids and for performing venipuncture and other vascular access procedures.

• Masks and protective eye wear or face shields should be worn during procedures that are likely to generate droplets of blood or other body fluids to prevent exposure of mucous membranes of the mouth, nose and eyes.

• Gowns or aprons should be worn during procedures that are likely to generate splashes of blood or other body fluids.

• Hands and other skin surfaces should be washed immediately and thoroughly if contaminated with blood or other body fluids. Hands should be washed immediately after gloves are removed.

• All health-care workers should take precautions to prevent injuries caused by needles, scalpels and other sharp instruments or devices.

• Although saliva has not been indicated in AIDS transmission, to minimize the need for emergency, mouth-to-mouth resuscitation, mouth pieces, resuscitation bags or other ventilation devices should be available for use in areas where the need is predictable.

• Health-care workers who have sores or weeping dermatitis should refrain from all direct patient contact and from handling patient-care equipment.

• Pregnant health-care workers are not known to be at a greater risk of contacting AIDS, but during pregnancy, the infant is at risk resulting from prenatal transmission. Because of this risk, pregnant workers should be especially familiar with and strictly adhere to precautions.

Activities that have no risk of transmitting HIV include:
- Living in the same home or apartment with an HIV-infected person
- Hugging, touching, shaking hands, or other casual contact with an HIV-infected person
- Sharing a car, a bus, or a waiting room with an HIV-infected person

What Scientific Progress Has Been Made in Understanding AIDS/HIV?

Since the first recognition of AIDS/HIV disease, the scientific response has been dramatic. Despite accomplishments (a) there is no ready cure for AIDS/HIV, (b) there is not vaccine to prevent HIV infection, and (c) AIDS/HIV disease remains uniformly fatal in its most advanced stages.

Reference:
The above sections on "Understanding AIDS/HIV Disease" were adapted from the Columbus/Franklin County AIDS Community Plant 1989-1990 (Columbus AIDS Community Advisory Coalition, 1989, pp. 54-56) with the permission of the Columbus Health Department.

Notes

1. _____ refers to a disease that is not genetic.

    a. Required
    b. Immune
    c. Acquired
    d. Deficient

2. Refers to the body's protection system against any particular disease:

    a. susceptible
    b. acquired
    c. immune
    d. deficient

3. Refers to a gap in the body's immune system which leads to an increase in illness:

    a. deficiency
    b. immune
    c. susceptibility
    d. acquired

4. Refers to a set of symptoms which occur together:

    a. calamity
    b. syndrome
    c. paladrone
    d. synopsis

5. Which of the following does not belong with those most likely to contract AIDS?

    a. homosexuals
    b. Intrvenous Drug Users
    c. Babies of AIDS infected mothers
    d. persons who practice "safe sex"

6. What percent of carriers will develop AIDS?

    a. between 10-20%
    b. between 20-50%
    c. between 50-90%
    d. Between 75-100%

7. How long of a period of time is AIDS at threat to an individual who has contracted the HIV virus?

    a. 10 years
    b. a lifetime
    c. 1 year
    d. 50 years

8. Some populations of female prostitutes carry a percentage of positive AIDS tests of over _____%

    a. 60
    b. 50
    c. 100
    d. 10

9. Which of the following is not a sympotoms of AIDS?

    a. fatigue
    b. enlarged lymph glands
    c. fever
    d. weight gain

10. Which of the following will not transmit the HIV virus?

    a. sharing restroom facilities
    b. anal intercourse
    c. drug abuse
    d. sexual contact with suspected AIDS carriers

THE EFFECTIVE SECURITY OFFICERS TRAINING MANUAL

Chapter XIII

Emergency Preparedness

Emergency Preparedness

Security officers can provide a valuable service in a facility's overall Emergency Preparedness plan. While many organizations have a formal, well-developed plan which addresses many emergencies which may occur, there are still many businesses, particularly those which are small, that do not have formal written plans which direct employees and arriving emergency services personnel. Therefore, if a security officer or student of this manual realizes that the organization where they work is lacking a formal Emergency Preparedness plan, a valuable service can be offered!

Role of Security in an Emergency

Generally, security personnel will plan an active, key role in any emergency situation. Security officers may be called upon to notify local emergency services of an emergency, assist in the evacuation of personnel, render first aid to injured employees, announce emergency instructions over the public address system, or in certain situations, the security officer on duty may be required to assume primary responsibility for initiating the emergency response.

Additionally, security officers can provide a key role in the overall planning and development of the emergency plan, the testing of the plan, coordinating in any follow-up action required, provide a resource for information such as maps, diagrams, etc. of the facility, and in general, assist in anyway possible.

Overview of the Emergency Preparedness Plan

In planning any response to an emergency the first question which must be addressed is in identifying the objectives of the plan. Generally, the overall objective of any emergency plan is to:

1. protect the lives of all employees, visitors, and nearby residents of the facility.

Notes

Reading For A Purpose
Look for these key words:
• Emergency Plan Coordinator
• Emergency Preparedness Team
• CPR   • Search
• Watch   • Warning
• Evacuation   • MSDS
• Bloodborne Pathogens
• Right-to-know

Look for the answers to these
      Questions:
1. What are the objectives of any
      emergency plan?
2. How could an organization
      begin to develop an
      emergency plan?
3. What is security's role in
      fire prevention?
4. Should security personnel
      become involved in
      developing emergency
      plans if none exist?
5. Should a total evacuation of a
      facility be ordered after
      receipt of a bomb threat?

Security's role in an emergency:
1. notify outside emergency
      services (police, fire)
2. assist in evacuation
3. give first aid
4. announce instructions
5. direct the response

If a plan has not been developed, security personnel should start one.

2. protect all property and physical assets belonging to the organization.

3. provide a minimum amount of disruption in the daily operation of the business and to restore the daily routine and operation of the business as soon as possible.

4. provide outside agencies such as local police and fire departments with information and resources which allow them to carry-out their duties and responsibilities without delay.

Development of the Emergency Plan

Organizations which fail to take the necessary time to properly prepare for an emergency, will normally suffer greater loss and possible embarrassment during an emergency than those organizations which have a well defined, comprehensive, and tested emergency plan. The following elements are essential for any plan:

1. The plan must be written.
2. The plan must identify objectives and what emergencies will be addressed:
    a. Fire
    b. Serious Injury
    c. Tornado/Severe Weather
    d. Flood
    e. Winter Storm
    f. Bomb Threat
    g. Civil Disturbance
    h. Chemical Spill

This section will address certain emergencies. Other emergencies such as earthquakes will be similar in pre-emergency planning.

3. An Emergency Plan Director or Coordinator must be identified as the person primarily responsible for initiating the plan. Each shift must have a designated coordinator and alternates in the event of absence from the facility by the primary coordinator.

Notes

Are copies of the plan easily made available for quick reference?

230

4. An Emergency Preparedness Team should be formed on each shift comprised of both hourly and salary employees who would provide the following services during an emergency:

a. Extinguishment of small fires.
b. Assist in evacuating the facility.
c. Assist in the search of the facility during a bomb threat.
d. Assist in the orderly shut-down of electricity and/or machinery.
e. Provide first aid to injured persons.
f. Assist arriving emergency services units in entering the facility.
g. Assist in clean-up procedures after the emergency.

FIRE

The first step in the preplanning process in identifying what response is needed in a fire situation, is to have a well-developed and written Fire Prevention plan which minimizes the exposure to fire. This plan should include written policies which address:

1. the need to keep all areas clear and free of combustible material.

2. the need to keep all aisles and hallways clear of obstructions which would restrict egress in an evacuation.

3. enforcement of "No Smoking" policy.

4. the monthly inspection and repair of all fire equipment including extinguishers, fire pumps, fire hoses, etc.

5. the duties of each employee during a fire emergency.

Notes

Training of all personnel assigned to an emergency preparedness team must comply with any federal, state or local regulations which address emergencies

To be effective, a fire prevention plan must be supported by all employees, especially those in management

Responsibilities

After a plan has been written which addresses fire emergencies this plan should be communicated to all employees and every member of the Emergency Team must know their assignment and who their identified alternate is in the event of an absence from work. Department managers, supervisors, foremen, and secretaries should be trained as "Fire Marshals" who will assist during an emergency.

1. Have Fire Marshals assist in developing evacuation maps and drawings which quickly and easily identify to all employees and visitors where they must go during an evacuation. Evacuation maps should be prevalent and visible throughout the facility.

2. Fire Aid kits should be obtained and strategically located throughout the facility.

3. An "In-House" Fire Brigade should be formed and trained in the use of fire extinguishers and possibly 1 1/2" fire hoses. Personal Protective Equipment such as fire helmets, coats, gloves, boots, face shields, and self-contained breathing apparatus (air-paks) may be required if fire brigade members are expected to do more than just extinguish small fires which can be extinguished with fire extinguishers. Depending on the duties required, fire brigade members may need to undergo annual physical examinations.

Security Responsibilities

Generally, security personnel will have primary responsibility for initiating the emergency evacuation alarm and contacting the local fire department to respond to the facility. In addition, security personnel will often be assigned to monitor special fire protection equipment such as fire pumps to be certain they operate as required.

Additional Responsibilities

Besides what has been previously addressed the following elements of the Fire Emergency plan must be addressed:

Notes

For each person who has an assigned responsibility, a back-up or alternate must be identified and trained.

Fire Marshals will assist employees in the event of a fire emergency.

Most businesses decide that their employees will attempt to extinguish only small fires. In the event a large fire develops, a total evacuation is often announced.

Security is often the first contact when a fire has been discovered.

1. Who will make the determination to evacuate the facility?

2. Who is responsible for communicating and answering questions of television, radio, and newspaper media personnel who respond to the facility? Will these individuals be segregated into one area in an attempt to control their access?

3. Who is responsible for notifying company officials who are not present at the facility? Is an emergency telephone call list up-to date and easily accessible?

4. Has the local fire department recently toured the facility? Have maps and diagrams of the location of hazardous material been given to them?

5. Who is responsible for testing the plan by conducting a fire drill? Who must approve the fire drill?

6. Who is responsible for writing the final report of the emergency?

7. Who is responsible for conducting follow-up on the items which need attention or follow-up after the emergency?

8. If an employee or visitor is seriously injured, what procedures will be followed in notifying their next of kin?

SERIOUS INJURY

To be adequately prepared to deal with emergencies involving serious injuries to people, security personnel should receive training in First Aid and CPR (Cardio Pulmonary Resuscitation) from a certified instructor from the American Red Cross or similar organization. The information presented in this section of The Effective Security Officer Training Manual is meant to provide only a brief introduction to the most serious injuries a security officer may encounter.

Notes

1. Normally the plant manager or shift superintendent.

2. Normally someone in public relations or personnel.

3. It is important that if more than one person is notifying individuals who are not at work about the emergency, the same exact information is relayed.

4. Most fire departments welcome the opportunity to tour a facility.

5. All plans have to be tested. It is during these drills that problem areas can be identified and addressed.

6. After the event, a report needs to be written.

7. Follow-up is essential.

8. Who will notify the relatives of injured employees?

BLEEDING

External bleeding is an injury that is the easiest for a person to identify and is one of the most serious. All adult human beings possess between five to six quarts of blood. The average, healthy adult can lose a pint of blood without any problems. A pint of blood is the amount withdrawn from a blood donor. However, if a quart or more of blood is lost rapidly, shock and possible death will most certainly occur without emergency care.

One of the best ways to treat external bleeding is to place clean material on the wound until the bleeding stops. By elevating the wound above the victim's heart, bloodflow will normally subside.

There are two major pressure points used to control bleeding. One is the brachial point in the arm and the second is the femoral point, located in the groin. These pressure points should only be used if elevation and bleeding and direct pressure have not stopped the bleeding.

SHOCK

Shock often results after a serious injury and can lead to death itself, if emergency care is not given at once. Shock occurs when the body's vital functions such as blood pressure and breathing are serious threatened. Body tissues begin to incur damage and shock begins to develop. Some signs and symptoms of shock are:

- pale or bluish and cold skin
- moist and clammy skin
- overall weakness
- vomiting
- dull, sunken eyes
- widely dilated pupils of the eye
- unusual thirst

Shock requires intensive medical treatment to be reversed. Until emergency medical assistance arrives, a security officer should attempt to:

Notes

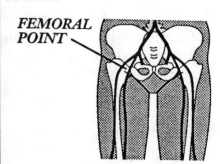

FEMORAL POINT

If necessary, use a handkerchief or clothing such as a jacket or shirt to cover the wound.

If it is necessary to use the pressure points to control bleeding, professional emergency care is needed immediately.

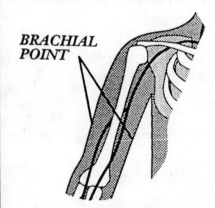

BRACHIAL POINT

- Maintain an open airway
- Control all obvious bleeding
- Elevate the legs about 12 inches unless the injury prevents this
- Place blankets over the person to prevent the loss of body heat
- Give nothing to eat or drink to the victim
- Keep the victim on his/her back unless the injury prevents this
- Handle victims gently

BREATHING

Besides excessive bleeding, a person who is not breathing is the most serious situation where emergency first aid must be administered immediately or death will result in a matter of minutes.

Upon coming to a person who is injured, tap the victim gently on the shoulder and ask them if they are O.K. If you do not receive a reply, call for "HELP" immediately. If a phone is nearby, call 9-1-1 or other number to notify the proper emergency response services.

Tilt the victim's head to open the airway, one hand goes on the victim's forehead, the other gently lifts the chin straight up. Fingers should be on the bony portion of the chin, not the throat.

Look, listen, and feel for breathing. Place your ear down and close to the victim's mouth. Look at the victim's chest, listen and feel for breathing for about 3-5 seconds.

If the victim is not breathing, give two full slow breaths. Maintain the head tilt position. Pinch the nose, place your mouth over the victim's mouth and give two full, slow breaths lasting approximately 1-1 1/2 seconds each. Allow time for the victim's lungs to deflate after each breath. Remove your mouth from the victim's mouth after each breath.

Notes

Even after suffering a fracture which may not seem serious, the victim may go into shock.

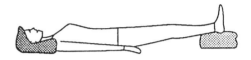

Within 3-5 minutes after breathing stops, damage to the brain will occur.

Shout for help while you tend to the victim.

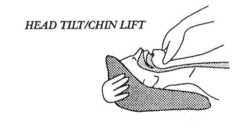

HEAD TILT/CHIN LIFT

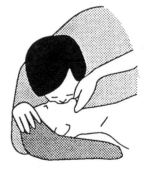

For infants, give gentle puffs of breath and blow through the mouth and nose. Do not tip the head back very far. If there is no exchange of air, reposition the victim's head and try again.

Check the pulse and breathing for about 5-10 seconds. Keep the head tilted with your hand on the victim's forehead. Place the fingertips of your other hand on the Adam's apple of the victim. Slide your fingertips into the groove at the side of the neck to check for a pulse. If the victim is still not breathing or you do not feel a pulse, begin to administer C.P.R. if you have been trained in this procedure. If you have not been trained in C.P.R., continue to administer mouth-to-mouth resuscitation until emergency help arrives.

BURNS

Burns are a common injury which first aid responders may come into contact. Burns are generally regarded as:

First Degree: redness, mild swelling of the skin and some mild pain.

Second Degree: deeper burn, blisters develop, more extensive pain.

Third Degree: deeper destruction of the skin and which may involve muscle damage, severe pain.

First degree burns should receive first aid consisting of applying cool water (not ice), and or a dry sterile dressing.

Second degree burns should be immersed in cool water and the skin blotted dry. A sterile dressing should also be applied and the person treated for shock. If the burn seems severe, medical attention should be obtained promptly.

Third degree burns should be covered with a sterile cloth to protect from further contamination. The victim should be treated for shock. Breathing difficulties should be closely monitored and medical attention quickly obtained.

Notes

Remember! To properly administer first aid or CPR, security officers should enroll in a class certified by the American Red Cross or the American Heart Association.

For any type of chemical burns, the area of the skin should be flushed with large quantities of water for at least 15 minutes. All surrounding clothing should be removed and medical attention quickly obtained.

Electrical Shock

When someone is in direct contact with an electrical current, it is critical that the rescuer does not try to immediately free them. A serious electrical shock could also affect the rescuer. The only safe way to rescue the victim is to stop the current which is going through the victim. If an appliance chord is not damaged, attempt to pull the plug. If the plug is damaged, the power should be turned off at the switch box. Be careful not to touch the victim or the appliance until the power has been turned off.

If the electrical injury is a result of a downed power line, do not approach the victim until after the power has been turned off. Emergency services should be notified at once of the injury. Arrange a barrier around the power line in order to prevent injury to others. Don't move the wire with a stick or rope and don't attempt to cut the wire. Wait for professional assistance.

If a victim's vehicle is in contact with a downed power line, advise the victim to remain in the vehicle. Do not approach the victim until the power has been shut off. If there is immediate danger of the car becoming engulfed in fire, advise the victim to jump out of the vehicle without touching the electrical wire.

The seriousness of the electrical shock injury depends on how much current the victim was exposed to and for how long. If the victim is unconscious, emergency rescue breathing may need to be administered. The victim may have experienced third degree burns where the current entered and exited the body. The victim should be treated for third degree burns by covering with sterile dressing and elevating the area.

Notes

Choking

If someone is believed to be choking, the first thing which should be done is to ask the victim if they can cough, speak or breathe. If they can, do nothing but monitor the situation. The universal distress signal for choking is a hand or hands around the neck. If someone is choking and cannot breathe, try the Heimlich maneuver to get rid of the obstruction and to clear the airway. If the victim is standing or sitting, (conscious) stand behind the victim, wrap your arms around the victim's waist, and:

- make a fist with one hand
- place the thumb side of the fist against the victim's abdomen, slightly above the navel
- grab the fist with the other hand
- press the fist into the victim's abdomen with a quick upward thrust.

If the victim is lying unconscious:

- kneel astride the victim's thighs
- place the heel of one hand against the victim's abdomen, slightly above the navel
- place the other hand on top of the fist and press into the abdomen with a quick upward thrust

Heart Attack

A heart attack occurs when the blood supply to some part of the heart has been cut off or severely reduced. Common symptoms of heart attack are:

- pressure in the middle of the chest, sometimes a little left of the sternum, the pain is not confined to the left side of the chest.
- sometimes the pain can come from the pit of the stomach, vomiting may accompany this pain
- excessive sweating
- rapid and shallow breathing
- nausea/vomiting
- weakness and dizziness
- sensation that the heart is skipping a beat.

Notes

CONSCIOUS VICTIM

UNCONSCIOUS VICTIM

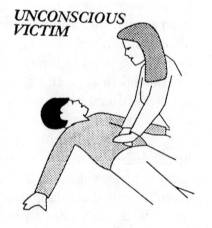

About 40 percent of all victims of heart attacks die within the first few hours following the attack. If it is believed a person may be suffering a heart attack or if a person displays the symptoms of a possible heart attack, immediate action must be taken.

The victim should be placed in the least painful position which is usually sitting with their legs up and bent at the knees. Loosen clothing around the neck.

If the victim looses consciousness, check for a pulse near the Adam's apple and administer rescue breathing and C.P.R. if necessary.

Review of Security Officers in an Emergency

While duties and responsibilities for security officers in dealing with an emergency will vary between companies, for the most part, security officers are responsible for ensuring the following during an emergency:

1. Assist in Pre-Emergency Planning
2. Notification of Emergency Services
3. Notification of first aid responders
4. Provide first aid/C.P.R.
5. Document the emergency events

OSHA Regulations - Infection Control Program and Exposure to Bloodborne Pathogens

The Occupational Safety and Health Administration (OSHA) of the U.S. Department of Labor issued as a final rule its Occupational Exposure to Bloodborne Pathogens Standard, which became effective on March 6, 1992. Among other things, this rule is applicable to all healthcare facilities that are required to comply with OSHA regulations. For organizations whose employees provide emergency first aid services, special care and attention must be given in protecting first aid responders from contracting infections which result from the care given to an emergency victim.

Notes

OSHA Regulation 1910.1030 -- Occupational exposure to bloodborne pathogens.

239

Organizations which provide first aid and C.P.R. response to injured employees are not currently mandated to comply with all of the new regulations recently enacted by OSHA, if these employees who provide emergency care are not "paid rescuers".. However, serious consideration should be given to incorporating certain aspects of the new regulation into the overall emergency plan of a facility.

As part of the Emergency Preparedness plan, first aid responders should be advised in writing of the steps which will be taken in an effort to minimize exposure to bloodborne pathogens, which include the following:

1. All body fluids should be considered potentially infectious materials and care needs to be given when exposed to these body fluids.

2. Provide personal protective equipment to first aid responders which include protective gloves and face or eye shields/goggles.

3. If a responder has sustained an exposure, the exposed area should be washed thoroughly and immediately using water on mucosal sur faces, and soap and running water on skin surfaces.

4. Disinfectant material or spray, should be provided to first aid responders to use to clean their hands and equipment after use. Gloves are to be properly disposed of after use.

5. Should a first aid responder be exposed to a possible infection resulting from their actions, medical guidance, evaluation, and where appropriate, treatment as soon as practical should be pro-video.

6. All exposures should be recorded in writing as soon as possible after the incident.

Notes

Organizations which provide first aid and CPR training to their employees with the intent that the trained employees would voluntarity assist an injured person in an emergency, may not need to comply with the OSHA correct. These employees would be considered as acting as "good samaritans.

Organizations which expect employees such as security officers to respond to an injured employee and provide emergency care, will in all likelihood, need to comply in full with the OSHA regulation.

Provided that employees are merely assisting their fellow employees in providing first aid or C.P.R., the new OSHA regulations pertaining to an Infection Control Program do not apply. However, as a practical manner, and since it is likely that in the future, OSHA may address first aid responses and infection control, organizations should implement the practical precautions outlined in this section. Organizations which have taken the time to properly prepare and identify these concerns, will head-off any undue stress or concern on the part of those employees who receive first aid and C.P.R. training and who are asked and expected to come to the aid of their fellow employees during an emergency.

TORNADOES & SEVERE WEATHER EMERGENCIES

Tornadoes are short-lived local storms containing high-speed winds usually rotating in a counter-clockwise direction. These tornadoes are often observable as a funnel-shaped cloud associated with a thunderstorm cloud. The funnel is initially composed of nothing more than condensed water vapor and is itself a cloud. However, when the circulation of the funnel reaches the ground, it usually picks up dust and debris, which eventually darkens the entire funnel. Tornado damage can occur on the ground even though the visible funnel does not seem to reach the ground.

Scientists now believe that tornadoes begin within an intense thunderstorm cloud and then develops downward to the earth's surface. Not all thunderstorms will create tornadoes, but when the proper weather conditions are present (unseasonably warm and humid air at the earth's surface, cold air at middle atmospheric levels, and strong upper level "jet stream" winds), severe thunderstorms and tornadoes are more likely to occur. Tornadoes sometimes occur with several smaller vortices rotating inside and around the wall of the parent tornado.

On the average, tornado paths are only a quarter of a mile wide, and seldom more than 15 miles in length. Tornadoes usually move from the south, southwest or west at about 30 m.p.h.. Other tornadoes may move as rapidly as 40

Notes

241

m.p.h. and these types are the most dangerous. During the afternoon and evening of April 3 and the early morning hours of April 4, 1974, 148 tornadoes across 13 States killed over 300 people, injured more than 6,000, and caused $600 million in damage. There were many large, long-lived tornadoes in that "super outbreak" of tornadoes. On March 18, 1925, the Tri-State tornado traveled 219 miles across Missouri, Illinois, and Indiana in 219 minutes and killed 689 people.

Tornadoes occur in many parts of the world and in all 50 States. No area is more favorable to their formation than the continental plains and Gulf Coast of the USA. Normally, the number of tornadoes is at its lowest in the United States during December and January, and at its peak in May. The greatest frequency of tornadoes occur in April, May, and June.

Tornado Watches are issued by the National Severe Storms Forecast Center in Kansas City, Missouri, for areas potentially threatened by tornadoes and severe thunderstorms. These watches specify a time period and an area where tornado probabilities are highest. Tornadoes may still occur outside the watch areas or time frames. Watches are relayed to National Weather Service offices and to the general public via radio and television. The watch also activates law enforcement officials, civil defense personnel, organized radio spotter groups, and others to be prepared in case a warning is issued.

A **Tornado Watch** means tornadoes are possible. During a watch, security personnel should notify on-site facility management representatives of the situation, and watch for threatening weather.

Tornado Warnings are issued by local National Weather Service Offices when a tornado has been sighted or indicated by radar. Warnings describe the area that could be affected. Since tornadoes are not always indicated by radar or sighted, warnings may not always be given. Security personnel should always be alert to these storms whenever threatening weather conditions occur.

Notes

The National Oceanic and Atmospheric Administration (N.O.A.A.) produced a film entitled: The Day of the Killer Tornadoes. This film describes the damage caused by the tornadoes in April, 1974. Your local civil defense or emergency preparedness office or local library, may have a copy of the film.

TORNADO & SEVERE WEATHER EMERGENCY PREPAREDNESS

Security personnel can provide a valuable service to their employers by assisting in emergency preparedness before severe weather such as a tornado affects an area.

A weather radio should be included in the essential equipment used by security personnel. As part of the Emergency Preparedness plan, certain key members of management should be notified immediately after learning that a **tornado watch** has been issued for the area. By notifying management personnel who are on duty that a **watch** is in affect, this allows time for certain planning decisions which should be made. Even though most **tornado watches** do not ultimately develop into **tornado warnings**, some actions may need to be taken. For example:

a. A construction or maintenance manager should be advised of a **watch** condition since often they have personnel who work outdoors and who may even work in elevated stations. Provided these workers are aware that conditions exist for severe weather, they should have time to seek shelter if weather become threatening.

b. Some manufacturing facilities leave windows, doors and even roof vents open during warm weather months to help in ventilating the facility. These openings may be chosen to be closed at the **watch** stage. Remember, even during Tornado Watches where tornadoes do not develop, severe weather such as torrential rain downpours, high winds, and lightning often occur and cause extensive damage.

NOTIFICATION OF TORNADO WARNING

Tornado Warnings must be taken very seriously and action must be taken immediately to notify key management personnel and employees of the danger. **Tornado Warnings** are issued when either weather radar has detected a funnel cloud, or whenever an actual tornado or funnel cloud has been observed.

Tornado warnings are often issued for an entire area or county. Therefore, a **warning** may be issued for a county which is 25 square miles in size. Your facility may be 10 miles from the exact location of the tornado. This may create a dilemma for management as to whether to instruct employees to go to shelter areas or to continue operations. Once again, the key point for security personnel to remember is to notify key management personnel of the warning in order for them to make whatever decisions they deem prudent.

SHELTERS

In the workplace, safe shelter from possible tornado damage is not as simple as one would think. In a fire, employees would simply evacuate to the outside. But, in a tornado condition, the safest place is inside, preferably in a basement area. Facilities where several hundred or even thousands of people are working may it impractical to evacuate everyone to a basement area.

As with any emergency situation, pre-emergency preparedness planning is essential. Practical questions such as the following must be addressed BEFORE an emergency:

1. where are safe shelters from a tornado?
2. when will a decision be made and by whom, to enter the shelters?
3. how long do employees remain in the shelters?

The National Oceanic and Atmospheric Administration advises the following safety steps be followed in a tornado warning situation:

- Stay away from windows, doors, and outside walls. Protect your head!
- In homes and small buildings, go to the basement or to an interior part of the lowest level— closets, bathrooms, or interior halls. Get under something sturdy.

Notes

Very often, the area of the country will determine the level of care and response management personnel implement. Parts of the country in Oklahoma, Texas, Kansas and Missouri are referred to as "tornado alley" because of the frequency of tornadoes. In these states, management may be eager to take action earlier.

- In schools, nursing homes, hospitals, factories, and shopping centers, go to predesignated shelter areas. Interior hallways on the lowest floor are usually best.
- In high-rise buildings, go to interior small rooms or hallways.
- In mobile homes or vehicles, leave them and go to a substantial structure. If there is no shelter nearby, lie flat in the nearest ditch, ravine or culvert with your hands shielding your head.

Tornadoes are only one of a thunderstorm's killers. Others include lightning, flash floods and high winds.

Lightning Safety Precautions: stay indoors and away from electrical appliances when storms are nearby. If you are caught outside, stay away from metal objects.

Thunderstorm rains can cause flash floods. Be careful where you take shelter.

High winds can cause great damage. Large hail can be very damaging but rarely kills.

FLOODS

Most facilities' property is surveyed prior to construction to be certain that the land is not part of any flood plain. Studies of previous floods are maintained by state, city and county engineering departments. Some land areas may be built on what is called a "100-year flood plain". Stated simply, this means the statistical probability that the land which is part of this plain, will flood on average, one time every 100 hundred years. Other studies may indicate various areas of land will flood more often.

Flood plain: an area of land which floods with water from a river or creek that has overflowed its normal levels.

In recent years, companies have gone to great lengths to insure their buildings are not built on flood plains. The cost associated with floods, including business interruption and damaged products is significant. Often, companies are unable to obtain flood insurance or if they can, the insurance is very expensive.

However, even with proper building construction planning, it is obvious that not all facilities are protected from flooding. Once again, as with any potential emergency, pre-emergency planning is essential!

1. What is the likelihood of a flood at this location?
2. If early warning is given, what steps can be taken to minimize loss?
   a. Can water be blocked using sandbags or other equipment?
   b. Can product be protected or should it be moved off-site?
   c. If a flood occurs, will employees be unable to come to work or to leave the facility?

In all likelihood, most security personnel will not become involved in flooding situations which are a result of a river flooding. More than likely, flooding situations will occur involving severe rain which causes small, nearby creeks to flood, or storm sewers which back-up into a facility.

As with the recent man-made flood disaster in Chicago, where a leak in a dike wall allowed for millions of gallons of water to flood basements in the city's business district, consideration must be given to at least some minimum pre-emergency planning.

While loss of life will usually not occur with regard to a flood of a business, product or equipment damage may be great. Computers which are located in basement areas are susceptible to water damage. Finished product should not normally be stored in basement areas. There is a much higher probability that security personnel will be confronted with rampaging water emitting from either a backed-up storm sewer, a ruptured fire protection pipe, or even a toilet which has run for several hours, rather than flooding from a river.

Notes

Usually the same sewer line back-ups each time a heavy rain occurs. By knowing the location of these "trouble spots" security personnel are better able to respond quickly.

It is critical for security personnel to know the following:

1. Location of fire-protection shut-off valves and how to close the valves.
2. Location of plastic tarps to protect product and equipment.
3. Location of mops, brooms, and "squeegees" to clean-up excessive water.
4. Phone numbers of key management personnel who must be immediately notified.

WINTER STORMS

In September, the sun leaves the Northern Hemisphere. Until the sun's return in March, polar air controls the northern continental atmosphere, pushing back the tropical warmth of summer. Winter storms are generated in much the same way as spring and summer thunderstorms. Disturbances occur from cold polar air meeting warm tropical air. These disturbances may become intense low-pressure systems, churning over tens of thousands of square miles in a great counter-clock-wise direction.

Every winter is a bad year for some portion of the country and winter storms can kill without breaking climatological records. From 1936-1969, snowstorms caused more than 3,000 deaths, more than a third were attributable to automobile and other accidents; one third to over-exertion, exhaustion, and consequent fatal heart attack; and about one-third to exposure and fatal, freezing, home fires, carbon monoxide poisoning in stalled cars, falls on slippery walks, electrocution from downed power lines, and building collapse.

The terms **watch** and **warning** are used for winter storms, as for other natural hazards. The **watch** alerts the public that a storm has formed and is approaching the area. The **warning** means that a storm is imminent and immediate action should be taken to protect life and property.

Security personnel, should notify key management personnel of an impending storm, and know where basic snow removal equipment such as brooms and shovels are

Notes

If water is damaging equipment or product, security personnel must intercept to stop the source of the water and take whatever steps are necessary to protect the equipment.

located, and have the phone numbers of key management personnel and snow removal crews at immediate disposal. Personal safety precautions will be extremely important for security personnel who will need to brave the winter elements.

Notes

During winter storms, security personnel may be the only individuals at a facility, particularly if the storm occurs during a weekend. Unfortunately, the security personnel who are on-duty when the storm develops, will often be required to remain at the facility for extended periods since their relief may be unable to reach the facility. There are many examples of security officers remaining at their posts for 24-48 hours without relief during winter storms. Therefore, security personnel must consider personal safety factors when preplanning for a winter storm:

1. Have your vehicle "winterized" in autumn. Be certain your vehicle is in proper working order.
2. Be certain to have your vehicle's fuel tank full before starting out to your worksite.
3. Maintain a battery-powered flashlight and radio in your vehicle.
4. Keep some food which does not require refrigeration in your vehicle. Bread, peanut-butter, canned food, beverages and candy will suffice. (Be certain to pack a can-opener!).
5. Keep extra clothing and blankets in your vehicle.
6. Dress to fit the elements. Wear loose-fitting, light-weight warm clothing in several layers; layers can be removed to prevent perspiring.

If in route to work, a winter storm traps you, it is safer to remain in your vehicle than to attempt to walk to a shelter.

1. Keep fresh air in your vehicle. Freezing, wet snow can completely seal the passenger compartment.

2. Run the motor and heater sparingly, and only with the downwind window open for ventilation. Carbon monoxide poisoning and oxygen starvation can kill quickly!

3. Exercise by clapping hands and moving arms and legs vigorously from time to time. Don't stay in one position too long.

4. Turn on the dome light at night to make the vehicle visible to work crews.

5. Keep watch. If someone else is in the vehicle with you, don't sleep at the same time.

BOMB THREATS

In developing a bomb threat response plan, there are four general areas of consideration:

1. Planning and Preparation
2. Receiving a Threat
3. Evacuation
4. Search

Planning & Preparation

Only with a properly organized plan will those organizations affected by a bomb threat know how, when, and in what order to proceed. Prevention is another factor that must be stressed. By making access to a facility restrictive as possible, the likelihood of an actual bombing is greatly minimized. Tightened security and controlled entry to the facility will assist in this regard.

With a well thought-out plan, a bomb threat situation can be resolved with a minimum of risk to people and property, while minimizing the disruption of normal operations. Proper preparation by security personnel includes assistance in the development of the plan and the evaluation of its effectiveness.

Key management personnel must be assigned primary and alternate levels of authority in order for decisions to be made regarding the threat. Each management member

---

Notes

Bomb threats are a common occurrence for most businesses today.

While the likelihood of an actual bombing of a facility is remote, to ensure the safety of all employees and visitors and to protect the corporation's assets, bomb threat planning must be addressed.

All threats must be taken seriously and should never be ignored.

of this team must be familiar with the scope and responsibility of their assignment, and have full authority to make necessary decisions. Probably the most important decision to be made will be whether to evacuate or not. A single person should be given the authority to order and direct the evacuation, search, facility shutdown, re-entry of personnel, and any other emergency procedures.

Once an evacuation is ordered, the person-in-charge should be centrally located at a bomb threat control center (often this is the security office or control center). If a mobile control center is more appropriate, primary and alternate locations should be designated for a stationary control center.

Evacuation and search teams must also be selected during the planning stages. The most likely candidates are volunteers from among those employees who work in the facility on a daily basis. Security personnel and maintenance employees are logical choices because of their knowledge of both the public and out-of-the-way areas of the facility. Usually, members of local police and fire departments can be solicited to assist in the training of the emergency team. It must be stressed that assignments need to be carried out in a swift and confident manner.

One person should be selected to serve as the media spokesperson. Although publicity in a bomb threat situation is usually not sought, a spokesperson can ensure the availability of accurate information to media representatives, and could help prevent additional bomb threats resulting from publicizing erroneous information.

RECEIVING A THREAT

In pre-emergency planning for a possible bomb threat which usually occur over the telephone, all personnel who answer incoming calls, should be supplied with a bomb threat checklist. When a bomb threat is received, it may be advisable for the person receiving the call to give a prearranged signal. This would allow monitoring of the call by more than one person. Since this may be sometimes difficult

Notes

The "chain of command" in the implementation of a bomb threat response is essential.

Most searches involve the inspection and examination of various areas of a facility where a suspicious object could be placed.

Security personnel should never volunteer information to members of the media.

to accomplish, serious consideration should be given to recording all incoming telephone calls. Federal law allows for this type of recording since one party (the company receiving the call) agrees to the tape recording. Applicable state laws should be reviewed prior to installing tape recording devices on telephones.

While comprising a smaller percentage of bomb threats, the written threat must be evaluated as carefully as one received over the telephone. Written bomb threats often provide excellent document-type evidence. Once a written threat is received, further handling should be avoided to preserve fingerprints, handwriting, typewriting, postmarks, and other markings for appropriate examination. It is imperative to save all items connected with the bomb threat document.

After a bomb threat is received, the next step is to immediately notify the people responsible for carrying out the bomb threat response plan. It is important during pre-emergency planning that a list of these individuals and outside agencies be prepared and readily available. These emergency phone numbers should include key management personnel, as well as police, fire, FBI, utility company, etc...

Once received, the bomb threat must be evaluated. During the decision making process, all threats should be treated as though they involved an actual bomb. A **specific** threat is more likely to be actual where an actual explosive device exists. This type of threat usually provides information regarding the bomb, its placement, rationale for the attack, and when the bomb is going to explode. The type of threat which is not specific, but just merely states that a bomb has been placed in a facility, will normally not involve an actual explosive device.

The most common reasons for a person making a bomb threat are:

1. they want to disrupt normal activities.
2. the caller has definite knowledge of the bomb and wants to reduce the risk of injury.

Notes

Be certain that the appropriate management personnel have agreed to allow for the use of a tape recorder, prior to its installation.

Security officers who come upon a written bomb threat should take steps to perserve possible evidence such as fingerprints. The letter should be properly secured and retained for future investigation.

Often a code is used to notify members of the Bomb Threat Response team that a threat has been received. Something as simple as "Mr. Strong, please report to personnel," may be used.

As a rule, the more specific a threat, the greater likelihood the threat is genuine.

Terrorists usually select a target according to the potential publicity and political or psychological gain that might be achieved by a bombing. Generally, terrorist bombings are meant to destroy property, however this is not always true. Criminal bombers select targets for a variety of reasons which include revenge, extortion, and intimidation.

EVACUATION

Once the credibility of the threat has been evaluated, it is necessary to determine what action if any should be taken regarding an evacuation. It is necessary to determine whether to:

1. take no action.
2. search without evacuation.
3. initiate a partial evacuation.
4. conduct a complete evacuation and search.

To avoid any possibility of risk and possible litigation from a charge of negligence, a policy to evacuate any time a threat is received could be made during pre-emergency planning. However, since most threats are hoaxes, such a policy could result in considerable production down-time and would be costly. Many threats are pranks perpetrated by employees or students who know that once a threat is received a complete evacuation of the facility will occur. A more viable alternative is to evaluate each bomb threat on its own merits and evacuate if only deemed necessary.

When considering an evacuation the following items should be evaluated:
1. Publish evacuation maps which show at least two ways to quickly evacuate the facility.
2. Establish an evacuation signal or alarm system.
3. Select and train evacuation teams. Training should encompass the control and direction of personnel during an evacuation. Properly trained teams familiar with evacuation procedures, possible hazards, primary and secondary evacuation routes will greatly assist in an actual evacuation. Evacuation and search team

Notes

Often, former or disgruntled employees are responsible for bomb threats.

The United States has been fortunate with regard to the relatively few terrorist bombings which have occurred to American companies.

"better safe than sorry"

Security personnel can assist in the development of evacuation maps.

members should wear some sort of identification (i.e. baseball hats) which indicate their authority.

4. Establish areas outside the facility where personnel are to gather and to wait for further instructions. Develop procedures for knowing all personnel are out of the building. Consideration has to be given to visitors at the facility and for employees who may be absent from work on the day of the evacuation.

5. Provide for effective communications through use of two-way radios or telephone communication.

6. Determine procedures for shutting off certain utilities, such as natural gas.

Before leaving office space, employees should unlock doors, desks, lockers and file cabinets, and turn-off machinery. Lights should be left on. People who are evacuating should remove all purses, briefcases, personal packages, and lunch boxes which may cause added distraction during the search process. As a precaution in the event of explosion, windows and doors should be opened to ventilate and minimize destruction in the event of an explosion.

SEARCH

A decision needs to be made as to whether a search will be conducted in the open with everyone's knowledge and whether or not the search will be initiated prior to an evacuation. A discrete search where few employees are notified of the threat allows for less panic and the continuation of business. Individuals on the search team should be instructed to search their own work areas looking for strange or suspicious objects which appear out of place.

Many factors regarding the search should be considered during the pre-emergency preparedness stage:

Notes

During an emergency, certain people must have the authority to direct and assist others.

Where will personnel meet once they are out of the facility and who will take a count to verify everyone is out of the facility?

Some organizations may choose to suspend all radio communication during a threat.

It is essential for some maintenance employees to serve as members of the emergency team.

Notes

1. Select search teams. A practical and effective approach is to select employees who are familiar with specific areas of the facility. Floor area wardens may also be designated to direct specific floor or area searches and relay information to the control center.
2. Train search teams in thorough search procedures. Searchers should familiarize themselves with normal building sights and sounds.
3. Determine search sequence and procedures. The usual search sequence is to start on the outside and work toward the inside. Once inside, start at the lowest level and work upward.
4. Designate control center locations and control center operators.
5. Provide for bomb disposal, fire fighting, rescue, medical and other emergency assistance.
6. Maintain strict key control. Availability of master keys is important because limited access is a common obstacle to speedy searches.

If a suspicious object is located, DO NOT TOUCH IT and do not assume that it is the only possible device. Note its location, description, and proximity to utility lines (gas, water and electric). Relay this information to the control center. A discovery of this object does not end the search. More objects may be found. The entire facility must be completely inspected.

Since a thorough search can be lengthy, fatigue is an important consideration. Effective training will help lessen the effect of hours of tedious searching. If a prolonged search is unavoidable, search teams should be given break periods.

CIVIL DISTURBANCE

For the past several years, civil riots or disturbances in the United States have not been as prevalent as those which occurred during the 1960's and the 1970's. In those years, the country was undergoing rapid changes with regards to the civil rights movement and opposition to the Vietnam War.

In recent years, most civil disturbances have resulted from protests involving work stoppages or issues such as the abortion controversy.

However, in May of 1992, the city of Los Angeles was the scene of several days of rioting resulting from the acquittal of the four white policemen charged in the beatings of African American motorist Rodney King.

As previously mentioned in every other emergency discussed in this chapter, preplanning is the single most effective means for minimizing loss during a civil disturbance.

Organizations must evaluate their own unique situations:

1. Is the business or operation located in an area which is susceptible to civil violence?
2. What type of incident could stimulate a disturbance?
3. At what point will the organization implement its Civil Disturbance Emergency Plan?
4. Can the facility be adequately protected or shielded from damage with additional security personnel, fencing, boarding-up of windows and doors?
5. How much time is needed to address protection needs?

Crowds turn into mobs when a few leaders or agitators incite the group. Individuals then lose their personal identity and become ruled by emotion. Feeling that they are anonymous, many people will then begin to riot and loot surrounding businesses. Riots are not confined to large metropolitan areas. They can occur in any city or town. When riots occur, law enforcement and fire protection services will be strained to the limit and may be unable to respond to all emergency calls.

If a riot reaches catastrophic levels, the loss to an organization equals the value of all buildings and equipment. In addition, losses associated with business interruption could be significant.

Notes

Civil Disturbances can "explode" with little or no warning.

Known as "mob psychology"

To reduce the risk potential at a facility, management representatives can start by assisting in civic projects that are designed to relieve community tension. Meeting with local law enforcement personnel and other businesses in the area to coordinate protection strategy is a key element in pre-emergency planning. Be aware of the social climate in the area and watch for danger signals which may indicate the need to initiate emergency protective measures.

If rumors of an impending disturbance are learned, try and obtain verification and an indication of severity so that the correct plan of action can be taken. Consideration for sending employees home early and for the removal of valuables susceptible to looting should be discussed.

Measures to protect the building which are detailed in the Physical Security chapter of this manual will greatly assist in protecting the facility. Since civil disturbances often develop rapidly, with little warning, a detailed physical security survey should be conducted on an annual basis at each facility to measure the effectiveness of protection measures.

CHEMICAL SPILLS

In recent years, environmental protection has received increased attention from most businesses as well as local, state and federal regulatory agencies. With various "Right to Know" laws designed to protect employees, visitors, and emergency response personnel, most organizations have taken the necessary pre-emergency planning steps to minimize chemical leaks and or spills. However, accidents and incidents will occur and often security personnel will be required to be involved in the emergency response to a chemical spill.

The first consideration for security personnel is to learn as much information as possible and which is available on the various chemicals and other materials used at the facility. Material Safety Data Sheets (MSDS), are required to be available at various locations at a facility for employees to review if they desire. These MSDS's provide information on a particular chemical or material such as:

Notes

Security personnel can provide a valuable service by informing management of rumors of possible disturbances or unrest.

Right -to-know: term given to the various federal, state or local regulations which require businesses to inform all personnel of the various hazardous materials used on the premises. Individuals must also be advised in the proper methods of protection from hazardous materials.

All security personnel should be familiar with the location of MSDS, as well as the areas where hazardous chemicals and materials are in use.

1. whether the material is flammable
2. how corrosive the material is to skin
3. what to do if the material touches the skin, mouth eyes, etc..
4. what to do if the material is inhaled
5. whether personal protective equipment such as gloves, face shields, boots, coats, aprons, and self-contain breathing apparatus are required to be worn by a person when handling the material
6. what to do if a spill occurs

It is extremely important for security personnel to know where the Material Safety Data Sheets are stored. In the event of an emergency which does not involve a spill, but may involve a fire, emergency responders will want to know precisely what chemicals are used at the facility and their exact location.

Usually if a spill occurs during normal operations, security personnel will be basically responsible for notifying emergency response units and for directing them to the spill location. However, if a spill or leak is discovered over a weekend, holiday or otherwise facility shutdown time, on-duty security personnel will need to implement the Emergency Preparedness plan.

If a security officer discovers a possible spill, it is critical that they use extreme caution in attempting to evaluate the seriousness of the situation. To simply enter a spill area without personal protective equipment or without knowledge of the source of the spill is extremely foolish and puts not only the health and safety of the security officer at risk but also further endangers the facility!

If a spill is suspected, attempt to first determine what might be the source? Are you familiar with the material used in the area? Can you see the container or pipes near the spill? Can you read any warning signs or numbers? Can you smell anything? What does it smell like? Can you see condensation or a fog-like mist? What can you hear?

Notes

Personnel safety is the first consideration when responding to a possible spill.

Be Careful!
Observe!
Document!

If you are still uncertain as to the source of the spill or you know for certain what material has spilled, notify the key management officials responsible for controlling a spill, immediately! Continue to contact management personnel until you have received appropriate instructions. At some facilities, security personnel may be required and expected to notify outside emergency services prior to contacting local management. However, it is advisable, that if in doubt, security personnel should first attempt to notify a key management official.

Once a management official has been notified, security personnel may be expected to attempt to contain the spill or leak. Never attempt to contain a significant spill or leak unless you have been properly trained in the used of personal protective equipment including self-contained breathing apparatus. However, if properly trained, security personnel may be able to contain the spill by using a clay-like substance or other absorbing material which will serve to absorb the material.

Security personnel may be instructed by the management representative or if outlined in writing in the Emergency Preparedness plan, to contact the local fire department or Hazardous Material Response team. At this time, an evacuation of the facility and adjacent homes and businesses may be ordered. Again, each facility's emergency response to a chemical spill will vary depending upon the material which has been spilled, the amount of the spill, the toxicity of the material, and the instructions detailed in the pre-emergency planning stages.

At all times, the safety of personnel is the single most important element in responding to a chemical spill. Failure to use personal protective equipment has injured and killed many emergency responders who failed to evaluate the situation prior to entering the contaminated area. Even if a rescue of another person is necessary, be certain that appropriate safeguards are taken into consideration before rushing into an emergency.

Notes

Security personnel must know who to contact in the event of a spill. Keep accurate notes of all attempted phone calls.

In order to use self-contained breathing apparatus (SCBA) security personnel must be trained in their use. Annual physicals may also be a requirement.

SUMMARY

Security officers can provide a valuable service in a facility's overall Emergency Preparedness plan. Security personnel will generally plan an active, key role in any emergency situation. Security officers may be called upon to notify local emergency services, assist in the evacuation of personnel, render first aid to injured persons, announce emergency instructions, and in certain situations, may be required to assume primary responsibility for initiating the emergency response.

In planning any response to an emergency the first question which must be addressed is in identifying the objectives of the Emergency plan. An Emergency plan must be developed and detailed in writing addressing a variety of emergencies which might affect an organization.

The plan should be in writing and should identify the following:

1. An Emergency Plan Director or Coordinator
2. An Emergency Preparedness Team

Detailed instructions addressing emergencies such as fire, serious injury, tornadoes and severe weather, floods, winter storms, bomb threats, civil disturbance and chemical spills are just some of the emergencies which could affect an organization and which should be addressed.

The safety of individuals and protection of property are the essential objectives of any effective Emergency Preparedness plan. A great deal of time in planning for a possible emergency is required to insure a proper response in an actual emergency.

References

Standard First Aid Personal Safety, American Red Cross, 1990.

Tornado, US Dept. of Commerce?NOAA, National Weather Service, US Government Printing Office, 1978.

Winter Storms, IBID, 1975.

The Bomb Threat Challenge, FBI Bomb Data Center, US Dept. of Justice, FBI, Washington D.C., 1987.

Notes

SAMPLE BOMB THREAT PROCEDURE FOR SECURITY OFFICERS

SUBJECT: BOMB THREAT PROCEDURE

PURPOSE: To provide instructions to be followed upon receipt of a bomb threat.

PROCEDURE: Bomb threats are generally received through telephone messages. At the time the call is received, it is almost impossible to determine the validity of the threat. Prompt decisive action is required. Information derived from the calling party may prove invaluable and could help to determine subsequent action to be taken.

1. Receipt of Bomb Threat

Although any employee may receive a bomb threat, they are most often received by the switchboard operators or security officers. The person receiving the threat may be faced with one or two situations:

    a. They will be asked to connect the caller with some employee, or

    b. They will be required to accept the message themselves.

2. Relaying the Call

Even if the operator or security officer has an indication of the nature of the call, follow the callers instructions and relay the call.

After relaying the call, notify management and advise them of any and all information you were able to obtain.

3. Accepting the Call

Listen, do not interrupt the caller except to ask when is the bomb set to explode? Where is it? What does it look like? Take notes. Keep in mind the items outlined in the checklist. If the call is received at the switchboard, signal another

---

Notes

Questions To Ask:
1. When is bomb going to explode?
2. Where is it right now?
3. What does it look like?
4. What kind of bomb is it?
5. What will cause it to explode?
6. Did you place the bomb?
7. Why?
8. What is your address?
9. What is your name?

Exact Wording of the Threat:

Sex of caller:
Race:
Age:
Length of call:
No. at which call is received:
Time:
Date:

Caller's Voice
Calm	Nasal
Angry	Stutter
Excited	Lisp
Slow	Raspy
Rapid	Deep
Soft	Ragged
Loud	Clearing Throat
Laughter	Deep Breathing
Crying	Crackling Voice
Normal	Disguised
Distinct	Accent
Slurred	Familiar
Whispered	

Background Noises:

Language:

Remarks:

operator or security officer who will notify security or assist in any possible way.

After the caller hangs up, immediately report the call to security. Notify your supervisor.

4. It is the responsibility of the Security Department to notify the Senior Executive available.

5. Notification of Employees - Option to Work or To Leave

The decision to evacuate should be made by the Senior Executive in conjunction with the Director/Manager of Security and the Vice President of Human Resources.

The vast majority of bomb threats are a hoax. In most instances, the employees should be informed that a threat has been received, however, we believe it to be a hoax and everyone is continuing to work. (Some companies will allow for employees to leave the building.) If any employee wants to leave the premises, he or she may do so but should remain on the premises away from the building and await further instructions.

6. Mandatory Evacuation of the Facility - No Option to Work

The decision to evacuate will be made by the Senior Executive in conjunction with the Vice President of Human Resources and the Director/Manager of Security.

Once the decision to evacuate the building has been made, the emergency notification alarm will be sounded. This signal will mean all employees should proceed in an orderly manner to the nearest exit. Employees are to proceed to their prearranged staging areas outside the facility to await further instruction and to sign-in with their Emergency Team captain.

In the event an order is given to evacuate the building, supervisory personnel will be responsible to ensure that their particular areas of responsibility have been evacuated. Before leaving their area, supervisory personnel will inspect their area for a possible bomb device.

Notes

If the responsible officials mentioned above are unavailable, the supervisor or lead security officer assumes responsibility for ensuring that the notification and possible evacuation procedures are carried out in the following manner:

1. Notify the local law enforcement agency.
2. Notify facility supervisors that a bomb threat has been received which is believed to be a hoax and that employees have the option to work.
3. If a decision is made to evacuate the building, sound the notification alarm.
4. In the event a decision is made to evacuate, designate supervisory personnel to insure the facility has been evacuated.
5. Direct employees to a safe distance from the building until the emergency is evaluated.
6. Do not initiate a bomb search unless directed to do so by appropriate management personnel.
7. Make certain that any device, if found, is not disturbed. Notify the proper law enforcement authorities.
8. Report the situation and current status to the appropriate management representative at the earliest opportunity.
9. Sound the all-clear signal once the building is determined to be safe by a responsible person.
10. Document the incident with a detailed written report.

EMERGENCY PREPAREDNESS

1. The person primarily responsible for initiating an emergency plan is:

   a. Fire Marshall
   b. Master of Disaster
   c. Emergency Plan Coordinator
   d. none of the above

2. The following elements are essential for any plan:

   a. it must be written
   b. it must identify objectives
   c. it must identify the emergencies which are to be addressed
   d. all of the above

3. An Emergency Preparedness Team would provide the following services during an emergency:

   a. extinguish small fires
   b. provide first aid
   c. assist in evacuation
   d. all of the above

4. The first step in the preplanning process is a written fire prevention plan. True or False? _____

5. The enforcement of a NO SMOKING policy will usually have little effect upon fire prevention. True or False? _____

6. Company Fire Marshalls should be professionally trained fire protection professionals. True or False? _____

7. First-Aid kits should be strategically located throughout a facility. True or False? _____

8. After initiating the emergency evacuation alarm, the responsibilities of the security staff are completed. True or False? _____

9. The duties of each employee should be explained during the fire emergency. True or False? _____

10. Security Officers need not worry about C.P.R. because the EMS teams are usually no more than five minutes from a facility. True or False? _____

11. The easiest injury for a person to recognize is external bleeding. True or False? _____

12. The average healthy adult usually possesses between:

    a. 8-9 quarts of blood
    b. 5-6 quarts of blood
    c. 11-12 quarts of blood
    d. none of the above

13. The best way to stop bleeding is to clean the wound, and elevate it above the victim's heart. True or False? _____

14. One of the major pressure points used to control bleeding is the femoral point in the arm. True or False? _____

15. Shock will usually develop when a person is seriously injured. True or False? _____

16. When a person goes into shock, it is wise to give them something to eat. True or False? _____

17. When assisting a victim's breathing, pinch the nose and place your mouth over the victim's, and give two breaths of approximately:

    a. 2-3 seconds each
    b. 3-5 seconds each
    c. 5-6 seconds each
    d. 1-1 1/2 seconds each

18. For infants, give gentle puffs of breath and blow through the mouth and nose. True or False? _____

19. Before giving C.P.R., check a person's pulse and breathing for about 20-30 seconds. True or False? _____

20. The worst type of burn is a first degree burn. True or False? _____

21. Ice should be used on a second degree burn. True or False? _____

22. For any type of chemical burn, the area of the burns should be flushed with large quantities of water for at least:

  a. 10 minutes
  b.   5 minutes
  c. 15 minutes
  d. two minutes

23. When someone is in direct contact with an electrical current, it is critical that the rescuer immediately free them. True or False? _____

24. The safest way to rescue a victim is to stop the current which is going through them. True or False? _____

25. If a victim's vehicle is in contact with a downed power line, advise the person to remain in their vehicle. True or False? _____

26. The seriousness of an electrical shock has little to do with the amount of current the victim was exposed to. True or False? _____

27. The universal distress signal for choking is a hand or hands around the neck. True or False? _____

28. To diagnose a heart attack, the pain must be confined to the left side of a person's chest. True or False? _____

29. Weakness, dizziness, rapid and shallow breathing are symptoms of a heart attack. True or False? _____

30. What percentage of all victims die within the first few hours following a heart atack?

  a. 100%
  b. 60%
  c. 25%
  d. 40%

31. Tornadoes are easily recognizable by their funnel shaped cloud. True or False? _____

32. Tornadoes usually rotate in a clock-wise direction. True or False? _____

33. Tornadoes are usually no longer than a quarter of a mile wide and thirty miles in length. True or False? _____

34. Most tonadoes move from the south, southwest, or west at about 30 M.P.H. True or False? _____

35. The first duty of a security officer when informed of a tornado watch is to notify a responsible member of management. True or False? _____

36. In schools, hospitals, and factories, interior hallways on the lowest floor are usually best for shelter from tornadoes. True or False? _____

37. The best place to store computers and finished products are in basement areas of a facility. True or False? _____

38. One of the first questions a security officer should ask themselves is, "Where are the water shut-off valves?" True or False? _____

39. Because of the threat of long hours at a facility during a winter storm, security personnel should take steps to insure their vehicle is "winterized" and that they have some extra food and clothing in their vehicle. True or False? _____

40. By making access to a facility restrictive as possible, the likelihood of a actual bombing at a facility is greatly reduced. True or False? _____

41. In the event of a bomb threat, the most important decision to make concerns the location of the bomb. True or False? _____

42. The most logical choice for members of the search team would be management personnel who are familiar with the facility. True or False? _____

43. Written bomb threats provide better document evidence than threats which are telephoned-in to a facility. True or False? _____

44. Preplanning is the single most effective means of minimizing damage during a civil disturbance. True or False? _____

45.	Laws designed to protect employees, visitors, and emergency response personnel are referred to:

	a. In the Know Laws
	b. Right to Know Laws
	c. Right to Protect Laws
	d. Right to Work Laws

46.	The single most important responsibility of a security officer in the event of a spill is to rush to the scene as quickly as possible to stop the source of the spill. True or False? _____

Practical Exercises

1.	Is there an emergency preparedness plan in effect at the facility where you work?

2.	Do all security officers know their duties and responsibilities during an emergency?

3.	How often are evacuation drills conducted at this facility?

4.	How often are employees trained in emergency preparedness?

5.	What types of emergencies have occurred at this facility? What was the result of these emergencies?

THE EFFECTIVE SECURITY OFFICERS TRAINING MANUAL

Chapter XIV

Human Relations

Human Relations

Notes

Reading for a Purpose
Look for these Key Words:
- Theory X   • Satisfiers
- Theory Y   • Dissatisfiers
- Motivation   • Competition
- Need Hierarchy
- Non-verbal Communication
- Value System Programming
- Conflict   • Stress

Look for Answers to these
       Questions:
1. What is value system
       programming?
2. What is the Need Hierarchy?
3. How is a person motivated?
4. What are the four elements
       of communication?
5. Why is conflict inevitable?
6. What is stress?

A great deal of interest in the human aspects of business and industrial organizations began in the 1930's and continued during and after World War II. The human relations movement introduced great changes in the thinking of many people.

In industry today, fair and humane treatment of employees is more than just good business or a moral obligation. It is the law.

The Human Relations Movement

The beginning of the human relations movement is usually associated with studies conducted by Elton Mayo and the Western Electric Hawthorne plant near Chicago. These studies showed that at a particular time and place, productivity could be increased in the workplace. Originally, the study was conducted to monitor the affect of lighting in the workplace. The researchers were surprised to find that the employees felt important because of the attention they were receiving. Another reason for the human relations movement was an attempt to stop the advances made by unions. Business owners were dealing with better educated employees who expected a higher standard of living. From that time to today, human relations training for supervisors is very popular.

The Challenge to Management

The manager who relies primarily on wage incentives, controls and authorities to motivate workers is influenced by ideas about human nature which are different from the manager who attempts to maximize workers' self esteem. The effectiveness with how managers relate to individuals and groups in organizations is a result of their ideas about human nature. It is very important that a manager's ideas about human nature are correct and make sense.

Elton Mayo in his Hawthorne Experiment revealed that if given attention, employees work better and are more productive.

Union's made great strides in the 1930's and 1940's

Elton Mayo: considered to have founded the Human Relations movement with his studies at the Western Electric Hawthorne plant.

Managers/Supervisors have different views on what motivates employees.

Motivation: the reason why a person does certain things.

Employees cannot be treated as if all of their needs are alike. Everyone has certain needs but they vary in degrees.

There are still large numbers of people in the work force whose childhood memories of the Depression of the 1930's are very real. Employees are influenced by events which occurred by previous employers and even by their family and friends.

The concept of creating a positive human relations attitude within a security department should be the goal of every officer, supervisor, and manager. Problems which are peculiar and inherent within this industry, may hamper those efforts however. Most security officer jobs are systematic, routine, and in many cases boring. Adding to this dilemma is the nature of the job which involves the enforcement of policies, rules and regulations, the fact that many jobs are fixed assignments, and the fact that flexibility and creativity are not included in job descriptions. The effective security manager or supervisor of the 1990's must be creative in developing a positive atmosphere which fosters a high regard for security personnel.

Theory X and Y

Douglas MacGregor defined two types of management theories which identify various human nature traits as Theory X and Y.

Theory X states that the average person dislikes work and is lazy, selfish and does not care about their employer. Because of these traits, the person must be threatened, forced and controlled in doing things. This person wants security more than anything else in life and avoids responsibility. Because these people are immature, managers must use a highly directive and forceful style.

Theory Y states that people enjoy work and are not lazy. If these people are lazy, it is because of their work and supervision. When properly motivated, these people develop interest in their work and are committed to company objectives. They usually work with need for few controls.

The assumptions which are made about most people tend to influence management style. A person cannot ignore individual differences. Some employees fit the Theory X model. The supervisor who attempts to lead

Notes

No two people view things the same way. Human beings are very unique. The way people think and behave is in large part a result of their life experiences.

Many security departments have problems with and between department members. Working together in a harmonious manner is essential but not common among security departments.

Theory X: *theory created by Douglas MacGregor, states the average person dislikes work and is lazy and selfish; must be forced to do things by employer.*

Theory Y: *theory created by Douglas MacGregor, states the average person enjoys work and is not lazy and can work with few controls.*

them with Theory Y ideas will probably fail.

The difficulty in managing a security organization is in determining which theory best suits security personnel, Theory X or Theory Y?

This point can be hotly debated within the security industry as to which theory works best for security departments. While this author sees value in each theory, it has been his experience that, Theory X is used for the most part in security organizations. Consider the fact that many security managers and supervisors have years of experience within law enforcement and/or the military and you can see why Theory X may dominate. In addition, due to the nature of many security assignments, Theory X is popular simply because a task must be accomplished at a particular date and time. Often, security departments are inundated in paperwork and procedures which inhibit creative approaches to work. Managers and supervisors easily fall into the trap of doing it this way because, "we've done it that way for 20 years!" Often, security departments take on the atmosphere and personality of their parent organization. If the parent organization stifles creativity, it is likely that a Theory X management philosophy will be practiced within a security department.

Nature of Work

The concept of work is interpreted differently. Some people's work becomes an obsession. These people postpone vacations and voluntarily work long hours with little concern for external rewards. Other persons may watch the clock, looking forward to the end of the workday.

In real life, work is uniquely personal, depending upon philosophy, specific situations and a variety of other factors. Work "is an activity that produces something of value for other people."[1] While an organization deals with work primarily for payment to a person, compensation is not limited to money.

Most employees do not work just for pleasure. They work because they want certain things. Most people work to earn money and provide for security and fun activities. This does not mean that work is done only for money. Studies show that most employees would continue to work even if

Notes

Theory X is a common foundation from which security organizations are managed.

A participative management philosophy that encourages employees to "speak out" and accept responsibility reflects a Theory Y management style.

Work is considered a four-letter by many people.

they did not need the money. Many employees identify with their work or employers. Some are engineers, maintenance workers or even security officers. Some people look with pride upon their work because they can see what they have done in a day. One problem with assembly line manufacturing work is that employees perform a minor operation that they are unable to identify with in the finished product.

Security personnel often fail to identify themselves with the organization for which they work. In large part because security assignments are often located on the exterior perimeter of the facility, security personnel feel "outside" the organization. Managers and supervisors must make a concentrated, conscious effort to include security personnel in identifying with the goals and objectives of the organization where they work. Including security personnel in employee meetings and activities is a step in bridging this gap.

Employees' Dislike of Work

Many employees dislike their jobs because their work is boring and does not present challenges. Many companies have attempted to reduce employees' dislike of work by involving them more in decision making. By involving employees, companies hope to increase morale and reduce job boredom.

Motivation

Every person has needs which must be satisfied. Needs are divided into two groups, physiological and psychological. Physiological needs include air, water, food, etc... and must be satisfied in order to live. Psychological needs include self esteem which is everything and everybody with which a person identifies such as family, friends, school, profession, religion and material possessions.

Many people have needs for power, achievement and/or affiliation. Persons with a high need for power have learned that by obtaining power they can control certain aspects of their life. A person with a high need for power is willing to take risks involved in competition with others. This person usually tries for promotions and is willing to become involved in confrontations.

Notes

Security officers may identify with their positions, if they feel challenged and that they contribute.

Goals and objectives for security personnel need to be clearly identified and measurable.

Many Americans simply do not enjoy their jobs. Often, people feel trapped in a job and they are reluctant to make any changes.

Physiological Needs: include air, water and food.

Psychological Needs: Self-esteem.

Affiliation: a sense of belonging to a group.

Most politicians have a high need or desire for power.

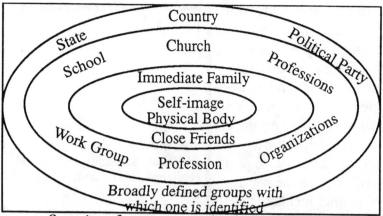

Country

State

Church

Political Party

School

Professions

Immediate Family

Self-image
Physical Body
Close Friends

Organizations

Work Group

Profession

Broadly defined groups with which one is identified

Notes

All of these elements affect a person in different ways. These elements will motivate a person in varying degrees. Graphic adapted from Human Behavior in Organizations, J. Clifton Williams, (South Western Publishing Co., Cincinnati, 1978, p. 97)

Do you want to work as a security officer to provide a service to people or do you want power?

Security often attracts individuals who seek or desire power. In May of 1983, The Wall Street Journal devoted a front-page article to the problems facing the security industry, entitled: "Hired Guns."

"...In addition, all law-enforcement work attracts, along with many perfectly competent people, a special brand of undesirable-impulsive, macho types with a strong need for power and authority. Security managers call it the John Wayne syndrome."

For the most part, security personnel possess what might be more appropriately call "perceived power." While in many situations, security personnel have broader power or authority than police officers, this power or authority is rarely used. Security personnel often complain about the lack of support received by management to enforce various policies and procedures. **Persons who are interested in working in the security industry, should be more interested in providing service to others as opposed to exerting power or authority.**

Persons with a high need for achievement want to accomplish things. These people are usually more interested in successfully completing a job instead of competing for power. Persons with a high need for achievement and a low need for power often work in positions in accounting or engineering. People with a high need for power prefer a position is sales or line management.

Management positions will usually have a good deal of power or authority.

Many people find greater satisfaction in being liked than in having power or achievement. They want to avoid power because people with power are often disliked. People who want affiliation care a lot about what people think about them. Their first goal is to be accepted, to be part of the group.

Need Levels

People's needs are usually never fully satisfied. As a person becomes reasonably satisfied their need level will increase to a higher level.

Abraham Maslow was a psychologist who developed the Need Hierarchy. Maslow believed that most people have 5 levels of needs:

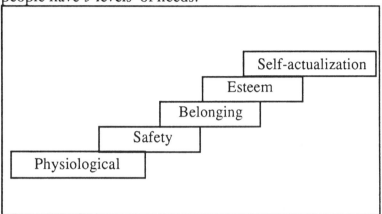

1. Physiological Needs: food, water, air, etc..

2. Safety Needs: includes protection from danger, desire to have money and job security including having savings accounts and life insurance.

3. Social Needs: includes the need for acceptance, love and friendship.

4. Esteem Needs: are greater than the need for acceptance; these needs include being highly respected by other people; very often referred to as self respect.

5. Self-actualization: need to be what a person is best suited for; to become everything that one is capable of becoming; these needs are never fully realized.

If a person agrees with Maslow then it must be understood that needs which are satisfied no longer motivate a person.

For most people who live in the United States the need for job security is weak when compared with the 1920's and 1930's. Because of opportunities to find work, seniority

---

Notes

Need Hierarchy: developed by psychologist Abraham Maslow, 5 levels of needs: physiological, safety, social, esteem and self-actualization; according to Maslow as one need is satisfied, another level will increase.

Required to live.

Basic needs that all persons have to one degree or another.

People want to be liked and to have friends.

People who "feel good" about themselves. Sometimes arrogance is displayed by people.

Persons should always be striving until death, "I have fought the good fight. I have finished the race. I have kept the faith!"

Once monetary needs are met, money will often fail to motivate.

provisions and programs of unemployment compensation, most people's needs for a reasonable level of job security can be attained. However, recently because of mergers, acquisitions, and the general downsizing of the workforce by many organizations, job security is becoming increasingly more difficult to attain.

More and more people have recently lost their jobs.

A second point is that employees' needs will change depending upon economic conditions. When a person is working 6 days a week, 12 hours a day and is paid for overtime, this person will not be as concerned about money. However, if this person is laid off from work for three months, their need for money becomes more critical.

While Maslow's theory has received a great amount of attention, there is no convincing objective evidence to support it. According to the Need Hierarchy, as one need is satisfied, the desire for that need should decrease. When one need desire decreases another should increase. While this may occur with some people, everyone does not experience this. Some psychologists suggest a two step theory regarding Maslow's theory. As an example, the two step theory would argue that a person who is unemployed or new on the job is likely to be thinking about physiological and safety needs. But as these needs are satisfied by money, other needs emerge. The two step view avoids any attempt to predict which higher level needs are satisfied.

People are different and have different needs. No two individuals respond in exactly the same manner in a given situation.

For security officers and supervisors needs such as belonging and esteem can be provided in their jobs but usually only if they feel a part of the organization and that what they do really counts. Security jobs which tend to suggest that the personnel working in the positions are simply statues, will normally not provide an opportunity for a security officer to feel a sense of belonging or esteem about their jobs.

Security personnel want to feel part of the organization and they want to make a contribution.

Frederick Herzberg

Frederick Herzberg developed a two-factor theory regarding motivation and needs satisfaction. Herzberg concluded from his research that many factors which managers have always believed to be motivators such as money do not really motivate. His two-factor idea is that job factors

Frederick Herzberg: developed a two-factor theory of motivation and needs satisfaction; one group of factors are satisfiers while the second group are dissatisfiers.

which are generally regarded as motivators should be divided into two groups: one consisting of motivational factors or what he called satisfiers and the other consisting of maintenance factors or dissatisfiers.

SATISFIERS	DISSATISFIERS
o achievement	o company policies
o recognition	o supervision
o responsibility	o relations - co-workers
o work itself	o pay
o growth possibilities	o working conditions

Herzberg believed that money, good working conditions, good benefits, being treated fairly etc... do not motivate a person. Instead, he believed that if these factors (money, benefits, etc...) do not exist, a person is demotivated. His theory implies that employees have an "all or nothing" attitude about their work and benefits. If the pay and the benefits are unattractive, a person will be difficult to motivate.

Herzberg's theory has been criticized by his peers. However, his theory is useful in focusing on job content factors. It has long been recognized that a high level of job satisfaction does not mean a person is highly motivated to do a good job.

Interests as Motivators

Some people are motivated in their jobs simply because of their high level of interest in their work. Most people have had work experience which did not seem like work because of their interest in the job. In these jobs, time passed quickly, concentration was strong and despite hard work, the job was enjoyable. Interest in work is an ideal motivator. A company that compensates an employee with an enjoyable work experience in addition to pay will usually have a worker who is a high producer, is creative and who creates few problems. Because interests are learned, interest in a particular subject or type of work will differ between people. People with low interest levels will disagree more

Notes

Herzberg believed that money does not motivate a person.

Just because a person is satisfied with his/her job does not mean they are motivated to do a good job.

Satisfaction: a state of being happy or content.

Motivation: provide a reason or a cause for a person's actions.

If people are interested in their work, they will normally be motivated to do a good job.

As security officers, what can be done to make work more interesting.

275

with management objectives than persons who have a high level of job interest.

Interests are not always motivational in terms of increasing productivity. Some people are highly motivated to be productive because they have high expectations for themselves. Interests have little effect on their productivity. Likewise, people with low work standards will usually do well in areas where interest is high. For example: some high ability students always make A's in courses they enjoy while their grades in other courses range from A to F. If possible, security personnel should be given assignments based upon their interest level. For example: an officer who likes fire protection may enjoy inspecting fire extinguishers and may perform this task excellently.

Coercive Motivation

Coercive motivation is usually unproductive since it demotivates a person. However, some degree of fear is present in individuals and is a deterrent to poor behavior. The employee who does what he/she is told because of fear usually resents their supervisor and/or organization. The employee will eventually become resentful and perhaps hostile. Resentment may be expressed in reduced production.

Fear however is not all bad. Highly successful people usually have a fear of failure because they constantly accept new challenges which may exceed their abilities. For these people, fear is a warning against carelessness. In general this type of fear is healthy, similar to the fear when crossing a busy intersection before a light changes. Fear is never absent as a possible motivator but it should only be used as a last resort when positive forms of motivation have failed.

Coercive motivation is usually relied upon within security organization when employee discipline becomes an issue. Most organizations have clear policies on attendance and appearance. A security officer who continues to be late or miss work, or whose appearance is judged to be improper, will no doubt experience coercive motivation. When an employee is counseled or reprimanded for their conduct and advised that further behavior will result in greater discipline, coercive motivation is being utilized.

Notes

Where does security fit?

Give security officers duties that interest them.

Coercive motivation is also known as..."Do it this way or else!"

Great athletes may perform better because they don't want to fail.

Unfortunately, coercive motivation is required when counseling poor performance.

Money as a Motivator

For practically everybody, money is an important motivator. If money had the same meaning to everyone it would be easy to make generalizations. But money means different things to different people. For the poor, money symbolizes the immediate satisfaction of food, health care, clothing and shelter. For most employed Americans this is not the case. At higher economic levels, money may symbolize security, status, power and prestige. Materialism is a part of our basic value system.

Whether money will motivate is to some degree a matter of the amount of money involved and the amount a person already has. Generally, the more people earn, the more they must receive to be motivated to work harder. Money usually does not motivate when a person has reached a comfort level. Reaching a comfort level is usually a choice to live within one's income by controlling wants and spending.

Another important factor of whether money motivates is the price one must pay for it. An employee who is paid on a piecework basis must decide whether the needs satisfied with increased earnings will offset being rejected by co-workers as a rate buster. The behavior required to earn more money may also conflict with the need for love, self respect or family life. In many situations, increased effort to earn more interferes with leisure time activities and the employee may reject a promotion or request to work overtime.

Money will motivate increased effort only if employees believe that working harder or producing more will result in more money. Unfortunately, money compensation systems reward performance and nonperformance equally. Money motivates best when it is received immediately after the behavior it is to reward.

Persons who work in security may be motivated by money but usually they are working in the profession as a second or supplemental job to provide extra income. While pay has improved in the security profession, particularly at the management level, security officers often receive low pay. This is usually the case with regard to the contract security industry.

Notes

Money means different things to different people.

Consider the many high priced athletes whose performance declines dramatically after signing a new contract. Perhaps, some of these athletes become contented and they don't work as hard as they did prior to the new contract.

How hard is a person willing to work for more money?

How much is free time or leisure time worth to a person?

A child who receives an allowance after completing certain duties or "chores" will be motivated differently than the child who receives an allowance for no work.

While security officer positions are plentiful in most areas of the United States, most are not well paying.

Competition

Competition within organizations has advantages and disadvantages. Competition is a secondary need which is learned. Since all kinds of games reward the winner, most children learn to enjoy competition and this continues into adulthood. People learn to compete in areas where they are most likely to succeed. Successfully competing with worthy opponents is ego enhancing. It contributes to self worth. People also learn not to be seriously hurt if they lose. Many average performers who think that they are as good as the next person may only desire to avoid being classified at the bottom of the ladder, Competition does not always involve a desire to be the best. The level which a person desires depends upon past experience as what is perceived as realistic aspirations.

Improving Communications

"What we got here is a failure to communicate," is a classic line from the Paul Newman movie, <u>Cool Hand Luke</u>. That statement summarizes a general belief by most employees about their jobs and company for which they work. Communications on the job are normally believed to be poor by many employees. Perhaps the lack of communication complaint is only an excuse for a general dislike for the job. But why do so many people complain about the lack of good communication?

It is important to understand exactly what communication means. What one person believes is good communication, another person might find unsatisfactory.

Interpersonal communication in organizations is defined as the process by which messages are transmitted from one person to another. Messages may be expressed in the form of bulletins, letters, memos, job descriptions, policy statements, telephone communications and other forms of verbal information. Some definitions imply that communication occurs only when the sender is successful in sending the intended message. A problem with this definition is that people seldom are totally effective in transmitting their intended messages.

Notes

Most people enjoy competition, provided they are successful.

Competition between security personnel is often destructive and detrimental to the security organization.

Security officers often complain that communication within their departments is poor.

Communication: messages which are transmitted from one person to another.

Most of the time people don't completely understand what another person is trying to tell them.

278

The goal in studying communication is to narrow the gap between the intended message and the message which is actually transmitted.

Communication involves four elements:
- Sender
- The Message
- A Medium or Device for sending the message
- A Receiver

It is important that the sender and the receiver have similar backgrounds for communication to be totally effective. In communicating a person never knows for certain what another person is thinking. We make assumptions from verbal and physical signs about what other people are thinking and feeling.

Encoding

Before a message can be transmitted from one person to another it must be encoded. Encoding is the process of transmitting into words, gestures, facial expressions, etc... the message the sender hopes to communicate. It is important to know that only symbols are transmitted. The meaning depends upon the receiver's interpretation of those symbols. A small child responds favorably to an adult who speaks in a soft tone of voice no matter what the adult is saying.

Medium

The medium or device of a message can be a face-to-face meeting, a letter, telephone call, etc... A different medium is used depending on the nature of the communication. Most persons want to discuss serious or important matters in person. The telephone is usually used for less formal communication.

Notes

A child who is a receiver of a message will interpret the meaning differently than an adult.

Encoding: as part of communication; Encoding is the process of transmitting into words, gestures, etc... the message the sender wants to communicate.

Message
- smiles, frowns
- tears
- clenched fist
- moving hands
- closed eyes
- clenched jaws

Medium: device used to transmit a message in communication.

A phone, television, walkie-talkie, letter, computer terminal and written note are all examples of a medium to transmit a message.

Decoding

The sender's message must be understood or interpreted. Words and other symbols have multiple meanings. There is no assurance that the intended meanings of the sender are the same as the receiver or decoder. The more experiences the sender and receiver have in common, the more likely it is that the intended message will be understood. In order for people with different experience fields to communicate, at least one must learn to speak the language of the other. Managers who want to communicate with their employees must learn how their employees think and feel. With this knowledge a person can usually predict with accuracy how a message will be decoded.

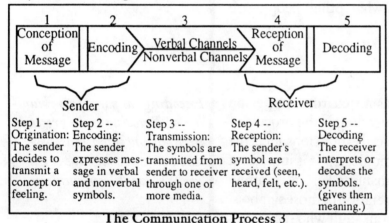

1	2	3	4	5
Conception of Message	Encoding	Verbal Channels / Nonverbal Channels	Reception of Message	Decoding

Sender — Receiver

| Step 1 -- Origination: The sender decides to transmit a concept or feeling. | Step 2 -- Encoding: The sender expresses message in verbal and nonverbal symbols. | Step 3 -- Transmission: The symbols are transmitted from sender to receiver through one or more media. | Step 4 -- Reception: The sender's symbol are received (seen, heard, felt, etc.). | Step 5 -- Decoding The receiver interprets or decodes the symbols. (gives them meaning.) |

The Communication Process 3

Non-Verbal Communication

Most of what a person communicates is transmitted nonverbally. Any gesture which serves as a word substitute may be classified as sign language. Examples are head movements for yes and no. A wave of the hand may mean both hello and good-bye.

Action language or body language is physical movement which conveys a message but are not specifically used as a word substitute. The way people work, sit or laugh tells something about them.

Object language can be an intentional or unintentional display of material things which communicate certain messages to other people. A person's clothes or automobile often communicate a message.

Notes

Decoding: process of understanding or interpreting another person's message.

Decoding involves attempting to understand what a person is saying and meaning.

To communicate effectively a person must try very hard to understand what the speaker is saying.

Human Behavior in Organization, J. Clifton Williams, (Cincinnati: South Western Publishing Co.) 1978, p. 328.

Non-Verbal Communication: body gestures or expressions which are a form of sign language communication.

Besides listening to what the person is saying, observe the speaker's body and facial movements. A person may say they agree with another person, but their non-verbal body and facial movements and expressions indicate that they disagree. The way a person dresses and the jewelry he/she wears, says something about the person.

Personality Factors & Communication

People differ in their ability to communicate. The differences are the result of skills in writing, grammar and even spelling. Other personality characteristics are important in communicating.

Empathy is the awareness of the needs and motives of others. A person can improve their sensitivity by consciously trying to understand how other people think and feel.

Talkativeness is talking too much or too little. Usually quiet people are poor communicators. Likewise, a good communicator motivates people to talk freely.

Assertiveness is shown by people who are persistent and forceful in stating a point of view. A person who gives a good presentation and is convincing in their speech is usually very persuasive.

Character is trust in a person. The ability to express oneself means little if trust is low. When trust is high people will accept a message and expect honorable motives from the sender. Maturity in the treatment of information is very important. Employees who believe supervisors can be trusted will usually confide in that person. Trust develops only over a long period of time. People's behavior not their words builds trust. Simply stated, "actions speak louder than words."

The People Puzzle

Dr. Morris Massey wrote The People Puzzle in 1979 which describes his theory of why people behave as they do. He states that if people take time to understand why a person acts a certain way you can develop more positive relationships.

Value System Programming

Dr. Massey identified Value System Programming which occurs in everyone. By this he means that society shapes a person. Everyone behaves differently depending on the value programming experienced. The major sources of value programming are:

Notes

Consider the difficulty in understanding the directions to assemble children's toys. Is an engineering degree necessary a bicycle.

Empathy: understanding the needs and motives of other people.

Do you really try to feel and understand what the speaker really believes about a situation?

Do you encourage people to tell you what's on their mind?

As security officers, we must be convincing in supporting the policies and procedures we enforce.

Do you respect the sensitivity and confidentiality of information?

Morris Massey: author of The People Puzzle which describes his theory of why people behave as they do; identified Value System Programming which describes how a person is shaped in terms of the way they think and act.

Dr. Massey's theory is very popular and accepted by many people.

Value System Programming: developed by Dr. Morris Massey, describes why people behave as they do; society shapes a person according to factors such as education, religion, the media, money, etc...

o family

o education

o religion

o the media

o friends

o where we grew up geographically

o amount of money

o other formal and informal teachers

The common traits of these factors will create highly similar patterns of behavior of people. An example of this are the people who were raised and programmed during the 1930's. A common value among these people is financial security. While not all of the people in the Depression generation refuse to use credit cards, a majority prefer dealing in cash.

As children develop certain values and behavior are reinforced. A programming sequence develops which creates very similar "gut level" values within each generation. Massey identifies three main periods in Value Systems Programming:

Imprinting (age 0 to 7)

At 3-4 years of age, scientists agree that basic personality is formed. A child learns how to behave as an adult by oberving others. "That's what a mother is like", etc...

Modeling (age 8 to 13)

As a child enters the formal learning process in school, intense modeling begins. People the child would like to be are carefully observed. "Heroes" can be parents, teachers, television or movie personalities, sports or political figures.

Socialization (age 14 to 20)

It's everyone, everyone, everyone, - our "significant others." The peer group, friends and families of friends are extremely important during this stage of our development. Birds of a feather DO flock together.

Notes

Dr. Massey believes people are the way they are based upon events and situations that occurred early in life.

Little girls play with dolls, little boys play with toy guns and cars.

Who were your heroes?

"But everybody is doing this or everybody is going, why can't I?"

Values Lock In: (Approximately age 20)

Around 20 years of age our value system programmed during childhood and adolescence locks in, and we then test it against the reality of the world. This value set is our operating filter for viewing the world for the rest of our lives.

Dr. Massey also coined the phrase Significant Emotional Event (S.E.E.). Massey believes that dramatic changes in our gut-level value system can occur at any time during our life. If something significantly effects us at a gut level, we may change our beliefs and alter our behavior. A Significant Emotional Event may be something as simple as reading a book, or watching a movie, or as complex as being fired from a job, winning a lottery, getting a divorce, or a brush with death. Typical reactions to a Significant Emotional Event are bewilderment, frustration and hostility. A person may fight to maintain his beliefs or values because to accept the possibility that a completely different way is as normal as our own can be a scary situation.

MAJOR FACTORS INFLUENCING VALUE PROGRAMMING:

FAMILY

Dr. Massey believes that the influence of the family occurs during the ages of infancy until 7. It is during this period that a child learns behavior from his/her family as to love and affection. Do parents and children hug and kiss? How does the family communicate? How are problems solved? Are the men macho, little boys tough, women weak and fluffy and little girls cute?

The way the family cooperates, laughs, cries, survives, etc.. all impact the development of children.

FRIENDS

As the family decreases in importance, a person will turn to those with whom they associate. Friends and families of friends are important because they provide a tremendous amount of reinforcement for values, especially during the teen years.

Notes

You are what you are! People usually don't change after values lock in.

Significant Emotional Event (SEE): describes the process or action which changes the way a person thinks and behaves according to Dr. Morris Massey.

When a significant emotional event occurs in a person's life, it causes a person to review and reflect on their life. Are they happy? Have they attained what they want in life? What is really important in life? Do I want to change jobs? What is really important?

Children who learn violence and hatred in their home will usually repeat this as an adult.

"The family that prays together, stays together."

Parents are always concerned with whom their children's friends are. The statement, "He/she hangs around with a bad crowd" refers to friends who are a poor influence.

RELIGION

Church or religion is another major source of values. When a child becomes ten, eleven or twelve he begins to deal with religious concepts and values. He/she will ask him or herself, "Do I really believe all this religion dogmas all these 'Thou shalt do these things, thou shalt not do these things'?"

SCHOOL

Teaching techniques that were used in the programming of young children will be reflected in the behavior of adults. Did your teacher talk with you or at you? Were you programmed to believe that the world would exist with absolute right answers and absolute wrong answers? Were you taught with another technique that said the world is not pure white or pure black, but in reality is grey? Was your school integrated or segregated? In textbooks, what were the roles of girls versus boys? The question is not whether schools program values, but HOW they program values.

GEOGRAPHY

Geography can be significant because there are differences: sunbelt, frostbelt, East, West, North, South, urban, rural. There are unique customs, foods, life styles and attitudes. All become part of a person's developing value systems.

INCOME OF FAMILY

The family income has a direct impact on values by programming what financially-based things and experiences to expect and not expect from the family. How does one family live compared to another family?

ELECTRONIC MEDIA

Music reflects the values of a generation. Advertising makes it seem that life is always exciting and that problems are solved in 60 seconds or less. Television has become a baby-sitter with intense exposure programmed values of instant satisfaction, instant gratification and "nowness." Television shows solve problems immediately. People are programmed to believe problems in real life can be solved that easily and quickly.

Notes

Religion means different things to different people. Religious people believe that God influences their lives and has definite plans for their lives.

How many names of your teachers do you remember? How many good teachers did you have? Did teachers motivate you? Did teachers encourage you? Did you play sports? What type of coach did you have? Were the majority of your teachers men or women?

How does a "Connecticut Yankee" feel when visiting the deep South. Is "you all" plural or singular?

Children from wealthy families have different values than children from poor families.

How much television do children watch today versus 20 years ago? Was your family life like the "Munsters, Addams Family, Ozzie and Harriet, or the Huxtables."

According to Dr. Massey, by the time a person reaches ten years of age, 90% of their gut-level value system is locked in. This value system is then used to filter the world through the rest of our lives. There may be some change, experimentation and modification during the latter portion of the value programming sequence. Massey's theory includes the notion that while it is important to recognize and allow for individual differences, you can learn a great deal by looking at groups of people holding similar values.

CURRENT AGE	VALUE YEAR	INFLUENCING FACTORS & ATTITUDES
70's	1920's	World War I - patriotic Close family, male was the breadwinner, female was home-maker, sense of responsibility and commitment to job.
		Good time was driving in a Model T drinking bootleg gin;
		It was a good world, a black and white world.
60's	1930's	The Great Depression- value programmed to worry;
		Security oriented-money motivates, put away for a rainy day, it could happen again;
		Immobile - flying is not normal.

Notes

As people reach adulthood, their ideas, values and the way they look at things are set.

Massey's theory is that if you understand the reasons why a person acts or behaves in a certain way, you could communicate better and enjoy a better relationship with the person.

285

50's	1940's	World War II-commitment to win;
		Family Decay-male was soldier, female kept the country going "Rosie the Riveter";
		Schools-kindergartens grow, schools takeover value programming.
		Mobility; "after they've seen Paris..."
40's	1950's	Family Income-Affluence, the good life arrived, kids were over-indulged.
		Television became the baby-sitter; hair, Elvis, Martin Luther King; Schools-integrated; Mobility-jet planes.
30's	1960's	Space program-man on the moon;
		Vietnam War-resistance, demonstrations,
		Schools-cause civil rights, riots;
		Television-Beatles, Kennedy elected on TV; Lived in Camelot on TV; died for REAL on TV.
		Media-bad guy heroes; bad guys win.

Notes

20's	1970's	Space program-rather be entertained;
		Watergate-don't get caught;
		Schools-sex education, ecology;
		Family and Friends-Identity crisis;
		Media-entertainment, Joe Namath
Teens	1980's	Media-heroes are media created, media hyped, media destroyed; no great American heroes-sleazy heroes;
		Schools-computers are normal.

CLASH OF VALUE SYSTEMS:

World War I patriotism	vs. Vietnam War Demonstrations
Stable family unit	vs. Divorced/remarried families
Close family unit	vs. Dispersed family unit
Homemaker mother	vs. Working mother
Save for a rainy day	vs. Get It Now
Ford marketing concept	vs. GE Marketing Concept
Short hair styles	vs. Long hair styles
Cash economy	vs. Credit card economy
Easy listening music	vs. Hard rock music
Commitment to work	vs. Punching out when time is up.

Notes

Where do you fit in? Where does your supervisor fit in?

Are you programmed for clashes?

These clash of value systems examples help to explain generation gaps and why it is often difficult for people to relate to one another.

Solving Your Own People Puzzles

There are no simple solutions for understanding how to solve the conflicts between ourselves and those who are "different." Acceptance of our own "normality" and that of others, and an open minded willingness to try to relate and communicate are the first critical steps in dealing effectively with other people according to Dr. Massey.

A complete and final solution to why people are different can never be obtained since the world and persons are always changing. In the past, things were simpler. In today's world a person must constantly be willing to change, to accept new ideas or new ways of doing things.

Massey states that there is a strong urge to see checklist recipes to solve our problems. No single recipe can possibly solve all of the problems for all of the people all of the time. Massey adds that any solution which does not start with a basic acceptance of self and others cannot be productive and may lead to unrealistic expectations about how people feel and what life should be all about. Massey contends that happiness and meaningful productive relationships grow out of commitment and responsibility. He believes people will be happier and more effective in life if they are willing to accept who and why we are and grant this acceptance to others.

Conflict & Stress

A company can achieve its objectives only if its members cooperate with each other. For cooperation to occur each person must to some degree give up individual freedom. Normally, conflict and stress occur when this freedom is given up. Conflict is a disruptive force within an organization and is also the cause of a person's stress. The goal of any organization should be to control conflict, not eliminate it.

Notes

As security officers, are we willing to try to understand why people behave as they do?

As security officers, are we willing to experiment and to try different approaches?

"Different strokes for different folks."

As security officers certain freedoms are given up when working. Patrols, inspections, etc., have to be conducted at certain times -- No exceptions.

Conflict is Going to Happen

It would be nice if all people were good. But within every individual is a blend of good and bad, selfish and unselfish. The United States is unique in its acceptance of conflict as a way of life. The court systems, labor relation laws, competition between business and the entire system of government (from the election of officials to debate over laws) is all based on the fact of conflict.

In organizations there are many sources of conflict:

- labor - management
- organization vs. individual goals
- personality clashes
- production vs. quality

It is obvious that both individuals and organizations are hurt by conflict. However, there are positive aspects of conflict:

1. better ideas are sometimes produced
2. people have to look for new approaches
3. long standing problems are surfaced and can be corrected.
4. people are forced to clarify their views.
5. the tension can increase interest and creativity.

Like an electrical shock, conflict attacks the foundation which makes people complacent, lazy and satisfied.

Stress

Stress occurs in response to a demand upon a person. The degree of stress depends upon the individual. Stress is influenced by a person's ability and self confidence.

Hans Selye, an authority on stress describes what he called the General Adaption Syndrome (GAS). The GAS occurs in three phases:

1. Alarm Reaction
2. Resistance Stage
3. Exhaustion Stage

In the alarm reaction phase a person deals with stress

Notes

What conflicts do you face every day in your own life -- with family, co-workers, roommates, friends? Big or small, we all face conflict daily.

Conflict, although integrally involved all around us, often only has a negative connotation.

What causes stress in your life?

either by confronting or by withdrawing from the situation which causes stress. This is commonly referred to as flight or fight. In this stage the heart beats faster, blood pressure rises and breathing becomes deep and rapid.

In the resistance stage, the stress threat continues and the body develops an increased resistance to it. In this stage the body functions return to normal.

If stress continues the person will continue into a stage of exhaustion. Eventually energy is deleted and lifespan is shortened. Many diseases such as ulcers, heart ailments and high blood pressure are in some cases directly related to stress.

Stress can be caused by many factors. Often stress can be minimized if a person's self image is such that they believe they can deal with most problems or situations. Resistance to stress can be due to other factors. Under the same situation people will react differently to stress. A person who has a flexible personality will handle stress better than a rigid person. A person who "blows off steam" or laughs at themself will normally control stress better than the person who never expresses their feelings.

An organization by its very nature will create the likelihood of stress. Examples include:

- Lack of leadership for employees
- Boring, routine jobs
- Little chance of promotion
- Too much responsibility
- Too much work
- Inconsistent procedures or direction
- Conflicts with personal values
- Conflicts with co-workers
- Poor communication
- Low pay, long hours

The most important consideration for the security officer is how to deal with stress. Many people try to escape from stress. Some of these escape techniques can be harmful such as excessive daydreaming, television watching, excessive alcohol consumption and overeating. Healthier forms of escape include hobbies, participation in sports, involvement

Notes

Flight or fight theory or dealing with stress: either avoid the source of stress or attack it and attempt to conquer it.

The body's defense mechanism begins.

Stress is reality. Everyone has some stress in their lives. Now a person copes with stress will vary among individuals.

Identify stresses in your life:
1.
2.
3.
4.
5.
6.
7.
8.
9.
10.

Being able to deal with stress in a healthy, productive manner in crucial to one's happiness and longevity.

in civic or religious activities, relaxing with families or friends and other activities which are not related to work.

     If stress in a person's life is caused for the most part by work, an excellent way to reduce stress is to identify and associate with other persons who have similar jobs. This is what occurs when people form "support groups." Organizations and associations have been founded for the main purpose of bringing people together who have similar jobs in order for them to share their experiences. Almost everyone enjoys talking with a person who agrees with you, supports you and can generally understand you.

Notes

Footnotes

1. Homo Faber, <u>Work in America</u> - Report of a Special Task Force to the Secretary of Health, Education, and Welfare, James O'Toole, Chairman (Cambridge, Mass: The MIT Press, 1973) p. 2.

2. J. CLifton Williams, <u>Human Behavior in Organizations</u>, (Cincinnati: South Western Publishing Co.), 1978, p. 97.

3. IBID, p. 329.

References

Dr. Morris Massey, <u>The People Puzzle</u>, Understanding Yourself and Others, Preston Publishing Co., (Preston, VA: 1979).

<u>The Wall Street Journal</u>, "Hired Guns" May 1983.

SUMMARY

The beginning of the human relations movement is usually associated with studies conducted by Elton Mayo. These studies showed that at a particular time and place productivity could be increased in the workplace.

Theory X and Theory Y were principles developed by Douglas MacGregor. Theory X states that the average person dislikes work and is lazy, selfish and does not care about their employer. Theory Y states that people enjoy work and are not lazy.

The Nature of Work for people is different. Some people's work becomes an obsession. Work is uniquely personal depending on a variety of factors. Most people do not work for pleasure. They work because they want certain things. Many people dislike work because it is boring and not challenging.

Motivation is a person's needs which must be satisfied. Needs are either physiological or psychological. Many persons have needs for power, achievement and/or affiliation.

People's needs are usually never fully satisfied. Abraham Maslow was a psychologist who developed the theory of Need Hierarchy which states people have five need levels: physiological, safety, social, esteem and self actualization.

Frederick Herzberg developed a two-factor theory regarding motivation and needs satisfaction. He believed that job factors can be divided into satisfiers and dissatisfiers.

Some people are motivated in their jobs simply because of their high level of interest in their work. Interests are not always motivational in terms of increasing productivity.

Coercive motivation creates fear in a person to perform the job in a particular way. While considered

Notes

unproductive, some degree of fear is present in everyone and be a deterrent to poor behavior.

For most people, money is also an important motivator. But money means different things to different people. Whether money motivates is to some degree a matter of the amount of money involved and the amount a person already possesses. Another important factor of whether money motivates is the price one must pay to get it.

Competition within organizations has advantages and disadvantages. Competition is a secondary need which is learned.

Communication is defined as the process by which messages are transmitted from one person to another. Communication involves a sender, the message, a device for sending the message and a receiver. Encoding is the process of transmitting into words, gestures, etc... the message the sender hopes to communicate. Decoding is the process by which the receiver attempts to understand the sender's message.

Most of what a person communicates is transmitted non verbally. Action language are physical movements which convey a message. Object language can be a display of material things which communicate certain things to other people.

People differ in their ability to communicate. Characteristics such as empathy, talkativeness, assertiveness and character affect a person's ability to communicate.

Dr. Morris Massey wrote The People Puzzle in 1979 which describes his theory of why people behave as they do. Massey identified Value System Programming which describes the way society shapes a person. Imprinting occurs for a person between the ages of 0 - 7. At this stage a person learns how to behave by observing others. Modeling occurs between the ages of 8 - 13. Socialization occurs between the ages of 14 - 20. Values are locked in around 20 years of age. A Significant Emotional Event occurs when a dramatic change occurs in a person's life. Massey believes that factors such as family, friends, religion, school, geography, income and the electronic media greatly affect a person's values. Massey offers no simple solutions for understanding how to solve the conflicts between people.

Conflict and stress are present in every organization. In organizations there are many sources of conflict. Stress occurs in response to a demand upon a person. Stress is influenced by a person's ability and self confidence.

Hans Selye, an authority on stress describes his theory of General Adaption Syndrome (G.A.S.). Three phases occur in the G.A.S.: alarm reaction, resistance stage and exhaustion stage.

Stress can be caused by many factors. An organization or company by its existence creates stress. Stress affects people differently. Some persons try to escape stress through unhealthy means while others escape from stress via healthy activities.

Notes

QUESTIONS

1. Who is associated with the beginning of the Human Relations movement with studies conducted at a Western Electric plant near Chicago?

    a. Frederick Herzberg
    b. Morris Massey
    c. Elton Mayo
    d. Douglas MacGregor

2. What was the original intent of the Hawthorne experiment?

    a. To reduce work
    b. To study the affects of lighting
    c. To speed up work
    d. To replace workers with machines

3. Who developed Theory X and Theory Y?

    a. Frederick Herzberg
    b. Morris Massey
    c. Elton Mayo
    d. Douglas MacGregor

4. Explain Theory X:

5. Explain Theory Y:

6. Every person has needs which must be satisfied. Needs are divided into two groups:

    a. Conscious and unconscious
    b. Lateral and bi-lateral
    c. Proactive and reactive
    d. Physiological and psychological

7.   What type of need is the need for power?

a. Conscious and unconscious
b. Lateral and bi-lateral
c. Proactive and reactive
d. Physiological and psychological

8.   Persons with a high need for achievement and a low need for power often work in positions in:

a. Finance and marketing
b. Production and quality
c. Personnel and safety
d. Accounting and engineering

9.   Persons with a high need for power prefer a position in:

a. Sales
b. Accounting
c. Line management
d. a and c

10.   Who developed the Need Hierarchy?

a. Frederick Herzberg
b. Elton Mayo
c. Abraham Maslow
d. Douglas MacGregor

11.   Name the 5 levels which make-up the Need Hierarchy:
a. _____

b. _____

c. _____

d. _____

e. _____

12.   Frederick Herzberg believed that money does not motivate a person. True or False?

13.   Coercive motivation relies upon _____ to motivate.

   a. Money
   b. Fear
   c. Maturity
   d. Responsibility

14.   Competition is a secondary need which is learned. True or False?

15.   What four elements are involved in communication?

   a. _____

   b. _____

   c. _____

   d. _____

16.   Symbols are a form of encoding. True or False?

17.   For decoding to be successfully understood in communication it is important that people understand one another. True or False?

18.   _____ is the awareness of needs and motives of others.

   a. Respect
   b. Sympathy
   c. Empathy
   d. Esteem

19.   _____ _____ wrote The People Puzzle in 1979 which describes his theory of why people behave as they do.

   a. Elton Mayo
   b. Frederick Herzberg
   c. Douglas MacGregor
   d. Morris Massey

20. Value System Programming describes:

    a. What is important to a person
    b. The way people treat one another
    c. The way society shapes a person
    d. The value of money

21. Name 3 sources of Value Programming:

    a. _____

    b. _____

    c. _____

22. _____ is referred to as the age (0-7) where most scientists agree that basic personality is formed.

23. Modeling occurs between the ages of:

    a. 8 - 13
    b. 15 - 18
    c. 4 - 7
    d. 2 - 6

24. At approximately what age are values locked in?

    a. 8
    b. 10
    c. 16
    d. 20

25. Peer group, friends and families of friends are part of _____ which occurs between the ages of 14 - 20.

26. What is a Significant Emotional Event?

27. What are typical reactions to a Significant Emotional Event?

28. Dr. Massey believes that the influence of the family occurs during the ages of:

    a. 7 - 14
    b. 14 - 21
    c. 0 - 7
    d. 10 - 12

29. Friends and families of friends are important because they provide a tremendous amount of reinforcement for values, especially during the _____ years.

    a. Infancy
    b. Adolescent
    c. Teen
    d. Adult

30. According to Dr. Morris Massey when a child becomes ____, ____ or ____ he/she begins to deal with religious values and concepts.

31. According to Dr. Massey, the question is not whether schools program but HOW they program. True or False?

32. According to Dr. Massey, family income has no direct impact on values. True or False?

33. According to Dr. Massey, by the time a person reaches _____ years of age, 90% of their "gut-level" value system is locked in:

    a. 7
    b. 10
    c. 16
    d. 21

34. According to Dr. Massey, a complete and final solution to why people are different can never be obtained since the world and persons are always changing. True or False?

35. Name two sources of conflict within organizations.

    1. _____

    2. _____

36. Name three positive aspects of conflict.

    1. _____

    2. _____

    3. _____

37. What are the three phases of the General Adaption Syndrome (G.A.S.) developed by Hans Selze?

    1. _____

    2. _____

    3. _____

38. What is a healthy way of dealing with stress?

    _____

Practical Exercises and Questions

1. Identify or give examples of attention you receive from the management of the organization where you work?

2. What motivates you? List those items.

3. Are you a Theory X or Y worker? How do you know? Give some examples.

4. Why do you work in this job as a security officer or supervisor?

5. List five examples of how security officers serve others.
   1.   4.
   2.   5.
   3.

6. Where are you currently in Maslow's Need Hierarchy? Where are your co-workers or classmates?

7. Does money motivate you? Why or why not? How do you know for certain?

8. What are you afraid of? Does fear motivate you?

9. How much competition exists in your life? Is this competition destructive?

10.   Identify the ways in which communications are handled where you work?

11.   Do people consider you to be a good listener? Are successful investigators good listeners? Why do you think so?

12.   What are your values in your life? Who influenced these values? Who or what influences your values now?

13.   Is there conflict within your work group?

14.   How much stress is created by your job?

Introduction to the Value Appraisal Scale

Dr. Morris Massey believes that all humans are value programmed beginning in infancy. The purpose of the questionnaire that follows is to provide the participant an opportunity to determine what is and is not important in his or her life. Is money more important than fame and religion? Are family issues more important than social issues?

The information provided to this person completing this questionnaire can greatly assist him or her in determining what profession he or she should consider when planning a career. Since over one third of an adult's life is spent working, does it not seem important to find a field or profession that supports one's values? For instance, if money and fame are extremely important to a person, studying to be a good diesel mechanic will most likely not support or enhance said person's values.

People should attempt to work at jobs which at a minimum do not conflict with their individual values. Hopefully, if the person is fortunate, he or she will work in a field or profession that reinforces his or her core values and that allows the worker an opportunity to obtain what is important in his or her life.

What are your values? Complete the questionnaire and then record your answers on the Value Appraisal Scoring Sheet. After totals are determined for each category, chart your scores on the graph included. Compare what is important to you with what is important to other students.

VALUE APPRAISAL SCALE

The purpose of this activity is to let you appraise your own values and compare them to those of other individuals throughout the USA.

You will read 100 statements indicative of 10 defined values. Circle your number answer, particular to you, in the following manner:

> 10 = definitely true
> 7 = mostly true
> 5 = undecided whether statement is true or false
> 3 = mostly false
> 0 = definitely false

1. I have a regular physical checkup by my doctor every year.   10   7   5   3   0

2. I will regularly take my children to church service, or attend myself.   10   7   5   3   0

3. I enjoy attending musical concerts.   10   7   5   3   0

4. It is important to me to have a lot of friends.   10   7   5   3   0

5. I donate to charities that I feel are worthwhile.   10   7   5   3   0

6. I envy the way celebrities are recognized wherever they go.   10   7   5   3   0

7. I would like to have enough money to retire at age 50.   10   7   5   3   0

8. I would rather spend an evening at home with my family than out with friends.   10   7   5   3   0

9. I enjoy making decisions which involve other people.   10   7   5   3   0

10. If I had the talent I would like to write music and songs.   10   7   5   3   0

11. I have, now or in the past, a close relationship with either my father or mother.   10 7 5 3 0

12. I have taught a Sunday school class or otherwise taken an active part in my church.   10 7 5 3 0

13. I am willing to spend time helping another individual who is having personal problems.   10 7 5 3 0

14. Even at the same salary, I would rather be the boss than just another employee.   10 7 5 3 0

15. I have a special appreciation for beautiful things.   10 7 5 3 0

16. If I had the talent, I would like to appear regularly on television.   10 7 5 3 0

17. I would like to counsel people and help them with their problems.   10 7 5 3 0

18. I would enjoy associating with movie stars and other celebrities.   10 7 5 3 0

19. I have a regular dental checkup at least once a year.   10 7 5 3 0

20. I enjoy writing short stories or fiction.   10 7 5 3 0

21. I would rather spend a summer working to earn money than to go on a paid vacation.   10 7 5 3 0

22. I like to attend parties.   10 7 5 3 0

23. I think it would be fun to write a screenplay for television or the movies.   10 7 5 3 0

24. I believe in a God who answers prayers.　　　10　7　5　3　0

25. I prefer being an officer rather than just a club member.　　　10　7　5　3　0

26. I would spend my last $100 for needed dental work rather than for a week's vacation at my favorite resort.　　　10　7　5　3　0

27. I enjoy giving presents to members of my family.　　　10　7　5　3　0

28. If I were an instructor, I would rather teach poetry than calculus.　　　10　7　5　3　0

29. I often have daydreams about things that I would like to do if I had the money.　　　10　7　5　3　0

30. I enjoy giving parties.　　　10　7　5　3　0

31. I am willing to write letters for old or sick people.　　　10　7　5　3　0

32. It would be very satisfying to act in movies or television.　　　10　7　5　3　0

33. When I feel ill, I usually see or call a doctor.　　　10　7　5　3　0

34. I beleive in tithing (giving 1/10th of one's earnings to the church) is one's duty to God.　　　10　7　5　3　0

35. I enjoy taking part in the discussion at the family dinner table.　　　10　7　5　3　0

36. I enjoy visiting art museums.　　　10　7　5　3　0

37. I like to write my own poetry.　　　10　7　5　3　0

38. I like to be around people most of the time.　　　10　7　5　3　0

39. When with a friend, I like to be the one who decides   10   7   5   3   0
what we will do or where we will go.

40. Someday, I would like to live in a large expensive house.   10   7   5   3   0

41. I pray to God about my problems.   10   7   5   3   0

42. If I knew a family that had no food for Christmas dinner,   10   7   5   3   0
I would try to provide it.

43. I like to spend holidays with family and relatives.   10   7   5   3   0

44. I like to see my name in print.   10   7   5   3   0

45. I would rather take a class in freehand drawing and art than   10   7   5   3   0
a class in math.

46. I do not like to spend an evening alone.   10   7   5   3   0

47. If the salary were the same, I would rather be an   10   7   5   3   0
administrator than an instructor.

48. I have expensive tastes.   10   7   5   3   0

49. I can tell the difference between a really fine painting   10   7   5   3   0
or drawing, and an ordinary one.

50. If I had regular headaches, I would consult a doctor even   10   7   5   3   0
if aspirin seemed to less the pain.

51. I have several close friends.   10   7   5   3   0

52. I expect to provide music lessons for my children or   10   7   5   3   0
my grandchildren.

53. It is important to me that grace be said before meals.   10   7   5   3   0

54. I sometimes miss sleep to visit late with company.   10   7   5   3   0

55. I usually get eight hours sleep each night.   10   7   5   3   0

56. I like to design things.   10   7   5   3   0

57. I like to be looked up to for my accomplishments.   10   7   5   3   0

58. I would feel a sense of satisfaction from nursing a sick person back to health.   10   7   5   3   0

59. I care what my family thinks about the things I do.   10   7   5   3   0

60. I daydream about making a lot of money.   10   7   5   3   0

61. I like to be the chairpersons at meetings.   10   7   5   3   0

62. It is thrilling to come up with the original idea and put it to use.   10   7   5   3   0

63. I believe there is life after death.   10   7   5   3   0

64. I would welcome a person of another race as a neighbor.   10   7   5   3   0

65. If I were in the television field, I would rather be an actor than a script writer.   10   7   5   3   0

66. I enjoy decorating my house or apartment.   10   7   5   3   0

67. I enjoy a picnic with my family.   10   7   5   3   0

68. I want to earn a much higher salary than the average worker, wage earner.   10   7   5   3   0

69. I am careful to have a balanced diet each day.   10   7   5   3   0

70. I often influence my peers concerning specific training which I think they should take.   10   7   5   3   0

71. I would like to be written up in professional journals.   10   7   5   3   0

72. I read the bible or other religious writings regularly.   10   7   5   3   0

73. If I were in the clothing industry, I would enjoy creating new styles.   10   7   5   3   0

74. I look forward to an evening out with a group of friends.   10   7   5   3   0

75. When I am with a group of people, I like to be the "one in charge."   10   7   5   3   0

76. I dislike being financially dependent on others.   10   7   5   3   0

77. When a friend is in trouble, I feel I must confort him/her.   10   7   5   3   0

78. I love my parents and family.   10   7   5   3   0

79. I almost never skip meals.   10   7   5   3   0

80. I have a collection of albums or tapes (music).   10   7   5   3   0

81. I have a particular friend with whom I discuss problems.   10   7   5   3   0

82. I believe that God created man in his own image.   10   7   5   3   0

83. I enjoy buying clothes for members of my family.   10 7 5 3 0

84. I enjoy having people recognize me wherever I am.   10 7 5 3 0

85. I like planning activities for others.   10 7 5 3 0

86. I do not smoke.   10 7 5 3 0

87. I feel good when I do things which help others.   10 7 5 3 0

88. Someday, I would like to write a novel.   10 7 5 3 0

89. I would put up with undesirable living conditions in order   10 7 5 3 0
    to work at a job that paid extremely well.

90. I belong to several clubs and organizations.   10 7 5 3 0

91. If I ask God for forgiveness, my sins are forgiven.   10 7 5 3 0

92. I would enjoy having my picture in local newspapers more   10 7 5 3 0
    than it has been in the past.

93. I often organize group activities.   10 7 5 3 0

94. When I see a newly constructed building, I consider its   10 7 5 3 0
    beauty as much as its practical use.

95. I respect my father and mother.   10 7 5 3 0

96. I like to design or make things that have not been made   10 7 5 3 0
    before.

97. Some of the hobbies I would like are quite expensive.   10 7 5 3 0

98. I enjoy classical music.   10 7 5 3 0

99. I would never use potentially harmful drugs because of   10 7 5 3 0
       what they might to do my body.

100. I am kind to people.   10 7 5 3 0

Value Appraisal Scoring
For each of the 10 values, record the answer circled for the statement indicated.

Fame	Money	Power	Religion	Humanism	Family	Health	Aestheti	Creative	Social
6	7	9	2	5	8	1	3	10	4
16	21	14	12	13	11	19	15	20	22
18	29	25	24	17	27	26	28	23	30
32	40	39	34	31	35	33	36	37	38
44	48	47	41	42	43	50	49	45	46
57	60	61	53	58	59	55	52	56	51
65	68	70	63	64	67	69	66	62	54
71	76	75	72	77	78	79	80	73	74
84	89	85	82	87	83	86	94	88	81
92	97	93	91	100	95	99	98	96	90
Total	Total	Total	Total	Total	Total	Total	Total	Total	Total

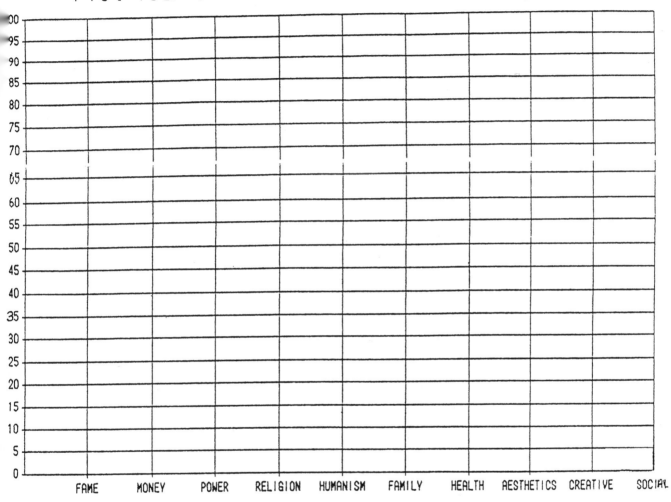

PROFILE OF VALUES
Plot Your Own Profile from the Scoring Scale

THE EFFECTIVE SECURITY OFFICERS TRAINING MANUAL

Chapter XV

Handling Disruptive People

Handling Disruptive Persons in the Work Place

THE WORK PLACE AND THE POTENTIAL FOR VIOLENCE

It seems almost on a regular basis you can pick up a newspaper or watch the 6 o'clock news and learn about some disgruntled employee or former employee who returns to his place of employment and opens fire on his boss and co-workers. You don't necessarily always think of the work place as an environment which would induce violence but over the past five or ten years there have been numerous violent episodes which have resulted in serious physical injury and even death to employees.

It is imperative today's security officer understand his role in potentially violent situations and have the training required to respond appropriately. In most instances, the security officer's role is preventative in nature. The security officer must develop excellent skills at being able to recognize potentially violent situations and be able to utilize appropriate verbal skill management techniques to diffuse them.

A closer examination of the work place environment reveals a number of situations which could turn violent:

* Employees being severely disciplined.
* Employees being discharged.
* Disgruntled former employees returning to the property.
* Employee suspected of drug abuse being sent for a drug test.
* Employees under the influence of drugs or alcohol which causes a reduced "threat threshold".
* Severe personality conflicts between employees and employees and their supervisors.
* Employees involved in relationships who are now feuding.
* Employees who are psychotic or have who developed severe mental problems due to personal

Notes

Reading For A Purpose
Look for these key words:
• Threat Threshold
• "Team Approach"
• Verbal Skill Management
• Emotional Behavioral Symptoms
• Threat Cues
• Mild Physical Arousal
• Defensive Alternatives
• Physical Intervention
• Debriefing
Look for answers to these Questions:
1. What are the most effective ways to prevent violence and provide assistance when violent situation occur?
2. What is the "Team Approach"?
3. What are the emotional behavioral symptoms of a disruptive person?
4. What are the appropriate verbal interventions to use with a disruptive person?
5. What is debriefing and why is it necessary?

Threat Threshold: The point at which an individual feels endangered (physically or emotionally). It is at this point where violence is most likely to occur.

problems or in some cases brought about by the work environment.
* Stress related incidents of "acting out".

THE SECURITY OFFICER'S ROLE IN PREVENTING VIOLENCE AND PROVIDING ASSISTANCE WHEN VIOLENT SITUATIONS OCCUR

This training is provided to the security officer for the purpose of learning to recognize and appropriately respond to disruptive instances in the work place. As a professional in public relations and law enforcement, the security officer's skillfulness in carrying out his duties is a reflection of him/her and the organization they represent.

The security officer's primary goal in a potentially violent situation is to defuse the situation - not incite a physical confrontation.

In order to become effective in his role, the security officer must become proficient at recognizing or assessing potentially violent behavior, utilizing verbal skills designed to minimize the risk of agitating the potentially violent individual and learning and utilizing only non-offensive physical techniques when appropriate.

The presence of a uniformed security officer is usually a visual deterrent to violence, particularly when there is a show of force. Security officers should be requested to "standby" in the immediate vicinity when management anticipates a violent situation might occur, such as when an employee with a past history of violence is being terminated. A "standby" may be referred to as a precautionary measure taken by management to permit security to intervene early with a potentially violent person. Prior to any management person giving the potentially violent person any ultimatum, the presence of uniformed security officers should be ensured. This may cause the situation to de-escalate. This form of early intervention is utilized in most mental health care settings and is deemed very appropriate when handling potentially violent individuals.

Notes

A security officer's primary goal in a potentially violent situation is to defuse the situation.

Standby: precautionary measure taken to permit security to intervene early with a potentially violent employee.

315

The primary goal, of preventing violence whenever possible, must always be remembered. There are times when a person becomes violent regardless of the presence of several security officers standing by in the immediate area and regardless of the skill level of the person verbalizing with the individual. When management is aware of an individual's potential for violence and that individual is going to be disciplined or discharged, etc., the security officers should be called early and a "game plan" developed in the event violence occurs.

This plan should include:

* Who is going to call the police?
* When should the police be called?
* When should the security officers move to restrain the individual?
* Where should the person be taken once restrained?
* Should handcuffs be utilized?
* Does anyone have handcuffs?
* Should the person be physically ejected from the property rather than restrained?

(The legal aspects of restraining someone are discussed in another section of this manual.)

The security officer-in-charge should discuss and assist in developing the plan with the appropriate management person on the scene.

A subject that rears it's ugly head during times of violence, although it is the most inappropriate time for such discussion is "I don't get paid enough to do this". Anyone considering a career in security must be aware that violence can and does occur in the work place. Wage rates are not a factor in determining our role in potentially violent situations.

Notes

ASSESSING BEHAVIOR AND THE POTENTIAL FOR VIOLENCE

There are several points to be aware of when assessing behavior and the potential for violence.

- All behavior is motivated.

    Acting-out, like other types of behavior, is intended to achieve some goal. This goal may or may not be apparent to you or the person who is upset. The first question you must ask yourself is "What is the reason for this person's behavior"? You need to become aware of the person's vital interests and how the environment might be perceived by the person as a threat to that vital interest. Examples of vital interests commonly threatened in the work place have been previously discussed, such as loss of job, loss of stature with co-workers, and in general, a feeling of helplessness as one places their well-being in the hands of others.

- The more basic the vital interest being threatened, the higher the risk of violence.

    All people have a threat threshold - that is a certain tolerance for perceived threat. If the intensity of perceived threat in the environment is more than the individual can handle, the risk of that person becoming violent is high. This threat threshold will differ from person to person.

- Violence-Prone individuals have a condensed threat threshold.

    The individual with a condensed threat threshold is more likely to escalate toward a physical confrontation than the average person. There are numerous reasons for someone to be or become violence-prone. Factors such as personality, past experience, learning, and the present circumstances shape a person's reactions. Typical examples of individuals that might have a condensed threat threshold include:

    * the criminal or antisocial individual
    * the intoxicated individual

Notes

Acting-out: Aggressive behavior demonstrated by verbal abuse and possible physical confrontation.

 * the psychotic individual
 * the physically and/or emotionally traumatized individual or family member

• The more intense a person's emotional reaction, the less likely they are able to think rationally.

Acting-out always involves some emotional force associated with the situation. Fear is the most common emotion related to aggression.

In understanding that the emotionally upset person is unable to think rationally, we can see the sense in taking deliberate steps to de-escalate the emotional components of a situation so that the person can rationally cooperate.

• When upset, if given an option, an individual will usually choose a non-violent way over a violent way of dealing with a stressful situation.

Common causes of acting-out:

• Frustration   • Tension (anxiety)
• Being ignored/rejected   • Lack of positive attention
• Confinement   • Loss of person power
• Psychological confusion/misperception
• Lack of impulse control   • Boredom
• Overcrowding   • Competition
• Staff behavior
• Need to establish/maintain self-esteem (MACHO MAN)

Impulse Control: Ability to rationally deal with frustration, tension, stress, anger, etc. without displaying overly aggressive behavior.

Person Power: Freedom and ability to make basic decisions in daily life such as freedom of movement.

Cues to potential acting-out:

• Mood swings
• Changes in body language/activity
• Physical tension
• Changes in verbal behavior
• Stimulus events - certain dates such as anniversary of termination date, etc.
• Depression, suicide attempt
• Past history data

318

THE TEAM APPROACH

The most effective "Crisis Management" approach is the TEAM APPROACH. Management and security should work together as a team. Security is an integral part of that team as they are usually relied upon to physically intervene with the person, if it becomes necessary.

Security officers must always remember that initially any management person who might call for their assistance in handling a disruptive person situation is ALWAYS the team leader. This leadership may be turned over to security at some point during the crisis but management is ultimately responsible for what occurs. Security may be asked to assist in this endeavor but is not ultimately responsible and therefore does not always have the final say about what should be done.

Even though management may be in charge, they rely a great deal on security's ability to deal with violent people who are acting-out. This reliance extends to security occasionally assuming the role of team leader, particularly with extremely violent people who have a past history at the organization for disruptive behavior.

When a person demonstrates behavior which indicates he is becoming upset, management should respond appropriately by having a single manager (designated team leader - usually the manager deemed to have the best rapport with the potentially disruptive individual) verbally intervene and attempt to calm the person down or de-escalate the situation. Other available staff should contact security in the event they have not yet been notified. If several security officers are available to respond, they should initially remain out of the potentially violent individual's sight until a plan is discussed, whenever possible.

Most potentially violent incidents can be handled smoothly if everyone knows their role and performs their function properly. Only one person (designated team leader) should verbally communicate with the potentially violent person. Even if the potentially violent person directs verbal abuse or questions to another person on the scene, including

Notes

The management person who calls for security assistance is handling a disruptive person situation is ALWAYS the team leader.

319

security, that person being spoken to by the potentially violent person MUST NOT RESPOND! The team leader should respond for him or her by stating that the person must speak with him and no one else. What the person is attempting to do, by trying to get other people talking is to DIVIDE AND CONQUER. If the potentially violent person is successful in getting everyone talking at the same time, he is getting everyone's attention away from what should be their primary goal, which is to calm or control the person who is potentially violent.

Notes

When the team leader is speaking with the potentially violent person, security officers on the scene should not interfere, regardless of what is said. Frequently, the potentially violent person becomes verbally abusive. Security officers must not take insults or verbal abuse personally. They must not take this as a challenge to fight. The manager dealing with the individual should inform security when he or she feels they have exhausted all of their verbal interventions and they desire to turn the situation over to security for continued verbal intervention or to restrain and remove the individual from the area. In the event the person attempts physical violence toward any of the team members, security should immediately move in and physically restrain the person and prevent anyone, including the violent individual from being injured.

VERBAL SKILL MANAGEMENT

Communication with words and gestures can be one of the safest, simplest, and most readily available interventions that people working with a potentially violent individual have available to them. The risks are few and the gains are many. Through effective verbal communication, problem resolution can be accomplished with minimum risk of injury. Verbal techniques can be used as a tool in helping persons to calm down; to discuss concerns; to regain an inner sense of control and to explore alternatives. As physical pain and emotional stress may reduce a person's ability to cope, effective verbal interventions can help the person deal with feelings of frustration and fear, and ultimately help restore a sense of balance and control.

The escalation or de-escalation of a crisis may depend on our ability to verbally intervene.

As previously stated, the team leader is the ONLY person to communicate and verbally intervene with the disruptive person. The rest of the team works to be supportive to their leader and a resource for future help. This approach will provide the disruptive person with structure and help focus their attention. If more than one staff member is talking to the disruptive person, the chance is MUCH GREATER that the team will lose control of the situation.

Verbal interventions should be based on the emotional/behavioral response to a crisis. Following are examples of a disruptive person's emotional behavior and symptoms, and the appropriate verbal interventions.

EMOTIONAL/BEHAVIORAL SYMPTOMS

• Mild anxiety and tension; defensiveness; scanning the environment for threat cues; reduced communication; some sweating; mile shakiness; mild physical arousal.

APPROPRIATE VERBAL INTERVENTIONS

* What is your name?
* My name is _____.
* You seem upset. Tell me what's going on.
* How can I help?
* What is it you're concerned about?
* It's not unusual to feel so concerned. I'm sure I would feel the same way.
* Let's go over here and sit down and talk about it.
* Let me get you a cup of coffee.
* How might we work this out?
* What would be most helpful right now?

EMOTIONAL/BEHAVIORAL SYMPTOMS

• Moderate anxiety, heightened physical arousal; increased defensiveness; scanning area for defensive alternatives; evaluating consequences of threats and actions; increased

Notes

Threat Cues: *People, things, or events that make an individual feel endangered.*

Mild Physical Arousal: *Behavior displayed by pacing, perspiration, quietness and general anxiousness.*

Defensive Alternatives: *Escape routes or protection devices for personal protection.*

talkativeness (asking questions); aversion to physical contact (Don't touch me!); tightening of muscles, clenching teeth; urge to move about; growing resistance to direction

APPROPRIATE VERBAL INTERVENTIONS

- Use diversion to redirect their attention.
* Let's get a cup of coffee.
* It's difficult to cooperate with you when.... so please......
* This is a tough situation right now, so how about sitting down and discussing what our alternatives might be.

EMOTIONAL/BEHAVIORAL SYMPTOMS

- High anxiety; assessing perceived adversary's vulnerability; verbal threats; abusive language; personal threatening gestures; open refusal to cooperate; intimidation.

APPROPRIATE VERBAL INTERVENTIONS

- Set limits by consequences.
* I know you are upset but you cannot continue to behave this way.
* Either you calm down and discuss the problem or we will escort you off the property.
* Either you calm down or we will help you control yourself.
- Never give an ultimatum unless you are prepared to "back it up" and follow through.
* Either you go to your room like the Nurses have asked or we will take you to your room.
- All communication should be short, simple and to the point.
- Do not yell or shout but be very clear that if he or she doesn't calm down, the team will help him or her control themselves.

Notes

EMOTIONAL/BEHAVIORAL SYMPTOMS

• Violence; action is quick and impulsive; striking out with hands, feet, biting; bodily attack; ability to assess consequences for actions is severely reduced; "they do not hear what you are saying and even if they do they don't care".

APPROPRIATE VERBAL RESPONSE

- • None
- • All talking should cease between team leader and disruptive person.
- • The only verbal communication should be between team members.
- • Once the disruptive person turns physically violent, ALL ATTENTION SHOULD BE DIRECTED TOWARD RESTRAINING HIM OR HER.
- • Verbal communication may resume after the person is secured and their aggressiveness has been reduced.

PHYSICAL INTERVENTIONS

As tension levels rise and people become more disruptive, ignoring verbal interventions, security officers must rely on physical management techniques. Disruptive people must be prevented from hurting themselves or others. The environment must be kept safe.

Once the decision is made to intervene physically, security officers should respond without hesitation or guilt, and with the idea that you are really helping that person regain control. Whenever possible, security officers should plan the manner in which they are going to "secure" the disruptive person. Depending upon the number of staff present, everyone should know exactly what he or she is to do once the officers "move in" on the person. The ideal situation would have five (5) security officers present. If there are more than five (5) officers or staff available, the others should stay in the immediate area and provide back-up. One officer should be

Notes

Five security officers are needed to most effectively and safely remove an individual causing a disruption.

323

assigned to each arm and each leg with the remaining officer responsible for controlling the person's head in the event he attempts to bite.

Specific non-offensive physical maneuvers have been developed for security personnel. It is difficult to discuss specific physical maneuvers in a written manner but there are a number of ideas that can be conveyed to security personnel who have the responsibility of responding to such emergencies.

* Staff must maintain a caring and concerned attitude.

* Staff must refrain from taking the disruptive person's verbal and physical abuse personally.

* Staff must continue to work as a team throughout the crisis and until the goal is reached of securing the environment.

* If time permits, remove personal items that may get broken such as watches, glasses, jewelry, etc.

* How you stand and move can aid in a fast response if struck by a disruptive person.

* Without special training, it is natural to respond with techniques that may not be effective or non-offensive.

• Legally, you must demonstrate that every effort has been made to control the situation utilizing NON-OFFEN-SIVE PHYSICAL CONTROL TECHNIQUES prior to utilizing any technique which might be construed as offensive such as punching, kicking, full nelson, etc.

* Non-offensive techniques are designed to minimize risk of injury to both the disruptive person and the staff.
* Any technique which by design causes pain or discomfort such as a full nelson, pressure points, etc. should be considered offensive.

Non-offensive Physical Control Techniques: Actions which attempt to restore accepted behavior without the use of physical force (i.e. holding hands up, palms open while talking to the person; gently placing a hand on the person's shoulder; motioning for a person to sit while requesting the same.)

* You do have the right to protect your life.
* Be aware of surroundings - anything the person may try to use as a weapon.
* Always try and call for back-up before giving ultimatums to the disruptive person.
* Use only that amount of force necessary to effectively control the situation.
* By gaining control of the person's wrist, you in affect can manipulate the movement and balance of the individual.
* Utilize the element of surprise whenever possible.
* Your first priority is to free and protect yourself so that you can intervene.
* Take advantage of your ability to think more rationally than the disruptive person.
* Be aware of your own physical limitations and plan accordingly.
* Execute physical interventions quickly.
* Another special consideration is handling people with injuries, physical ailments, which should involve getting specific instructions from the Nursing Staff.

DEBRIEFING

It is recommended that all personnel involved in handling a violent or potentially violent situation stay together for a short period to discuss what occurred, in general how the situation was handled, and could it have been handled better? This process is known as debriefing. These sessions should not be held for the purpose of personal attacks or stinging criticism of each others performance. In the event any one person performs far below expected standards, this should be discussed with him or her alone. Debriefing is held for the purpose of making the team perform better, if applicable, which is usually the case. Security officers need to be aware of their roles and perform at their very best during crisis situations.

At times it would seem easier to forget about having a debriefing or not make it into a big deal but the team will not reach it's potential in handling disruptive person situations

Notes

Offensive Physical Control Techniques: Any technique which by design causes pain or discomfort.

Debriefing: Discussion among the persons involved in an event, usually conducted immediately after the event or incident for the purpose of evalutating the performance of the responding officers or personnel.

unless everyone clearly understands what happened, what should have happened, and what everyone needs to work on. When a time period is offered to help staff discuss what occurred, a great amount of relief can result. The chances for dealing with disruptive person situations or crisis more efficiently in the future is greatly enhanced by the debriefing process. The debriefing process allows everyone present during the crisis to give each other support; confer about their roles; decide what might have gone wrong and why, and what can be done in the future to improve team performance.

Keeping all personnel present during the debriefing process may not always be practical. In these situations, it is advisable for the security supervisor to remain and instruct the remainder of his staff to return to their normal duties. The security supervisor should inform his staff of the events which took place at the debriefing.

Summary

It is imperative today's security officer understand his role in potentially violent situations and have the training required to respond appropriately. In most instances, the security officer's role is preventative in nature. The security officer must develop excellent skills at being able to utilize appropriate verbal skills and management techniques to defuse them.

The security officer's primary goal in a potentially violent situation is to defuse the situation — not incite a physical confrontation.

In order to become effective in his/her role, the security officer must become proficient at recognizing or assessing potentially violent behavior, utilizing verbal skills designed to minimize the risk of escalating the potentially violent individual and learning and utilizing only non-offensive physical techniques when appropriate.

A subject that rears it's ugly head during times of violence, although it is the most inappropriate time for such discussion is "I don't get paid enough to do this". Anyone considering a career in security must be aware that violence can and does occur in the work place. Wage rates are not a factor in determining a role in potentially violent situations.

Notes

All behavior is motivated. Acting-out behavior, like other types of behavior, is intended to achieve some goal. This goal may or may not be apparent to you or the person who is upset. The first queston you must ask yourself is "What is the reason for this person's behavior"? You need to become aware of the person's vital interests and how the environment might be perceived by the person as a threat to that vital interest. All people have a threat threshold — that is a certain tolerance for perceived threat. If the intensity of perceived threat in the environment is more than the individual can handle, the risk of that person becoming violent is high. This threat threshold will differ from person to person. The more intense a person's emotional reaction, the less likely they are able to think rationally. Acting-out behavior always involves some emotional force associated with the situation. Fear is the most common emotion related to aggression.

In understanding that the emotionally upset person is unable to think very rationally, we can see the sense in taking deliberate steps to de-escalate the emotional components of a situation so that the person can rationally cooperate.

When upset, if given an option, an individual will usually choose a npn-violent way over a violent way of dealing with a stressful situation.

Security officers must always remember that initially any management person who might always remember that initially any management person who might call for their assistance in handling a disruptive person situation is always the team leader. This leadership may be turned over to security at some point during the crisis but management is ultimately responsible for what occurs. Security may be asked to assist in this endeavor but is not ultimately responsible and therefore does not always have the final say about what should be done. The most effective "Crisis Management" approach is the team approach. Management and security should work together as a team.

When a person demonstrates behavior which indicates he/she is becoming upset, management should respond appropriately by having a single manager (designated team leader — usually the manager deemed to have the best rapport with the potentially disruptive individual verbally intervene and attempt to calm the person down or de-escalate the situation.

Most potentially violent incidents can be handled smoothly if everyone knows their role and performs their function properly. Only one person (designated team leader) should verbally communicate with the potentially violent person. Even if the potentially violent person directs verbal abuse or questions another person on the scene, including security, that person being spoken to must not respond! The team leader should respond for him/her by stating that the person must speak with him/her and not anyone else. What that person is attempting to do, by trying to get other people talking is to divide and conquer. If the potentially violent person is successful in getting everyone talking at the same time, he/she is getting everyone's attention away from what should be their primary goal — de-escalating the person who is potentially violent.

Communication with words and gestures can be one of the safest, simplest, and most readily available interventions that people working with a potentially violent individual have available to them. The risks are few and the gains are many. Through effective verbal communication, problem resolution can be accomplished with minimum risk of injury.

The escalation or de-escalation of a crisis may depend on the ability to verbally intervene.

The team leader is the only person to communicate and verbally intervene with the disruptive person. The rest of the team works to be supportive to its leader and a resource for future help. This approach will provide the disruptive person with structure and help focus his/her attention.

As tension levels rise and people become more disruptive, ignoring verbal interventions, security officers must rely on physical management techniques. Disruptive people must be prevented from hurting themselves or others. The environment must be kept safe.

Once the decision is made to intervene physically, security officers should respond without hesitation, guilt, and with the idea that you are really helping the person regain control. Whenever possible, security officers should plan the manner in which they are going to secure the disruptive person. Depending on the number of staff present, everyone should know exactly what he/she is to do once the officers move in on the person.

Notes

Specific non-offensive physical maneuvers have been developed for security personnel. It is difficult to discuss specific physical maneuvers in a written manner but there are a number of ideas that can be conveyed to security personnel who have the responsibility of responding to such emergencies. Legally, an officer must demonstrate that every effort has been made to control the situation utilizing non-offensive physical control techniques prior to utilizing any technique which might be construed as offensive such as punching, kicking, full nelson, etc. Take advantage of your ability to think more rationally than the disruptive person.

It is recommended that all personnel involved in handling a violent or potentially violent situation stay together for a short period to discuss what occurred, in general how the situation was handled, and could it have been handled better? This process is known as debriefing. Security officers need to be aware of their roles and perform at their very best during crisis situations.

Notes

QUESTIONS

1. In most instances, the security officer's role is preventative in nature.   True or False.

2. The security officer must develop excellent skills which enable him/her to recognize potentially violent situations and to utilize appropriate verbal skill management techniques to defuse them. True or False.

3. The security officer's primary goal in a potentially violent situation is to diffuse the situation - not incite a physical confrontation. True or False.

4. The presence of a uniformed security officer seldom deters to violence. True or False.

5. When management is aware of an individual's potential for violence and that individual is going to be disciplined or discharged, it's a good idea to wait until the last possible minute to inform security. True or False.

6. Management should confer with security prior to any potentially violent situation and develop a plan. This plan should include:

    a. When should the police be called?
    b. When should the security officers restrain the individual?
    c. Should the person be physically ejected from the property rather than restrained?
    d. All of the above.
    e. None of the above.

7. All behavior is:

    a Antisocial
    b. Psychotic
    c. Motivated
    d. Violence prone
    e. None of the above

8. Factors such as personality, past experience, learning, and present circumstances shape a person's reactions. A typical examples of a person who is likely to be disruptive is the:

    a. Criminal or antisocial individual
    b. Intoxicated individual
    c. Psychotic individual
    d. Emotionally traumatized worker
    e. None of the above
    f. All of the above

9. The more intense a person's emotional reaction, the less likely they are able to think rationally. True or False.

10. When upset, if given an option, an individual will usually choose a non-violent way over a violent way of dealing with a stressful situation. True or False.

11. Common causes of acting-out include:

    a. Frustration
    b. Tension
    c. Loss of personal power
    d. Overcrowding
    e. All of the above
    f. None of the above

12. Cues to potential acting-out include:

    a. Mood swings
    b Physical tension
    c. Past history data
    d. Changes in verbal behavior
    e. None of the above
    f. All of the above

13. Security officers must always remember that in any potentially violent situation:

    a. They are always the team leader
    b. They are never the team leader
    c. Leadership may never be turned over
    d. Management seldom relies on security officers
    e. All of the above
    f. None of the above

14. Most potentially violent incidents can be handled smoothly if everyone knows their role and performs their function properly. The only person who should verbally communicate with the potentially violent person:

    a. Security officer
    b. Security supervisor
    c. Team leader
    d. Highest level manager on scene
    e. None of the Above

15. If the disruptive person starts talking with everyone on the scene, each person must speak with him to ensure he feels like he is being given everyone's undivided attention. True or False.

16. If the disruptive person gets everyone talking at the same time he has succeeded in:

     a. Undermining management
     b. Undermining security
     c. Dividing and conquering
     d. All of the above
     e. None of the above

17. In the event the disruptive person attempts physical violence toward any of the team members, security should:

     a. Back-off immediately
     b. Back-off and contact police immediately
     c. Give the person breathing room
     d. Immediately restrain the person
     e. All of the above
     f. None of the above

18. Communication with words and gestures can be one of the:

     a. Best ways to make security look good
     b. Best ways to manipulate the person prior to restraining them non-offensively
     c. Safest, simplest, and most readily available interventions
     d. None of the above
     e. All of the above

19. Escalation or de-escalation of a crisis may depend on one's:

     a. Ability to verbally intervene
     b. Ability to physically intervene
     c. Ability to restrain non-offensively
     d. None of the above
     e All of the above

20. If more than one person is talking to the disruptive person, the chance is:

    a. Much greater the team will win over
    b. Much greater the team will lose control
    c. Much greater for de-escalation
    d. All of the above
    e. None of the above

21. In the event the disruptive person becomes physically violent:

    a. Everyone on the scene should speak with him or her to calm them down
    b. No one should talk to anyone
    c. All talking should cease with the disruptive person
    d. None of the above
    e. All of the above

22. Any technique which by design causes pain or discomfort such as a full nelson, pressure points, etc. :

    a. Should be used to Divide and Conquer
    b. Should be considered non-offensive
    c. Should be considered offensive
    d. Should be used to minimize risk of injury to the staff and disruptive person
    e. None of the Above
    f. All of the above

23. Security officers should be aware of their own physical limitations and plan accordingly. True or False.

24. All physical interventions should be executed:

    a. Slowly and methodically
    b. Quickly
    c. In an offensive manner
    d. By causing sufficient discomfort to overcome the disruptive person's threat threshold
    e. None of the above

Practical Exercises

1.   You are contacted by the personnel manager who informs you he is terminating an employee who has a history of violence. What factors do you consider and what is your plan for dealing with this individual?

2.   A trespasser, visitor, or client representative becomes very indignant with you when you ask them to leave the facility. He curses at you, utters every vulgarity and profanity you have ever heard of, and insults your family, profession and worth. How do you respond to this individual?

3.   A patient in the hospital where you work is unruly. Nursing has asked you to respond. You and another person are the only security personnel on duty. When you arrive to the scene you notice the patient is quite belligerent and is arguing with a nurse. You also notice the patient is 6'3" and weighs about 250 pounds. How do you respond to this situation?

THE EFFECTIVE SECURITY OFFICERS TRAINING MANUAL

Chapter XVI

Labor Relations

Labor Relations

Many companies which either employ their own employees as security officers or hire a company to provide contract security officers, may have a union to deal with which represents some or all of its workforce. For security officers who work at a facility where a labor organization exists, certain rules and regulations may affect the manner in which security policies are formulated and enforced.

Rights of Labor Unions

In 1935, after many years of violent work stoppages in the nation's coal fields, railroads, and automotive factories, Congress passed the National Labor Relations Act. This law is also referred to as the "Wagner Act" gave workers the right to representation and described specific management practices that were considered unfair.

In 1947 the Taft-Hartley Act, also called the Labor Management Relations Act, amended the earlier 1935 law and identified unfair labor practices which could not be engaged in by unions.

For security personnel, the most important areas of consideration to be familiar with are those actions which could be considered unfair. If security personnel were to engage in any behavior judged to be an unfair labor practice, the company employing the security officer could be cited and fined.

All unions will have some sort of contract with the company which employees the workers. Generally these contracts are for one, two, or three years in duration. The contract will usually cover a wide variety of subject areas including wages, benefits, work rules, and discipline.

Whenever a disagreement occurs between the union and the company over interpretation of the contract, the two sides normally arrange a series of meetings to discuss the dispute. This is normally considered part of a grievance hearing. After the various grievance meetings (often referred

Notes

Reading For A Purpose
Look for these key words:
- Grievance   • Strike
- Arbitration   • Economic Strike
- Unfair Labor Practice
- Unfair Labor Practice Strike

Look for answers to these
   Questions:
1. Are strikes regulated by law?
2. Under what circumstances could a security officer be charged with an unfair labor practice?
3. What is the role of security during a strike?

Wagner Act: First law giving workers right to representation and desciding specifc unfair management practices.

Taft-Hartley Act: Later law describing unfair union practices.

Grievance: complaint and process where a disagreement between two parties is discussed in the hope of settling the dispute.

to first step, second step, third step, etc.), have taken place, if there is still no agreement, the two sides will normally take the dispute to arbitration. During an arbitration hearing, both sides are permitted to present their side of their case. This includes calling on witnesses to testify and presenting material which supports their claim or disputes the other side's contention.

One or sometimes more than one person will hear the evidence and testimony presented at the arbitration hearing. This person is referred to as the arbitrator, who acts in much the same way as a judge in a court proceeding. After hearing the evidence, the arbitrator will normally not enter an opinion or judgment immediately. Usually, the arbitrator will review all of the material and re-read the testimony presented at the arbitration. It may be several weeks before the arbitrator issues their decision. Normally, the decision is submitted in writing to both parties along with the reasons which support the arbitrator's decision.

Binding arbitration is the type where both the union and company are legally bound to support the final decision made by the arbitrator. Sometimes, if the arbitration is not binding, the losing side may appeal the decision to the National Labor Relations Board or to a judicial court.

Unfair Labor Practices

Unreasonable Conduct: If the actions of a security officer are considered to be unreasonable, such as searching the locker or vehicle of an employee when a policy or practice concerning searches has never been addressed, a charge may be made by the union representing the employee. As discussed in the Legal Aspects module, the actions and behavior or security officers must always be judged to be reasonable. Provided the security officer's action are judged to have been consistent with existing policies, procedures, or past practice, a claim of unreasonable conduct will probably not be substantiated.

Notes

Often, attorneys are hired to present the case for the respective side of labor or management.
Arbitration: process where disputes are settled after facts have been determined.
Security officers who are involved in a situation where discipline has occurred involving a union employee, may be required to testify during the arbitration hearing.

Arbitrators will often attempt to resolve an issue by issuing a compromise ruling. In these situations, both sides are normally not satisfied.

Major league baseball uses arbitration to settle disputes between owners and players. In cases involving contract disputes in baseball. The arbitrator will rule for one side or the other with no compromises.

Forcible opening a locker or vehicle, conducting surveillance in a restroom, eavesdropping on telephone conversations are all examples of unfair labor practices.

Statements by Employees: In the Legal Aspects module, the Miranda warnings were discussed. To review, in virtually every situation, security officers are not required to advise a suspect of their constitutional rights before questioning. Exceptions apply if the security officer is commissioned or is acting as an agent of a law enforcement agency. Provided that statements given to security personnel by employees were given voluntarily, without any threats or promises, these statements would be admissible in a discipline hearing against the employee. If the statement made to security personnel is not written or tape recorded, it should be witnessed (heard) by at least two security officers.

Search and Seizure: Employees in the workplace may be afforded some basic rights to privacy which are considered reasonable. Areas such as lockers, desks, vehicles, etc. may fall under this category. Companies can normally avoid these restrictions by issuing clear written policy statements that the company reserves the right to search lockers, desks, vehicles, etc. Many companies will have written "letters of understanding" or policy statements which address these issues. Failure to notify employees, including those who are not represented by a collective bargaining unit, may result in evidence derived from such searches to be inadmissible by an arbitrator. Some companies inform their employees at the time of hiring that desks, lockers, vehicles, etc. are subject to search at the company's discretion.

Surveillance: Surveillances are an effective tool used by all security investigators. If a covert or hidden surveillance of a restroom was initiated by security investigators, in all likelihood any evidence uncovered as a result of the covert surveillance would be dismissed by an arbitrator. Most arbitrators would find surveillance of this type extremely offensive and an invasion of an employee's right to privacy.

Union Representation during Investigative Interviews: Courts have rules that generally, there is a right, under the National Labor Relations Act, for an employee to have union representation present during a management interview of a union member when there is the likelihood that discipline to the employee will result. The case which

Notes

When a security officer comes upon a situation where an employee is engaged in illegal or improper conduct, it is essential to obtain another witness from management or security who will be able to support your testimony.

Written statements made by employees or those which are tape recorded, should also be witnessed.

Provided notice is given to employees that the company reserves the right to conduct inspections, most searches will be permitted and not considered to be an unfair labor practice.

is generally regarded as the cornerstone of this right is called the Weingarten decision. In the Weingarten case, the Court ruled that when an employee is being interviewed and he/she believes that the information discussed during the interview may lead to discipline, up to and including termination, the employee has the right to request a union representative be present during the interview. An employer must grant the union representation if requested but is under no duty to discuss the matter or bargain with the union representative.

If an employee does not request union representation, the company is under no obligation to provide it. Some companies have decided that they will always offer union representation to an employee even if the employee has not requested it. Some companies may even require an employee to have union representation, whether or not the employee has asked for the representation.

Security Personnel as Union Members

There may be situations where individuals employed as security officers are they themselves members of a union. There is a specific rule against combining security officers and non-officers within the same union. However, some companies have allowed this practice. The reason to exclude security personnel from belonging to the same union as employees is that security personnel have to enforce rules and regulations. A situation could easily develop where security officers would be in a conflict of whether to enforce a rule or regulation against a fellow union member or ignore the offense.

Strikes

Security personnel will be relied on a great deal in a strike situation in order to maintain order and protect company property. Because of the serious impact of strikes on the public, courts have ruled that strikes are to be regulated by law. Laws pertaining to strikes are far from settled. New laws continue to shape strike behavior on the part of management and labor.

Notes

Weingarten Decision: gave the right to employees who believe an interview may result in disciplinary action to request a union representative to be present.

The union representative may be instructed not to disrupt or interfere with the interview.

The policy of always offering union representation during an interview is an example of "past practice". Past practice is a term used to describe the manner in which issues have been settled before. Even if there is no written agreement regarding a particular issue, past practice may be cited by either party to support their actions.

In the past, large factories such as the many automotive plants, would employ proprietary security officers who belonged to a separate union (i.e. Protection Workers of America). It is unclear how many security officers are currently represented by a labor union.

Under the law, strikes fall into three major categories: economic strikes, unfair labor practice strikes and illegal or unprotected strikes. The rights of both labor and management depend on the kind of strike involved.

An economic strike is a strike over wages, hours or working conditions. Economic strikers may be permanently replaced by replacement workers which occurred during the 1980 Air Traffic Controllers Strike. Then President Ronald Reagan, ordered all of the striking air traffic controllers to return to work or risk being permanently fired. The union representing the striking controllers advised the workers to remain on strike. The controllers who refused to return to work were subsequently fired. Many labor law experts believe that the 1980 Air Traffic Controllers Strike changed the way in which management dealt with economic strikes.

An unfair labor practice strike is one that is caused by management's unfair labor practices. Unfair labor practice strikers are entitled to reinstatement, even though it may be necessary to discharge the replacement workers.

Illegal or unprotected strikes are prohibited by law. A strike in violation of a non-strike clause in the agreement has been held to be an unprotected activity and such strikers may be discharged or otherwise disciplined.

Right Not to Strike

Under the law there is also a right not to strike. Employees may refuse to join a strike and are protected from coercion or restraint from striking workers. Mass picketing to prevent entrance to or exit from a facility is illegal, as are threats of physical violence and destruction of an employer's property in the course of picketing. The threat of violence is often employed by striking workers to create an atmosphere of fear and to intimidate non-striking workers.

Notes

Economic strike: strike over wages, hours or working conditions. Economic strikers may be permanently replaced.

Unfair labor practice strike: strike as a result of an employers unfair labor practices. Strikers may not be replaced.

Illegal strike: striking in spite of a non-strike clause is illegal and strikers may be replaced or disciplined.

Any type of illegal or criminal behavior can be photographed and/or videotaped and used in a legal proceeding. Lawful activity on the part of strikers may not be photographed.

Employer's Legal Rights During a Strike

An employer may not discharge employees for planning a strike. Once a strike has begun, management may use every legal means to break the strike. The company operation can be maintained by hiring replacement workers, or by having supervisors perform the work. Protection and security can be given to those employees who continue to work. Newspaper advertisements and other forms of publicity may be used to inform the strikers and public of the facts. If the strike violates the law, the government and the courts may be appealed to for legal assistance.

Role of Security Personnel During a Strike

Security personnel will be relied on extensively during a strike to protect the facility and the employees who continue to work. During most strikes, security personnel will be permitted to cross picket lines by striking workers without a great deal of verbal threats or intimidation from strikers. However, if the strike is an extremely bitter one where emotions are high are both sides, security personnel may also be targets for violence.

Most organizations who successfully operate during a strike, have gone to great lengths to adequately prepare for a strike. This would include a plan of how many additional security officers may be needed or if management personnel would be utilized to supplement the existing security force. Provided proper advance planning has occurred prior to the strike, sufficient security personnel and equipment will greatly assist in providing adequate protection to persons and property.

Security personnel must demonstrate great restraint and discipline during a strike situation. Responding to verbal threats will serve only to heighten tension and may be the cause of physical violence. When crossing picket lines, security personnel should not demonstrate an aggressive or cocky attitude. Rather, an attitude displaying patience, restraint, and calmness will serve the security officer well and strikers will probably eventually allow security personnel to cross the picket line.

Notes

In the past ten years many companies have adopted a more aggressive manner in dealing with striking employees. In 1992 the United Auto Workers (UAW) struck the Caterpillar Corporation for five months. When it became apparent that Caterpillar was prepared to replace all of the striking employees, the UAW ordered its striking workers to return to work without a contract.

They are no guarantees, no certainties during a strike. Non-striking employees and security personnel may be instructed to remain at the facility to sleep and eat in order not to attempt picket line crossings. Companies have many different viewpoints in dealing with strikes.

Most violence occurs when replacement workers or shipments of products are moved across picket lines.

Remember that in large groups, individuals take on the attitude of a mob. Persons whom you consider to be friends, may act as enemies during a strike.

Security personnel must remember that while they may need to display an outward attitude and demeanor of being objective and neutral during a strike, management has hired them and management pays their wages. Security personnel are to enforce and carry-out the legal duties and responsibilities assigned to them during a strike. In virtually every strike, remember that eventually the strike will end. Workers will normally return to work. Words or actions by security personnel that create animosity, will not soon be forgotten by the returning workers. As always, a calm, professional manner displayed by security personnel will minimize problems.

Real-Life Example

A security officer employed at a facility for several years, was attempting to cross a picket line during a long, bitter strike. A striking worker who knew the security officer on a first name basis commented, "Hey Ed. That sure is a nice car you've got there. You know Ed, it sure would be a shame if your vehicle was damaged while you were crossing this picket line. Maybe you shouldn't go into work today." Ed calmly looked at the striking worker that he knew for several years and replied, "You know Joe, one of these days this strike is going be over and you and your co-workers will be back to work and me and the rest of the security officers will still be working everyday. While you're inside the plant I'll be outside patrolling the parking lot making sure your car is protected. And you know that I will always do my best to protect that new Cadillac of yours. Know what I mean?"

The striking worker reflected for just a moment and as he moved out of the way to allow the security officer entrance the plant, he said, "Have a nice day Ed."

REFERENCES

Protection of Assets Manual, Timothy J. Walsh, CPP and Richard J. Healy, CPP, The Merrit Company, Santa Monica, California, 1987.

Front-Line Supervisor's Labor Relations Handbook, Stephen F. Byrd, National Foremen's Institute, Waterford, CT., 1978.

Notes

Remember, if the facility is damaged or the business suffers losses resulting from the actions of security officers, the damage done to your credibility and reputation may never recover.

SUMMARY

For security officers who work at a facility where a labor organization exists, certain rules and regulations may affect the manner in which security policies are formulated and enforced.

In 1935, after many years of violent work stoppages in the nation's coal fields, railroads, and automotive factories, Congress passed the National Labor Relations Act. This law is also referred to as the "Wagner Act" gave workers the right to representation and described specific management practices that were considered unfair.

In 1947 the Taft-Hartley Act, also called the Labor Management Relations Act, amended the earlier 1935 law and identified unfair labor practices which could not be engaged in by unions.

For security personnel, the most important areas of consideration to be familiar with are those actions which could be considered unfair.

Whenever a disagreement occurs between the union and the company over interpretation of the contract, the two sides normally arrange a series of meetings to discuss the dispute. This is normally considered part of a grievance hearing. After the various grievance meetings (often referred to first step, second step, third step, etc.), have taken place, if there is still no agreement, the two sides will normally take the dispute to arbitration. During an arbitration hearing, both sides are permitted to present their side of their case. This includes calling on witnesses to testify and presenting material which supports their claim or disputes the other side's contention.

Binding arbitration is the type where both the union and company are legally bound to support the final decision made by the arbitrator. Sometimes, if the arbitration is not binding, the losing side may appeal the decision to the National Labor Relations Board or to a judicial court.

Security personnel could possibly be charged with unfair labor practices if there actions are not considered appropriate and reasonable. These unfair labor practices involve unreasonable conduct, statements by employees, search and seizure, surveillance and union representation during investigative interviews.

There may be situations where individuals employed as security officers are they themselves members of a union. There is a specific rule against combining security officers and non-officers within the same union. However, some companies have allowed this practice. The reason to exclude security personnel from belonging to the same union as employees is that security personnel have to enforce rules and regulations. A situation would easily develop where security officers would be in a conflict of whether to enforce a rule or regulation against a fellow union member or ignore the offense.

Under the law, strikes fall into three major categories: economic strikes, unfair labor practice strikes and illegal or unprotected strikes. The rights of both labor and management depend on the kind of strike involved.

An economic strike is a strike over wages, hours or working conditions. Economic strikers may be permanently replaced by replacement workers.

An unfair labor practice strike is one that is caused by management's unfair labor practices.

Illegal or unprotected strikes are prohibited by law. A strike in violation of a non-strike clause in the agreement has been held to be an unprotected activity and such strikers may be discharged or otherwise disciplined.

Under the law there is also a right not to strike. Employees may refuse to join a strike and are protected from coercion or restraint from striking workers. Mass picketing to prevent entrance to or exit from a facility is illegal, as are threats of physical violence and destruction of an employer's property in the course of picketing.

Notes

An employer may not discharge employees for planning a strike. Once a strike has begun, management may use every legal means to break the strike.

Security personnel will be relied on extensively during a strike to protect the facility and the employees who continue to work.

Security personnel must demonstrate great restraint and discipline during a strike situation.

Notes

QUESTIONS

1. The name of the law passed in 1935 which gave workers the right to representation and which described specific management practices that were considered unfair is
    _____.

    a. The Bush-Quayle Act   b. The Laguardia Act
    c. The Taft-Hartley Act   d. The Grahamm-Rudman Act

2. Name of the procedure in which management or labor discuss a disagreement involving interpretation of the labor contract.

    a. trial   b. grievance
    c. arbitration   d. subpoena

3. Unreasonable conduct on the part of a security officer against an employee who is a member of a labor union may be considered a _____.

    a. Violation   b. Citation
    c. Unfair Labor Practice   d. Grievance

4. The name of the court decision which allows an employee to have union representation during a meeting which may lead to discipline is called _____.

    a. The Taft-Hartley Act   b. The Miranda Warning Act
    c. The LaGuardia decision   d. The Weingarten decision

5. Name of the strike which is a strike over wages.

    a. Unfair Labor Practice Strike b. Illegal or Wildcat Strike
    c. Economic Strike   d. None of the above

PRACTICAL EXERCISES & QUESTIONS

1. Package inspections have never been conducted at the facility where you work. A supervisor calls you at the security office to advise you someone has stolen three air grinders which would easily fit into a lunchbox. He wants you to do a complete package inspection for all employees who exit the facility during the shift change which will occur in 20 minutes. What do you do?

2. You are asked by the plant manager to inspect all employees' lockers during a plant shutdown. Can you legally inspect the lockers and if so, how would you properly proceed in doing so?

THE EFFECTIVE SECURITY OFFICERS TRAINING MANUAL

Chapter XVII

Alcohol & Drug Dependence

Alcohol & Drug Dependency

Notes

Reading for a Purpose
Look for these Key Words:
- addiction
- tolerance
- depressants
- stimulants
- hallucinogens
- cirrhosis
- central nervous system
- antabuse
- dependence
  - -psychological
  - -physical

Look for the answers to these questions:
1. What is drug abuse?
2. What is the Comprehensive Drug Abuse and Prevention Act of 1970?
3. What is alcoholism?
4. What are indicators of drug abuse?
5. What is the role of security personnel in an organization's alcohol and drug program?

A single definition for drug dependence is impossible. The term drug dependence of a specific type emphasizes that different drugs have different effects. Addiction refers to a style of living that includes drug dependence. Usually this dependence is both physical and psychological. Dependence usually is considered to be a compulsive use and overwhelming involvement with a drug. In addition addiction implies the risk of harm and the need to stop use whether the addict agrees or not.

Drug or substance abuse is defined only in terms of society's disapproval and involves different kinds of behavior. Drug abuse can include:

1. experimental and recreational use of drugs

2. use of drugs to relieve problems or symptoms

3. use of drugs to relieve problems or symptoms which leads to a dependency

Recreational drug use has increasingly become a part of our culture even though not sanctioned by society. Users who apparently do not suffer harm tend toward sporadic use involving relatively small doses. Recreational use is seldom practiced alone. Most drugs used in this manner are used to obtain a "high" rather than to relieve distress. For this reason, depressant drugs are seldom used for the "recreational" user.

Two general aspects are common to most types of drug dependence:

1. Psychological dependence involves feelings of satisfaction and a desire to repeat the use of the drug in order to produce pleasure or avoid pain. The mental state is a powerful factor involved in chronic use of certain drugs.

2. Physical dependence is a state of addiction to a drug accompanied by development of tolerance displayed by a withdrawal or abstinence

Dependence: the need or "perceived" need of a person to continue taking a drug; related to cultural patterns and to socioeconomic factors; may include a physical and mental dependency.

Abuse: defined only in terms of society's disapproval, involves different types of behavior; may involve psychological and physical dependence.

Addiction: state of being that includes drug dependence; usually dependence is both physical and psychological; implies the risk of harm and need to stop use.

syndrome. Tolerance is a need to increase the dose progressively in order to produce the effect originally achieved by smaller amounts. A withdrawal syndrome is characterized by physiological changes that occur when the drug is discontinued, such as convulsions, violent shaking and twisting, sweating, vomiting, delirium, etc....

Drugs that produce dependence act on the Central Nervous System and produce one or more of the following effects: reduced anxiety or tension; elation, euphoria, or other pleasurable mood changes; feelings of increased mental and physical ability; altered sensory perception; and changes in behavior. These drugs can be divided into two categories: those which cause psychological dependence and those which cause both a physical and psychological dependence. Drugs which cause primarily a mental dependence include: cocaine, marijuana, amphetamine, bromides and the hallucinogens, such as LSD, MDA, and mescaline.

Notes

Recreational drug use: term used to describe drug use by people who apparently do not suffer harm due to sporadic use involving relatively small doses; most drugs in this definition are those which produce a "high".

Physical Dependence: state of adaption to a drug accompanied by a development of tolerance which requires an increase in dose to achieve the desired effect.

Psychological Dependence: involves feelings of satisfaction and a desire to repeat the use of the drug in order to produce pleasure or relieve pain; can be a powerful factor in the chronic use of certain drugs.

A person's mental state is a powerful factor involved in the chronic use of certain drugs.

Tolerance: need to increase the dose progressively in order to produce the effect originally achieved by smaller amounts.

Central Nervous System: main "electrical" system of the body involving the brain, spinal chord and nerves within the body; impulses are conveyed from the brain to the rest of the body involving motor and sensory nerves.

Drugs that produce dependence act on the Central Nervous Syndrome and are divided into two categories: those which cause psychological dependence and those which cause both a physical and psychological dependence.

COMMONLY USED SUBSTANCES WITH PO-TENTIAL FOR DEPENDENCE

Drug	Physical Dependence	Psychological Dependence	Tolerance
Depressants			
Opioids	++++	++++	++++
Synthetic Narcotics	++++	++++	++++
Barbiturates	+++	+++	++
Methaqualone	+++	+++	++
Alcohol	+++	+++	++
Minor Tranquilizers			
Meprobamate	+++	+++	+
Benzodiazepines	+	+++	+
Stimulants			
Amphetamine	?	+++	++++
Methamphetamine	?	+++	++++
Cocaine	0	+++	0
Hallucinogens			
LSD	0	++	++
Mescaline	0	++	+
Marijuana			
low dose	0	++	0
high dose	0	++	?

0 indicates no effect
+ indicates slight to ++++ significant effect

The Merck Manual of Diagnosis & Therapy, Merck Sharp and Dohme Research Laboratories, Rahway, N.J., 1987, p. 1477.

Notes

The chart on this page indicates the potential for dependence for certain drugs. Those drugs which have three or more `+' in each category:
    physical dependence
    psychological dependence
    tolerance
are the most common drugs of abuse.

In the United States, the Comprehensive Drug Abuse Prevention and Control Act of 1970 and subsequent changes require the drug industry to maintain physical security and strict record keeping over certain types of drugs. The Act also divided controlled substances into 5 schedules or classes on the basis for their potential for abuse, accepted medical use and accepted safety under medical supervision. Substances included in Schedule I are those with a high potential for abuse, no accepted medical use and lack of accepted safety. Those in Schedules II through V decrease in potential for abuse. Prescriptions for drugs in all these schedules must bear the physician's Federal Drug Enforcement (FDA) license number.

The development of drug dependence is complex and unclear. At least 3 components require consideration: the addictive drugs, predisposing conditions, and the personality of the user. The psychology of the individual and drug availability determine the choice of the addicting drug and the pattern and frequency of use.

Drug dependence is in part related to cultural patterns and to socioeconomic factors. Factors which lead to increased use can include peer or group pressure and emotional distress that is temporarily relieved by the specific effects of the drug. Factors which may lead to drug use include sadness, low self-esteem and stress.

Pharmacological Factors

Persons who become addicted or dependent have no known biochemical or physiological differences from persons who do not become addicted. With some drugs, after only 2 to 3 days of continued use some physical dependency may exist for some people. These persons generally have mild withdrawal symptoms which may have the same symptoms of the influenza (flu) but they do not become addicted. Even persons with chronic pain problems requiring long-term administration usually are not addicts. These persons may experience some problems with tolerance and physical dependency. Some substances have a high potential for physical dependence and are more prone to abuse even when used in a social or recreational setting. Pharmacological effects are important but not the only factors in the development of drug dependency.

Notes

The Comprehensive Drug Abuse Prevention and Control Act of 1970 requires the drug industry to maintain physical security and strict record-keeping for certain drugs. The act also divided controlled substances into five schedules or classes.

Schedule Drugs: *drugs regulated by the Food and Drug Administration; divides controlled drugs into 5 classes or schedules because of their abuse potential.*

-- Ask yourself again: what is meant by tolerance and physical dependency?

Personality Factors

The "addictive personality" has been a term used by behavioral scientists but there is little scientific evidence that characteristic personality factors exist. Some believe that addicts are escapists, people who cannot deal with life and choose to "run away." Others have described addicts as schizoid persons who are fearful, withdrawn and depressed. Addicts have also been described as basically dependent and grasping in their relations with others.

Abuse of prescription drugs and avoidance of illegal drugs may occur in persons with an advanced education and professional status. Before developing the drug dependence, they did not demonstrate the pleasure-oriented, irresponsible behavior usually attributed to addicts. Sometimes the patient justifies the use of medication because of a crisis, job pressure, or family catastrophe that produces temporary anxiety or depression. Most of these patients abuse alcohol or another drug at the same time and may have repeated admissions for overdose, adverse reactions, or withdrawal problems.

DEPENDENCE ON ALCOHOL

Alcoholism is a chronic illness showing recognizable symptoms and signs in direct relation to its severity. The Prohibition of alcohol existed in the USA from 1920 - 1933. Experts estimate that alcohol abuse costs the USA over $25 billion per year.

An alcoholic is identified by severe dependence or addiction and a pattern of behavior associated with drinking:

1. Frequent intoxication is obvious and destructive; it interferes with the ability to socialize and work.

2. Drunkenness may lead to marriage failure and work absenteeism.

3. Alcoholics may seek medical treatment; they may suffer physical injury and may be apprehended for driving under the influence.

4. Eventually alcoholics may be hospitalized for delirium tremors or cirrhosis of the liver.

Notes

delirium tremors: (D.T.'s) Body and Brain Withdrawal Reaction from prolonged alcohol use. May include muscle tremors and abnormal body movements or hallucinations.

cirrhosis of the liver: breakdown of liver function due to chronic alcohol abuse; cirrhosis can also be caused by non-alcohol related conditions.

Incidence of alcoholism among women, children, adolescents, and college students is increasing. Males outnumber female alcoholics 4:1. It is generally assumed that 75% of American adults drink alcoholic beverages and 1 in 10 will experience some problem with alcoholism.

Families of alcoholics tend to have a higher incidence of alcoholism. Genetic or biochemical defects leading to alcoholism are suspected but have not been clearly demonstrated although a higher incidence of alcoholism has been consistently reported in biological children of alcoholics as compared to adoptive children. Social factors affect patterns of drinking and consequent behavior. Alcoholics frequently have histories of broken homes and disturbed relationships with parents.

Children of alcoholics have a greater chance of becoming alcoholics than children of non-alcoholics.

Physiology & Pathology

Alcohol is absorbed into the blood, principally transmitted from the small intestine. It accumulates in the blood because absorption is more rapid than oxidation and elimination from the body. Depression of the central nervous system is a principal effect of alcohol. A blood alcohol level of 50 mg/dL produces sedation or tranquility; 50 to 150 mg/dL produces lack of coordination; 150 to 200 mg/dL produces intoxication (delirium) and 300 to 400 mg/dL produces unconsciousness. Blood levels greater than 500 mg/dL may be fatal. The legal driving level is 100 mg/dL or less in most states. From 5 to 10% of ingested alcohol is excreted unchanged in urine, sweat, and expired air; the remainder is oxidized to carbon dioxide (CO_2) and water.

Continued consumption of alcohol without stopping over a short period of time, will eventually result in intoxication. The body can only dispose of alcohol at a rate of about one beer per hour. Alcohol leaves the stomach and enters the bloodstream. Like a river swollen by driving rain, alcohol "spills out" from the stomach into the blood system without having been filtered completely through the liver.

The most common forms of specific organ damage seen in alcoholics are cirrhosis of the liver, brain damage and cardiomyopathy (heart disease). Gastritis is common and pancreatitis may also develop. Irreversible impairment of liver function occurs in some alcoholics. Both the direct action of alcohol and the accompanying nutritional deficiencies are considered responsible for the frequent nerve problems and brain damage. Alcoholic cardiomyopathy (heart disease) may develop after approximately 10 years of heavy alcohol abuse and is attributed to a direct toxic effect of alcohol on the heart muscle.

Continued abuse of alcohol damages the liver, brain and heart similar to wood losing its texture and strength with prolonged contact with water.

351

Persons who drink large amounts of alcohol repeatedly become somewhat tolerant to its effects. The physical dependence accompanying tolerance is great, and withdrawal produces a series of adverse effects that may lead to death. Symptoms and signs of alcohol withdrawal usually begin 12 to 48 hours after the intake of alcohol has stopped. The main withdrawal symptoms include tremor, weakness and sweating.

Treatment

Medical evaluation is needed initially to detect any illness that might complicate withdrawal and to rule out any central nervous system symptoms from injury that might be covered by the withdrawal symptoms. Some drugs are frequently used to treat alcohol withdrawal. All patients entering withdrawal are candidates for depressant drugs but they may not need them.

No other approach has benefited so many alcoholics as effectively as Alcoholics Anonymous (AA). A person must find an AA group that he/she is comfortable with, preferably one where they have common interests with other members in addition to the alcohol problem. These groups provide the person with nondrinking friends who are always available and an area in which to socialize away from a tavern.

Disulfiram (Antabuse) is used in therapy since it interferes with oxidation process of alcohol creating acetaldehyde in the body which produces nausea, vomiting and great discomfort. Discomfort is so intense that few patients will risk taking alcohol as long as they are taking dislufiram.

DEPENDENCE OF THE OPIOID TYPE

The first major attempt to control opium use came in 1909 with a Federal Act that limited the use of opium and derivatives except for medical purposes. Opioid type drugs are considered narcotic which are a most effective pain reliever, used by physicians for surgery, fractures, burns, etc. Opium itself is a dark brown, plastic like substance which is smoked through a long stemmed pipe. Opium is the dried milk of unripe opium poppy. For the most part, opium has been replaced by its more powerful derivatives: morphine and heroin.

Notes

People who drink a lot require more alcohol to feel the effect. While many of these people may be legally drunk, they may appear to function without noticeable problems.

A tremor is a violent shaking of the body.

Antabuse: drug which is used in the treatment of alcoholics; it interferes with the oxidation process of alcohol creating acetaldehyde in the body which causes nausea, vomiting and great discomfort if a person consumes alcohol when taking the drug.

Recovering alcoholics are often given antabuse (a pill which is swallowed). If they consume any alcohol whatsoever, they will become violently ill. The reason antabuse is given to a person is to provide a deterrent. If the person chooses to consume alcohol, they will be sick. The learned behavior is to then avoid alcohol.

Opium: dark brown, plastic like substance which is smoked in a long-stemmed pipe; it is the dried milk of the unripe opium poppy; narcotic which relieves pain; has been replaced by its more powerful derivatives: morphine and heroin.

Morphine is the preferred drug for relief of pain and is derived from crude opium. Morphine is an odorless, light brown or white crystalline powder in tablets, capsules or powder form. It is either injected or taken orally. It acts on the Central Nervous System as a pain killer (analgesic).

Heroin is the synthetic alkaloid form of morphine and is 2-10 times as potent. It is popular because of the "high" it produces.

Codeine is a weak derivative of opium and is most commonly used in cough medicine and milder pain medicine and is less addictive than morphine or heroin.

Methadone is a synthetic opiate developed during World War II in Germany. It is considered more addictive than heroin and is used to block the withdrawal symptoms of heroin. Methadone may be taken orally or injected. It is now also being used in treatment of severe, prolonged pain in cancer patients.

A strong mental dependency can occur which creates an overpowering compulsion to continue taking the drug. Tolerance develops so the dosage must be continually increased in order to obtain the initial effect. Physical dependency will occur with increased dosage and continued use.

Tolerance and physical dependence on the opioids and synthethic narcotics develop rapidly. Therapeutic doses taken regularly over a 2 to 3 day period can lead to some tolerance and dependence and the user may show symptoms of withdrawal when the drug is discontinued. Opioid drugs induce cross-tolerance. Abusers may substitute one drug for another.

Symptoms & Signs

Acute intoxication with opioids is characterized by euphoria, flushing, itching of the skin, drowsiness, decreased respiratory rate, hypertension and decreased body temperature. During withdrawal, symptoms begin to appear as early as 4 to 6 hours after cessation and reach a peak within 36 to 72 hours for heroin. The initial anxiety and craving for the drug are followed by other symptoms increasing in severity and intensity. A reliable early sign of withdrawal is an increased respiratory rate usually accompanied by yawning and perspiration.

Notes

Morphine: derived from crude opium; preferred drug for relief of pain; odorless, light brown or white crystalline powder; can be taken orally or injected; acts on the Central Nervous System as a pain killer.

Heroin: synthetic alkaloid form of morphine, 2-10 times as potent as morphine, popular because of the "high" it produces.

Codeine: weak derivative of opium which is widely used in cough medicine to stop coughing.

Methadone: synthetic opiate developed during World War II in Germany; considered more addictive than heroin and is used to block the withdrawal symptoms of heroin; may be take orally or injected.

Opiate type drugs are very powerful and a person taking these drugs can develop a serious drug dependency problem very quickly. Physicians should closely monitor a patient's behavior when an opiate type drug is being used.

Opioid drug users may switch back and forth between morphine, heroin and methadone.

Euphoria: a feeling or sense of happiness, well-being.

Complications

Many but not all complications of heroin addiction are related to unsanitary administration of the drug. The more frequent complications include pulmonary problems, hepatitis, arthritic conditions, and neurological disorders. The treatment of these addicts is extremely difficult.

DEPENDENCE OF THE BARBITURATE TYPE

Mental dependence may lead to periodic or continuous use of the drug which in turn can result in a physical dependence after a user ingests amounts considerably above the therapeutic or socially acceptable levels.

Barbiturates are depressants and are used to induce sleep or to act as mild sedatives or tranquilizers.

Symptoms & Signs

In general, those dependent on sedatives and hypnotics prefer the rapid onset drugs such as secobarbital and phenobarbital. In susceptible persons, psychological dependence on the drug may develop rapidly and after only a few weeks. Attempts to discontinue use may result in insomnia, restlessness, disturbing dreams and feelings of tension early in the morning. The extent of the physical dependence is related to the barbiturate dose and length of time that it has been taken. Barbiturate users may appear as if they are alcohol intoxicated.

An abrupt withdrawal from large doses of barbiturates or tranquilizers produces a severe, frightening and potentially life-threatening illness similar to delirium tremens. Withdrawal from barbiturates carries a significant mortality rate and should always be conducted under medical supervision.

The procedure for treating dependence on depressants, particularly barbiturates, is to reintoxicate the patient and then withdraw the drug on a strict schedule, being alert for signs of marked withdrawal.

Notes

Opioid type drug users may appear very happy, show redness in their face or skin, may become sleepy, appear almost drunk.

Barbiturate: drugs which are depressants, used to induce sleep or act as mild sedatives or tranquilizers.

Persons who abuse barbiturates may believe that they have to continue taking the drug in order to sleep or simply "get through the day." Continued abuse will result in a physical dependence.

DOSES OF SOME COMMON SEDATIVES AND TRANQUILIZERS THAT HAVE PRODUCED PHYSICAL DEPENDENCE

Drug	Doses Producing Dependence (mg/day)	Time Necessary to Produce Dependence (days)
Secobarbital	500 - 600	30
Pentobarbital (yellow jackets)	500 - 600	30
Amobarbital (blues)	500 - 600	30
Amobarbital- Secanol combination (rainbows)	500 - 600	30
Glutethimide	1250 - 1500	60
Methprylon	1200 - 1500	60
Etchlorvynol.	1500 - 2000	60
Meprobamate	2000 - 2400	60
Chlorodiazepoxide	200 - 300	60
Diazepam	60 - 100	40
Methaqualone	1800 - 2400	30
Chloral hydrate	2000 - 2500	30

DEPENDENCE OF MARIJUANA

Chronic or periodic use of marijuana (cannabis) or cannabis substances produces some mental dependence because of the desired effects but no physical dependence occurs. Marijuana can be used on a periodic basis without evidence of social or psychic (mental) problems. For many users, the term dependence is probably a misconception.

Marijuana use is widespread in the United States and is commonly used in the form of a cigarette. Recently, synthetic tetrahydrocannabinol (THC) an active ingredient of marijuana, has become available for research and chemical use. Some controversy exists whether THC is available on the "street" for drug dealers and users.

Marijuana: Cannabis; commonly smoked in a cigarette; derived from the cannabis plant, leafy material which produces a dreamy state of consciousness and feeling of "well-being" or "high."

THC: tetrahydrocannabinol; active ingredient in marijuana. **Persons who abuse marijuana may develop a mental dependence or belief that they need the substance but no real physical dependency results from use.**

Symptoms & Signs

Marijuana produces a dreamy state of consciousness in which ideas seem disconnected, uncontrollable and free flowing. Time, color and perceptions are distorted. In general, there is a feeling of "well-being", exaltation, and excitement that has been termed a "high." Many of the psychological effects seem to be related to the setting in which the drug is taken.

Metabolic products of marijuana are retained in the tissues for a long time. For this reason, many persons who undergo a drug screen urinalysis may show by-products of marijuana in their urine for 30 days after use. Lowered testosterone (sperm count) levels have been reported in some males.

DEPENDENCE OF THE COCAINE TYPE

Psychic or mental dependence sometimes leads to an extreme psychological addiction when cocaine is used in high doses. In the study of cocaine use physical dependence or a tolerance to the drug has never been proven. However, there is usually a strong desire to continue to take the drug.

Symptoms & Signs

When cocaine is either injected or inhaled it produces a condition of euphoria and feelings of great power. The "high" produced is similar to that produced by injection of high doses of ampehtamines. Because cocaine is such a short acting drug, users may continue to repeat dosages.

Hallucinations may develop with continued use as well as violent behavior. An overdose of cocaine produces tremors, convulsions and delirium. Death may result from a cardiovascular collapse or respiratory failure.

Cocaine use and the development of addictive behavior has continued to increase in the United States. The smoking of "free-base" cocaine (crack) has become popular. This requires the conversion of the hydrochloride salt to the more combustible form. A flame is held to the material and the smoke inhaled. The speed of onset is quicker and the intensity of the "high" is magnified. Because this process utilizes flammable liquids, there have been serious explosions and burns.

Procaine when snorted produces local sensations not unlike cocaine and may even produce some "high."

Notes

Marijuana is normally smoked and produces a sense of well-being. Time, color and perceptions are distorted which slows a person's senses and reactions. For this reason, a person having recently smoked marijuana may have impaired driving reactions and would often be susceptible to injury in a factory job setting. Applicants for jobs often fail drug screens because traces of marijuana remain in the body and show up in the urine for up to 30 days after use.

Cocaine: powdery drug extracted from the cocoa plant; injected or inhaled it produces a condition of euphoria and feelings of great power.

Cocaine is a short acting drug, "the high" lasts for only a short time. Therefore, repeated dosage often accompanies its use.

Death can result from acute cocaine intoxication.

Hallucinations: illusions in the mind, "seeing" things which do not actually exist.

Crack: "free-base" cocaine, conversion by flame of the salt of cocaine to form a combustible substance which is then inhaled; the "high" of cocaine is greatly magnified.

Procaine: powdery substance; synthetic cocaine used primarily to "cut" cocaine or is mixed with cocaine; can produce a "high."

Powered procaine is widely used to cut cocaine and is occasionally mixed with mannitol or lactose and sold as cocaine. It is sometimes called "synthetic cocaine."

Treatment of acute cocaine intoxication is generally unnecessary because of the extremely short action of the drug. If an overdose requires intervention, schedule 4 barbiturates may be used. However, the difficulty in breathing which accompanies cocaine intoxication can be worsened with the use of sedatives. Discontinuing the use of cocaine requires considerable assistance and the depression that may occur requires close supervision and treatment.

DEPENDENCE OF THE AMPHETAMINE TYPE

Some psychological dependence occurs with the continued use of amphetamines. Previously these drugs were used in control of weight and obesity. However, recent studies have shown that their effectiveness in reducing a appetite decreases after 30 days of use and therefore they have little or no place today in treatment of overweight patients. These drugs are widely used as stimulants and generally cause elevated mood, increased wakefulness, alertness, concentration and physical performance. They may also produce a feeling of well-being. There is significant sale of fake amphetamines so much so the FDA has outlawed the manufacture of fakes by declaring that any combination of a stimulant phenethylamine with caffeine is a new drug that must be registered with the agency.

Symptoms and Signs

The withdrawal syndrome, if one exists is not severe. Withdrawal is usually followed by a state of mental and physical depression and fatigue. The psychological dependence of the drug varies. Amphetamines are different from Cocaine, in that they induce tolerance. This tolerance develops slowly but an ever increasing dosage can permit the ingestion of amounts much greater than therapeutically prescribed. The tolerance to various effects is different. Nervousness and sleeplessness may occur along with hallucinations. Massive doses are rarely fatal. Abusers are prone to accidents because of their excited state and the excessive fatigue which follows usage.

Notes

Amphetamine: drugs which are widely used as stimulants which generally cause elevated mood, increased wakefulness alertness, concentration and physical performance; used to be prescribed to control weight and obesity.

Stimulants: term used to describe drugs which increase heart rate, blood pressure and concentration; amphetamines and cocaine are types of stimulants.

Amphetamines induce tolerance which requires increasing dosages for the same effect.

Abusers of amphetamines are prone to accidents because of their excited state. Employees with excessive accidents in the workplace <u>may</u> be abusing amphetamines.

Although there are no real withdrawal effects other than sleepiness and fatigue the abrupt discontinuance of the drugs may bring on depression, often with suicidal potential. Usually reassurance and a quiet, nonthreatening environment will encourage a patient to recover.

DEPENDENCE OF THE HALLUCINOGEN TYPE

Hallucinogens include LSD (lysergic acid diethylamide), psilocybin, mescaline and methylene dioxymethamphetamine (MDMA). Generally, other than LSD, the other hallucinogens are not available on the street. In recent years a number of samples of a street product called "Ecstasy" have contained relatively pure methylene dioxyamphetamine (MDA).

Symptoms and Signs

The substances induce a state of excitation and mood change from euphoric to depressive. Psychic dependence on hallucinogens varies greatly but usually is not intense. There is no evidence of physical dependence when the drugs are abruptly withdrawn. LSD can develop a high degree of tolerance but disappears quickly. Individuals who are tolerant to any one of these drugs are cross-tolerant to the others. The greatest dangers to the user are psychological effects and impaired judgement. Some persons, particularly those who are repeated users of the hallucinogens, especially LSD, may experience drug effects after discontinued use. These effects are commonly referred to as "flashbacks" which usually consist of visual illusions. "Flashbacks" can be brought on by use of marijuana, alcohol or barbiturates, by stress or fatigue or may occur without apparent reason. What produces "flashbacks" is not known, but they tend to decrease in frequency over a period of 6 months to one year.

Treatment

A person must be reassured that their bizarre thoughts, visions and sounds are due to the drug and not to a "nervous breakdown". Short-acting barbiturates or minor tranquilizers may help to reduce anxiety. For heavy users, withdrawal from the drug is the simplest part of treatment. Persistent psychotic states or other psychological disorders require psychiatric care.

Notes

Hallucinogens include LSD.

Hallucinogens: drug type such as LSD; induce a state of excitement and mood change, may create psychological impairment and effect judgement.

LSD: lysergic acid diethylamide; a hallucinogen; popular during the 1960's induces an excited state and may psychologically affect the user.

Persons who have a tolerance to LSD may also have a tolerance to the other hallucinogens. The greatest dangers to the user are psychological effects and impaired judgement.

Flashbacks which are visual illusions can occur with persons who are repeated users of hallucinogens, especially LSD. Flashbacks usually decrease in frequency over a period of 6 - 12 months.

DEPENDENCE ON PHENCYCLIDINE (PCP)

PCP has merged as an important drug of abuse. It is not easily classified and should be considered separately from the hallucinogenic drugs.

PCP was tested as an anesthetic agent in humans in the late 1950's. It was withdrawn because people experienced severe anxiety and delusions. Clinical testing stopped in 1962 and PCP appeared as a street drug in 1967. Initially sold as "THC" in recent years it has established its own market. Occasionally injected or ingested, it is most frequently sprinkled on smoking material and inhaled. Since the frequent reports of problems with PCP in 1978 the number of reports have declined significantly.

Symptoms and Signs

A giddy euphoria usually occurs with low doses often followed by bursts of anxiety. Effects of higher doses include a withdrawn catatonic state. In treatment, diazepam (valium) is often helpful.

INDICATORS OF DRUG ABUSE

Individuals while at work may continue their drug dependency and/or habit. Signs which may indicate drug abuse include:

- Frequent absence or tardiness.
- Unexplained absences from work during normal working hours.
- Frequent telephone calls.
- Frequent and lengthy visits to washrooms, lockerooms, or the parking lot.
- Frequent non-work related visits by strangers or employees from other areas.
- A change in the disposition of the employee.
- Frequent mood changes.
- Poor appetite and weight loss.
- Bloodshot eyes, runny nose, irritation in eyes.
- Unusual pupil size (i.e. very contracted or dilated in all types of light).
- Wearing of long-sleeved shirts in warm weather.

Notes

PCP is usually injected or ingested, it is most frequently sprinkled on smoking material and inhaled.

PCP: phencyclidine; tested in the late 1950's to relieve affects of anesthesia; injected or smoked it produces an euphoric feeling in low doses and a withdrawn, catatonic state in high doses.

THE ROLE OF SECURITY PERSONNEL IN ALCOHOL & DRUG ABUSE

Virtually no company or organization which exists in the 1990's is immune from the problem of alcohol and drug abuse by employees. Security personnel should be primarily concerned with alcohol and drug use by employees at the workplace. Information received which indicates an abuse problem away from work, should be communicated to the proper management authorities however.

Corporate America has become more sensitive to the negative publicity and potential liability resulting from an incident at a company sponsored event where alcohol is served. More and more companies are prohibiting the sale or consumption of alcohol at sponsored events.

The role of security in addressing the problem of alcohol and drug abuse in the workplace should remain consistent and similar to other policies and procedures. Security personnel are best suited to provide information, gather intelligence, and conduct observation concerning alcohol and/or drug use on company property. In particular, security officers who are stationed at or near parking lots can provide a significant amount of information concerning:

- employee trips to their vehicles
- non-employees visiting the facility
- use of pay phones by employees
- parking lot activities before and after work
- condition of employees reporting to work
- evidence of drinking (empty cans and bottles)

Additionally, employee informants may often confide in a security officer if they know their identity will remain anonymous. Any information received by a security officer either through his/her own observations or from an informant, must be treated confidentially and sensitively. Speculation, rumor and innuendo are often given as fact so as to embarrass or discredit an employee or the security officer reporting the information. Security personnel should always document reports of drug or alcohol activity at the workplace and report the same to their supervisor.

Notes

Security personnel should be primarily concerned with alcohol and drug abuse by employees at the workplace.

Security personnel are best suited to provide information, gather intelligence, and conduct observation concerning alcohol and/or drug abuse on company property.

Any information received by a security officer concerning possible alcohol or drug related activity at work should never be discussed with anyone other than the officer's immediate supervisor.

Security personnel may be asked to serve as a witness for a supervisor who suspects employees may be engaged in drug or alcohol use on company property. It should be the responsibility of the security department to properly recover, record, identify, secure and store the evidence of suspected alcohol/drug activity. Plastic, self-sealing envelopes can often be purchased from a local supplier or law enforcement agency.

Security can provide a valuable service in conjunction with the Human Resources department by providing and/or coordinating the training of all supervisors and security personnel to drug awareness and to the procedures which are to be followed when an employee is suspected of drug/alcohol use at work. Local law enforcement agencies are usually an excellent resource in providing some basic training and indoctrination of drug awareness to management personnel. These presentations will often allow the participants to view first-hand what a particular drug looks like and smells like when used. Educating the entire workforce to the problems associated with alcohol and drug abuse is a key role that security can provide for any organization.

Often, to accurately detect whether or not a drug problem exists within an organization, undercover investigators are employed to obtain and gather information. Security officers would normally never be informed than an undercover investigator is being utilized. Naturally, if a security officer would suspect that a person is an undercover investigator, this suspicion should never be discussed with anyone for fear of endangering the person's safety.

Notes

It should be the responsibility of security personnel to properly recover, record, identify, secure and store the evidence of suspected alcohol or drug activity.

Security departments should be utilized as a resource for coordinating employee drug awareness programs.

SUMMARY

A single definition for drug dependence is impossible. Addiction refers to a style of living which includes drug dependence. Dependence is usually both physical and psychological.

Recreational drug use has increased in society. Most drugs used in a "recreational" manner are done to attain a "high."

Psychological dependence involves the mental state of a person. Physical dependence occurs as the body adapts to a drug. Tolerance is the need to increase the dose in order to produce the same effect. A withdrawal syndrome is described as a physical change which occurs when the use of the drug is stopped. Drugs which produce dependence act on the Central Nervous System.

The drug industry is required by law to maintain physical security and strict record keeping over certain types of drugs. The Comprehensive Drug Abuse and Prevention Act of 1970 divides controlled substances into 5 classes or schedules. Those in Schedule I have the highest potential for abuse with no accepted medical use. Prescriptions for drugs in all these schedules must show the physician's Federal Drug Enforcement (FDA) license number.

Drug dependence in part is related to cultural patterns and to socioeconomic factors. Factors which may lead to drug use include: peer pressure, low self-esteem and stress.

Persons who become addicted to or dependent on drugs have no known physiological differences from people who do not become addicted. Some substances have a high potential for physical dependence and are more prone to abuse even when used in a social or recreational setting.

Alcoholism is a chronic illness which costs the US economy over $25 billion per year. Males outnumber female alcoholics 4 to 1. One in ten Americans will

Notes

experience some problem with alcoholism. Families of alcoholics tend to have higher incidence of alcoholism. Alcoholics frequently have histories of broken homes and disturbed relationships with parents.

Alcohol accumulates in a person's blood. From 5-10% of ingested alcohol is excreted unchanged in urine, sweat and expired air; the remainder is oxidized to carbon dioxide (CO2) and water. The most common forms of specific organ damage are cirrhosis of the liver, brain damage and heart disease. Persons who drink large amounts of alcohol repeatedly are somewhat tolerant to its effects.

No other approach has benefited alcoholics as much as Alcoholics Anonymous (AA). Antabuse can be taken by a person who is an alcoholic and if they drink while using this medication they will become violently ill.

Since 1909 the federal government has attempted to control opium use. Opioid type drugs are considered narcotic and are effective pain relievers. Opium is usually smoked through a long stemmed pipe. Opium for the most part has been replaced by morphine and heroin.

Morphine is preferred for the relief of pain. It is odorless and is either injected or ingested. It acts on the Central Nervous System.

Heroin is the synthetic alkaloid of morphine and is 2-10 times as potent.

Codeine is a weak derivative of opium and is used mostly in cough medicine.

Methadone, a synthetic opiate is considered more addictive than heroin and is used to block the withdrawal symptoms of heroin.

Tolerance and physical dependence on the opioids and synthetic narcotics develop rapidly. Many but not all complications of heroin addiction are related to unsanitary administration of the drug. The more frequent complications include lung problems, hepatitis and neurological disorders.

Notes

Barbiturates are a depressant and are used to induce sleep or to act as mild tranquilizers. Barbiturate users may appear as if they are alcohol intoxicated. The extent of physical dependence to barbiturates is related to dosage and length of time the drug has been regularly taken.

Notes

Marijuana use is widespread in the US. Continued used of marijuana may produce some mental dependence but usually there is not a physical dependence. Marijuana produces a dreamy state of consciousness or "high." By-products of marijuana are retained in the body's tissues for a long time (up to 30 days).

Mental dependence on cocaine can occur quickly. When cocaine is either injected or inhaled it produces an euphoric condition. Because cocaine is such a short acting drug, users may continue to repeat doses. Death may result from cardiovascular collapse or respiratory failure. The smoking of "free-base" cocaine or "crack" has become popular.

Treatment of acute cocaine intoxication is generally not necessary because of the extremely short action of the drug. Cocaine poisoning is much more severe and is life threatening.

Amphetamines are used as stimulants and generally cause elevated mood, alertness and concentration. Amphetamines induce tolerance. Massive doses are rarely fatal.

LSD is considered a hallucinogen. These drugs induce a state of excitation. There is no evidence of physical dependence when drug use is stopped. The greatest dangers to the user are psychological effects and impaired judgement. "Flashbacks" may occur after discontinued use.

Individuals who abuse drugs usually experience frequent absences from work and may be involved in more job related accidents.

QUESTIONS

1. _____ refers to a style of living that includes drug dependence.

   a. Tolerance
   b. Abuse
   c. Intoxication
   d. Addiction

2. _____ is usually considered to be a compulsive use and overwhelming involvement with a drug.

   a. Tolerance
   b. Abuse
   c. Addiction
   d. Dependence

3. _____ has increasingly become a part of the culture of the USA.

   a. Recreational drug use
   b. Psychological dependence
   c. Treatment centers
   d. LSD use

4. Recreational drug use usually involves:

   a. Depressants
   b. Hallucinogens
   c. Narcotics
   d. Stimulants

5. Drugs that produce dependence work on the:

   a. Heart and lungs
   b. Bloodstream
   c. Central Nervous System
   d. Bone structure

6. Name 3 drugs which cause primarily a mental or psychological dependence.

    1. _____

    2. _____

    3. _____

7. Cocaine produces a strong psychological dependence but no real physical dependence. True or False?

8. What law enacted in 1970 in the USA requires the drug industry to maintain physical security and strict record keeping over certain types of drugs?

    a. Omnibus Safe Street Act
    b. Health and Human Services Act
    c. Comprehensive Drug Abuse Prevention and Control Act
    d. Federal Opium Act

9. Specifically, what does the above law require regarding drug classifications?

    _____

    _____

    _____

10. The development of drug dependence is complex and unclear. The addictive drug, pre-existing conditions and the personality of the user must all be considered regarding drug dependence. True or False?

11. Factors which may lead to drug use include:

    a. Low self-esteem
    b. Peer pressure
    c. Emotional distress
    d. Stress
    e. All of the above

12.   Persons who become addicted or dependent have no known biochemical or physi-ological differences from people who do not become addictive. True or False?

13.   Abuse of prescription drugs and avoidance of illegal drugs may occur in persons with:

    a. Low education and low professional status
    b. Criminal backgrounds
    c. Advanced education and professional status
    d. None of the above

14.   Prohibition existed in the USA from:

    a. 1910 - 1920
    b. 1920 - 1933
    c. 1905 - 1920
    d. 1940 - 1945

15.   Male alcoholics outnumber female alcoholics:

    a. 2 to 1
    b. 3 to 1
    c. 4 to 1
    d. 10 to 1

16.   Families of alcoholics tend to have higher incidence of alcoholism. True or False?

17.   Alcohol is absorbed into the blood primarily transmitted from the:

    a. Kidney
    b. Brain
    c. Liver
    d. Small intestine

18. Depression of the _____ is a principle effect of alcohol.

    a. Liver
    b. Brain
    c. Heart
    d. Central Nervous System

19. The most common form of specific organ damage seen in alcoholics is:

    a. Cirrhosis of the liver
    b. Brain damage
    c. Heart disease
    d. All of the above

20. People who drink large amounts of alcohol repeatedly, become somewhat tolerant to its effects. True or False?

21. The one thing that has benefited alcoholics the most has been:

    a. Antabuse
    b. Use of depressants
    c. Alcoholics Anonymous
    d. Prohibition

22. A person who drinks alcohol while on the medication antabuse will become violently ill. True or False?

23. There is no real scientific or medical benefit with any of the narcotics. True or False?

24. Morphine and heroin are derived from:

    a. Codeine
    b. Cocaine
    c. Hashish
    d. Opium

25. _____ is the preferred drug for intense pain relief.

    a. Heroin
    b. Methadone
    c. Aspirin
    d. Morphine

26. Heroin is a synthetic form of:

    a. Cocaine
    b. Methadone
    c. Aspirin
    d. Morphine

27. _____ is used in cough medicines.

    a. Codeine
    b. Cocaine
    c. Caffeine
    d. Methadone

28. _____ is the drug developed during World War II used in the treatment of heroin addiction.

    a. Codeine
    b. Cocaine
    c. Morphine
    d. Methadone

29. Tolerance and physical dependence on the opioids and synthetic narcotics develops rapidly. True or False?

30. Barbiturates are a _____ and are used to induce sleep or to act as mild sedatives or tranquilizers.

    a. stimulant
    b. hallucinogen
    c. depressant
    d. pain reliever

31. The procedure for treating dependence on depressants, is to reintoxicate the patient and then withdraw the drug on a strict schedule. True or False?

32. No physical dependence occurs with marijuana use. True or False?

33. _____ is an active ingredient of marijuana.

    a. LSD
    b. PCP
    c. THC
    d. PDQ

34. Many persons who undergo a drug screen urinalysis may show the by-products of marijuana in their urine for up to:

    a. 7 days
    b. 14 days
    c. 21 days
    d. 30 days

35. In cocaine use, physical tolerance or dependence has never been proven. True or False?

36. A strong desire to continue to take cocaine is usually present with the user. True or False?

37. Cocaine is a "short-acting" drug. True or False?

38. What is "crack" and how is it produced?

    _____

    _____

    _____

39.   Cocaine poisoning can quickly induce death because of interruption of breathing and heartbeat. True or False?

40.   Amphetamines are classified as:

    a. Depressants
    b. Stimulants
    c. Hallucinogens
    d. Barbiturates

41.   Amphetamines are different from cocaine because they induce tolerance. True or False?

42.   Massive doses of amphetamines are rarely fatal. True or False?

43.   Hallucinogens induce excitement and can mentally impair the user. True or False?

44.   "Flashbacks" may be common for people who have used:

    a. Marijuana
    b. Amphetamines
    c. LSD
    d. Cocaine

45.   PCP was first developed to isolate people from the side effects of anesthesia. True or False?

46.   Name 5 indicators of possible drug use by an employee.

    1. _____

    2. _____

    3. _____

    4. _____

    5. _____

Practical Questions and Exercises

1. How often do security personnel inspect the parking lot and "out of the way" places at a facility for signs of alcohol or drug use at work (i.e.. empty beer cans, liquor bottles or roach clips)?

2. What is a security officer to do if they suspect an employee is "unfit to work" upon arrival?

3. What is a security officer to do if they encounter an employee drinking a can of beer in a locker room? Smoking a marijuana cigarette?

4. What is a security officer to do if they see an empty liquor bottle in the lunchbox of an employee during a package inspection?

5. What should a security officer do if he/she suspects that the security officer arriving to work as his/her relief has been drinking?

6. How long before reporting to work should a security officer abstain from drinking?

7. What should a security officer do if he/she sees the same visitor in the parking lot on most pay days, talking with employees and exchanging money?

The party begins.

I can drive when I drink.

2 drinks later.

I can drive when I drink

After 4 drinks.

I can drive when I drunk.

After 5 drinks.

I can drin when I drin

7 drinks in all.

I can drwrecknlrmk

The more you drink, the more coordination you lose. That's a fact, plain and simple.

Still, people drink too much and then go out and expect to handle a car.

When you drink too much you can't handle a car. You can't even handle a pen.

The House of Seagram

THE EFFECTIVE SECURITY OFFICERS TRAINING MANUAL

Chapter XVIII

Ethics

Ethics

Much has been written recently concerning ethics in our country. Most of the time, when we read about violations of recognized ethical standards we associate the conduct with business fraud of some sort. As security officers, the foundation of our very existence rests on the refusal of certain people to act in an ethical manner at all times. If people did not steal, cheat, rob, vandalize or otherwise destroy that which belongs to someone else...why would there be a need for security?

Unfortunately, because of evil, there is a need for persons to protect themselves and property. By and large that is why security exists! However, if as security professionals we accept the theory that security personnel must conduct themselves in a highly proper and ethical manner at all times, then we must also accept the notion that ours is an **integrity** profession. Without **integrity**, security personnel are no better than criminals. In fact, many would argue worse than criminals, for if a person has been assigned the responsibility of protecting someone else's property, to damage or steal the property is the greatest wrong!

What is Ethics?

This question has been debated for hundreds of years. A study conducted several years ago by the Ethics Resource Center found that over 86% of all people who were interviewed, associated ethics with standards and rules of conduct, morals, right and wrong, values and honesty. Unfortunately, only those who display a lack of ethics are identified. Those who "do the right thing" are not often publicized. Rather, individuals who violate recognized standards of behavior are apparent.

Dr. Albert Schweizter defined **ethics** as, "*the name we give to our concern for good behavior. We feel an obligation to consider not only our own personal well-being, but also that of others and of human society as a whole.*" 1. Ethical behavior includes a shared interest which affects all humans. Ethical behavior needs to be recognized and accepted. Behavior becomes unethical when a special interest of one individual or a

Notes

Reading For A Purpose
Look for these key words:
• Integrity   • Morals
• Bribes
• Sexual Harassment
Look for answers to these
        Questions:
1. What are the three elements of theft?
2. What are common ethical violations committed by security personnel?
3. What should a security officer do when he/she suspects wrongdoing?

Integrity: Honest behavior characterized by following a code of values or principles.

Ethics includes standards and rules of conduct, values and honesty.

Morals: Principles of right behavior; conforming to a standard of right behavior.

Dr. Albert Schweitzer: Philosopher, theologian and physician, considered to be a genius, often cited for his views and opinions.

374

number of individuals is considered more important than the interest of society.

For security professionals, it is essential that we understand and accept what is considered ethical behavior. Since securty personnel are often enforcing rules and policies, an example which demonstrates high ethical standards must be the rule and not the exception for all security personnel.

Ethical Violations or Cardinal Sins of Security Officers

When hired, most security officers are instructed by their employer what is considered improper or unethical behavior. Often a statement to the affect that, *"anyone who violates any of the beforementioned rules and regulations will be subject to discipline, up to and including discharge,"* is signed by all new hires. Normally these rule violations include: theft, sleeping while on duty, destruction of property, misuse of equipment , etc.

Dishonesty-Theft

Without question, security personnel who exhibit dishonest behavior discredit the entire profession. Security personnel who are assigned to a facility to protect and insure that product is not damaged or stolen, but decide to engage in the theft of that product, have commited the most serious and damaging offense possible. Security and cleaning personnel are considered prime suspects in any theft investigation because of their opportunity to have access to various areas of a facility.

As discussed in the Internal Threat module, people steal for a variety of reasons but a need or desire to steal is always present. When security officers are found to have been responsible for a theft, they will usually display the second element of theft...rationalization. Security officers will often rationalize that they chose to steal becaue they were not appreciated, or they were overworked, underpaid, etc... The fact remains that **no legitimate reason ever exists** for a security officer to engage in theft. Opportunity is the final

Notes

Security personnel must always conduct themselves in a highly professional manner.

Security personnel who engage in theft will be subject to both civil and criminal penalties including monetary fines and jail time. In addition, these criminal offenses may prevent the person from working in the security field in the future.

The need and desire to steal is usually driven by greed. Security officers who steal are normally involved in the theft of product or material.

element that is present in any theft situation. Usually a security officer has more of an opportunity than anyone in an organization to steal.

Security personnel have a great opportunity for theft since they may be the only person working at the facility or one of only a few people working. It may seem easy for a security officer to have an accomplice come into a facility, back-up a truck to the rear loading dock and remove property. This can often be accomplished without detection. Usually, thieves who find a facility so susceptible to theft will often come back and become more daring. If the thefts continue, the odds are great that the thefts will eventually be discovered and the perpetrators apprehended. Some facilities may discover a theft immediately while other organizations may not learn of the loss for weeks or month. The point to be remembered is that the odds increase that eventually a security officer who engages in theft will be identified.

Dishonesty-Theft of Time

Security officers are required to record the actual hours worked in many different ways. Some officers will punch-in using a timeclock. Others will simply write their hours in a log, or telephone a central office to record their call-on and off times. No matter what system is utilized to record the time worked, security personnel are often afforded the opportunity to misrepresent their actual hours worked.

Security officers who walk off-duty at a facility are not only leaving the facility unprotected, they are leaving their employer possibly liable for any loss or damage which occurs while the facility is left unprotected. In addition, if the security officer is a contract employee, his employer may unintentionally be cheating the client for hours worked. Again, eventually the truth will come to the service and the security officer who is leaving their post will be identified. Usually a situation of this type is extremely embarassing to all parties.

Notes

Organizations with effective inventory control precedures will normally discover a loss or theft within a short period of time.

Many security companies have checks and balances to insure that a security officer cannot misrepresent their time, thereby cheating their employer or client.

Occasionally, low-paid contract security officers decide to quit their employer and simply walk-off from their post. These individuals show a great lack of respect and courtesy. If a security officer chooses to quit a job, providing their employer with proper notice is necessary and essential.

Destruction of Property

Because of boredom, unethical security officers will often decide to use a computer, take a "spin" on a forklift, take a drive in a company vehicle, or simply perform some "knucklehead" action which damages or destroys property.

Damage to property can often be repaired or replaced no matter how costly. Damage to the reputation of the security officer, security department, or contract providing company will often be damaged beyond repair.

Real-Life Example

A relatively new security officer locked himself out of the security post early one Sunday morning. Not certain as to what he should do, he telephoned his field supervisor from a near-by payphone to receive advice.

The field supervisor asked the officer if the locked office door had a window. When he was informed it did, he instructed the security officer to break the window in order to gain access to the locked office.

The security officer dutifully followed the instructions of the field supervisor. Unfortunately, the window to the office door was made of reinforced glass and it took several tries with a chair before the glass was broken. The security officer gained access and continued his rounds. Since he was not instructed to clean-up the broken glass he did not.

Now one can imagine what the client would say when he arrived to work the following morning to find a broken window, glass strewn about and an overall level of disarray.

Fortunately, an executive with the security company had decided to make some random field inspections this same Sunday morning and he visited the facility in discussion at about 7:00 a.m.

Upon his arrival, the executive was shocked to find the mess! When questioned, the security officer informed the executive of all that had happened. The executive telephoned the field supervisor to ask why he had given the advice to break the window as opposed to

Notes

There is never a legitimate excuse or reason for misusing or damaging equipment belonging to a client.

What are your instructions if this occurs to you?

Was the field supervisor using good judgment? Was this an emergency?

When the security officer realized that the window was made from reinforced glass, he should have stopped trying to break the glass. After breaking the window, the mess should have been cleaned up.

The client probably would have fired the security company.

Inspections of facilities and security officers are essential.

The executive could not believe the supervisor would have instructed the security officer to break the window.

contacting the client at his home in an effort to obtain another key to the office. The field supervisor did not have a satisfactory answer to this question.

> *The executive pondered his dilemma: What should he do?*
> * *Call the client representative at home and advise him of the situation?*
> * *Clean-up the mess and ignore the problem?*
> * *Clean-up the mess, fix the window and say nothing with the hope the client would never find out what had happened?*

The executive chose to call an emergency glass repair company who arrived at the facility within 45 minutes. In less than two hours, the window was repaired at a cost of $300.00 since the incident occurred on a Sunday. The executive had cleaned-up the entire mess and he started to feel a little better about the situation.

Yet, he still knew he was not finished. He wrote a brief note and slipped it under the office door of the client representative with these words, "Bill: I stopped out at the facility today to take care of a problem we had. I'll call you first thing on Monday morning and advise you of the situation. Best Regards!"

When the security executive contacted the client the following day, he informed the client exactly of what had happened. The client was not pleased with the decision made by the field supervisor but the client was delighted to have a security company whose executive had the honesty and integrity to "do the right thing." His opinion of the security company improved dramatically.

Dishonesty-Telephone Abuse and Misuse

As with every other Code of Conduct violation, telephone misuse or abuse is discussed with security offcers before their first day of work. Everyone knows that on occasion, a security officer will need to use the telephone for legitimate reasons and few would question this moderate use. However, since telephone calls are logged by most organizations which describe the phone use, date and time of the call, whether the call was incoming or outgoing, telephone number called, length of the coversation, and cost of the call, it is very easy to determine if a security officer was abusing telephone privileges.

Notes

What do you think is the "right" thing to do in this situation?

The essence of providing good service is responding to a situation or problem and resolving it effectively.

Truth is always the best way to deal with any situation.

Since the client knew the problem was immediately corrected, he did not feel the reputation of the security company had been seriously damaged.

Again, because of boredom, security officers will often misuse the telephone.

If the security officer decides to make a long-distance call or call a 900 number, not only is communication often impossible, an expense is being incurred for the phone call. Additionally, the security officer is being paid to perform their job, not talk on the phone! And eventually, the facts will become clear who was working on a particular date and time and who in all likelihood is responsible for the phone abuse!

Dishonesty-Falsification of Records

Security officers who attempt to take shortcuts by stating that patrols or inspections were made when, in fact, they were not, have committed a very serious offense. Acts of omission are those where something should occur and does not. Acts of comission are those where something occurs which should not.

Falsifying records or logs are acts of omission and are more serious because a security officer had to have thought out in advance how they were going to misrepresent or falsify a record.

Falsification of records is the equivalent of lying and a very dishonest act. Whether the security officer is falsifying a travel expense or indicating that a patrol was made which did not occur, serious discipline will result when discovered, and these actions should result in the termination of the security officer.

Even security officers who fill-in their daily logs in advance are violating accepted codes of conduct. Since many shifts result in similar reports and activities, dishonest security officers will often complete their logs in advance. Naturally, when an incident occurs which changes the pre-completed log, a problem exists. Usually, logs are completed in advance because of boredom or laziness on the part of the security officer. No matter what the reason, completing logs in advance is dishonest and is falsification of records!

Notes

A complete lack of honesty and integrity occurs when 900 phone numbers are called by security officers. This type of conduct seriously detracts from the image of every person who works in the security department.

Falsification of records are acts of omission and may be considered to be acts of negligence.

A security officer who is tired from having worked 12 straight hours and skips a patrol should truthfully state why the patrol was missed rather than lying that the patrol was made.

Once a person begins to lie or deceive someone on small things, it is only a matter of time until the dishonesty involves something of significance.

Just because shift activities are identical on most days, a security officer cannot justify completing his log in advance.

Use of Alcohol or Drugs

As with all of the previously discussed rules of conduct, the use of alcohol or drugs while on duty is strictly prohibited. In addition, consumption of alcohol prior to reporting for duty is prohibited. As discussed in the Alcohol and Drug Awareness Module, the liver can detoxify only one ounce of alcohol per hour. Therefore, if a security officer consumes two or three beers one hour before the start of their shift, they will be considered unfit to work!

The security industry attracts a great many individuals who have a variety of emotional problems. Coupled with the low pay associated with most contract security agencies, it is obvious why some people who work in security may suffer from alcohol or drug abuse.

Since security positions will often allow a person a good deal of privacy, away from others, persons with an abuse problem can indulge themselves without immediate fear of being detected. However, signs and symptoms will eventually become apparent to co-workers, superiors or even visitors. Once again, the credibility and reputation of the entire security organization is tarnished when incidents of alcohol and/or drug abuse are discovered.

Sleeping on Duty

There is sleeping on duty and then there is **sleeping on duty!** The first type of sleeping on duty has occurred to just about everyone who has worked in the security field. This situation occurs as a security officer is sitting in a chair legitimately attempting to perform his/her duties. Before long the eyelids become heavy and the head begins to nod and before you know it...! Usually, this type of brief sleep is interrupted by the security officer realizing what is occuring and he/she immdiately gets up, walks around the desk, splashes cold water on their face, and stands up for several minutes. Sometimes the ring of the telephone or worse yet, someone entering the security office awakens the officer. While this situation is embarassing, it will normally not lead to immediate termination after only one offense.

Notes

Security officers who drink while on duty should be discharged with no consideration given as to the reasons for this inappropriate conduct.

Security officers who suspect other officers may be coming to work unfit, or who believe co-workers may be drinking on the job, must notify their superiors.

When a person is in a relaxed position, even if they have good sleep habits, drowsiness may develop. It is at this time a person must take steps to prevent sleep from occuring.

The second type of sleeping on duty occurs when the security officer deliberately attempts to sleep while on duty. Evidence supporting this occurrence usually includes the officer finding an "out-of-the-way" place where he/she can lie down; removal of shoes and socks; and general absence from their assigned duties for extended periods of time. This type of sleeping on duty is normally discovered by an executive who enters their office early one morning to begin their workday and finds the security officer "sacked-out." To say the least, this is a very embarassing situation which discredits the security officer and his/her employer.

There are no reasonable excuses for sleeping on duty. Even if a security officer has had to work 12 or 16 hours straight, sleeping is not reasonable or excusable. Sleeping on duty is strictly forbidden and will usually result in immediate termination. Proper rest is a condition of employment. Clients expect security officers to be alert and awake while on duty.

Bribes

Bribes are defined as, *anything offered or given to someone in a position of trust to induce him/her to act dishonestly.* Security officers who accept money from persons in order for the security officer to "look the other way," are guilty of accepting bribes and should be terminated at once!

Attempted bribes of security personnel will often occur if other dishonest employees believe that in order to commit an act, they must protect themselves from the likelihood of security observing their conduct. Bribes will usualy not be offered if the person offering the bribe believes their offer will be refused. Acceptance of a bribe will result in immediate termination of a security officer.

Gambling, Betting and/or Borrowing Money

Security officers who bet with other officers or with employees of a facility are violating the accepted code of conduct for security personel. Gambling or betting debts can become quite excessive and result in compromises in the overall security of a facility.

Notes

Examples of this type of conduct will normally lead to the immediate termination of the security officer.

Security officers who work two jobs are prime candidates to fall asleep while on duty.

Excuses such as, "I'm underpaid, overworked, nobody will ever know," etc. are <u>not acceptable</u>.

Many security executives believe that capital punishment is acceptable for security officers who accept bribes.

There's nothing wrong with discussing a ballgame with a co-worker, but gambling with employees is strictly prohibited.

Borrowing money from employees and/or co-workers is also an unacceptable practice. Borrowed money is often never paid back which causes resentment and hard-feelings. Co-workers and client employees should never be asked to loan money for any reason.

Sexual Harassment

Security officers who attempt to solicit attention from members of the opposite sex, may find themselves on the receiving end of a sexual harassment complaint if their advances are unwarranted and not acceptable. Security officers should never attempt to date employees of the facility where they work for obvious reasons. Conflicts of interest can easily develop and compromises in the security operation are possible.

Any verbal or physical conduct of a sexual nature that can create an intimidating or offensive work environment cannot be tolerated. Any undesirable activity such as sexual, racial, or ethnic jokes, unwelcome sexual advances or requests for sexual favors in exchange for special treatment cannot be tolerated.

Companies and organizations who condone or tolerate behavior which is considered to be of a harassing nature, can be sued in a federal court and subjected to severe financial penalties.

Reporting of Ethical Violations

It can be very difficult for a security officer to report to his or her superior that they believe a fellow security officer is invovled in improper conduct. To report to a superior that a co-worker may be involved in improper conduct, requires a great deal of courage on the part of the reporting security officer. In addition, the reporting security officer must have a strong feeling of trust in the people he/she is providing this information to. If after a report has been filed, the security officer is accosted by the co-worker because information "leaked" regarding the suspicions, a greater problem now exists.

Notes

When a security officer borrows money from a co-worker, their credibility and image is damaged in the eyes of other employees.

Ever since Adam and Eve, men and women have been attracted to one another. This attraction will often occur in the workplace.

Once a person has been informed that their actions are inappropriate and undesirable, all contact should immediately cease with the person in question

Security officers are to conduct themselves in a professinal manner at all times. "Affairs of the heart" have no place at work for security officers.

Have you ever witnessed improper conduct on the part of another security officer? Did you say anything to anyone?

Reporting wrongdoing is never easy, never pleasant. But as security professionals, we are required to report this wrongdoing, no matter how difficult. Many organizations have initiated "hot-lines" for anonymously reporting wrongdoing. Other companies encourage security officers to telephone a key executive or security director to report their suspicions. Others may encourage individuals to write an anonymous letter to report the information. Whatever avenues are available to report the wrongdoings or suspicions, the security officer must choose one and report the information. Failure to do so casts a shadow of suspicion over all security officers. Sometimes, investigations are underway before the security officer's suspicions are made known. By reporting this information, security officers are not only doing the right thing, they are doing their job and removing themselves from the cloud of suspicion.

CODE OF ETHICS FOR PRIVATE SECURITY EMPLOYEES

In recognition of the significant contribution of private security to crime prevention and reduction, as a private security employee, I pledge:

1.   To accept the responsibilities and fulfill the obligations of my role: protecting life and property; preventing and reducing crimes against my employer's business, or other organizations and institutions to which I am assigned; upholding the law; and respecting the constitutional rights of all persons.

2.   To conduct myself with honesty and integrity and to adhere to the highest moral principles in the performance of my security duties.

3.   To be faithful, diligent, and dependable in discharging my duties, and to uphold at all times the laws, policies, and procedures that protect the rights of others.

4.   To observe the precepts of truth, accuracy and prudence, without allowing personal feelings, prejudices, animosities or friendships to influence my judgements.

Notes

Spreading blatantly false rumors or innuendo is not the pupose of information "hot lines." Information or suspicions based on objective evidence should immediately be reported to a responsible management official.

5.   To report to my superiors, without hesitation, any violation of the law or of my employer's or client's regualtions.

6.   To respect and protect the confidential and priviledged information of my employer or client beyond the term of my employment, except where their are contrary to law or this Code of Ethics.

7.   To cooperate with all recognized and responsible law enforcement and government agencies in matters within their jurisdiction.

8.   To accept no compensation, commission, gratuity, or other advantage without the knowledge and consent of my employer.

9.   To conduct myself professionally at all times, and to perform my duties in a manner that reflects credit upon myself, my employer, and private security.

10.   To strive continually to improve my performance by seeking training and educational opportunities that will better prepare me for my provate security duties.

Source: *Report of the Task Force on Private Security*, Washington, D.C.: U.S. Government Printing Office, 1976.

SUMMARY

Notes

Dr. Albert Schweizter defined **ethics** as, "*the name we give to our concern for good behavior. We feel an obligation to consider not only our own personal well-being, but also that of others and of human society as a whole.*" Ethical behavior needs to be recognized and accepted. Behavior becomes unethical when a special interest of one individual or a few individuals is considered more important than the interest of society.

Security personnel who exhibit dishonest behavior discredit the entire profession. Security personnel who are assigned to a facility to protect and insure that product is not damaged or stolen, but decide to engage in theft, have commited the most serious and damaging offense possible. Security and cleaning personnel are considered prime suspects in any theft investigation because of their opportunity to have access to various areas of a facility.

When security officers are found to have been responsible for a theft, they will usually display the second element of theft...rationalization. Security officers will often rationalize that they chose to steal becaue they were not appreciated, were overworked, underpaid, etc... Opportunity is the final element that is present in any theft situation. Usually a security officer has more of an opportunity than anyone in an organization to steal.

Security officers are required to record the actual hours worked in many different ways. No matter what system is utilized to record the time worked, security personnel are often afforded the opportunity to misrepresent their actual hours worked.

Damage to property can often be repaired or replaced no matter how costly. Damage to the reputation of the security officer, security department, or contract providing company will often be damaged beyond repair.

Telephone misuse or abuse is discussed with security offcers before their first day of work. If the security officer decides to make a long-distance call or call a 900 number, not only is communication with the security officer often impossible, an expense is being incurred for the phone call. Additionally, the security officer is being paid to perform their job, not talk on the phone! And eventually, the facts will become clear who was working on a particular date and time and who in all likelihood is responsible for the phone abuse!

Officers who attempt to take shortcuts by stating that patrols or inspections were made when in fact, were not, have made a very serious offense. Acts of omission are those where something should be occur and does not. Acts of comission are those where something occurs which should not.

The use of alcohol or drugs while on duty is strictly prohibited. In addition, consumption of alcohol prior to reporting for duty is prohibited. The security industry attracts a great many individuals who have a variety of emotional problems. Coupled with the low pay associated with most contract security agencies, it is obvious why many people who work in security may suffer from chemical abuse.

Since security positions will often allow a person a good deal of privacy, away from others, persons with an abuse problem can indulge themselves without immediate fear of being detected. Once again, the credibility and reputation of the entire security organization is tarnished when incidents of alcohol and/or drug abuse are discovered.

Sleeping on duty is strictly forbidden and will usually result in immeidate termination. Proper rest is a condition of employment. Clients expect security officers to be alert and awake while on duty.

Security officers who accept money from persons in order for the security officer to "look the other way," are guilty of accepting bribes and should be terminated at once! Acceptance of a bribe will result in immediate termination.

Security officers who bet with other officers or with employees of a facility are violating the accepted code of conduct for security personel. Gambling or betting debts can become quite excessive and result in compromises in the overall security of a facility.

Security officers who attempt to solicit attention from members of the opposite sex, may find themselves on the receiving end of a sexual harassment complaint if their advances are unwarranted and not acceptable. Security officers should never attempt to date employees of the facility where they work for obvious reasons.

It can be very difficult for a security officer to report to his or her superior that they believe a fellow security officer is invovled in improper conduct. To report to a superior that a co-worker may be involved in improper conduct, requires a great deal of courage on the part of the security officer.

Notes

QUESTIONS

True or False

1. ___ Without integrity, security personnel are no better than criminals.

2. ___ Generally speaking, security officers have less opportunity to steal than most other employees.

3. ___ Damage to a reputation is far more costly than damage to property.

4. ___ Acts of omission are those where something occurs which should not.

5. ___ Falsifying a record or log is considered very serious.

6. ___ Completing your daily log in advance shows that the security officer is prompt and on the job.

7. ___ Having two or three beers before reporting to work is harmless.

8. ___ Finding an "out-of-the-way" place to sleep is considered good taste and not a serious violation of the rules of conduct.

9. ___ Borrowing money from co-workers is a good way to build up a "good working relationship."

10. ___ Security officers should never attempt to date employees of a facility for fear of sexual harassment reprisals.

11. ___ By not reporting wrong-doings by fellow security officers, a security officer casts doubt upon himself.

Fill-In the Blank

1. The name we give to our concern for good behavior is called _____ .

2. Security officers normally have a greater _____ to steal than most other employees.

3. Taking a spin on a forklift, drawing pictures on a client's property, are examples of a security officer's _____ on the job.

4.   Security officers who attempt to take _____ by stating that patrols are being made, have committed a very serious offense.

5.   _____ of records is the equivalent of lying and is a very dishonest act.

6.   Anything offered or given to someone in a postion of trust to induce hime/her to act dishonestly is called a _____.

7.   Security officers who attempt to force their intentions upon a fellow employee could very well be acussed of _____ _____.

8.   Many organizations have initiated _____ _____ for anonymously reporting wrongdoing.

PRACTICAL EXERCISES & QUESTIONS

Case Study #1

Imagine that you are a security officer at a prestigious world headquarters of a Fortune 500 company. You had been unemployed for the over 18 months before a friend of yours, Tommy Smith helped you obtain a job for the company. Tommy Smith is a local boy who has "made good." Tommy spent the early part of his career in the Army, having served two tours of duty in Vietnam. Tommy is now the third shift supervisor of security for the Acme Company, whom you report to.

1.   On three occasions you have found an hourly maintenance mechanic asleep, in a remote location of the facility. On each occasion you have immediately informed your supervisor, Tommy Smith, who told you he will handle the situation. To your knowledge, the maintenance employee has never been disciplined for sleeping.

2.   You notice that when employees are leaving work, they talk to Tommy Smith about meeting for a drink later. Tommy tells them he'll meet them at the "usual spot" in about 20 minutes. You ask Tommy if he could get in trouble with his superiors for fraternizing with employees. Tommy tells you its nobody's business what he does after work.

3.   There are strong suspicions that a group of employees are involved in alcohol and drug use on the third shift. Some of the employees suspected of being involved are the same ones that Tommy meets after work for a drink. Tommy has told you that these employees are nothing but a bunch of "good ol' boys" who just like to have a little fun at work.

The Acme Corporation's security department has a very clear policy regarding the behavior of all security personnel. All security department employees are required to report to the Manager of Security, any suspicions regarding the possible misconduct of employees. You believe that your supervisor, Tommy Smith may be involved in some improprieties with some other employees but you don't know for certain. What if anything, should you do?

Case Study #2

You have just been named the Loss Prevention Manager for a the ABC Company which operates a large warehouse distribution center for which you are responsible. Rumors abound that the Distribution Manager, whom you report to, is a recovering alcoholic. You have heard that he once had a very bright career before he became involved with alcohol. While he had abstained from alcohol for several months, he recently has missed several days of work. You heard that the Assistant Distribution Manager had to drive the Manager home from work one day last week because the Manager was intoxicated.

While at the local courthouse where you are waiting to testify in a shopifting case, you notice the Distribution Manager's name on the court docket for a "driving under the influence" charge. You notice the arresting officer's name as someone you know. You seek out this officer who informs you that on the previous Saturday night he arrested the Distribution Manager for drunk driving. The officer told you that the Distribution Manager's blood alcohol content was .18. The officer added that the Distribution Manager begged the officer not to arrest him since he would lose his job if anyone from the company learned of the charge.

You notice that the Distribution Manager sees you speaking with the officer. When you return to work the Distribution Manager calls you into his office for a private meeting. He politely tells you that he has always been impressed with your work and that you have a bright career ahead of you. He also advises you that a person of your age should do all that is possible not to have enemies within the corporation and that he has a lot of friends at the corporate offices who can either help or hinder you in your career. You thank him for his time and quickly leave his office.

When you were hired, you signed a statement that you would report to management any behavior on the part of any other employee which detracts from the overall good of the company or reflects poorly on the company's reputation. **Do you report what you know about the Distribution Manager?**

THE EFFECTIVE SECURITY OFFICERS TRAINING MANUAL

Chapter XIX

Non-Security Duties

and

Creating a Positive Impression

Non-Security Duties and Creating a Positive Impression

A popular television commercial's catch phrase, "You never get a second chance to make a first impression," is never more true than in the security profession.

Security officers are judged in large part, by the impression created in dealing with people in 15-30 seconds. Most security officers are wearing a uniform, consisting of a shirt, possible tie, hat, shoes and perhaps a jacket. The security officer who arrives to work unshaven, with a soiled, wrinkled shirt, unpolished shoes, and in general an appearance that looks like the officer has just climbed out of bed, might as well find another job! The visual impression given to the client, supervisor and co-workers is that this officer just doesn't care and will never become an effective member of the security department. This person may be the most qualified individual in their field of study, but they have already impaired their potential for success.

Beside visual appearance, the tone of one's voice, the willingness to offer a "good morning," or a "may I help you?" creates a positive impression in the minds of the listener.

As security officers, to improve our chances of success follow these simple guidelines:

1. Arrive to work 15 minutes early, in a clean uniform.
2. Bathe or shower just before leaving for work.
3. Greet your co-workers with a friendly hello and smile.
4. Ask the officer you are relieving, what happened on the preceding shift that you need to be aware of.
5. Leave you personal problems and hang-ups at home.
6. Smile when on the telephone or giving directions.
7. Ask at least once a day, "How can I help you?"
8. Clean your work area before the end of your shift.
9. Ask your relief, if there is anything they need before you leave.
10. Remember that you agreed to perform this job for a agreed amount of money. If you find a better job, treat your employer as you would like to be treated and give at least two weeks notice.

Notes

Reading For A Purpose
Look for answers to these Questions:
1. How can a security officer create a positive first impression?
2. Why do so many security officers have non-security duties to perform?
3. What is the best way in dealing with non-security responsibilities?

Some may feel that it is unfair for a security officer to be judged by an executive in a very limited interaction. Unfair or not this is what happens. When 3 or 4 security officers are seen together most executives don't consider a shift change may be occuring. They usually think that security must by overstaffed and underworked.

Ask yourself if you really want to assist and serve others as a security officer? If you really are serious, show it by your actions and attitudes.

Good personal hygiene and grooming is essential.

Be friendly.

Show some interest.

Don't let personal problems affect you work.

Be willing and eager to help.

Don't leave a messy work area.

Treat your employer and client with respect.

NON-SECURITY DUTIES

This entire Security Officer Training Manual was written with the hope and intent of upgrading the training and professionalism of all security officers. Unfortunately, many security officers work for organizations where they are asked to perform a multitude of duties which are not truly security in nature.

A question often asked by the inexperienced security officer or student is, "Why are security officers expected to perform these non-security duties? Management should be told to have someone else perform these tasks!" It is not as simple as it may appear.

The main author of this manual was once the supervisor of a small, eight-person security department. Two security officers worked each shift on a daily basis. Three days a week, one of the day-shift security officers was to drive the plant manager's vehicle into the nearby city to have the vehicle washed and filled with fuel. Whenever a maintenance problem occurred with the vehicle, security was responsible for driving the vehicle into the repair shop to have whatever problems corrected. It was not uncommon for the security supervisor to be summoned by the plant manager early on a Monday morning. The security supervisor initially thought that a serious problem must have occurred at the plant over the weekend. Unfortunately, the security supervisor's ego was usually bruised after he was informed that while driving with his wife the plant manager had noticed a noise with their car . The supervisor was asked if he would take care of the problem as soon as possible. Since the security supervisor was young, early in his career, and not independently wealthy, he "cheerfully" always complied with these requests.

It is extremely difficult to upgrade the image and professionalism of a security department if some many duties performed by security officers are seemingly trivial, unproductive and often demeaning. The problem faced by security officers, supervisors and managers, is how to transfer the mundane job duties to some other department?

Reasons for Non-Security Responsibilities

If a contest were held throughout the United States to determine what was the most ridiculous non-security duty performed by security officers, the list of entries would probably be long and quite humorous. There may be many reasons or past history as to why security is responsible for certain duties. In a large, general and broad sense, the primary reason security officers perform non-security duties is that currently, or in the past, someone other than a true security professional was given responsibility for managing or supervising the security department. This person while perhaps well-intentioned, may not have had a clue as to what security officers should be doing on a daily basis. Worse yet, they may have preconceived notions of what security officers should be doing which are totally inconsistent with projecting a professional image.

Consider these analogies: Would it make sense to give a maintenance supervisor responsibility for accounting? Would it make sense to have an engineer responsible for all personnel activities? Or would it make sense to have the supervisor of janitorial staff responsible for the chemical laboratory?

Naturally, few executives in their right minds would consider implementing any of the examples just mentioned. But why do so many executives and other managers think that just about anyone can manage the security function? For the most part, managers and executives have preconceived ideas about security based upon their own experiences, (even if these experiences are few). If their experience with a security problem or security officer was positive and pleasant, then there is a much higher degree of probability that they have a positive view security. Unfortunately, if there security experiences were negative or left a very poor impression of the duties and responsibilities of the security, they are likely to have a poor image of the function.

Notes

List non-security duties you are responsible for performing:

1._____

2._____

3._____

4._____

5._____

The professionalizing of the security field is continuous with improvement still needed.

Find out what executives and managers think about the overall level of service provided by security officers. Is it low or poor? Do something about it.

Removing Non-Security Duties

Attempting to eliminate security officers from performing non-security duties is difficult at best. Unless the duties are so obsolete that if no one assumed their responsibility, no one would notice, it will be very difficult to remove the functions from security.

The first, most basic question to ask is who needs the service? Secondly, if no one performs this service will it matter? Finally, if the service is needed and security does not plan to provide it, who will? The last question is the most difficult to answer. Who will provide the service if security does not?

Typical Non-Security Duties

TELEPHONE

Most security officers are required to answer the telephone for some minimum amount of time on a daily basis. This may require the security officer to simply answer telephone calls which come into the security post from another interior telephone, or as often the case, security personnel are required to act as the main telephone operator during evening and weekend hours. No matter the level of telephone service provided by security, it is critical that all security personnel answer the telephone in a professional manner.

Since a person who is calling on the telephone cannot see the other person who is answering the call, perceptions are made about the person on the other end of the phone. If the caller has never met the person who is receiving the phone call, a mental picture is formed. This mental picture is shaped by perceptions on the part of the caller. People have a natural tendency to guess what a person looks like. Often, these mental pictures are totally inaccurate. The soft, sweet, and even sexy female voice on the other end of the phone, may belong to a woman who bench presses 500 pounds and looks like a linebacker for the Green Bay Packers.

Notes

Identify how many hours per day/ per shift security personnel are required to answer the telephone.

Project a positive mental picture on the telephone.

People make assumptions and reach conclusions about a person based upon the tone of voice and way in which a person speaks on the telephone. A person's mood and mental outlook are expressed in the voice. The mood of a person who is tired, angry, happy, frustrated, etc., is often very obvious by their tone of voice. Therefore, if a security officer is not very happy with having to answer the telephone, this resentment is often transferred through his/her tone of voice in their unfriendliness or willingness to help the caller.

As security officers, image and perceptions go a long way in the way workers and executives view the entire security operation. Security officers who are required to answer the telephone for extended periods of time, may be accepting a telephone call from the president or chief executive officer of the corporation. For an executive of the corporation to hear an impolite, rude, uncaring security officer answer the telephone, will greatly erode and damage the reputation of the entire security department. Security officers should accept to responsibility of answering the telephone and perform this task to the best of their abilities.

Suggestions for Answering the Telephone

1. Always answer the phone within three rings.

2. Answer the phone by saying, "Good morning, afternoon, evening, ABC company, Security Officer Jones speaking, may I help you?"

3. Try to help the person. If they ask for someone who is not at work, don't just say, "There not in." Help the caller by saying, "Is there someone else who can help you."

4. If the person has a problem or complaint, listen to them and attempt to offer them a suggestion or alternative.

5. If the caller asks for the home phone number of anyone, don't give it out. If the caller persists that they must speak to the person ask the caller for their

---

Notes

The telephone is a medium for conversation. It is essential for a positive manner to be expressed when using the telephone.

Practice these suggestions.

name and phone number. Advise the caller that you will call the employee at home and give them the caller's name and phone number.

6. If the caller is a customer or client, be certain to obtain specific information to their questions or problems and then attempt to contact the appropriate executive at home.

7. If the caller states that they must speak to someone because of an emergency, take notes of their statements and be certain to notify the employee or if required, their supervisor as soon as possible.

8. Security personnel must not convey their emotions in their voice. If the security officer is tired, or angry at someone, he/she must remember that in all likelihood, the caller is not responsible for their mood. Therefore, don't make the caller the victim.

9. Security personnel when answering the telephone should always assume their boss is the person calling. Never think that you can play jokes or games on the phone because you know the caller. You "might think" you know the identity of the caller, but you may often be mistaken.

10. Smile on the telephone. Project a positive image.

VEHICLE MAINTENANCE

Security personnel may be responsible for insuring company vehicles are kept in good working order and clean at all times. If security personnel are required to wash vehicles, information on car wash locations should be obtained. Discounts are often given if a book or coupons of several car washes are purchased at one time.

Logs should be maintained for each vehicle which document when the vehicle last received fuel, lubrication, oil, engine tune-up, tire rotation, etc. If at all possible, consideration should be given to transferring the responsibility of vehicle maintenance to another department. If this is not possible, security personnel must perform this task in as professional manner as possible.

Consideration must also be given as to how vehicle maintenance work will be paid. If cash is used, proper documentation and retention of all receipts must be maintained and submitted for review and approval on a regular basis. If credit cards are used, clear instructions must be given to credit car recipients to the description of vehicles which are permitted to have work charged on the card. Instances have occurred where a person with access to a company credit card had work charged to the credit card for work performed on a personal vehicle.

DELIVERING THE MAIL

If mail moves the country, and zip code moves the mail, then why do so many security officers deliver the mail at the locations where they work?

Once again, some bright, non-security professional no doubt thought that it would be a good idea for security to deliver the mail. Think about the reasons this executive found!

1. Security has to patrol anyway, so why not have them do something useful with their time.

2. What else do they have to do anyway?

3. It allows a person who has really important things to do like a secretary, to be able to do more important things.

4. By keeping the security officers busy they are less likely to fall asleep.

5. We've done this way for years. If we change now, who will do it?

Notes

If you happen to be a security officer who is responsible for mail delivery or posting of notices on bulletin boards, etc...there is not much you can do to alleviate this problem except by performing the task in the best way possible. Unless clear alternatives can be addressed to remove mail delivery from the security officer's area of responsibility, little chance exists of someone else becoming the mailman.

CLEANING & JANITORIAL SERVICES

If you are a security officer who delivers mail, consider yourself luckier than the officers who are also expected to mop floors and clean restrooms.

Once again, some wise-guy came up with this idea for much the same reasons security was given responsibility to deliver the mail.

As security professionals, this is one area where the proverbial "line in the sand" must be drawn. Individuals who are applying for a security officer position, should refuse the position if it involves basic janitorial responsibilities of any kind other than maintaining a clean work area for the security officer himself. If contract security companies refused to accept these assignments because no one would serve in these capacities, the level of professionalism would immediately improve.

The author of this manual is very adamant about security officers not performing basic janitorial services. However, it would be expected for a security officer to use a mop, bucket, broom, etc. to assist in the clean-up after a spill, leak, or otherwise emergency. Aside from assisting in these emergency situations, as security professionals we have to politely and diplomatically refuse to become janitors.

LAWN CARE

Other than having the responsibility of turning a lawn sprinkler system on and off, the author believes that lawn care also falls into a similar category as janitorial services.

If a security officer enjoys planting flowers and cutting the lawn, etc. at the facility where they are employed, this work should be conducted after normal working hours. In addition, the person should not be performing this work while dressed in the security uniform.

Notes

Once again, impression and professionalism is the central point to be made. A security officer who possesses a Ph.D. will not gain the respect of workers and visitors if they are viewed as the gardener.

GENERAL GOPHER ("GO-FOR")

Some companies give security officers the responsibility of driving a company vehicle to retrieve spare parts and maintenance items from local suppliers.

While this function is much more acceptable from an image standpoint, it is very unacceptable from the standpoint that security exists to protect a facility. By removing the person who has primary responsibility to protect the facility in order to retrieve a item that can be delivered or picked-up by other means is not conducive to building a professional image.

Again, the same reasons as before are often used to justify why security personnel have this responsibility. If one accepts the premise that an objective of the organization is to have a professional security service, then one has to also make some tough decisions by removing certain of these non-security responsibilities.

CHAUFFEUR

Perhaps one of the best typical non-security duties is that of being a chauffeur. Since being a chauffeur allows the driver to often come into close personal contact with key executives, opportunity is presented to converse with the people who possess the power within an organization.

In recent years, the task of being a chauffeur has become increasingly more important from a security standpoint. Since executives are often the possible targets of kidnappers or extortionists, it is critical that security personnel who serve as chauffeurs take their jobs very seriously and go to great length to protect their passengers.

Most chauffeurs should be schooled not only in defensive driving techniques, but also in detecting if they are being followed by another vehicle. Some common sense tips such as varying routes and times of departure will greatly assist in deterring the possible kidnapping of an executive.

Security personnel who are asked to be chauffeurs should take their jobs seriously and accept the assignment as a compliment as opposed to a demotion.

In conclusion, non-security duties for officers are standard operating procedure at many facilities. For officers facing these responsibilities, there are two different yet parallel courses to take.

On one hand, officers must execute all of their duties, security or otherwise, with the utmost professionalism and dedication. On the other, there must be a concerted effort to make employers and management aware of the compromises made when security officers are expected to perform duties unrelated to their purpose.

SUMMARY

Security officers are judged in large part, by the impression created in dealing with people in 15-30 seconds. Most security officers are wearing a uniform, consisting of a shirt, possible tie, hat, shoes and perhaps a jacket. The security officer who arrives to work unshaven, with a soiled, wrinkled shirt, unpolished shoes, and in general an appearance that looks like the officer has just climbed out of bed, might as well find another job! The visual impression given to the client, supervisor and co-workers is that this officer just doesn't care and will never become an effective member of the security department.

Notes

Beside visual appearance, the tone of one's voice, the willingness to offer a "good morning," or a "may I help you?" creates a positive impression in the minds of the listener.

It is extremely difficult to upgrade the image and professionalism of a security department if some many duties performed by security officers are seemingly trivial, unproductive and often demeaning. The problem faced by security officers, supervisors and managers, is how to transfer the mundane job duties to some other department.

There may be many reasons or past history as to why security is responsible for certain duties. In a large, general and broad sense, the primary reason security officers perform non-security duties is that currently, or in the past, someone other than a true security professional was given responsibility for managing or supervising the security department.

For the most part, managers and executives have preconceived ideas about security based upon their own experiences, (even if these experiences are few). If their experience with a security problem or security officer was positive and pleasant, then there is a much higher degree of chance that they have a positive view concerning the role of security. Unfortunately, if there security experiences were negative or left a very poor impression of the duties and responsibilities of the security, they are likely to have a poor image of the function.

Attempting to eliminate security officers from performing non-security duties is difficult at best. Unless the duties are so obsolete that if no one assumed their responsibility, no one would notice, it will be very difficult to remove the functions from security.

Most security officers are required to answer the telephone for some minimum amount of time on a daily basis. This may require the security officer to simply answer telephone calls which come into the security post from another interior telephone, or as in often the case, security personnel may be required to act as the main telephone operator during evening and weekend hours.

Notes

Since a person who is calling on the telephone cannot see the other person who is answering the call, perceptions are made about the person on the other end of the phone.

People make assumptions and reach conclusions about a person based upon the tone of voice and way in which a person speaks on the telephone. A person's mood and mental outlook are expressed in the voice. A person who is tired, angry, happy, frustrated, etc., is often very obvious by their tone of voice.

As security officers, image and perceptions go a long way in the way workers and executives view the entire security operation. Security officers who are required to answer the telephone for extended periods of time, may be accepting a telephone call from the president or chief executive officer of the corporation.

Security personnel may be responsible for insuring company vehicles are kept in good working order and clean at all times. If security personnel are required to wash vehicles, information on car wash locations should be obtained.

If you happen to be a security officer who is responsible for mail delivery or posting of notices on bulletin boards, etc...there is not much you can do to alleviate this problem except by performing the task in the best way possible. Unless clear alternatives can be addressed to remove mail delivery from the security officer's area of responsibility, little chance exists of someone else becoming the mailman.

Individuals who are applying for a security officer position, should refuse the position if it involves basic janitorial responsibilities of any kind other than maintaining a clean work area for the security officer himself. If contract security companies refused to accept these assignments because no one would serve in these capacities, the level of professionalism would immediately improve.

Other than having the responsibility of turning a lawn sprinkler system on and off, the author believes that lawn care also falls into a similar category as janitorial services.

Some companies give security officers the responsibility of driving a company vehicle to retrieve spare parts and maintenance items from local suppliers. While this function is much more acceptable from an image standpoint, it is very unacceptable from the standpoint that security exists to protect a facility. By removing the person who has primary responsibility to protect the facility in order to retrieve a item that can offer be delivered or picked-up by other means is not conducive to building a professional image.

Perhaps one of the best typical non-security duties is that of being a chauffeur. Since being a chauffeur allows the driver to often come into close personal contact with key executives, opportunity is presented to converse with the people who possess the power within an organization.

In recent years, the task of being a chauffeur has become increasingly more important from a security standpoint. Since executives are often the possible targets of kidnappers or extortionists, it is critical that security personnel who serve as chauffeurs take their jobs very seriously and go to great length to protect their passengers.

Security personnel who are asked to be chauffeurs should take their jobs seriously and accept the assignment as a compliment as opposed to a demotion.

Notes

Questions

1.   Identify at least 5 ways of creating a favorable first impression?

a._____

b._____

c._____

d._____

e._____

2.   State in writing how a security officer should answer each and every telephone call.

_____

_____

3.   You work as a security officer at a facility where security officers are expected to deliver mail and maintain the plant manager's vehicle in clean and proper working order. How do you deal with these regulations and how would you try to change them?

_____

_____

_____

_____

_____

_____

_____

PRACTICAL EXERCISE FOR EVALUATING FIRST IMPRESSIONS

Next to the following names indicate whether or not you have a positive impression of the person or a negative impression. Use a + for positive and a - for negative. Picture the person in your mind and mark immediately whether you have a positive or negative impression. Discuss with other students their responses.

___ Kevin Costner		___ Sean Connery	
___ Kim Bassinger		___ Minnie Pearl	
___ Archie Bunker		___ Charles Barkley	
___ Madonna		___ Charles Manson	
___ Adolf Hitler		___ Bob Hope	
___ Pope John Paul II		___ Richard Nixon	
___ John Kennedy		___ Martin Luther King	
___ Henry Fonda		___ Jane Fonda	
___ Jose Canseco		___ George Bush	
___ Frank Sinatra		___ Donald Trump	

THE EFFECTIVE
SECURITY OFFICERS
TRAINING MANUAL

Chapter XX

Future of Security

Future of Security

By all indicators and recent studies, the future of security over the next 10-15 years is considered very bright. Very bright in the sense that the industry will continue to grow, technological advancements will continue, and jobs will be plentiful. However, like other growing industries, those persons who have special technical skills and abilities or education, will have the best opportunity to command the better, higher paying jobs.

Recent studies have detailed the trends in the security profession which include:

1. The security industry will continue growth in jobs and technology.

2. A continued emphasis on security personnel training.

3. Continued expansion of the contract security industry with a subsequent reduction in the use of proprietary security.

4. Expansion of security job functions to include functions such as: basic safety inspections, hazardous material control, and certain environmental concerns.

5. Continued pressure to reduce overall security costs with regard to wages and benefits.

6. Continued aggressiveness and competition among contract security companies with varying degrees of quality of service.

7. Greater government regulation of the security industry with regard to standards, training, licensing fees, and taxes.

8. Continued expansion of security in assuming many traditional, law enforcement functions (i.e. parking and traffic enforcement, response to alarms, etc.).

A summary of the major findings, recommendations, and forecasts of the security industry contained in the Hallcrest II study reflect similar trends as previously outlined:

Fear of Crime is increasing among citizens and businesses.

Business and governmental efforts are not effectively preventing, detecting, or controlling economic crime.

A growing concern exists among businesses that lawsuits arising from claims against security personnel and their employers for inadequate or improper security will continue.

Active involvement of security personnel in enforcing policies and procedures will increase as executives continue to stress business ethics. Security personnel will be more involved in ensuring ethical behavior.

There is a reasonable expectation that the crime rate will decrease if citizens can reduce the availability and use of illegal drugs.

There is little evidence of a serious international terrorist threat in the United States.

Private security personnel in 1990 are better educated and this trend will continue.

The rapid growth of security technology (closed-circuit television systems, access control systems, etc.), will not necessarily reduce the number of security personnel but will change the functions they perform.

The Hallcrest II study concludes that four major reasons account for the increasing growth of private security and limited growth of law enforcement:

1. increasing workplace crime
2. increasing fear of crime
3. decreasing rate of government spending for public

Notes

protection

    4. increasing awareness and use of private security products and services as cost-effective protective measures.1.

1. William C. Cunningham, John J. Strauchs, and Clifford W. Van Meter, **The Hallcrest Report II: Private Security Trends**, (Boston: Butterworth-Heinemann, 1990), p. 327.

CONCLUSION

This Security Officer Training Manual has presented a great deal of information in the hope of better educating the security personnel who read and study its contents. It should be evident from the information presented, that the private security industry continues rapid growth and changes. Unfortunately, for the basic private security officer, much of this growth and change has not necessarily resulted in an increase in one's standard of living. Security personnel, especially those employed in the contract security field earn meager wages and few benefits. Proprietary security officers while earning more money and receiving greater benefits are an endangered species, which will continue to decline in the years to come.

The student of this manual may then ask him or herself, "What does the future hold for me in the security profession?"

No one knows for certain the answer to that question. But what is known that the person responsible for the implementing this training program has made an investment in the student. Whether the provider of this manual is the owner of a contract security company, the security director of a hospital, or an instructor at a vocational or continuing education school, all have one thing in common—their desire to better train and educate security personnel!

The student of this manual needs to take their new-found knowledge and evaluate their lives and to ask him or herself where do they want to be in the next year, two years, five years, or ten years from now in regard to their careers. The best avenue for improving one's life is to invest in

Notes

oneself. The student who continues to pursue education or to obtain a technical degree will be better prepared to obtain a position of worth within the security industry. To simply complain that wages and benefits provided by an employer are not enough or non-satisfactory is not a viable excuse. Security personnel who are not satisfied with their jobs and/or career must decide to improve themselves for no other reason other than benefiting themselves.

"The Quality of a person's life is in direct proportion to their commitment to excellence, regardless of their chosen field of endeavor." Vincent T. Lombardi

Notes

THE EFFECTIVE SECURITY OFFICERS TRAINING MANUAL

Appendix I

Security Survey

Effective Security Officer Training Manual
Security Survey

The purpose of this survey is to assist the security officer in determining what areas need attention, clarification, or further information in order that all security personnel can successfully implement all appropriate policies and procedures.

		YES	NO	NOT NEEDED
1.	Security personnel employed at this facility know completely what legal authority they possess?	___	___	___
2.	Security personnel are permitted to detain persons suspected a stealing from this company?	___	___	___
3.	Security personnel are permitted to use reasonable force against a person?	___	___	___
4.	A job description exists for all security positions?	___	___	___
5.	A minimum amount of training is provided all security personnel prior to training?	___	___	___
6.	The training provided for all new security personnel is adequate?	___	___	___
7.	A training checklist is used at this facility to verify training?	___	___	___
8.	On-going and in-service training is provided to all personnel?	___	___	___
9.	Security personnel are encouraged to pursue additional training and education?	___	___	___

		YES	NO	NOT NEEDED
10.	The local law enforcement agency is aware of who provides security at this facility?	___	___	___
11.	The turnover rate of security personnel at this facility is satisfactory?	___	___	___
12.	Security personnel are required to have a high school diploma or G.E.D.?	___	___	___
13.	The hourly wage paid at this facility is considerably higher than the federal minimum wage?	___	___	___
14.	Security personnel receive regularly scheduled evaluations?	___	___	___
15.	Security officers have been trained to look for fire hazards while on patrol?	___	___	___
16.	Security personnel know which doors and windows are to be secured?	___	___	___
17.	Security personnel are given a patrol checklist to be used when patrolling?	___	___	___
18.	Security personnel have been given clear instructions in reporting and correcting problems with leaks, electricity, etc..?	___	___	___
19.	Incident reports are written for all serious conditions noted while on patrol?	___	___	___
20.	External or perimeter patrols are conducted on a regular basis?	___	___	___

		YES	NO	NOT NEEDED
21.	Vehicles are used to assist security personnel when conducting external patrols?	___	___	___
22.	All persons authorized to drive a motorized vehicle possess the proper licensing and insurance requirements?	___	___	___
23.	Are vehicles inspected prior to use and are logs maintained reflecting maintenance and repair work?	___	___	___
24.	Do all security personnel know what they should do if they find machinery left-on during patrols?	___	___	___
25.	Are problems from the previous shift communicated to the next shift in written logs?	___	___	___
26.	Are patrol times and routes varied so as not to develop patterns?	___	___	___
27.	Are all entrances/exits checked while patrolling?	___	___	___
28.	Are keys used when patrolling properly protected?	___	___	___
29.	Are keys retained on a large key ring which deters an officer from removing the keys from the facility by accident?	___	___	___
30.	Are two-way radios needed for proper communication when patrolling?	___	___	___
31.	Are a notebook, pen and flashlight provided for officers when patrolling?	___	___	___
32.	Are shift or daily logs maintained to record all pertinent information?	___	___	___

	YES	NO	NOT NEEDED

33. Are vehicle logs used and properly maintained?

34. Are visitor and contractor logs used and properly maintained?

35. Are material control or package passes used and properly maintained?

36. Are all security personnel properly instructed in the manner in which to write security reports?

37. Are all security reports properly safeguarded from unauthorized persons?

38. Are all security personnel properly instructed in conducting a preliminary investigation?

39. Are all security reports written before the end of the shift?

40. Are all security reports distributed to the appropriate people without delay?

41. Is all evidence properly collected, marked for identification, and safely secured?

42. Are electronic alarm systems used at this facility?

43. Have all security personnel been instructed in the proper use of the alarm systems?

44. Do all security personnel know what appropriate action needs to be taken once an alarm has been received?

		YES	NO	NOT NEEDED

45. Are CCTV systems in use and have all security personnel been instructed in their use? ⎯⎯ ⎯⎯ ⎯⎯

46. Is a sprinkler systems in use at this facility? ⎯⎯ ⎯⎯ ⎯⎯

47. Are all security personnel knowledge-able to the location of all sprinkler risers, valves, fire extinguishers and other fire protection equipment? ⎯⎯ ⎯⎯ ⎯⎯

48. Are fire extinguishers inspected on a monthly basis and is a chart or map used to record the inspection? ⎯⎯ ⎯⎯ ⎯⎯

49. Are special fire protection systems such as Halon, CO_2 or other systems used and are all security personnel familiar with their operation? ⎯⎯ ⎯⎯ ⎯⎯

50. Are monthly or bi-monthly shift meetings conducted for all security personnel in order to maintain proper communication? ⎯⎯ ⎯⎯ ⎯⎯

51. Weekly/Monthly inspections are made of perimeter fencing by security? ⎯⎯ ⎯⎯ ⎯⎯

52. Alarms are tested on a weekly basis to ensure their proper operation. ⎯⎯ ⎯⎯ ⎯⎯

53. Weekly inspections of all outside lights are made by security with documentation of any deficiencies? ⎯⎯ ⎯⎯ ⎯⎯

54. An annual physical inventory of all keys and their issuance is conducted by security personnel? ⎯⎯ ⎯⎯ ⎯⎯

		YES	NO	NOT NEEDED

55. Current recordkeeping of all keys is maintained by security? ____ ____ ____

56. Combination locks are changed when an employee with access leaves the employment of the company? ____ ____ ____

57. Security personnel are knowledgeable of all keys and the areas which they access? ____ ____ ____

58. Safes are checked by security during patrols and if found unlocked, a report is immediately written and a person-in-charge notified? ____ ____ ____

59. Security is notified on a regular basis about inventory shortages? ____ ____ ____

60. Package inspections of all personnel as they exit the facility are conducted on a regular basis? ____ ____ ____

61. A clear policy exists which regulates the conduct of all employees as it pertains to package or vehicle inspections? ____ ____ ____

62. A program exists which encourages employees to report theft and other improper behavior of others? ____ ____ ____

63. A clear practice and policy exists which states clearly, employees will be terminated for theft? ____ ____ ____

64. Known thefts are immediately reported to the security department? ____ ____ ____

65. The theft of time is considered a serious offense at this facility? ____ ____ ____

		YES	NO	NOT NEEDED

66. Sensitive information is shredded or properly destroyed before being discarded?   ___ ___ ___

67. A Code of Conduct exists and is well publicized?   ___ ___ ___

68. Security personnel are familiar with the policies and procedures which govern their behavior with employees represented by a union?   ___ ___ ___

69. Unionized employees at this facility must be afforded representation as part of a security investigation?   ___ ___ ___

70. A clear strike contingency plan is prepared several weeks in advance of a possible strike?   ___ ___ ___

71. Security personnel are given clear instructions regarding their behavior during a strike?   ___ ___ ___

72. The appropriate law enforcement agency is notified in advance by security of a possible strike?   ___ ___ ___

73. Security personnel have been properly trained in dealing with disruptive or combatant individuals?   ___ ___ ___

74. A weather radio is located at a central security post?   ___ ___ ___

75. A clear chain-of-command exists for security personnel to notify in the event of a severe weather watch?   ___ ___ ___

76. An emergency telephone call list exists with the phone numbers of all key personnel and outside agencies?   ___ ___ ___

		YES	NO	NOT NEEDED
77.	Evacuation maps and outside meeting locations are posted throughout the facility?	___	___	___
78.	A written Emergency Preparedness plan exists and is updated regularly?	___	___	___
79.	Evacuation drills are conducted at least on an annual basis.	___	___	___
80.	An emergency audible alarm or an effective public address system is used to notify all personnel of an emergency?	___	___	___
81.	A sufficient number of two-way radios are available during an emergency?	___	___	___
82.	Following an emergency or a drill an analysis is conducted in order to identify problems?	___	___	___
83.	A policy or program whereby security personnel can report the improper behavior of other security officers exists?	___	___	___
84.	Clear written policies addressing theft, dereliction of duty, sleeping, sexual harassment, etc... are reviewed with all security personnel on a regular basis?	___	___	___
85.	Security personnel are instructed in reporting and observing unsafe conditions while patrolling?	___	___	___
86.	Statistics on accidents are well publicized and understood by employees?	___	___	___

		YES	NO	NOT NEEDED

87. Security personnel are trained in first aid and C.P.R.? ___ ___ ___

88. Security personnel are expected to transport injured personnel to a hospital? ___ ___ ___

89. Security personnel are responsible for notifying outside emergency services in the event of a serious accident. ___ ___ ___

90. Security personnel are expected to coordinate any hazardous material spills? ___ ___ ___

91. Security personnel are expected to answer the telephone for the entire organization on a daily basis? ___ ___ ___

92. Security personnel are given training in the proper manner to answer the telephone and in transferring calls? ___ ___ ___

93. Security personnel are required to deliver mail and post notices at this facility? ___ ___ ___

94. Security personnel maintain vehicle maintenance logs for all company vehicles? ___ ___ ___

95. Security officers are expected to report 10-15 minutes before the start of their shift in order to communicate with the off-going shift? ___ ___ ___

96. Security personnel are given instruction prior to hiring regarding their appearance? ___ ___ ___

		YES	NO	NOT NEEDED
97.	Security personnel are given an adequate number of uniforms?	___	___	___
98.	Security personnel who serve as chauffeurs are provided defensive driving lessons?	___	___	___
99.	Security personnel are often promoted to positions other than in security?	___	___	___
100.	Security personnel are encouraged to interact with security personnel from other facilities/companies?	___	___	___

Appendix II

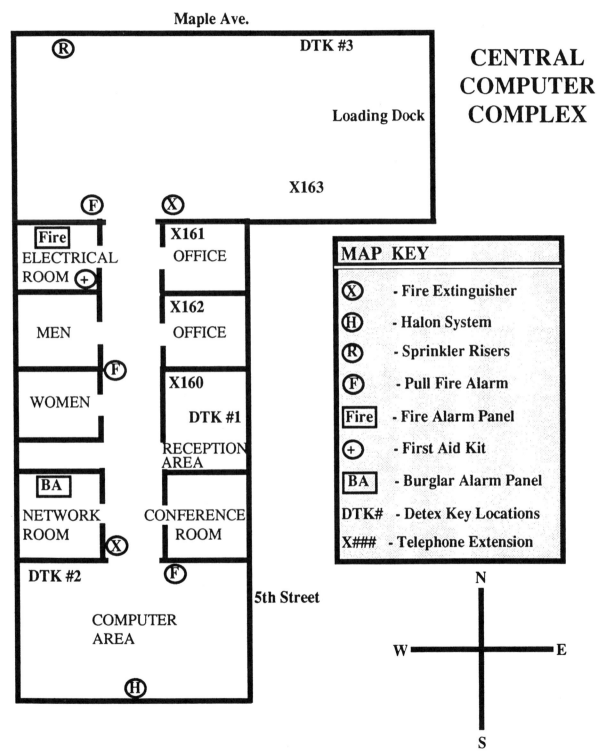

Sample Security Officer Facility Diagram

THE EFFECTIVE SECURITY OFFICERS TRAINING MANUAL

Bibliography

&

Recommended References

BIBLIOGRPAHY & RECOMMENDED REFERENCES

Principles of Security: An Introduction, Truett A. Ricks, Bill G. Tillet & Clifford W. VanMeter, Anderson Company, (Cincinnati: 1981).

Private Security: Standards and Goals, The Official Private Security Task Force Report, Anderson Company, (Cincinnati: 1977).

Security Management Magazine, American Society for Industrial Security, (Arlington, VA).

The Hallcrest Report II: Private Security Trends 1970-2000, William C. Cunningham, John J. Strauchs & Clifford W. VanMeter, Butterworth-Heinemann, (Boston: 1990).

Security Supervision, Eugene D. Finneran, Butterwoth-Heinemann, (Boston: 1981).

Hospital Security, Russell L. Colling, Butterwoth-Heinemann, (Boston: 1976).

The Protection of Assets Manuals, Timothy J. Walsh & Edward J. Healy, Merritt Company, (Santa Monica, CA: 1986), 213-450-7234.

Honeywell Product and Services Manual, Honeywell Protection Services, (Minneapolis: 1990).

Legal Aspects of Private Security, Arthur J. Bilek, John C. Klotter, R. Keegan Federal, Anderson Company, (Cincinnati: 1981).

Principles of Fire Protection, Percy Bugbee, National Fire Protection Association, (Quincy, MA: 1978).

The People Puzzle: Understanding Yourself and Others, Morris E. Massey, Reston Publishing Co., (Reston, VA: 1979).

Video Available from Reston Publishing Co., 800-336-0338

Human Behavior in Organizations, J. Clifton Williams, South Western Publishing Co., (Cincinnati: 1978).

Front-Line Supervisor's Labor Relations Handbook, Stephen F. Byrd, National Foremen's Institute, (Waterford, CT: 1978).

The Merck Manual of Diagnosis & Therapy, Merck Sharp and Dohme Research Laboratories, (Rahway, NJ: 1987).

BIBLIOGRAPHY & SELECTED REFERENCES

Standard First Aid: Personal Safety, American Red Cross, 1990.

U.S. Department of Commerce/NOAA, National Weather Service, US Government Printing Office, (Washington: 1978).

The Bomb Threat Challenge, FBI Bomb Data Center, US Department of Justice, (Washington, D.C.: 1990).

Effective Report Writing for the Security Officer, Ralph F. Brislin, Bonita Cirignano, Carolyn Varner, Practical Education Services, (Akron, OH: 1991).

Loss Control: A Safety Guidebook for Trades and Services, George J. Matwes, Helen Matwes, Van Nostrand Reinhold Company, (New York: 1990).

THE EFFECTIVE
SECURITY OFFICERS
TRAINING MANUAL

Answer Key

to

Chapter Questions

Answer Key to Chapter Questions

Introduction to Security

1.	d	3.	a	5.	d	7.	d
2.	d	4.	c	6.	a	8.	b

Chapter I: Security Personnel

1.	True	6.	True	11.	c	16.	True
2.	False	7.	d	12.	d	17.	True
3.	True	8.	False	13.	True	18.	$6.50–$7.00
4.	True	9.	d	14.	c	19.	False
5.	True	10.	Newspaper advertisements	15.	c	20.	True

Chapter II: Physical Security

1.
   - Define property boundaries
   - Deter entry
   - Delay and impede unauthorized entry
   - Channel and restrict flow of traffic
   - Provide for more efficient and effective use of security forces

2.
   - Chain link: secure permanent facilities
   - Barbed wire: less permanent facilities
   - Concertina wire: emergency situations

3. Sentry dogs are use in conjunction with a security officer, while guard dogs roam an area by themselves.

4.
   - Four walls
   - Roof
   - Floor

5.
   - Reinforced with bars or grates
   - Use of window alarm foil
   - Glass breakage alarms

6.
   - Advertising
   - Assists traffic
   - Deters unauthorized entries

7.
   - Continuous
   - Glare
   - Controlled

8.
   - Mechanical
   - Electro-mechanical
   - Electronic
   - Combination

9. Master keying allows for the opening of all locks with special keys of the same key systems.

10.
   - Issue all keys
   - Note changes
   - Conduct regular inventories
   - Maintain a written log of all keys

11. Moisture

12. The safe should withstand temperatures up to 2,000 degree (F) for four hours

13. 150 degrees (F) and 85%

14. Reinforced or solid steel

15. Vaults protect valuables and are usually part of a building with walls of 12" reinforced concrete with steel doors and a combination lock.

Chapter III: Patrol Procedures

1.	True	c.	Patrolling	e.	Ingress
2.	True	a.	Pattern Variations	h.	Simultaneously
3.	False	f.	External Patrol	g.	Sixth Sense
4.	True	b.	Egress	j.	First Patrol
5.	False	d.	Internal Patrol	i.	Loss Prevention

Chapter IV: Electronic Alarms

1.
   - Detect fire
   - Detect unauthorized entry
   - Notify authorities during an emergency
   - Monitor equipment and report malfunctions

2. Quick response

3.
   - Perimeter or point of entry
   - Area Protection
   - Object Protection

4.
   - Intrusion
   - Magnetic

5.
   - Capacitance
   - Wire/Screen

6.
   - Psychological deterrent
   - Damage should be minimized
   - Inexpensive

7.
   - Easy to defeat
   - Intruder will probably not be apprehended
   - The alarm may be disregarded if no one is near to hear

8.
   - Local
   - Central Station
   - Direct
   - Proprietary

9.
   - System can be designed to meet the needs of the owner
   - System is owned and operated by the owner
   - Cost of providing personnel to monitor the system
   - Additional costs if the system has not been designed properly

10.
   - User error or negligence
   - Poor installation or servicing
   - Faulty equipment

11. User error or negligence

12.
   - Sell the system correctly
   - Don't use space protection excessively

Chapter V: Investigations

1. Gathering, evaluation
2. Preliminary
3. Follow-up
4. Evidence
5. Mental
6. Scene, evidence
7. Interviews
8. Interrogations

Exercises

1. Render assistance; Effect arrest; Locate and identify witnesses; Interview; Maintain scene; Interrogate; Note; Arrange; Report incident; Yield responsibility

2. Who; What; When; Where; Why; How

3. Date; Time; Location; Weather conditions; Witnesses; Complaint; Physical descriptions; Clothing; Odor or smells; Statements

4. Skid Marks; Broken glass; Damaged vehicles; Empty liquor containers;

5. Fingerprints; Footprints; Scratches/dents; Burglary tools

Chapter VI: Report Writing

1.
   - To provide a permanent record or an incident
   - To verify the job duties performed
   - To explain confusing events
   - To provide evidence in a legal proceeding
   - To provide information for follow-up action

2.
   - Who; What; When; Where ;Why; How; Conclusions

3. False

4. True

5. d

6.
   - Officer's name
   - On duty time
   - Name of officer relieved
   - Notation as to obtaining keys
   - Times of Patrols
   - Number of personnel/vehicles on site
   - Doors/windows open or unlocked
   - Coffee pots left on

7.
   - Weight Measurement
   - Driver assistance
   - Recording of tractor and trailer numbers
   - Recording of manifest and bills of lading
   - Time in/out
   - Seals and locks

8. To determine if a shipment has been opened or tampered with

9.
   - Unescorted: an employee does not have to accompany the person

10.
    - Escorted: an employee must accompany the person

11.
    - Date and time
    - Name of employee/person removing the material
    - Description of material
    - Ownership
    - Length of time material is loaned
    - Reason if material is not to be returned
    - Person authorizing removal

12. True

13. Chronological

14. c

15.
    - Possible legal action
    - Documentation of the facts

Chapter VII: Legal Aspects

1. • Citizen power
   • Deputation of commissioned power
   • Combination of citizen and commission
2. c
3. b
4. c
5. True
6. True
7. c
8. • Right to remain silent
   • Anything said can be used against a person in court
   • Right to an attorney
   • If a person cannot afford an attorney, one will be provided
9. True
10. False
11. Any force, less than deadly
12. Shopkeeper's Law
13. To protect persons and property
14. True
15. True
16. 4th
17. True
18. Rights of a store owner to detain a person for determining his/her identity and ownership of property in question
19. Actual threatening of a person
20. Unauthorized touching of a person
21. Tort
22. False imprisonment
23. Emotional distress
24. Libel, slander
25. Negligence

Chapter VIII: Testifying in Court

1. Tell the truth
2. Reporting the facts
3. An administrative hearing is usually not a part of a legal proceeding and is conducted within a business or organization.
4. There is no judge present.
5. It creates a good impression and suggests the witness is credible.
6. The moment you are assigned to write a report
7. To prove their innocence
8. Telling a story from the point of view of the witness
9. The challenging of the witness' story by the opposing side
10. The party who has brought the legal action

Chapter IX: Internal Threat

Questions

1. • They don't believe the problem exists
   • They are unsure what to do about it
   • They believe there is nothing that can be done cost effectively
   • They believer more serious problems will result
   • They believe the investigation may involve key employees
   • Inventory shortages

2. • Evidence discovered
   • Information received
3. • Person lives beyond his/her means
   • Dislike for policies and procedures
   • Bitterness
   • Gambling habit

• Alcohol/drug abuse
4. Reporting unusual events
5. A kleptomaniac has a psychological need to steal
6. Valuable proprietary information may not be recovered

Multiple Choice/True False
1. c
2. a
3. True
4. True
5. False
6. True
7. c

Matching
a. Opportunistic
e. Kleptomaniac
f. Rationalization
c. Kickback
d. Positive Variance
b. Negative Variance

Chapter X: Fire Protection

1. a
2. • Prevent; starting
   • Prevent; life; property
   • Confine
   • Extinguish
3. c
4. b
5. d
6. • Fuel
   • Heat
   • Oxygen
   • Reaction time of oxidation
7. • Consumed or removed
   • The level
   • Cooled below its ignition point
   • Chemically
8. • Conduction
   • Convection
   • Radiation
9. A piece of paper laid on a hot pipe
10. • Chemical
    • Electrical
    • Mechanical

• Nuclear
11. c
12. • Segregate the hazard by distance
    • Confine or enclose the hazard
    • Ventilate
    • Install explosion venting
    • Eliminate sources of ignition
    • Education
    • Provide adequate fire protection
13. Water
14. Human error
15. • Dry-pipe
    • Wet-piper
    • Deluge
16. True
17. • 1211
    • 1301
18. 1301
19. False
20. • Petroleum
    • Chemical
21. Pipe and hose system in building that are used to provide water

Chapter XI: Safety

1. Occupational Safety and Health Administration
2. d
3. True
4. e
5. c
6. c
7. False
8. False
9. b
10. c
11. d
12. b
13. • OSHA Recordable Incidence Rate
    • OSHA Lost Workday Case Incidence Rate
    • OSHA Lost Workday Incidence Rate
14. True
15. True
16. The seriousness or severity of injuries
17. True
18. • Workers' Compensation
    • Public Liability
    • Product Liability
    • Fire
    • Business Interruption
    • Automobile Damage
19. • Death
    • Permanent Total Disability
    • Permanent Partial Disability
    • Temporary Total Disability
    • Temporary Partial Disability
20. False
21. • Comprehensive Public Liability
    • Product Liability

Chapter XII: AIDS & HIV

1. c
2. c
3. a
4. b
5. d
6. c
7. b
8. b
9. d
10. a

Chapter XIII: Emergency Preparedness

1. c
2. e
3. d
4. True
5. False
6. False
7. True
8. False
9. False
10. False
11. True
12. b
13. True
14. False
15. True
16. False
17. d
18. True
19. False
20. False
21. False
22. c
23. False
24. True
25. True
26. False
27. True
28. False
29. True
30. d
31. True
32. False
33. False
34. True
35. True
36. True
37. False
38. True
39. True
40. True
41. False
42. False
43. True
44. True
45. b
46. False

Chapter XIV: Human Relations

1. c
2. b
3. d
4. Average dislike work and is lazy.
5. Average worker enjoys work and is not lazy.
6. d
7. d
8. d
9. d
10. c
11. • Physiological
    • Safety
    • Belonging
    • Esteem
    • Self-actualization
12. True
13. b
14. True
15. • The sender
    • The message
    • A medium or device for sending the message
    • The receiver
16. True
17. True
18. c
19. d
20. c

21. • Family
    • Education
    • Religion
22. Imprinting
23. a
24. d
25. Socialization
26. An incident that changes the way a person thinks and behaves
27. A person reviews and reflects on his/her life
28. c
29. c
30. 10, 11, or 12
31. True
32. False
33. b
34. True
35. • Labor and management
    • Organization vs. individual goals
36. • Better ideas are sometimes produced.
    • People have to examine new approaches.
    • Tension can increase interest and creativity.
37. • Alarm
    • Resistance
    • Exhaustion
38. Exercise

Chapter XV: Handling Disruptive People

1. True
2. True
3. True
4. False
5. False
6. d
7. c
8. f
9. True
10. True
11. e
12. f
13. f
14. c
15. False
16. c
17. d
18. c
19. a
20. b
21. c
22. c
23. True
24. b

Chapter XVI: Labor Relations

1. c
2. b
3. c
4. d
5. c

Chapter XVII: Alcohol and Drug Dependency

1. d
2. d
3. a
4. d
5. c
6. • Cocaine
   • Marijuana
   • LSD
7. True
8. c
9. Requires the drug industry to maintain physical security and strict record keeping for certain drugs, and it divides controlled substances into five schedules or classes.
10. True
11. e
12. True
13. c
14. b
15. c
16. True
17. d
18. d
19. d
20. True
21. c
22. True
23. False
24. d
25. d
26. d
27. a
28. d
29. True
30. c
31. True
32. True
33. c
34. d
35. True
36. True
37. True
38. "Free base" cocaine: conversion by flame of the salt of cocaine to form a combustible substance which is then inhaled.
39. True
40. b
41. True
42. True
43. True
44. c
45. True
46. • Frequent trips to his/her vehicle
    • Non-employees visiting the facility
    • Use of pay phones
    • Parking lot activities before and after work
    • Evidence of drinking

Chapter XVIII: Ethics

True/False Questions

1. True
2. False
3. True
4. True
5. True
6. False
7. False
8. False
9. False
10. True
11. True

Fill-in-the-blanks

1. Ethics
2. Opportunity
3. Boredom
4. Shortcuts
5. Falsification
6. Bribe
7. Sexual harassment
8. Hot lines

<u>Notes</u>

Notes

<u>Notes</u>

Notes